JOURNAL FOR THE STUDY OF THE OLD TESTAMENT
SUPPLEMENT SERIES
315

Sheffield Academic Press

Abraham, Israel and the Nations

The Patriarchal Promise and its Covenantal Development in Genesis

Paul R. Williamson

Journal for the Study of the Old Testament
Supplement Series 315

Copyright © 2000 Sheffield Academic Press

Published by
Sheffield Academic Press Ltd
Mansion House
19 Kingfield Road
Sheffield S11 9AS
England

www.SheffieldAcademicPress.com

Typeset by Sheffield Academic Press
and
Printed on acid-free paper in Great Britain
by Bookcraft Ltd
Midsomer Norton, Bath

British Library Cataloguing in Publication Data

A catalogue record for this book is available
from the British Library

ISBN 1-84127-152-7

CONTENTS

From the impact of the enlightenment on historical-critical study in the eighteenth century until the development of new literary approaches in the 1970s, much of the focus of Old Testament scholarship was on 'the world behind the text'. Rather than focusing on the final edited product, scholars were somewhat preoccupied with issues of authorship, date and provenance. The identification and reconstruction of underlying sources and traditions tended to dominate the study of the Hebrew Bible in general, and the Pentateuch in particular—so much so that the skilful literary artistry and theological understanding reflected in the final form of the text were generally passed over without comment.

Since the advent of 'new literary criticism' the pendulum has swung decidedly in the other direction. Articles and books espousing holistic readings of the biblical text have mushroomed in the past two decades. Diachronic and synchronic approaches are now vying for supremacy (in practice, if not in theory). Despite some calls for caution and balance, these two very different approaches are often pitted against each other as mutually exclusive enterprises.

There is a danger, therefore, that this present study may become simply another statistic—notched up on the synchronic scoreboard—in the battle of methodologies that rages at the end of the second millennium CE. However, this is certainly not the intention. While a synchronic approach to the text has been adopted, the reason for doing so is a pragmatic one: the aim of this work is to establish the theological relationship between two core pericopes within the Abraham narrative, viz. Genesis 15 and 17. Whatever their source or tradition history, both these passages have been artistically woven into the final framework of the Abraham narrative in such a way that suggests that the compiler intended each to make its own distinct theological contribution to the narrative as a whole. As this investigation will demonstrate, the theological significance of these pericopes within the final compilation of Genesis—and the ramifications of this for our understanding of the Pentateuch and beyond—have largely been lost on previous Old Testament scholarship, albeit for different reasons. This study seeks not only to establish the legitimacy of a new reading of the Abraham narrative, but also to defend it as the best reading for undestanding the intricacies and complexities of the narrative's final compilation.

Admittedly, in the present postmodern era a search for *one* 'correct' reading of any text might be considered not only audacious, but also rather naïve. Nevertheless, even within the plurality of possible interpretations, the superiority of one reading over another is clearly recognized. It is hoped, therefore, that the final-form reading presented in this study will be seen as more than just one of several alternative interpretations of the Abraham narrative.

ACKNOWLEDGMENTS

This book is a slightly revised version of a PhD dissertation submitted to The Queen's University of Belfast in 1998. Like any research project, it could not have been undertaken without the moral support and practical assistance of others. I want, therefore, to express sincere thanks to all who in various ways have contributed to the publication of this present volume.

I am deeply indebted to Desmond Alexander for his unflagging assistance and guidance offered in his capacity as supervisor of my doctoral research, and also for encouraging me in so many ways, not least in his suggestion to submit my work for publication. I am also grateful to those who commented helpfully on earlier drafts of the material contained in this volume: Raymond Banks and Stanley McIvor read it in its earliest form; James McKeown and Gordon Wenham, in their role as examiners, commented on its more polished version. While an attempt has been made to incorporate the various improvements suggested to me, I assume full responsibility for deficiencies that remain.

The constant support and encouragement of my colleagues at the Irish Baptist College, as well as the use of the library and facilities, has also been of great help. The assistance of the library staff at Queen's University, the personnel at Tyndale House, Cambridge, and the co-operation of the staff at Cambridge University Library in obtaining scarce titles and obscure journal articles proved invaluable.

I am especially grateful to Philip Davies for his initial interest in the manuscript, John Jarick for accepting it for inclusion in the JSOT Supplement Series, and Frances Mawer for improving the final product in her capacity as desk editor.

My greatest debt, however, is to my family. My children—Matthew and Andrew—have grown to appreciate that their father has more than a passing interest in reading rather dull books with no pictures in them. My wife, Karen, freely admits to being less than enthusiastic about academic theology, but her unfailing moral support throughout my musings on Abraham has shown her to be a true daughter of both Abraham and Sarah. This book is therefore dedicated to her and the boys with love.

ABBREVIATIONS

AB	Anchor Bible
ABD	D.N. Freedman (ed.) *The Anchor Bible Dictionary* (6 vols.; New York: Doubleday, 1992)
ABQ	*American Baptist Quarterly*
AnBib	Analecta biblica
ANF	*Ante-Nicene Fathers*
AnOr	Analecta orientalia
AOAT	Alter Orient und Altes Testament
ATR	*Anglican Theological Review*
AusBR	*Australian Biblical Review*
AUSS	*Andrews University Seminary Studies*
BangTF	*Bangalore Theological Forum*
BASOR	*Bulletin of the American Schools of Oriental Research*
BBB	Bonner biblische Beiträge
BBR	*Bulletin for Biblical Research*
BDB	F. Brown, S.R. Driver and C.A. Briggs, *A Hebrew and English Lexicon of the Old Testament* (Oxford: Clarendon Press, 1907)
BETL	Bibliotheca ephemeridum theologicarum lovaniensium
BHS	*Biblia hebraica stuttgartensia*
BHT	Beiträge zur historischen Theologie
Bib	*Biblica*
BibInt	*Biblical Interpretation: A Journal of Contemporary Approaches*
BJRL	*Bulletin of the John Rylands University Library of Manchester*
BKAT	Biblischer Kommentar: Altes Testament
BN	*Biblische Notizen*
BR	*Bible Review*
BSac	*Bibliotheca Sacra*
BT	*The Bible Translator*
BTB	*Biblical Theology Bulletin*
BWANT	Beiträge zur Wissenschaft vom Alten und Neuen Testament
BZ	*Biblische Zeitschrift*
BZAW	Beihefte zur *ZAW*
CB	Century Bible
CBC	Cambridge Bible Commentary

CBQ	*Catholic Biblical Quarterly*
ConBOT	Coniectanea biblica, Old Testament
CovQ	*Covenant Quarterly*
CRBS	*Currents in Research: Biblical Studies*
CTJ	*Calvin Theological Journal*
CTM	*Concordia Theological Monthly*
CTR	*Criswell Theological Review*
CurTM	*Currents in Theology and Mission*
DBAT	*Dielheimer Blätter zur Alten Testament*
DCH	D.J.A. Clines (ed.), *The Dictionary of Classical Hebrew* (8 vols.; Sheffield: Sheffield Academic Press, 1993–)
DSB	*The Daily Study Bible*
EncJud	*Encyclopaedia Judaica*
EstBíb	*Estudios bíblicos*
EvRT	*Evangelical Review of Theology*
EvQ	*Evangelical Quarterly*
EvT	*Evangelische Theologie*
ExpTim	*Expository Times*
FOTL	The Forms of the Old Testament Literature
FRLANT	Forschungen zur Religion und Literatur des Alten und Neuen Testaments
FzB	Forschung zur Bibel
GKC	*Gesenius' Hebrew Grammar* (ed. E. Kautzsch, rev. and trans. A.E. Cowley; Oxford: Clarendon Press, 2nd edn, 1910)
GTJ	*Grace Theological Journal*
HAHAT	W. Gesenius, *Hebräisches und aramäisches Handwörterbuch über das Alte Testament* (ed. F. Buhl; Berlin: Springer, 17th edn, 1915; ed. R. Meyer and H. Donner; Berlin: Springer-Verlag, 18th edn, 1987–)
HALAT	L. Koehler, W. Baumgartner and J.J. Stamm (eds.), *Hebräisches und aramäisches Lexicon zum Alten Testament* (6 vols.; Leiden: E.J. Brill, 1967–96)
HALOT	*The Hebrew and Aramaic Lexicon of the Old Testament* (5 vols.; Leiden: E.J. Brill, 1994–) (ET of *HALAT*)
HKAT	Handkommentar zum Alten Testament
HSAT	Die heilige Schrift des Alten Testamentes
HSM	Harvard Semitic Monographs
HTS	Harvard Theological Studies
HUCA	*Hebrew Union College Annual*
IBHS	B.K. Waltke and M. O'Connor, *An Introduction to Biblical Hebrew Syntax* (Winona Lake, IN: Eisenbrauns, 1990)
IBS	*Irish Biblical Studies*
ICC	International Critical Commentary
IDB	G.A. Buttrick (ed.), *The Interpreter's Dictionary of the Bible* (4 vols.; Nashville: Abingdon Press, 1962)

IDBSup	*IDB*, Supplementary Volume
Int	*Interpretation*
ISBE	G.W. Bromiley (ed.), *The International Standard Bible Encyclopaedia* (4 vols.; Grand Rapids: Eerdmans, rev. edn, 1979–88)
ITC	International Theological Commentary
JAOS	*Journal of the American Oriental Society*
JB	Jerusalem Bible
JBL	*Journal of Biblical Literature*
JES	*Journal of Ecumenical Studies*
JETS	*Journal of the Evangelical Theological Society*
JJS	*Journal of Jewish Studies*
JLT	*Journal of Literature and Theology*
Joüon	P. Joüon, *A Grammar of Biblical Hebrew* (rev. and trans. T. Muraoka; 2 vols.; Rome: Pontifical Biblical Institute, 2nd edn, 1993)
JQR	*Jewish Quarterly Review*
JRE	*Journal of Religious Ethics*
JSOT	*Journal for the Study of the Old Testament*
JSOTSup	*Journal for the Study of the Old Testament*, Supplement Series
JSS	*Journal of Semitic Studies*
KAT	Kommentar zum Alten Testament
KHAT	Kurzer Hand-Kommentar zum Alten Testament
MelT	*Melita Theologica*
N-A^{27}	*Novum Testamentum Graecum*, Nestle-Aland's 27th edition
NASB	*New American Standard Bible*
NCB	New Century Bible
NCBC	New Century Bible Commentary
NEB	*New English Bible*
NICOT	New International Commentary on the Old Testament
NIDOTE	W.A. VanGemeren (ed.), *New International Dictionary of Old Testament Theology and Exegesis* (5 vols.; Grand Rapids: Zondervan, 1997)
NIV	New International Version
NJB	New Jerusalem Bible
NJPSV	The Tanach: New Jewish Publication Society Version
NKJV	*New King James Version*
NPNF	*Nicene and Post-Nicene Fathers*
NRSV	New Revised Standard Version
NTS	*New Testament Studies*
OBO	Orbis biblicus et orientalis
OBT	Overtures to Biblical Theology
OTG	Old Testament Guides
OTL	Old Testament Library
OTM	Old Testament Message

OTS	Oudtestamentische Studiën
RB	*Revue biblique*
REB	*Revised English Bible*
RelSRev	*Religious Studies Review*
RevExp	*Review and Expositor*
RHPR	*Revue d'histoire et de philosophie religieuses*
RivB	*Rivista biblica*
RSO	*Revista degli studi orientali*
RSV	Revised Standard Version
RTR	*Reformed Theological Review*
RV	Revised Version
SBA	Stuttgarter biblische Aufsatzbünde
SBET	*Scottish Bulletin of Evangelical Theology*
SBFA	Studium Biblicum Franciscanum Analecta
SBLDS	Society of Biblical Literature Dissertation Series
SBLMS	Society of Biblical Literature Monograph Series
SBLSS	Society of Biblical Literature Semeia Studies
SBM	Stuttgarter biblische Monographien
SBS	Stuttgarter Bibelstudien
SBT	Studies in Biblical Theology
ScEs	*Science et esprit*
Sem	*Semitica*
SJLA	Studies in Judaism in Late Antiquity
SJOT	*Scandinavian Journal of the Old Testament*
SJT	*Scottish Journal of Theology*
SOTBT	Studies in Old Testament Biblical Theology
SP	The Samaritan Pentateuch
SR	*Studies in Religion*
SSN	Studia Semitica Nierlandica
StudBT	*Studia Biblica et Theologica*
TBT	*The Bible Today*
TDOT	G.J. Botterweck and H. Ringgren (eds.), *Theological Dictionary of the Old Testament* (10 vols.; Grand Rapids, Eerdmans, 1974–)
TEV	Today's English Version *(The Good News Bible)*
Them	*Themelios*
TJT	*Toronto Journal of Theology*
TLOT	E. Jenni and C. Westermann, *Theological Lexicon of the Old Testament* (3 vols.; Peabody: Hendrickson, 1997) (ET of *Theologisches Handwörterbuch zum Alten Testament* [2 vols.; Munich: Chr. Kaiser Verlag, 1971–76])
TLZ	*Theologische Literaturzeitung*
TOTC	Tyndale Old Testament Commentaries
TV	*Theologia Viatorum*
TWOT	R.L. Harris, G.L. Archer, B.K. Waltke (eds.), *Theological*

	Wordbook of the Old Testament (2 vols.; Chicago: Moody Press, 1980)
TynBul	*Tyndale Bulletin*
TZ	*Theologische Zeitschrift*
UF	*Ugarit-Forschungen*
VT	*Vetus Testamentum*
VTSup	*Vetus Testamentum*, Supplements
WBC	Word Biblical Commentary
WMANT	Wissenschaftliche Monographien zum Alten und Neuen Testament
WTJ	*Westminster Theological Journal*
ZAW	*Zeitschrift für die alttestamentliche Wissenschaft*
ZBK	Zürcher Bibelkommentare
ZTK	*Zeitschrift für Theologie und Kirche*

Chapter 1

INTRODUCTION

1. *Approaching the Problem: Two Covenant Pericopes within the Abraham Cycle*

> Abraham, one easily notices, does certain things more than once. Twice he migrates on divine command. Several times he builds an altar. Twice he represents his wife to foreigners as a sister. Twice he has a hand, direct or indirect, in the expulsion of his servant Hagar. Other episodes that may or may not include Abraham happen more than once: of hospitality to strangers; of disaster at Sodom; of a parent driven into the wilderness with a seemingly doomed child...[1]

The first perceptible narrative repetition in the Abraham narrative concerns the making of covenants in Genesis 15 and 17.[2] Of all the events that are repeated in the Abraham cycle, however, this is undoubtedly the most significant theologically. Both covenant pericopes clearly elaborate on the divine promises in Gen. 12.1-3. The latter provides the programmatic agenda not only for the Abraham narrative, but also for the rest of Genesis and beyond. Therefore, the inclusion by the final redactor of the material contained in Genesis 15 and 17 raises important exegetical questions which to date have not been adequately explained: Why are there two pericopes relating the establishment of a divine–human covenant? Why do each of these two covenant-making episodes reflect different promissory foci? What is the theological relationship between the 'covenant between the pieces' (Gen. 15) and the 'covenant of circumcision' (Gen. 17)? How does the distinctive emphasis of each covenant pericope impinge upon a holistic reading of the Abraham narrative?

1.   J. Rosenberg, *King and Kin: Political Allegory in the Hebrew Bible* (Bloomington: Indiana University Press, 1986), p. 73.
2.   As Rosenberg highlights (*King and Kin*, p. 88) in his ensuing discussion of the symmetrical structure of the Abraham cycle.

In the following study each of these questions will be critically examined, and a more nuanced explanation (than those reflected in current diachronic and synchronic interpretations) of the relationship between these two covenant pericopes will be proposed.

Due to the presence and generally accepted literary function of the 'Toledot Formulae' in the book of Genesis,[3] the Abraham narrative is clearly demarcated. Commencing in 11.27 and concluding with 25.11, the cycle comprises episodic events in the life of the first of Israel's patriarchs. The cycle relates how Abraham migrated with his family from Ur of the Chaldees, separated from his clan to become a semi-nomadic tribesman in and around the land of Palestine, and eventually became a figure of considerable significance through a series of events involving both political strife and personal intrigue.

Central to the account are God's promises to the patriarch, and the denouement of various obstacles that stood in the path of their realization. The promissory agenda is established in Gen. 12.1-3, in which two distinct prospects are anticipated: the evolution (from Abraham) of both a 'great nation' and international blessing.[4] The subsequent episodes in the Abraham narrative focus mainly on the first stage in the outworking of this programmatic agenda: the establishment of a special line of

---

3.   Noted challenges to the consensus opinion that the formulae are introductory have come from P.J. Wiseman (*New Discoveries in Babylonia about Genesis* [London: Marshall, 1936]; more recently reissued as *Ancient Records and the Structure of Genesis* [Nashville: Nelson, 1985]), R.K. Harrison (*Introduction to the Old Testament* [Grand Rapids: Eerdmans, 1969], pp. 543-47; *idem*, 'Genesis', *ISBE*, II, pp. 436-37) and D.S. DeWitt ('The Generations of Genesis', *EvQ* 48 [1976], pp. 196-211). As V.P. Hamilton (*The Book of Genesis Chapters 1–17* [NICOT; Grand Rapids: Eerdmans, 1990], pp. 9-10) notes, however, there are several difficulties with the proposal that the *tôlᵉdôt* phrases are concluding summaries, the most serious of which is the lack of correspondence between the alleged colophon and the preceding material (that is, Gen. 25.12 does not sit easily as a colophon for all the material from 11.27b). It is unsurprising, therefore, that other interpreters have taken these statements (with the possible exception of 2.4a) as introducing a new section. In any case, however the *tôlᵉdôt* statement is understood, its presence in Gen. 11.27 and Gen. 25.12 serves to mark the outside parameters of the Abraham narrative; cf. D.M. Carr, 'Βίβλος γενέσεως Revisited: A Synchronic Analysis of Patterns in Genesis as Part of the Torah (Part 1)', *ZAW* 110.2 (1998), pp. 159-72.

4.   For a defence of this bipartite distinction see Chapter 7 below.

descendants through which God's promises of nationhood and international blessing will find fulfilment.[5]

Within this broad narrative framework, however, the structure of the cycle is far from established.[6] While a chiastic pattern of some sort is aesthetically appealing, one which incorporates all of the material (including 22.20–25.18) appears to be somewhat elusive. Moreover, as Goldingay has recently highlighted,[7] the 'watershed' location of Genesis 16 in several such chiasms elevates Ishmael's profile considerably, giving him more literary and theological significance than interpreters have previously discerned. While Ishmael's significance in the Abraham narrative should not be underestimated, to raise him to equal importance with Isaac seems rather to overplay his role, both in the Abraham narrative and beyond. In view, therefore, of their potential to distort the significance of any one episode in the narrative, elaborate structures which some readers discern in the text must be examined with cautious reserve.

The various chiastic structures alluded to above do draw attention, nevertheless, to the intriguing feature of the Abraham cycle under investigation: the fact that two quite separate pericopes focus on the establishment of a covenant between God and Abraham. As acknowledged above, this is but one of a number of repetitions in the Abraham

5.   Such a theme broadly encompasses the entire narrative, including the stories involving Lot (Gen. 13.1–14.24; 18.1–19.38), and the Hagar/Ishmael episodes (Gen. 16.1-16; 21.8-20), as is convincingly argued by J. McKeown ('A Study of the Main Unifying Themes in the Hebrew Text of the Book of Genesis' [PhD thesis, The Queen's University of Belfast, 1991], pp. 180-223), for whom Lot and Ishmael serve respectively as foils to Abraham and Isaac (p. 222).

6.   An observation only underscored by the *different* structural patterns which have been suggested; see G. Rendsburg, *The Redaction of Genesis* (Winona Lake, IN: Eisenbrauns, 1986), pp. 27-52; cf. Rosenberg, *King and Kin*, p. 84; G.J. Wenham, *Genesis 1–15* (WBC, 1; Waco, TX: Word Books, 1987), p. 263 (cf. *idem*, 'The Akedah: A Paradigm of Sacrifice', in D.P. Wright *et al.* [eds.], *Pomegranates and Golden Bells: Studies in Biblical, Jewish, and Near Eastern Ritual, Law, and Literature* [Festschrift J. Milgrom; Winona Lake, IN: Eisenbrauns, 1995], p. 98); D. Garrett, *Rethinking Genesis: The Sources and Authorship of the First Book of the Pentateuch* (Grand Rapids: Baker Book House, 1991), pp. 160-63; J. Magonet, *Bible Lives* (London: SCM Press, 1992), p. 25.

7.   J. Goldingay, 'The Place of Ishmael', in P.R. Davies and D.J.A. Clines (eds.), *The World of Genesis: Persons, Places, Perspectives* (JSOTSup, 257; Sheffield: Sheffield Academic Press, 1998), pp. 146-48.

cycle, to which the various chiasms that have been proposed bear eloquent testimony. Even so, the implication of this observation for a holistic reading of Gen. 11.27–25.11 seems generally to have been overlooked by previous scholarship. Moreover, the presence of two covenant pericopes impinges upon the interpretation of Gen. 12.1-3,[8] a text which outlines the promissory agenda that is developed in the ensuing Pentateuchal narratives and the Former Prophets, and is of such significance for the interpretation of the Abraham narrative reflected in the New Testament. Therefore the importance of the relationship between Genesis 15 and 17 cannot be overstated.

As the next chapter will show, the majority of exegetes have started with the assumption that God established a single covenant between Abraham and himself. Consequently, the presence of a second chapter within the Abraham narrative announcing the establishment of a divine covenant with Abraham has usually been explained in one of three ways:

1.   Genesis 15 and 17 reflect two separate stages (stressing, respectively, divine and human responsibilities) in the ratification of a single covenant established between God and Abraham;

2.   Genesis 17 constitutes a divine reaffirmation or renewal of the covenant that was formally ratified in Genesis 15, yet 'jeopardized' by the behaviour of Abraham and Sarah in Genesis 16;[9]

3.   Genesis 15 and 17 derive from different literary sources that have been incorporated into the final form of the book of Genesis;[10] thus the idea of two distinct covenantal events has been introduced artificially by a redactor.

However, not everyone shares the basic premise underlying each of these three interpretations; viz. that only one covenant was established

---

8.   As will be demonstrated below; cf. Chapter 7.

9.   Not all who interpret Gen. 17 as a reaffirmation of the covenant established in Gen. 15 relate such a confirmation directly to Abraham's lapse of faith in Gen. 16.

10.   Here and throughout this book reference to 'the final form' relates to the shape and contents of the Hebrew Bible as reflected in the MT, except where there are sufficient philological, syntactical or textual grounds for questioning the authenticity of any particular word or clause.

between God and Abraham. A fourth possibility has been suggested by several scholars, especially since the advent of more holistic readings of the biblical text: Genesis 17 draws attention to a covenant which is in many respects quite distinct from the covenant that had been ratified in Genesis 15. These differences are of sufficient importance to distinguish between the covenants spoken of in each chapter, and to identify the covenant in Genesis 17 as a separate development in God's dealings with Abraham (that is, God made two different covenants with Abraham, each with its own particular emphasis and function in the narrative as a whole).

Thus four distinguishable positions have been adopted on the question of the relationship between the covenant(s) in Genesis 15 and 17: (1) God established a single covenant in two stages; (2) God ratified a covenant with Abraham, and subsequently reaffirmed it; (3) two different accounts of the ratification of a single covenant have been incorporated within the composite Abraham narrative; (4) two distinct covenants were established between God and Abraham.

As will become evident from the historical review in the following chapter, it is not always possible to place every exegete neatly into one of these four interpretative camps. Some scholars seem to vacillate between some of these explanations.[11] Such lack of clarity and precision, however, simply serves to highlight the nature and complexity of the problem being discussed. Scholarship has not yet firmly established the precise relationship between Genesis 15 and 17 within the final form of the book of Genesis. Indeed, all too easily standard arguments proffered by respective schools of thought are simply repeated, without adequate thought being given to this important issue.[12]

---

11. As the following synopsis will illustrate, this is especially so in the case of the first two interpretations discussed; it is difficult to put some writers into one camp or the other, either because of the absence of explicit elaboration of their position or because of their ambiguous use of terminology.

12. This criticism applies especially (though by no means exclusively) to interpreters who accept the validity of the traditional source-critical analysis of the text. Too often such scholars assume rather uncritically that a source-critical labelling of the material explains adequately the relationship between these two covenant chapters. As Y. Zakovitch ('Juxtaposition in the Abraham Cycle', in Wright *et al.* [eds.], *Pomegranates and Golden Bells*, p. 509) has correctly pointed out, 'Scholars of biblical criticism have shown little regard for the rationale behind the editorial work of the Bible. For these scholars the prehistory of a text is more interesting than is the final product. By focusing either on the literary documents that preceded the

2. *Methodological Options*

Clearly the literary and theological relationship between the material in
Genesis 15 and 17 can be approached from two quite different perspectives. Those approaching the text from a diachronic framework generally assume the presence of a number of underlying literary and/or oral
traditions. While the utilization of some such traditions by the com-
piler(s) of Genesis is possible,[13] the labelling of individual units as different sources or traditions is of limited value in determining the literary and theological relationship between them in their present canonical
context. While it may provide some explanation for the diversity and
complexity reflected in the biblical text, it does so at the expense of the
integrity of the final form. Moreover, in the absence of any extra-biblical documentary evidence, the fruit of such research can never be
anything more than hypothetical.[14] Unfortunately there are no objective
criteria against which to measure the correctness of any such reconstructions.[15]

present puzzle, or on the "smallest literary units" and their *Sitz im Leben*, critics
have paid almost no attention to the editor—who, in any case, is considered to be
mildly senile, a state reflected in the apparent disorder of the texts.' Given the
present interest in the final shape and shaping of the biblical text, it is clear that a
source-critical analysis can at best offer only a partial answer to a question that is
much more complex than a previous generation of scholars acknowledged.

13. Even a single author, as recently postulated by R.N. Whybray (*The Making
of the Pentateuch: A Methodological Study* [JSOTSup, 53; Sheffield: JSOT Press,
1987]), had to collate existing information (see p. 242).

14. As is graphically illustrated by the present state of flux in source criticism;
in addition to Chapter 2 Section 4c below compare the recent appraisals by G.J.
Wenham ('Pentateuchal Studies Today', *Them* 22.1 [1996], pp. 3-13) and E.W.
Nicholson (*The Pentateuch in the Twentieth Century: The Legacy of Julius Wellhausen* [Oxford: Clarendon Press, 1998], pp. 132-221).

15. While J.H. Tigay (*Empirical Models for Biblical Criticism* [Philadelphia:
University of Philadephia Press, 1985], pp. 21-96) has shown that the sort of
conflation and inconsistencies which the Documentary Hypothesis finds in the Pentateuch is also reflected in other ancient texts (for instance the *Gilgamesh Epic*, the
Samaritan Pentateuch and the LXX), this merely demonstrates that such redactional
activity was practised and that, therefore, some source-critical reconstructions are
feasible; unlike Tigay's examples, there is no earlier documentary evidence (such as
a proto-Genesis) against which to measure the accuracy of any particular reconstruction, or indeed to establish the case for such redactional activity in the Pentateuch. Thus, in the absence of such documentary evidence, all source-critical recon-

The other perspective from which one can approach the relationship between these two chapters is a synchronic analysis of the text. This methodology, as the term 'synchronic' suggests, investigates the material at a single point in time; chiefly, the final form of the biblical text. Thus, rather than looking behind the text at the various reconstructed stages of its historical development, a synchronic investigation looks more holistically at the relationship between the component parts of the biblical narrative. Moreover, rather than investigating the relationships between hypothetical sources and traditions whose demarcation and very existence remains to be established with any degree of certainty, a synchronic analysis focuses on something that is tangible, and against which the validity of any proposed exegetical interpretation can be measured objectively. Such an approach is eminently suited to any attempt to understand Genesis 15 and 17, not in terms of priority and provenance, but in terms of their present literary and theological relationship.

Admittedly, as Boorer has illustrated,[16] diachronic investigation and the resultant analyses may have significance for how *some* readers approach the final form of the text. However, as she nevertheless admits, 'the interpretation of the present text [i.e. Genesis–Kings] that results from a diachronic reading is likely to be different from a synchronic reading of that text'.[17] Given that this is so, and that diachronic analyses may unduly influence synchronic readings, it is better to set aside (at least for the purpose of establishing a final-form reading) historical-critical questions altogether and focus on the literary shape and theological significance of the Abraham narrative as we now have it. Only when conclusions have been reached in relation to the latter is it wise to venture into the more speculative area of the text's prehistory.[18]

structions, however convincing, must remain hypothetical.

16. S. Boorer, 'The Importance of a Diachronic Approach: The Case of Genesis–Kings', *CBQ* 51 (1989), pp. 195-208; see also J. Barr's essay, 'The Synchronic, the Diachronic and the Historical: A Triangular Relationship?', in J.C. De Moor (ed.), *Synchronic or Diachronic? A Debate on Method in Old Testament Exegesis* (OTS, 34; Leiden: E.J. Brill, 1995), pp. 1-14.

17. Boorer, 'A Diachronic Approach to Genesis–Kings', pp. 204-205.

18. The case for such a methodology has been advanced by R.W.L. Moberly (*At the Mountain of God: Story and Theology in Exodus 32–34* [JSOTSup, 22; Sheffield: JSOT Press, 1983], pp. 22-27). As Moberly avers, 'It is only a rigorous examination of the final text, treated in its own right as a literary and theological

3. *The Synchronic Framework and Plan of this Investigation*

Since this study aims to establish the relationship between Genesis 15 and 17 within the *final* form of the Abraham narrative, the following investigation will operate within a synchronic framework. Given the obvious limitations (as outlined above) of a historical-critical approach in relation to this objective, the source and tradition history of specific text-units will be largely ignored. Rather, the relationship between these two important pericopes in the Abraham narrative will be explored primarily through careful exegesis of the canonical text.

After the various approaches to the relationship between Genesis 15 and 17 have been surveyed in Chapter 2, the two pericopes will be compared and contrasted in Chapter 3. This chapter will disclose the fundamental problem with the traditional source-critical explanation of the two covenant pericopes as records of the same event. Differences in both major and peripheral details will be highlighted in order to demonstrate that within the final form of the text (at least) Genesis 15 and 17 constitute two quite distinct episodes. Thus whatever the source or tradition history of these two chapters, the exegetical goal of the modern interpreter must be to understand their function within their present literary context.

Each pericope will then be examined in terms of its own literary structure and particular emphases, in order to illustrate the distinctive promissory foci which they reflect. The close analysis of Genesis 15 in Chapter 4 will illustrate how this covenant pericope relates specifically to the promise of nationhood (i.e. descendants and land). The specific

---

composition, that will enable one to pronounce with any certainty upon what are genuine difficulties in the text such as suggest a complex prehistory' (pp. 23-24). The ramifications of such an approach for a traditional diachronic analysis are articulated by P.R. Noble ('Synchronic and Diachronic Approaches to Biblical Interpretation', *JLT* 7.2 [1993], pp. 136-48), for whom 'a successful synchronic interpretation of a text renders a "sources-and-redactor" account of its prehistory highly improbable' (p. 148). Noble, however, is clearly assuming a degree of success beyond that anticipated by Moberly. Cf. the 'complementary' approach adopted by M. Sternberg (*The Poetics of Biblical Narrative: Ideological Literature and the Drama of Reading* [Bloomington: Indiana University Press, 1985], pp. 13-23) and the 'hermeneutical pluralism' advocated by M. Brett (*Biblical Criticism in Crisis? The Impact of the Canonical Approach on Old Testament Studies* [Cambridge: Cambridge University Press, 1991], esp. pp. 166-67).

emphasis of the 'covenant of circumcision' will be examined in Chapter 5. Here it will be shown that, despite some overlap with Genesis 15, the promissory focus of Genesis 17 is quite different, with prominence being given to promises that are not mentioned at all in relation to the 'covenant between the pieces'. This lends further weight to the conclusion that Genesis 15 and 17 relate not only to two chronologically distinct episodes in the Abraham narrative, but also to two theologically distinct covenants.

This latter possibility is explored further in Chapter 6, in which the specific literary and theological function of Genesis 17 is investigated to ascertain whether it is best understood as the renewal of an existing covenant, or the annunciation of a new one. This investigation will demonstrate that there are important elements of continuity and discontinuity, suggesting that the relationship between Genesis 15 and 17 is more complex than previous scholarship has acknowledged.

Finally, the relationship between the two covenant pericopes and the rest of the Abraham narrative will be explored in Chapter 7, and an attempt will be made to provide a coherent reading of chs. 15 and 17 within the context of the Abraham narrative as a whole.

Before doing any of this, however, it is important to see how this current investigation relates to previous research on the relationship between these covenant pericopes. The next chapter will analyse and synthesize the interpretations reflected in past and present scholarship, and so provide a framework for understanding how this study contributes to the scholarly debate.

Chapter 2

APPROACHES TO THE RELATIONSHIP BETWEEN GENESIS 15 AND 17

1. *Introduction*

It is not inconceivable that Abraham should relocate more than once at God's command; that he should build more than one altar; that he should lose his concubine a second time—even that he should twice attempt the same wife-sister ploy with a foreign king. But why should he enter a second time into a covenant with God (or more accurately, why does God initiate a second covenant with the patriarch)? As noted in the previous chapter, scholarship has explained the presence of a second divine–human covenant in Gen. 11.27–25.11 in one of four ways:

1.   Chapters 15 and 17 reflect two separate and distinctive stages in the ratification of a single covenant established between God and Abraham;
2.   Chapter 17 constitutes a divine reaffirmation or renewal of the same covenant that was announced and formally ratified in ch. 15;
3.   Chapters 15 and 17 derive from at least two different literary sources which have been incorporated into the final form of the Abraham narrative;
4.   Chapter 17 incorporates a covenant which is in many important respects quite distinct from the covenant that was ratified in ch. 15.

As was underlined, however, the demarcation between these four distinct interpretations is not quite as sharply defined as this classification may suggest. While the following historical survey will attempt to classify exegetical approaches according to these four positions, a certain degree of flexibility must be taken into account.

2. *Two Stages in the Ratification of the Same Covenant*

The interpretation of Genesis 15 and 17 as two stages in the covenant made between God and Abraham seems to have the greatest antiquity. This is apparently the interpretation adopted by the earliest Jewish exegetes.[1]

Josephus does not explicitly mention the 'covenant' between God and Abraham.[2] Nevertheless, in his re-telling of the Abraham narrative he seems to equate the promises of Genesis 17 (i.e. a son by Sarah from whom would come great nations and kings who would conquer the land of Canaan) with the promise of conquest in Genesis 15. In any case, Josephus places emphasis on the concept of numerical increase at the expense of territorial acquisition, reducing Genesis 15 to a prediction about the military successes of Abraham's future descendants. Thus for Josephus, Genesis 17 becomes simply a further stage in the divine revelation given to Abraham.

In his presentation of Abraham as the 'father of philosophy' Philo typically allegorizes the material in both Genesis 15 and 17, but in such a way that suggests not two distinct covenants, but rather two distinct stages of a single covenant (*Quaest. in Gen.* 3.15). Thus the 'my covenant' announced in Gen. 17.2, 4 is interpreted as 'the incorporeal word... Since he had previously used the expression, "treaty", he now proceeds to say, do not seek that treaty in letters, since I myself, in

---

1. It must be admitted that most of the early post-biblical (i.e. post-Hebrew Bible) Jewish literature offers simply a re-telling of the Abraham story, sometimes with interesting embellishments and changes; cf. *Jubilees*, *Testament of Abraham* and *Pseudo-Philo*, in J.H. Charlesworth (ed.), *The Old Testament Pseudepigrapha* (2 vols.; London: Darton, Longman & Todd, 1983–85). To a large extent this is also true of Josephus and Philo, thus the following comments are necessarily tentative.

2. Cf. *Ant.* 1.10. As T.W. Franxman observes, however, this is 'consistent with Josephus' policy of repressing all reference to a permanent possession of the land as promised and guaranteed by God...a point which might have delicate political consequences' (*Genesis and the Jewish Antiquities of Flavius Josephus* [Rome: Biblical Institute Press, 1979], p. 138). Franxman further adds, 'God's covenant with Abraham and with his descendants to be their God is not part of Josephus' religious purview. The eternal possession of Canaan is transmuted into a promise of future victory in war' (Franxman, *Genesis*, p. 141). For a somewhat similar assessment of Josephus's treatment of Gen. 15 and 17, cf. B. Halpern-Amaru, *Rewriting the Bible: Land and Covenant in Postbiblical Jewish Literature* (Valley Forge, PA: Trinity Press International, 1994), pp. 95-99.

accordance with what has been said before, am myself the genuine and true covenant'.[3]

Thus while Josephus and Philo do not address the relationship between Genesis 15 and 17 specifically, their treatment of the material contained in these two chapters appears to suggest that the two chapters are viewed simply as different stages in God's covenantal relationship with Abraham.

A somewhat similar situation is reflected in the Targums.[4] Like Josephus and Philo, the Targums do not expressly address the question of how the covenants in Genesis 15 and 17 relate to each other. Nevertheless, they appear to treat them as different stages of a single covenant between God and Abraham, so much so that the covenantal significance of Genesis 15 is almost bypassed altogether.[5]

What was implicit in the earlier Jewish literature becomes explicit in the Midrashim. *Genesis Rabbah* interprets the act of circumcision as part of the ratification of the covenant established between God and Abraham. The fourteen-year delay in the institution of circumcision was 'so that Isaac in particular [and not Ishmael] should be born of a holy seed [that is, of semen of a circumcised penis]'.[6] Citing R. Simeon ben Eleazar, the point is also made that Shammai (in contrast to Hillel) interpreted the blood spilt at circumcision as signifying the covenant of circumcision.[7] Thus interpreted, Genesis 17 is the second stage in the establishment of the covenant initiated in Genesis 15.

A 'two-stage' interpretation also seems to have been adopted by Justin Martyr, the first of the Church Fathers to focus considerable attention on the Abraham narrative. While in his *Dialogue with Trypho*

---

3.   C.D. Yonge (ed.), *The Works of Philo: Complete and Unabridged* (Peabody: Hendrikson, 1993), p. 854.

4.   Cf. M. Aberbach and B. Grossfeld, *Targum Onkelos to Genesis: A Critical Analysis Together with an English Translation of the Text* (Denver: Ktav Publishing House, 1982); M. McNamara, *Targum Neofiti: Genesis* (The Aramaic Bible, Ia; Edinburgh: T. & T. Clark, 1992); M. Maher, *Targum Pseudo-Jonathan: Genesis* (The Aramaic Bible, Ib; Edinburgh: T. & T. Clark, 1992).

5.   *Targ. Neof.* 15.17 comes closest to drawing out the covenantal significance of Gen. 15.7-21, making Abraham himself pass between the pieces. Both *Targ. Onq.* 17.4 and *Targ. Ps-J.* 17.4 insert an interpretative gloss ('I am making') into Gen. 17.4, apparently interpreting this episode as a further ratification of the covenant established between God and Abraham.

6.   *Gen. R.* 46.2.2.

7.   *Gen. R.* 46.12.3.

Justin appeals extensively to Abraham and the promise God made to him, he does not really address the question of how Genesis 15 and 17 are related.[8] His wholesale 'Christianization' of all the promises made to the patriarch would suggest,[9] however, that like Jewish writers before him, he read Genesis 17 simply as a further stage in God's covenantal dealings with Abraham.

Other Church Fathers pay little attention to the relationship between Genesis 15 and 17. Clement of Alexandria picks up Philo's idea that Gen. 17.2 cryptically suggests that God had told Abraham not to seek the covenant in writing, suggesting that he also identified the two chapters as two stages in the one covenant.[10] Not even Jerome appears to have given much thought to the relationship between the two covenant chapters within the Abraham narrative.[11] This key question of interpretation is not really brought into focus until it is addressed by Augustine in his *City of God*.[12]

Mediaeval Jewish exegetes, like their rabbinical predecessors, generally side-step the issue of how the covenants in Genesis 15 and 17 are related. Rashi differentiates between a covenant (relating to land) in Genesis 15 and a 'covenant of love' (relating to inheriting the land) in Genesis 17, but does not elaborate on this distinction.[13] Ibn Ezra notes the covenantal significance of the animal ritual in Genesis 15, but not that of circumcision in Genesis 17.[14] In contrast, the covenantal significance of Genesis 15 is ignored altogether by Rambam and Sforno.[15]

8.   *ANF*, I, pp. 258ff.

9.   See J.S. Siker, *Disinheriting the Jews: Abraham in Early Christian Controversy* (Louisville, KY: Westminster / John Knox Press, 1991), pp. 163-84.

10.   *ANF*, II, p. 341.

11.   *Saint Jerome's 'Hebrew Questions on Genesis'* (trans. with commentary by C.T.R. Hayward [Oxford: Clarendon Press, 1995]) is noticeably silent on this issue.

12.   *NPNF*, First Series, II, pp. 318ff. Augustine's interpretation is discussed in Section 4 below.

13.   Cf. *'Rashi' on the Pentateuchal Genesis* (trans. and annotated by J.H. Lowe [London: Hebrew Compendium, 1928]), pp. 174, 187.

14.   Cf. H.N. Strickman and A.M. Silver, *Ibn Ezra's Commentary on the Pentateuch: Genesis (Bereshit)* (New York: Menorah, 1988), pp. 183-88.

15.   Cf. M. Zlotowitz and N. Scherman, *Bereishis: Genesis/A New Translation with a Commentary Anthologized from Talmudic, Midrashic and Rabbinic Sources* (2 vols.; New York: Mesorah Publications, 1986), I, pp. 503-37; R. Raphael Pelcovitz, *Sforno Commentary on the Torah: Translation and Explanatory Notes* (New York: Mesorah Publications, 1987), pp. 73-76.

Ramban identifies the *everlasting* possession of the land as the principal difference between the promise in Genesis 17 and the earlier promise in Genesis 15, but otherwise the relationship between the two chapters is ignored.[16] It would seem, therefore, that these mediaeval exegetes also interpreted the two chapters as complementary, Genesis 17 constituting the second (and apparently for them, the main) stage in the institution of the Abrahamic covenant.

Calvin appears to be the first to state quite categorically that Genesis 15 and 17 are two stages in the same divine–human covenant.[17] He understands the Abrahamic covenant as consisting of two parts:

> The first was a declaration of gratuitous love; to which was annexed the promise of a happy life. But the other was an exhortation to the sincere endeavour to cultivate uprightness... He [God] does not...speak of this [covenant] as a new thing: but he recalls the memory of the covenant which he had before made, and now fully confirms and establishes its certainty... Therefore, by these words, he intends nothing else than that the covenant, of which Abram had heard before, should be established and ratified: but he expressly introduces that principal point, concerning the multiplication of seed, which he afterwards frequently repeats.[18]

The Puritan commentator Matthew Henry is another who interprets Genesis 15 and 17 as two separate stages of a single covenant. For Henry, the passing of the smoking furnace and burning lamp between the pieces in Genesis 15 'was the confirming of the covenant God now made with him'.[19] In the caption heading for Genesis 17 Henry ob-

---

16. Ramban, *Commentary on the Torah: Genesis* (New York: Shilo Publishing House, 1971), p. 211.

17. *Pace* H.C. Chew ('The Theme of "Blessing for the Nations" in the Patriarchal Narratives of Genesis' [PhD thesis, The University of Sheffield, 1982], p. 345 n. 55), who places Calvin among those who interpret Gen. 17 as a renewal of the covenant.

18. J. Calvin, *A Commentary on Genesis* (Geneva Commentaries; repr., London: Banner of Truth Trust, 1965), pp. 444-45. While Calvin differentiates between temporal/physical and eternal/spiritual aspects of the covenant, restricting the latter to Isaac's line, he does not, like Luther, draw a sharp distinction between the covenant God established with Abraham and that subsequently established with Isaac (pp. 461-62); cf. Section 5 below.

19. M. Henry, *Matthew Henry's Commentary on the Whole Bible* (6 vols.; McLean, VA: MacDonald Publishing Company, n.d.), I, p. 105. Henry defines 'covenant' here in terms of promise; on 'the Lord made a covenant with Abram'

serves that 'mention was made of this covenant (ch. xv. 18), but here it
is particularly drawn up, and put into the form of a covenant, that
Abram might have strong consolation'.[20] Thus, while not oblivious to
the differences in nature and emphasis between the covenants in each
chapter, Henry interprets the covenant as having been ratified in two
stages.

While the position advocated by Herman Witsius is certainly more
complex, its underlying tenet is essentially the same: God established a
single covenant with Abraham, but in different stages. Witsius identifies two covenantal dimensions: stipulations and promises.[21] Witsius
implies that the covenant was initiated in Genesis 12, Genesis 15 and
17 both representing further stages in its development. Thus for
Witsius, each key stage in the development of the covenant begins with
a stipulation (cf. Gen. 12.1; 15.1; 17.1). The covenant promises are of
two types, spiritual (of which some are general and common to all
believers, and of which others are special and peculiar to Abraham) and
corporal (i.e. external promises made to Abraham, yet at the same time
types of spiritual and heavenly things). Thus Witsius understands Genesis 15 and 17 as subsequent stages of the covenant that was initiated in
Gen. 12.1-3.

A similar, albeit much less complex, approach is adopted also by
John Flavel. In his 'Reply to Mr Cary's Solemn Call' Flavel maintains
(contra Cary) that the promises and stipulations in Genesis 17 do not
reflect two different covenants—a pure covenant of grace and a *restipu-
lation* amounting to a covenant of works.[22] Flavel insists rather that the
stipulations of Genesis 17 should be incorporated with the promises as
'just and necessary parts of one and the same covenant'.[23] Given that
Flavel speaks of Gen. 12.1-3 (and Gen. 22.2-3, 16-18) as 'God's covenant with Abraham',[24] presumably he thinks of the covenant as having

(Gen. 15.18) Henry writes: 'that is, gave a promise to Abram, saying *Unto thy seed
have I given this land*' (p. 105, emphasis his).

20. *Matthew Henry's Commentary*, p. 110.

21. H. Witsius, *The Economy of the Covenants between God and Man: Comprehending a Complete Body of Divinity* (trans. and rev. W. Crookshank; 2 vols.;
repr.; Escondido, CA: The den Dulk Christian Foundation, 1990 [1822]), II, pp.
146-47.

22. J. Flavel, *The Works of John Flavel* (6 vols.; repr.; London: Banner of Truth
Trust, 1968), VI, p. 344.

23. Flavel, *Works*, p. 344.

24. Flavel, *Works*, pp. 348, 351.

been initiated in ch. 12, and renewed and expanded in chs. 15, 17 and 22.

In the twentieth century the view that Genesis 15 and 17 are two stages of the same covenant has been advocated by a number of scholars. The Lutheran commentator, H.C. Leupold, contends that

> the basic fact to be observed for a proper approach to this chapter [Gen. 17] is that the covenant referred to is not a new one. For 15.18 reports the establishment of the covenant, whose essential provisions are the same as those here outlined... the one covenant promises certain blessings, the other the realization of these blessings when their appointed time has come.[25]

Thus Leupold understands the key verbs in Genesis 17 (נתן in Gen. 17.2 and הקים in Gen. 17.7) as 'to put in force/make operative' and 'uphold' respectively.[26] Not surprisingly, he also plays down the different emphases of both chapters, somewhat naïvely accusing others of magnifying 'incidental differences'.[27]

Kidner likewise maintains that the divine response to Abraham's request for reassurance (in Gen. 15) was

> a formal covenant...executed in two stages. The first is in this chapter [15], an inauguration of a particularly vivid kind. The second stage, in chapter 17, was the giving of the covenant sign, circumcision. For good measure, as Hebrews 6.13, 17 points out, there was finally an oath to reinforce it in 22.16ff.[28]

Kidner explains the reason for the delay in the second stage in terms of the testing of Abraham's faith, the rationale for the two stages of covenant-making being to highlight both dimensions of the covenant:

> The earlier chapter fixed the basic pattern of grace and answering faith; nothing was asked of Abram but to believe and 'know of a surety'. Now [in ch. 17] emerge the implications, in depth and extension: in depth, for faith must show itself in utter dedication (1); in extension, for the whole company must be sealed, one by one, down the generations (10ff.). Together then the two chapters set out the personal and corporate par-

---

25. H.C. Leupold, *Exposition of Genesis* (Columbus: The Wartburg Press, 1942), p. 511.

26. Leupold, *Genesis*, pp. 514, 517. Significantly, he reverts to the usual understanding of הקים as 'establish' in 17.19 and 21; cf. pp. 528-29.

27. Leupold, *Genesis*, p. 511.

28. D. Kidner, *Genesis* (TOTC; Downers Grove: InterVarsity Press, 1967), p. 124.

ticipation; the inward faith and the outward seal...imputed righteousness and expressed devotion (15.6; 17.1).[29]

While Kidner acknowledges that in Genesis 17 new promissory aspects come into view, he clearly does not consider these novel enough to warrant interpreting ch. 17 as a covenant distinct from the one that was formally established in ch. 15.[30]

Although his rationale is significantly different, Kline's conclusion is basically the same: Genesis 17 represents a further ratification of the same covenant whose formal establishment is recorded in Genesis 15.[31] Basing his analysis on ancient Near Eastern treaties, Kline distinguishes between 'law covenants' and 'promise covenants', so defined according to who (human or God) swears the oath of ratification.[32] For Kline, Genesis 15 is an example of the latter covenant-type, whereas Genesis 17 is an example of the former. It is important to stress, however, that Kline does not draw such a dichotomy too sharply in the context of these chapters, for he identifies a single covenant (or covenant process) which was confirmed or ratified on several occasions.[33] It is Kline's contention, therefore, that Genesis 17 is the natural corollary to Genesis 15: the latter is 'an example of a covenant sealed by divine oath';[34] the former is 'an oath of allegiance... an avowal of Yahweh as covenant Lord, a commitment in loyalty to him... a sign of consecration'.[35] Thus for Kline, Genesis 15 and 17 represent different aspects (stages) of the same divine–human covenant. Genesis 15 highlights God's unconditional commitment to Abraham; Genesis 17 emphasizes Abraham's consecration to God.

Several scholars advocated a two-stage interpretation of the Abrahamic covenant in the 1980s. Although somewhat ambivalent, Gros Louis appears to suggest that Genesis 15 and 17 represent respectively

29. Kidner, *Genesis*, p. 128.

30. For instance, Kidner notes the introduction in Gen. 17 of *kings* and *nations*, and the promise of a special divine–human relationship, but interprets these primarily in relation to God's promise to Abraham of nationhood (*Genesis*, p. 129).

31. M.G. Kline, *By Oath Consigned: A Reinterpretation of the Covenant Signs of Circumcision and Baptism* (Grand Rapids: Eerdmans, 1969), pp. 22-25, 39-49.

32. Kline, *By Oath Consigned*, p. 16. Kline's thesis is that the biblical covenants essentially conform to the ancient Near Eastern treaty patterns.

33. Kline, *By Oath Consigned*, p. 22.

34. Kline, *By Oath Consigned*, p. 16.

35. Kline, *By Oath Consigned*, p. 43.

the divine guarantee and the human reciprocation involved in this divine–human covenant.[36] Nelson's synchronic study, in contrast, is quite unequivocal.[37] For Nelson the two chapters are complementary, Genesis 15 emphasizing divine grace and Genesis 17 highlighting human responsibility. While expressed differently, Magonet's conclusion is rather similar:

> Both chapters 15 and 17 deal with God's discussions with Abraham and the establishment of the *brit*, the covenant, between them. It is made by God's promise in chapter 15, and reciprocated by Abraham's acceptance of circumcision, the sign of the covenant, in chapter 17.[38]

A two-stage interpretation of the Abrahamic covenant is also reflected in two quite different works on Genesis produced in the mid-1980s: a homiletical commentary by Baldwin,[39] and a short literary study by Rendsburg.[40] Baldwin suggests that

> though the covenant had already been sealed by sacrifice (chapter 15), one more preparatory stage remained to be fulfilled before the birth of the promised son. Whereas in chapter 15 the covenant made with Abram was private and personal to him alone, now the time had come for the matter to be made public... The covenant sacrifice established that the covenant was an unconditional act of God in which Abram had no part to play, and to which he could make no contribution. Now his response is stipulated, albeit in one all-embracing command.[41]

The rite of circumcision is for her the means by which Abraham and his heirs were to commit themselves unconditionally to God and to the covenant, as God himself had formerly done in the rite of Genesis 15.[42]

---

36. See K.R.R. Gros Louis, 'Abraham' (I and II), in K.R.R. Gros Louis and J.S. Ackerman (eds.), *Literary Interpretations of Biblical Narratives*, II (Nashville: Abingdon Press, 1982), pp. 53-84 (64-65); however, cf. pp. 75-76, where he seems rather to imply that Gen. 15 and 17 present two distinct covenants.

37. R.D. Nelson, 'Was Not Abraham Justified by Works?', *Dialog* 22 (1983), pp. 258-63.

38. J. Magonet, 'Abraham and God', *Judaism* 33 (1984), pp. 160-70 (162).

39. J. Baldwin, *The Message of Genesis 12–50* (Bible Speaks Today; Leicester: InterVarsity Press, 1986). A very similar interpretation is reflected in the earlier devotional study by R.S. Wallace, *Abraham: Genesis 12–23* (London: SPCK, 1981), pp. 59ff.

40. Rendsburg, *The Redaction of Genesis*.

41. Baldwin, *The Message of Genesis*, p. 62.

42. Baldwin, *The Message of Genesis*, p. 65.

Approaching the Abraham narrative from a very different perspective, that of redaction criticism, Rendsburg advocates seeing the two covenant chapters as 'matching sequences' in the chiastic structure which the redactor of the Abraham narrative has imposed upon his material.[43] Because of this premise, Rendsburg highlights the 'striking similarities' between both pericopes, rather than focusing on points of discontinuity and difference in emphasis.[44]

More recently, Hays has proposed a somewhat different analysis of the relationship between Genesis 15 and 17.[45] Attempting a canonical reading of the Abraham narrative, Hays correctly acknowledges the need to 'address the differences and similarities of the two, but from the perspective of relating them to each other and to their immediate context rather than relating them to a P or J document'.[46] Following Barr's lead in assuming that in the context of Genesis 17 the future hiphil of קוּם must carry the sense of 'to fulfil',[47] Hays maintains that Genesis 15 relates to the formal establishment of the covenant between God and *Abraham*, whereas in Genesis 17 the focus shifts to the continuation of that same covenant with Abraham's *descendants*. Hays supports such an analysis by comparing the use of the key verbs in the contexts of both the Abrahamic and Davidic covenants (2 Chron. 7.18):

> in both כרת is used of the one who initially received the covenant (David and Abraham) while הקים is used of their descendants. כרת is never used of God's covenant or oath to Isaac or Solomon, but only הקים is (Gen. 17.19; 26.3; Exod. 6.4). Also, הקים is never used of Abraham or David when referred to without their descendants, but rather כרת... If this distinction was truly present in the minds of the biblical writers, then it also explains the use of נתן in Gen. 17.2. For if כרת is reserved for the past event of Genesis 15, and if הקים is to be used primarily in reference to descendants or future fulfillment, then another term (נתן) would be

43. Rendsburg, *The Redaction of Genesis*, p. 41; cf. p. 44. Rendsburg follows and builds on the arguments of Cassuto (cf. Section 3 below).

44. Rendsburg, *The Redaction of Genesis*, p. 43.

45. J.D. Hays, 'An Exegetical and Theological Study of The Abrahamic Covenant in a Canonical Context' (PhD thesis, Southwestern Baptist Theological Seminary, Fort Worth, TX, 1992).

46. Hays, 'The Abrahamic Covenant', p. 37 n. 114.

47. J. Barr, 'Some Semantic Notes on the Covenant', in H. Donner, R. Hanhart and R. Smend (eds.), *Beiträge zur alttestamentlichen Theologie* (Festschrift W. Zimmerli; Göttingen: Vandenhoeck & Ruprecht, 1977), p. 33.

necessary for Gen. 17.2, where God is speaking of later fulfillment but still addressing only Abraham.[48]

Hays further suggests that such may explain the otherwise anomalous use of the divine name/title in Genesis 15 and 17, 'Yahweh' being used in the context of covenant ratification; 'Elohim' being substituted in the context of maintaining the covenant with Abraham's descendants.[49] He also identifies a widening or universalizing of the covenant blessings in Genesis 17, fitting in rather well with Cassuto's hypothesis concerning the use of 'Elohim' in such contexts.[50]

While for Hays Genesis 15 and 17 (along with ch. 12) 'combine to form one Abrahamic covenant/promise',[51] he is keenly aware that significant development is reflected in Genesis 17:

> Genesis 17 presents an elaboration or further explanation of the Abrahamic covenant, which was initiated in Genesis 15. In Genesis 15, God formally ratified his earlier promises to Abraham in a covenant. In Genesis 17 God restated the covenant, broadening the level of participation and also defining the obligations that the beneficiaries must carry out to enjoy the benefits of the covenant.[52]

Walton is another American scholar who has recently advocated reading Genesis 15 as simply the 'initiatory phase of the covenant'.[53] Although he does not address the role of Genesis 17 vis-à-vis Genesis 15, Walton implies that Genesis 17 reflects the second stage of a two-part covenant. In a non-specialist study,[54] Walton states such a position quite clearly, suggesting that Gen. 15.7-17 represents the 'initiation of agreement' (i.e. a ratification of the covenant with emphasis on the giving of land), whereas Gen. 17.1-8 reflects the 'initiation of fulfilment' (i.e. the acceptance of the covenant with emphasis on many

---

48. Hays, 'The Abrahamic Covenant', p. 47 n. 144. Hays notes the difficulty that the Noahic covenant thus presents for him (in that הקים is used), but avers that Noah must have already been in covenant relationship with God prior to the flood (even though it is difficult to pinpoint when such a covenant was initiated).

49. Hays, 'The Abrahamic Covenant', pp. 47-48, n. 145.

50. See Section 3 below.

51. Hays, 'The Abrahamic Covenant', p. 56.

52. Hays, 'The Abrahamic Covenant', p. 55.

53. J.H. Walton, *Covenant: God's Purpose, God's Plan* (Grand Rapids: Zondervan, 1994), p. 63.

54. J.H. Walton, *Chronological and Background Charts of the Old Testament* (Grand Rapids: Zondervan, 1994), p. 17.

descendants, nations and kings). What makes Walton's suggestion particularly noteworthy is his identification of two very similar (parallel) stages of development (first land, then many descendants, nations and kings) in the Jacob cycle (i.e. Gen. 28.13-15 and 35.10-12), where, interestingly, the divine names are deployed in a comparable fashion (i.e. *I am Yahweh* in Gen. 15 and 28; *I am El Shaddai* in Gen. 17 and 35).[55]

While one might have expected a distinguished literary critic such as Robert Alter to offer some valuable insights on the relationship between Genesis 15 and 17, unfortunately this is not the case.[56] The most Alter offers is a rather bland dismissal of the source-critical caricature of P's portrayal of Abraham, and the inference that Genesis 17 represents the 'sealing' of the covenant established in Genesis 15.[57]

In a recent and innovative holistic study E.T. Mullen implicitly adopts a two-stage interpretation.[58] Typical of the holistic approach, Mullen suggests that the Genesis 17 pericope 'involves much more than simple repetition of the divine promises'.[59] Rather, the earlier covenantal promises are here refined, especially in relation to the legitimate covenant heir. Thus understood, the Genesis 17 pericope serves to clarify which of the nations descended from Abraham will inherit the land of Canaan permanently.

Summary and Assessment

Given the lack of explicit comment before Calvin, it is difficult to pinpoint when and by whom the interpretation of Genesis 15 and 17 as two stages of a single covenant between God and Abraham was initially proposed. It is certainly implicit, however, in the comments offered by Jewish exegetes as far back as Philo. This, and its explicit articulation by Calvin and several early Puritan writers, certainly militates against seeing it as a recent innovation, artificially imposed upon the text to give the appearance of literary coherence. Rather, the number of advo-

---

55. Other links between Gen. 17 and 35 are highlighted below; cf. Chapter 5 Section 3c (n. 85).

56. R. Alter, *Genesis: Translation and Commentary* (New York: W.W. Norton, 1996).

57. Alter, *Genesis*, pp. 72-73.

58. E.T. Mullen, *Ethnic Myths and Pentateuchal Foundations: A New Approach to the Formation of the Pentateuch* (SBLSS; Atlanta: Scholars Press, 1997).

59. Mullen, *Ethnic Myths*, p. 138.

cates, ancient and modern, Jewish and Christian, would suggest that this is a rather obvious way of understanding the relationship between these two covenant pericopes. Thus understood, Genesis 15 and 17 are two sides of the same coin. Each chapter has a distinctive function, but this dichotomy is not sufficient to warrant distinguishing between two different covenants.

This interpretation has in its favour the virtue of being able to incorporate (at least to some extent) the different emphases reflected in the two chapters, and to provide some explanation for the introduction in Genesis 17 of obligations and promissory aspects not found at all in Genesis 15.

Its major drawback, however, is the lack of any convincing explanation for the chronological and literary gap between the two suggested 'stages' in the establishment of a single covenant.[60] Also problematic is the use of the future tense in relation to the establishment of the covenant in Genesis 17, and the introduction of what (for this interpretation) must constitute a rather anomalous third stage in Genesis 22.[61]

3. *Covenant Making and Covenant Renewal*

Unlike those who interpret Genesis 17 as a second stage in the ratification of a single covenant between God and Abraham, advocates of this second interpretation read Genesis 17 more as a reiteration and elaboration of the covenant established earlier. The distinction between advocates of this approach and those of the former is admittedly in some instances a rather subtle one. It is, nevertheless, important to distinguish between the two quite different premises involved: for the scholars now under review, Genesis 17 is read in terms of covenant renewal, not as a second stage of covenant-making.

This interpretation of Genesis 17 as a simple renewal or reaffirmation of a covenant previously established between God and Abraham does not appear until the seventeenth century.[62] The Puritan writer, John Owen, assumes that the covenant between God and Abraham was

---

60. See Chapter 6 Section 2d.3 below.

61. Unlike Gen. 17, Gen. 22.16-18 adds little distinctively new material to the promises already incorporated in the earlier covenant chapters. If anything, it further refines the promises of Gen. 17; cf. T.D. Alexander, 'Further Observations on the Term "Seed" in Genesis', *TynBul* 48 (1997), pp. 363-67.

62. It must be admitted that some such view may have been held earlier by both Jewish and Christian exegetes, but it is not clearly articulated.

established in Genesis 12. He thus speaks of Genesis 15 as a renewal of God's covenant with Abraham: 'When God solemnly renewed his covenant with Abraham, and he had prepared the sacrifice whereby it was to be ratified and confirmed, God made a smoking furnace to pass between the pieces of the sacrifice, Gen. xv. 17'.[63] Thus while Owen speaks of Genesis 17 in terms of the making of an everlasting covenant,[64] he apparently understands it as a further renewal of the covenant that had previously been established between God and Abraham. This is clearly so in the commentary of Matthew Poole, one of Owen's seventeenth-century contemporaries. While Poole rather loosely entitles Gen. 15.17-21 'The covenant concerning Canaan renewed', in his comments he seems to think more in terms of covenant-making. On Gen. 15.10 he writes: 'This [dividing of the pieces] was done…to ratify God's covenant with Abram and his seed; for this was a rite used in making covenants…partly that the persons entering into covenant might pass between those parts'.[65] It would thus appear that for Poole the covenant with Abraham is formally established in Genesis 15.

Poole also thinks of Genesis 17 as a renewal of the covenant. This is reflected not only in the description he gives to Gen. 17.1-4 ('God renews his covenant with Abram'), but also in his paraphrastic comment on v. 2: 'I am come to renew, establish and enlarge that covenant which I formerly made with thee'.[66] Thus for Poole, Genesis 17, while reflecting some development of the covenant established in Genesis 15, is essentially a renewal of the covenant that had been ratified previously.[67]

The suggestion that Genesis 17 is a reiteration and renewal of the covenant established in Genesis 15 reappears in the latter part of the nineteenth century, in the comments of C.F. Keil. In his 'Pentateuch'

---

63. J. Owen, *The Works of John Owen* (16 vols.; repr., London: Banner of Truth Trust, 1965–68), VI, p. 581; cf. IX, pp. 414 and 426 where Owen again refers to Gen. 15 as the renewing of God's covenant with Abraham.

64. Owen, *Works*, IX, p. 416.

65. M. Poole, *A Commentary on the Holy Bible* (3 vols.; repr., London: Banner of Truth Trust, 1962), I, p. 37.

66. Poole, *Commentary*, I, p. 39.

67. While Poole speaks of the covenant established with Isaac as almost a distinct entity in Gen. 17, his interpretation of this as 'the covenant of the promised Seed to come out of his loins' (Poole, *Commentary*, I, p. 41) seems to equate it with the spiritual significance that he gives to the promise of nations announced in the earlier part of the chapter.

contribution to the *Biblical Commentary on the Old Testament*, Keil entitles Genesis 17 'Sealing of the Covenant by the giving of new names and by the rite of circumcision', and writes:

> The covenant had been made with Abram for at least fourteen years, and yet Abram remained without any visible sign of its accomplishment, and was merely pointed in faith to the inviolable character of the promise of God. Jehovah now appeared to him again…to give effect to the covenant and prepare for its execution.[68]

Keil clearly speaks of Genesis 15 as 'the establishment of the covenant' and Genesis 17 as its 'maintenance and confirmation'.[69] Thus for Keil God's promise in Gen. 17.2 to 'give (נתן) my covenant' signifies 'not to make a covenant, but to give, to put, *i.e.* to realize, to set in operation the things promised in the covenant—equivalent to setting up the covenant'.[70]

The British commentator, M. Dods, gives clear articulation to the renewal interpretation, reasoning that 'the purpose of God's present appearance to Abraham [Gen. 17] was to renew the covenant'.[71] A similar position is espoused by W.J. Beecher.[72] Although Beecher speaks of the 'covenants between Deity and Abraham', he immediately elaborates this in terms of 'two formal covenant transactions'.[73] Moreover, he sees the promissory focus of each covenant chapter as essentially the same (each relating especially to the promise of 'seed'); thus it is clear that despite his ambiguous use of the plural, he recognises not two distinguishable covenants, but a single covenant made and subsequently reaffirmed.

An interpretation of Genesis 17 in terms of covenantal renewal is also

---

68. 'The Pentateuch', in C.F. Keil and F. Delitzsch, *Biblical Commentary on the Old Testament* (10 vols.; repr., Grand Rapids: Eerdmans, 1976–77), I, p. 222.

69. 'The Pentateuch', pp. 222-23.

70. 'The Pentateuch', p. 223. Although Delitzsch (*A New Commentary on Genesis* [trans. S. Taylor; 2 vols.; Edinburgh: T. & T. Clark, 1888]) adopted a diachronic approach, labelling Gen. 17 'Q' (i.e. P), he too speaks of this episode in terms of 'sealing' and 'confirming' the covenant (II, pp. 25, 26).

71. M. Dods, *The Book of Genesis* (The Expositor's Bible; London: Hodder & Stoughton, 11th edn, 1888), p. 162.

72. W.J. Beecher, *The Prophets and the Promise* (repr., Grand Rapids: Baker Book House, 1963 [1905]).

73. Beecher, *Prophets and the Promise*, p. 203. Beecher goes on to speak of 'the substance of the *covenant*' (emphasis mine), confirming that he recognizes only one divine–human covenant in these chapters.

advocated by the mid-twentieth century Dutch commentator, G. Ch. Aalders.[74] He too entitles Genesis 17 'the Renewal of the Covenant', maintaining that the significant differences in detail between Genesis 15 and 17 rule out treating the passages simply as parallels.[75] Aalders prefers, therefore, to interpret Genesis 17 as confirming and re-emphasizing the covenant already established in Genesis 15.

Against the traditional source-critical explanation that Genesis 17 is a parallel account of Genesis 15,[76] the Jewish scholars Cassuto and Segal both contend that Genesis 17 constitutes a reaffirmation of the covenant initiated in Genesis 15.[77] Cassuto maintains that the idioms כרת ברית and הקים ברית are not in fact synonymous; rather, ' "to cut a covenant" signifies to give a certain assurance; "to establish a covenant" connotes the actual fulfilment of an assurance that had been given at the time of the making of the covenant'.[78] Cassuto believes that this position is confirmed by the future tense used in Gen. 17.7: 'Seeing, however, that the covenant exists already in the present (v. 4), is it necessary to make another covenant in the future?'[79]

Cassuto's interpretation of the Pentateuchal compiler's use of the divine names is of particular significance for the relationship between the two covenant chapters. Cassuto suggests that one of the determining factors in the selection of these divine names was whether the theme of the passage focused on Israel (in which case 'Yahweh' would be employed) or on the rest of the world (when 'Elohim' would be used). Thus, as Hays has correctly observed, 'according to Cassuto, the theme of Gen. 17 is universal enough to require the use of Elohim'.[80] This 'universal' emphasis in Genesis 17 is further explored below.[81]

74. G.C. Aalders, *Genesis* (trans. W. Heynen; Bible Student's Commentary, 2 vols.; repr., Grand Rapids: Zondervan, 1981 [1949]).
75. Aalders, *Genesis*, I, p. 303. Aalders is arguing against the traditional source-critical explanation of the two covenant chapters that will be outlined below.
76. See Section 4 below.
77. U. Cassuto, *The Documentary Hypothesis* (trans. I. Abrahams; Jerusalem: Magnes Press, 1961); M.H. Segal, *The Pentateuch: Its Composition and its Authorship and Other Biblical Studies* (Jerusalem: Magnes Press, 1967).
78. Cassuto, *The Documentary Hypothesis*, p. 47.
79. Cassuto, *The Documentary Hypothesis*, p. 48. This assumes, however, that Gen. 17.4 should be read, 'My covenant is with you'. This is far from established.
80. Hays, 'The Abrahamic Covenant', p. 48.
81. Cf. Chapter 5 Section 3a.

While Segal agrees that the use of different names for God in Genesis 15 and 17 does not necessarily betray different literary sources, his explanation of this phenomenon is literary rather than theological: he explains them as simply 'for the sake of variety'.[82] He is in complete agreement with Cassuto, however, that Genesis 17 'only gives a reaffirmation of the covenant concluded many years before in xv, with additional details and promises'.[83]

Adopting a similar negative stance towards the standard source-critical interpretation of Genesis 15 and 17 as doublets, Victor notes concerning ch. 17 that

> there is no detailed representation of the covenant ceremony as in Gen. 15. It is presented in an altogether new way as a renewal of Abraham and Sarah through the change of their names. The words ברית אתך would suggest that the covenant is available to Abraham if he would only stand by it. In chapter 16 Abraham and Sarah have disregarded the covenant through their attempt to have the heir of promise through Hagar. Here in chapter 17 God warns Abraham and renews both Abraham and Sarah, reaffirms his promises and renews his covenant.[84]

Thus for Victor the final form of the narrative is to be understood as follows: In response to Abraham's request for confirmation of the promise, a covenant is established in Genesis 15. In ch. 16, however, Abraham and Sarah (because they misunderstand God's plan) attempt to provide the 'promised heir' through Hagar. In Genesis 17, therefore, God must renew the covenant and spell out the promise more clearly than before.[85] For Victor, the latter renewal takes place in Gen. 17.7,

---

82. Segal, *The Pentateuch*, p. 33.

83. Segal, *The Pentateuch*, p. 33.

84. P. Victor, 'The Theme of Promise in the Patriarchal Narratives' (PhD thesis, University of St Andrews, 1972), p. 143. Victor's position is rather enigmatic. While he appears to reject a source-critical dissection of the Abraham narrative (p. 143), in the following pages he frequently refers to the author of Gen. 17 as P, apparently assuming that the source-critical analysis is correct after all. For example, in view of his earlier dismissal of the source-critical explanation of Gen. 15 and 17 as doublets, Victor somewhat bizarrely concludes: 'P, while using older material, makes important changes in his account of Abraham in Gen. 17' (p. 154).

85. In line with his interpretation of Gen. 17 as a renewal of the covenant, Victor prefers to read Gen. 17.7 'I will fulfil my covenant' (NEB), correctly noting that the RSV's 'I will establish...' '[implies] that the covenant is not yet complete and that it will be established in the future' ('Theme of Promise', p. 149).

and only after the renewal of Abraham himself (by his change of name).[86]

In the latter part of the twentieth century this interpretation of Genesis 17 as a covenant renewal seems almost to have gained a consensus among scholars who are unhappy with a source-critical explanation for the presence of two distinct covenant chapters within the Abraham narrative.[87] There are some patent differences among these scholars in relation to specific details. Davis understands Gen. 12.1-3 to be the initiation of this covenant, describing both Genesis 15 and 17 in terms of a renewal or reaffirmation of the covenant,[88] whereas others imply that Genesis 15 is the inauguration of the covenant. Willis attempts to find traces of all three promises 'affirmed' in Genesis 17 within the previous narrative,[89] whereas others recognize at least some

86. Thus Victor (contra von Rad) does not consider Gen. 17.7a to be a repetition of Gen. 17.2a.

87. The following scholars all advocate some form of 'renewal' explanation: B.F.C. Atkinson, *The Book of Genesis* (The Pocket Commentary of the Bible; Chicago: Moody Press, 1957), p. 154; J.J. Davis, *Paradise to Prison: Studies in Genesis* (Grand Rapids: Baker Book House, 1975); J.T. Willis, *Genesis* (Austin: Sweet, 1979); O.P. Robertson, *The Christ of the Covenants* (Phillipsburg: Presbyterian and Reformed, 1980); V.P. Hamilton, *Handbook on the Pentateuch* (Grand Rapids: Baker Book House, 1982; see also *idem, Genesis 1–17*); W.J. Dumbrell, *Covenant and Creation: A Theology of the Old Testament Covenants* (Exeter: Paternoster Press, 1984); T.E. McComiskey, *The Covenants of Promise: A Theology of the Old Testament Covenants* (Leicester: InterVarsity Press, 1985) (although cf. Section 5 below); A.P. Ross, *Creation and Blessing: A Guide to the Study and Exposition of Genesis* (Grand Rapids: Baker Book House, 1988); N.M. Sarna, *Genesis* (JPS Torah Commentary; Philadelphia: Jewish Publication Society, 1989); R.F. Youngblood, *The Book of Genesis: An Introductory Commentary* (Grand Rapids: Baker Book House, 2nd edn, 1991); McKeown, 'Unifying Themes', pp. 73-74; G.J. Wenham, *Genesis 16–50* (WBC, 2; Dallas: Word Books, 1994), pp. 16-17; J.H. Stek, '"Covenant" Overload in Reformed Theology', *CTJ* 29 (1994), pp. 12-41 (29-30) (although cf. p. 33); D. Sheriffs, *The Friendship of the Lord: An Old Testament Spirituality* (Carlisle: Paternoster Press, 1996), pp. 37-51; B.T. Arnold, *Encountering the Book of Genesis* (Encountering Biblical Studies; Grand Rapids: Baker Book House, 1998), pp. 96-98. In addition, J.C.L. Gibson (*Genesis* [DSB; 2 vols.; Edinburgh: Saint Andrew Press, 1982], II, p. 66), while presupposing a traditio-historical reconstruction of the text, implies that in its final form Gen. 17 is to be read in terms of a covenant renewal.

88. Cf. Davis, *Paradise to Prison*, pp. 183-91.

89. Willis, *Genesis*, p. 246. Dumbrell adopts a somewhat similar stance, maintaining that in Gen. 17 'no definitive new content is attached to the covenant which

elements of promissory expansion within Genesis 17.[90] McComiskey distinguishes between two covenants in Genesis 17 (a renewal of the covenant instituted in Gen. 15 and the introduction of a distinct covenant of circumcision),[91] whereas others make no distinction in this chapter between the covenant of promise and the covenant of circumcision. Robertson explains the delay between the making and the sealing of the covenant in terms of the lapse of faith reflected in Genesis 16,[92] whereas for Hamilton 'the chronological gap between the institution of the covenant and Abraham's circumcision is to put divine promise and human obligation in perspective. The latter is subordinated to the former.'[93] Notwithstanding such differences among these scholars, they are agreed on the basic premise; viz. that Genesis 17 is a renewal or reaffirmation of the same covenant described in Genesis 15.

Some of these scholars, as indicated above, while interpreting Genesis 17 as a reaffirmation of the covenant of Genesis 15, nevertheless acknowledge some degree of expansion, development or difference in emphasis within Genesis 17. For Sarna, Genesis 17 serves 'not only to reaffirm the assurances of posterity and national territory but also broaden their scope and add a note of specificity'.[94] In a similar vein Hamilton notes that 'there is more here [Gen. 17], however, than reconfirmation. Two new items enter the covenant promises in chapter 17.'[95] For McComiskey, only the promise of land and offspring received covenantal confirmation in Genesis 15; other promissory elements (i.e. the promises of royal descendants and divine–human relationship) received such covenantal affirmation only in Genesis 17.[96] Youngblood

is "cut" at Gen. 15.18... Nothing new by way of content is being introduced by the notion of covenant here' (*Covenant and Creation*, p. 49).

90. See further discussion in the next paragraph.
91. McComiskey, *The Covenants of Promise*, p. 146.
92. Robertson, *The Christ of the Covenants*, p. 147.
93. Hamilton, *Handbook*, p. 107. Admittedly, however, the rationale offered in Hamilton's commentary is much closer to that of Robertson; cf. Hamilton, *Genesis 1–17*, p. 459.
94. Sarna, *Genesis*, p. 122.
95. *Handbook*, p. 106. Hamilton identifies these two new items as 'the new name which universalises Abraham's experience with God (he is to be the "father of a multitude of nations") and circumcision which particularises it (he is to be the father of the Jews)'.
96. *The Covenants of Promise*, p. 61. McComiskey implies that the promise of

acknowledges that whereas 'the land received the major emphasis in Genesis 15, so the descendants receive it in Genesis 17'.[97] Wenham correctly observes that Gen. 17.7 'is the first occasion that the covenant is extended to include Abraham's seed'.[98] However, while these features of development are acknowledged, it is questionable whether the full significance of this for their interpretation of the function of Genesis 17 has been appreciated by the scholars concerned.

The interpretation of Genesis 17 in terms of covenant renewal is not solely advocated by scholars opposed to the atomistic approach of source criticism. In a recent commentary Fretheim, while basically accepting the source-critical suggestion that Genesis 15 and 17 represent alternative accounts of the covenant, makes the tentative suggestion that

> the redactor of the present text probably does not so view the matter. Most likely we should view this covenant as a *revision* (not simply a renewal) of the earlier covenant in view of events that seem to take the future of the promise in directions not fully satisfactory... The promise of a son (15.4) has been fulfilled, and thirteen years pass between 16.16 and 17.1 (vv. 24-25), during which time Abram lives with what 16.15-16 and 17.18 suggest to be a settled matter. It may be that, during these years, everyone—including God—lives with Ishmael to see what opens up regarding the future. Experience shows (for reasons unknown) that Ishmael will not do. The story begins again this time with Sarai as mother (v. 19), not simply Abram as father. In a new moment for God, he reveals a new name and shapes a somewhat different future. This new divine identity, correlating with newly shaped promises, associates with *both* Abraham and Sarah, who are also given new names.[99]

In Fretheim's analysis, Genesis 17 represents not only a renewal of the covenant established in Genesis 15, but also a substantial modification of that covenant. The covenant is not simply reiterated; it is radically revised! However, while recognizing significant development and

---

international blessing only received such covenantal status in the context of the solemn oath of Gen. 22.

97. Youngblood, *The Book of Genesis*, p. 169.

98. Wenham, *Genesis 16–50*, p. 22. He also notes the introduction in Gen. 17 of the eternal dimension of the covenant (p. 22), and furthermore that, unlike the covenant of Gen. 15, Gen. 17 involves a human response (p. 20).

99. T. Fretheim, 'The Book of Genesis', in J.A. Keller *et al.* (eds.), *The New Interpreter's Bible* (12 vols.; Nashville: Abingdon Press, 1994), I, p. 457 (emphasis his).

highlighting the introduction of several new concepts in Genesis 17,[100] Fretheim stops short of labelling the covenant in Genesis 17 as either a second stage of the covenant established in Genesis 15 or indeed a separate entity altogether. Thus while his interpretation is more nuanced than simply reading Genesis 17 in terms of a covenant renewal, it is clearly within this category that his synchronic reading of the text belongs.

A similar position on the synchronic relationship between Genesis 15 and 17 is adopted by Sheriffs.[101] Sheriffs covers a much wider gamut than the Abraham narrative or even the book of Genesis, therefore he does not devote a lot of space to the issue under review. Nevertheless, his conclusions are worthy of note. Sheriffs agrees with Alexander that Genesis 22 must be read in association with the imperative of 17.1.[102] He further agrees that the covenant-making occasion of Genesis 15 is quite distinct from that of Genesis 17. He differs from Alexander, however, in the latter's analysis of Genesis 17 as merely the annunciation of the second covenant ratified in the Akedah account of Genesis 22. Sheriffs contends that

> the canonical form of the Abraham narrative and Near Eastern practice suggest rather that covenant and treaty were updated at royal or divine initiative, when guarantees or stipulations were extended or modified. This leaves both Gen 15 and 17 as covenant-making occasions, subsequently confirmed by Gen 22. After all, both Gen 15 and Gen 17 have explicit statements concerning covenant-making, and all three episodes have rituals, of which only the dismemberment of Gen 15 and the circumcision of Gen 17 tie in with covenant-making.[103]

In Sheriffs' reading of the Abraham narrative Genesis 15 records the making of a divine–human covenant, later updated and modified by the covenant of circumcision.[104] Both covenants were then subsequently confirmed by the divine oath in Genesis 22. For Sheriffs, therefore,

---

100. The novel aspects emphasized are a *multitude* of nations and kings, the *everlasting* nature of the covenant, the allusions to creation (1.28), the divine–human relationship and the human response to this covenant.

101. Sheriffs, *The Friendship of the Lord*, pp. 37-51.

102. See Section 5 below.

103. Sheriffs, *The Friendship of the Lord*, p. 51 n. 60.

104. While Sheriffs' comments do not preclude a staged or even a twin-covenant interpretation, personal correspondence with the author confirmed that he understands Gen. 15 and 17 as the making and renewal (updating) of a single covenant.

Genesis 17 is a covenant-making ceremony through which the covenant of Genesis 15 was modified and extended.

Summary and Assessment
While reading Genesis 17 in terms of covenant renewal does not seem to have a long history, it certainly has an impressive array of adherents (e.g. C.F. Keil, F. Delitzsch, U. Cassuto, N. Sarna, V. Hamilton, G. Wenham). Moreover, although mainly defended by scholars overtly opposed to a source-critical dissection of the Genesis text, this interpretation has also won the support of some scholars with no such axe to grind.[105]

The one obvious and important difference among those who advocate such a reading of the Abraham narrative relates to how they handle the novel material in Genesis 17. Not all advocates of this view have correctly acknowledged that such innovations have serious ramifications for reading Genesis 17 simply in terms of covenant renewal. Even those who do, however, do not give sufficient weight to this in their analysis.[106] It is somewhat unsatisfactory to suggest that the differences between Genesis 15 and 17 (in the promissory emphasis and in the nature of the covenant) can really be incorporated under umbrella terms like 'confirmation', 'elaboration' and 'expansion'. While Fretheim's 'revision' or Sheriffs' 'updating' is certainly to be preferred, the difference between this and the view that Genesis 17 presents a distinct covenant is rather semantic.

4. *Different Sources or Traditions*

The view that the presence of these two covenant chapters in the Abraham narrative can be explained by their distinct provenance (i.e. they derived from different underlying sources or traditions) was first introduced by scholars who adopted the source-critical method.

a. *The Allocation of the Chapters to Different Literary Sources*
The source-critical approach to the entire book of Genesis began in the eighteenth century with Jean Astruc's suggestion that Moses had

105. Delitzsch, Cassuto, Victor and Fretheim all, to a greater or lesser extent, embrace source-critical tenets.

106. Fretheim is a possible exception, in that he recognizes that the promissory differences are of such a nature to warrant labelling Gen. 17 a 'revision', rather than simply a reaffirmation.

composed the book from two main sources which could be distinguished by the divine name each employed.[107] With the ascendancy of source criticism by the latter half of the nineteenth century,[108] it soon became commonplace for scholars to divide Genesis 15 and 17 between the main literary documents which had allegedly been combined in the final redaction of the Pentateuch. Therefore the majority of commentaries produced in the latter decades of the nineteenth century (and indeed the greater part of the twentieth) explained the presence of the two covenantal chapters in the Abraham narrative in terms of different underlying documentary sources; viz. Genesis 17 represented the Priestly version of God's covenant with Abraham, whereas the material in Genesis 15 derived from the Yahwistic and the Elohistic accounts.

Dillmann typically lists 'the double covenant of God with Abram, chs. xv. and xvii' among the duplicate accounts reflecting the wavering of tradition, if not composite authorship.[109] This reflects what by the turn of the century was the standard source-critical analysis, understanding Genesis 17 as the Priestly parallel to the combined Yahwistic and Elohistic accounts in Genesis 15.[110] For Dillmann 'it is easy to see that the covenant, introduced in ver. 2ff. as something quite new, must

---

107. J. Astruc, *Conjectures sur les mémoires originaux dont il paraît que Moyse s'est servi pour composer le livre de la Genèse* (Brussels: Chez Fricx, 1753).

108. Influential in this respect were W.M.L. de Wette's *Beiträge zur Einleitung in das Alte Testament* (2 vols.; Halle: Schwimmelpfennig, 1806–1807) (trans. T. Parker, *A Critical and Historical Introduction to the Canonical Scriptures of the Old Testament* [2 vols.; Boston: Little, Brown, 1843]), H. Hupfield's *Die Quellen der Genesis und die Art ihrer Zusammensetzung von neuem untersucht* (Berlin: Wieganat und Grieben, 1853) and, most especially, J. Wellhausen's *Geschichte Israels: Erster Band—Prolegomena zur Geschichte Israels* (Berlin: G. Reimer, 1883; ET *Prolegomena to the History of Israel* [Edinburgh: A. & C. Black, 1885]). A useful and succinct historical summary of the development of the Documentary Hypothesis is presented by T.D. Alexander in his *Abraham in the Negev: A Source-Critical Investigation of Genesis 20.1–22.19* (Carlisle: Paternoster Press, 1997), pp. 1-16. For a more detailed survey, see Nicholson's recent monograph, *The Pentateuch in the Twentieth Century*, pp. 3-28.

109. A. Dillmann, *Genesis Critically and Exegetically Expounded* (trans. W.B. Stevenson; 2 vols.; Edinburgh: T. & T. Clark, 1897).

110. Interestingly Dillmann suggests (*Genesis*, II, p. 56) that the redactor 'instead of simply attaching the covenant narrative [i.e. Gen. 15.7-21, which he identifies as J] to B's [E] account, transformed it, with A's [P] parallel (ch. xvii.) in mind, into a solemnly assured promise of future possession of the land (vv. 7-18)'.

be described by a writer other than the author who described the covenant of ch. xv'.[111] A similar source-critical labelling of the material,
though employing what has become the more common sigla, is propounded in the German commentaries of Holzinger,[112] Gunkel,[113]
Procksch,[114] König,[115] and more recently in those of Ruppert,[116] Zimmerli,[117] the monumental work by Westermann (albeit with reservations
about labelling any of Gen. 15 as E),[118] and Scharbert.[119]

S.R. Driver was one of two British scholars who popularized the

111. Dillmann, *Genesis*, II, p. 76. Dillmann supports his interpretation of Gen. 17
as mainly unadulterated P on the grounds of its linguistic peculiarities and in
particular, its affiliation with the Noahic covenant in Gen. 9.9-17 (allegedly its most
theologically significant antecedent in the original Priestly work).

112. H. Holzinger, *Genesis* (KHAT; Tübingen: J.C.B. Mohr [Paul Siebeck],
1898), pp. 125, 147.

113. H. Gunkel, *Genesis* (trans. M. Biddle; Macon: Mercer University Press,
1997), pp. 258-59 (ET based on *Genesis übersetzt und erklärt* [Göttingen: Vandenhoeck & Ruprecht, 3rd edn, 1910]). Interestingly Gunkel suggests that in Gen.
17.19b (and elsewhere) the phrase הקים ברית means 'to maintain the (old) covenant', while recognizing, nevertheless, that in other passages such as 6.18; 9.9, 11,
17 it carries the connotation of 'establishing the (new) covenant' (p. 266).

114. O. Procksch, *Die Genesis, übersetzt und erklärt* (KAT; Leipzig: A. Deichertsche Verlagsbuchhandlung, 2nd edn, 1924). Gen. 15 is divided between *Die Jahve-
quelle* (vv. 1a, 3-4, 7-12a, 17-21) and *Die Elohimquelle* (vv. 1b-2, 5-6, 12b-16),
whereas Gen. 17 is discussed under *Die Priesterschrift*.

115. E. König, *Die Genesis eingeleitet, übersetzt und erklärt* (Gütersloh: C.
Bertelsmann, 3rd edn, 1925).

116. L. Ruppert, *Das Buch Genesis. I. Kap. 1–25, 18* (Düsseldorf: Patmos Verlag, 1975). Commenting on Gen. 17 Ruppert quite categorically affirms that 'der
erste Teil des Kapitels (1-14) bildet teilweise das priesterliche Gegenstück zu der
jawistischen Erzählung vom Abschluß des Gottesbundes mit Abraham (15, 7-21)'
(pp. 178-79).

117. W. Zimmerli, *1. Mose 12–25: Abraham* (ZBK; Zürich: Theologisher Verlag, 1976), pp. 49, 67.

118. C. Westermann, *Genesis 12–36* (trans. J.J. Scullion; London: SPCK, 1986;
ET of *Genesis 12–36* [BKAT; Neukirchen–Vluyn: Neukirchener Verlag, 1981]), pp.
217, 254-56. However, while Westermann adopts a source-critical analysis of Gen.
15 and 17, he does not use this to explain the relationship between the 'covenant'
mentioned in each chapter. For Westermann, a covenant between God and Abraham
is not in fact established until Gen. 17, thus Westermann's interpretation will be set
out below, in Section 5.

119. J. Scharbert, *Genesis 12–50* (Die Neue Echter Bibel, 5; Würzburg: Echter
Verlag, 1986), pp. 136 and 143.

source-critical approach in the English-speaking world,[120] and his commentary on Genesis not surprisingly advocates a typical source-critical analysis of Genesis 15 and 17.[121] The commentaries by Skinner and Ryle which followed likewise adopted the source-critical allocation of Genesis 15 and 17 to JE and P respectively.[122] For Skinner 'the marks of P's authorship appear in every line of the chapter [i.e. Gen. 17]',[123] while 'the close parallelism with ch. 15 makes it probable that that chapter, in its present composite form [i.e. JE], is the literary basis of P's account of the covenant'.[124] Observing that, strictly speaking, only the promise of land is embraced in the scope of the covenant in Genesis 15,[125] Skinner cautiously suggests that this is J's emphasis: 'in E the covenant had to do with the promise of a seed, and not with the possession of land'.[126] To make this distinction, however, he must excise Gen. 15.13-16 as 'the continuation of the E-sections of [vv.] 1-6', making the logic of his hypothesis rather circular. Skinner is on much less speculative ground when he identifies the covenant-promises in Genesis 17 as threefold: (a) Abraham will be the father of a numerous posterity; (b) God will be God to him and his seed; and (c) his seed will inherit the land of Canaan.[127] Nevertheless, as will be demonstrated below,[128] it is questionable whether this is comprehensive enough as a summary of the promissory material in Genesis 17.

The commentaries by Herbert and Speiser similarly use the source-critical method to explain why there are two chapters in the Abraham corpus that recount the establishment of a covenant between God and

---

120. The other was William Robertson Smith in his book, *The Old Testament in the Jewish Church* (Edinburgh: A. & C. Black, 1881).

121. S.R. Driver, *The Book of Genesis* (Westminster Commentaries; London: Methuen, 11th edn, 1920), p. 174 and p. 184.

122. Cf. J. Skinner, *A Critical and Exegetical Commentary on Genesis* (ICC; Edinburgh: T. & T. Clark, 2nd edn, 1930 [1910]), pp. 276-77 and 289; H.E. Ryle, *The Book of Genesis in the Revised Version with Introduction and Notes* (Cambridge Bible for Schools and Colleges; Cambridge: Cambridge University Press, 1914), pp. 184-85 and 196.

123. Skinner, *Genesis*, p. 289.

124. Skinner, *Genesis*, p. 290.

125. Skinner, *Genesis*, p. 276.

126. Skinner, *Genesis*, p. 282.

127. Skinner, *Genesis*, p. 290.

128. Cf. Chapter 5 Section 3.

the patriarch. [129] The latter, however, adopts a more tentative approach to labelling any of the material in Genesis 15 'E'.[130] For Speiser the verb נתן in Gen. 17.2 conveys the sense of establishing P's covenant (parallel to the initial step recorded in Gen. 15.18 by J), whereas the verb הקים is used to convey the sense of maintaining it.[131]

Several of the more recent studies on Genesis continue to promote the basic source-critical premise that Genesis 15 and 17 reflect different literary sources,[132] though there is a more cautious approach to

129. A.S. Herbert, *Genesis 12–50: Abraham and his Heirs* (Torch Biblical Commentaries; London: SCM Press, 1962), pp. 36 and 40; E.A. Speiser, *Genesis* (AB; New York: Doubleday, 1964), pp. 111 and 122.

130. Speiser's more tentative identification of E material in Gen. 15 is apparently due simply to its alleged similarity in form and subject matter with J, rather than any reservations about E per se as a parallel literary source in the Pentateuch; cf. *Genesis*, p. xxx.

131. Speiser, *Genesis*, p. 124. Speiser rather ambiguously writes: 'A lasting covenant must be established or concluded before it can be maintained. An initial step was recorded in xv 18, but by a different source (*J*)'.

132. For example, N. Lohfink, *Die Landverheissung als Eid: Eine Studie zu Gn 15* (SBS, 28; Stuttgart: Katholisches Bibelwerk, 1967), pp. 11-23; S.E. McEvenue, *The Narrative Style of the Priestly Writer* (AnBib, 50; Rome: Biblical Institute Press, 1971), pp. 145-55; B. Vawter, *On Genesis: A New Reading* (New York: Doubleday, 1977), pp. 203, 218; R. Davidson, *Genesis 12–50* (CBC; Cambridge: Cambridge University Press, 1979), pp. 42, 55; J.C.L. Gibson, *Genesis*, II, p. 3 and *ad loc.* (although see Section 3 above, n. 87); G.W. Coats, *Genesis, with an Introduction to Narrative Literature* (FOTL; Grand Rapids: Eerdmans, 1983), pp. 123, 133; J.G. Janzen, *Genesis 12–50: Abraham and All the Families of the Earth* (ITC; Grand Rapids: Eerdmans, 1993), p. 47; see also B.W. Anderson, *Contours of Old Testament Theology* (Minneapolis: Fortress Press, 1999), p. 99.

Other scholars, while embracing the source-critical differentiation between Gen. 15 and 17 (e.g. W. Brueggemann, *Genesis: a Bible Commentary for Teaching and Preaching* [Interpretation; Atlanta: John Knox Press, 1982], p. 151; T.W. Mann, *The Book of the Torah: The Narrative Integrity of the Pentateuch* [Atlanta: John Knox Press, 1988], p. 38; D.M. Carr, *Reading the Fractures of Genesis: Historical and Literary Approaches* [Louisville, KY: Westminster/John Knox Press, 1996], pp. 83ff.) also attempt to combine diachronic analyses with synchronic readings of the material. Thus Brueggemann sees in Gen. 17 an elaboration of 'the claim and reality of the covenant' (*Genesis*, p. 154). Mann similarly suggests that Gen. 17 constitutes a 'fresh clarification of the relationship between Yahweh and the Abrahamic line', showing that, among other things, 'the nature of the relationship between God and these characters (and their descendants) defines the constitutive content of the covenant' (*The Book of the Torah*, p. 38). Somewhat more vaguely

identifying E material within Genesis 15.[133] In addition to the commentaries, a number of important works focusing on the concept of covenant in ancient Israel understand the presence of two covenant chapters in the Abraham narrative along standard source-critical lines.[134]

b. *Refinements Resulting from Form and Traditio-Historical Analysis*
Largely through the influence of the pioneering form-critical work of H. Gunkel,[135] G. von Rad,[136] and M. Noth,[137] the documentary approach has not only been refined in the twentieth century, but also has been largely subsumed by interest in traditio-historical concerns.

Carr opines that 'Gen 17 is a complete replaying, and sometimes an expansion and/or systematization of non-P materials' (*Reading the Fractures*, p. 84).

133. This undoubtedly reflects the reservations that have arisen in some quarters over the existence of an independent, parallel E document. A concise summary of this twentieth-century development is presented by Alexander (*Abraham in the Negev*, pp. 11-14); for a fuller analysis of the recent scepticism over the P and E sources, see Nicholson, *The Pentateuch in the Twentieth Century*, pp. 196-248. The existence of E as a unified, extensive and parallel tradition to J still has its defenders; see, for example, A.W. Jenks, *The Elohist and North Israelite Traditions* (SBLMS, 22; Missoula, MT: Scholars Press, 1977) (see also his 'Elohist' entry in *ABD*, II, pp. 478-82) and R.E. Friedman, 'The Recession of Biblical Source Criticism', in R.E. Friedman and H.G.M. Williamson (eds.), *The Future of Biblical Studies: The Hebrew Scriptures* (SBLSS; Atlanta: Scholars Press, 1997), pp. 81-101 (see too his 'Torah [Pentateuch]' entry in *ABD*, IV, esp. pp. 609-19).

134. For example, D.R. Hillers, *Covenant: The History of a Biblical Idea* (Baltimore: The Johns Hopkins University Press, 1969), p. 102; J. Bright, *Covenant and Promise: The Future in the Preaching of the Pre-Exilic Prophets* (London: SCM Press, 1977), p. 25 (Bright does not mention Gen. 17, but given the sub-title of his book, this clearly reflects the typical source-critical understanding of this chapter as P); E.W. Nicholson, *God and his People: Covenant and Theology in the Old Testament* (Oxford: Clarendon Press, 1986) (again, the relationship between Gen. 15 and 17 is not discussed, but the traditional source-critical analysis of the two pericopes is clearly assumed—an inference which *The Pentateuch in the Twentieth Century* confirms as accurate; cf. p. 260).

135. Gunkel, *Genesis*.

136. Especially his essay, 'The Form-Critical Problem of the Hexateuch', in *idem, The Problem of the Hexateuch and Other Essays* (trans. E.T. Dicken; Edinburgh: Oliver & Boyd, 1966), pp. 1-78 (originally published as *Gesammelte Studien zum Alten Testament* [Munich: Chr. Kaiser Verlag, 1958]).

137. M. Noth, *A History of Pentateuchal Traditions* (trans. B.W. Anderson; Englewood Cliffs, NJ: Prentice-Hall, 1972) (originally published as *Überlieferungsgeschichte des Pentateuch* [Stuttgart: W. Kohlhammer Verlag, 1948]).

In broad agreement with the traditional source-critical analysis of Genesis 15 and 17, traditio-historical critics offer reconstructions of how pre-literary traditions may have been adapted by the various communities among whom they were transmitted. This throws up many fresh and interesting possibilities for the 'pre-literary' relationship(s) between the contents of Genesis 15 and 17.[138] Thus, rather than explaining the complex interweaving of themes in Genesis 15 and 17 simply in terms of different documentary sources that have been incorporated within the Abraham narrative, attention is focused on the evolutionary development of these sources from their original (and most pristine) form(s).

By applying such methodology Noth contends that 'in J the Abrahamic covenant was a traditio-historically secondary prelude to the Sinai covenant; but in P, who elaborated this prelude into an important act with its own significance, the Sinai covenant became superfluous'.[139] It is clear from what Noth says here and elsewhere, nevertheless, that he presupposes a traditional source-critical analysis of these texts.[140] Thus for Noth Genesis 17 reflects a Priestly elaboration and 'contemporization' (i.e. by linking it with the rite of circumcision) of an earlier covenant tradition which has been preserved in Genesis 15.

Whatever one thinks about Noth's source-critical premise, the idea that Genesis 17 does more than simply present an alternative version of the Abrahamic covenant is certainly worth careful consideration. Presumably, what is possible for the Priestly author of the material in Genesis 17 must equally be so for the final redactor of the Abraham narrative!

Von Rad is likewise convinced that, together, Genesis 15 and 17

138. Important differences (and disagreements) exist over precisely how traditio-historical criticism is to be applied: whether to the oral stage only, or both to the oral and written stage of a text unit's prehistory. Cf. R. Knierim's helpful observations on the resultant terminological confusion: 'Criticism of Literary Features, Form, Tradition, and Redaction', in D.A. Knight and G.M. Tucker (eds.), *The Hebrew Bible and its Modern Interpreters* (Minneapolis: Fortress Press, 1985), pp. 146-48.

139. Noth, *A History of Pentateuchal Traditions*, p. 240 n. 631.

140. Cf. his typical dissection of Gen. 15 as a redaction of J and E, and Gen. 17 as P (*A History of Pentateuchal Traditions*, p. 263); and his identification of Gen. 15 as 'the early tradition' whose covenant concept has been elaborated upon by P (*The Laws in the Pentateuch and Other Essays* [trans. D.R. Ap-Thomas; London: Oliver & Boyd, 1966], pp. 91-92).

reflect different stages of development in the covenant tradition(s).[141] While admitting that 'a satisfactory source analysis [of Gen. 15] seems absolutely impossible',[142] von Rad is nevertheless confident that 'the two parts [i.e. vv. 1-6 and vv. 7-21] are completely different as regards both their origin and their literary nature'.[143] Gen. 17.1-14, viewed by von Rad as 'essentially parallel to the Yahwistic report (ch. 15.7 ff.)', reflects 'various Priestly traditions about the covenant with Abraham [which] have been combined into a large unit'.[144] Likewise the rest of ch. 17 (i.e. vv. 15-22) 'corresponds basically...to the substance of ch. 18'.[145]

Like Noth, von Rad recognizes different emphases in these chapters as well as significant theological development in the way that the various traditions (i.e. those reflected in both chs. 15 and 17) have been shaped and reshaped by later redactors. Once again, the ramifications of such observations for a coherent reading of the final form of the Abraham narrative must not be overlooked.

Clements approaches the problem from a similar traditio-historical perspective.[146] Labelling Genesis 15 'J+' and Genesis 17 'P', he also maintains that a 'comparison of the two accounts shows that the later one is not the result of an independent historical tradition, but is the result of theological reflection upon the earlier narrative'.[147] For Clements the tradition of a covenant with Abraham can be traced back to a Hebrew clan who used it to justify their settlement in the Hebron-Mamre vicinity. Thus the concept of a covenant, the initial focus of which was the promise of land, has been expanded (and adapted) in order to 'anticipate' the Davidic covenant (i.e. 2 Sam. 7) until, at last, 'the Priestly authors circumvented the threat of failure attaching to the Sinai covenant by asserting that the promises declared made with

141. G. von Rad, *Genesis: A Commentary* (trans. J.H. Marks; OTL; London: SCM Press, rev. edn, 1972).

142. von Rad, *Genesis*, p. 183.

143. von Rad, *Genesis*, p. 190.

144. von Rad, *Genesis*, p. 197.

145. von Rad, *Genesis*, p. 202.

146. R.E. Clements, *Abraham and David: Genesis 15 and its Meaning for Israelite Tradition* (SBT, 2.5; London: SCM Press, 1967).

147. Clements, *Abraham and David*, p. 10. Again, such reflection (and subsequent revision) allegedly arose from the need to give contemporary significance to the Abrahamic covenant.

Abraham remained permanently in force'.[148] Yet again, such an analysis logically opens up various holistic readings of Genesis 15 and 17.

Van Seters, though very critical of the speculative nature of Clements' traditio-historical reconstruction, shares the same basic premise; viz. that Genesis 17 reflects the Priestly development of an earlier tradition.[149] For Van Seters, however, Genesis 15 is entirely the work of the Yahwist, and is designed 'to substitute the election and covenant of Abraham for the exodus election and Sinai covenant'.[150]

Genesis 17 is thought to be a literary unity also, dated after the restoration and not long before Ezra, preoccupied with 'reconstituting the religion of Israel for the condition and needs of the post-exilic period'.[151] Thus in Van Seters' analysis, the literary relationship between the two covenant accounts is as traditionally understood by source critics, albeit telescoped into a much shorter time period and with a different rationale.[152]

In his *Prologue to History* Van Seters addresses the most basic question that arises from a comparison of the two covenant passages: Why does each account reflect an entirely different emphasis? Why does the promise of land dominate Genesis 15, whereas the promise of seed receives the higher profile in Genesis 17?[153] For Van Seters this is

148. Clements, *Abraham and David*, p. 76. Clements also highlights (p. 71) the significant shift in emphasis reflected in the promissory aspects of Gen. 17 vis-à-vis Gen. 15, although he wrongly (in my opinion) limits the significance to the promise of divine–human relationship.

149. J. Van Seters, *Abraham in History and Tradition* (New Haven: Yale University Press, 1975), pp. 252-93.

150. Van Seters, *Abraham*, p. 292. While recognizing the number and complexity of genres reflected in Gen. 15, Van Seters maintains that 'there is no reason form-critically why any particular verse should be separated from the basic account and considered as secondary or why there should be a general source division into more than one source' (*Abraham*, p. 260). As for the date, Van Seters identifies a number of allusions to the Neo-Babylonian period (cf. pp. 266-68) and dates Gen. 15 in the early exilic period; such a context suits the setting allegedly presupposed by its author.

151. Van Seters, *Abraham*, p. 293. Van Seters sees as a major one of these needs, '[allowing] for the possibility of proselytism among the diaspora'.

152. Thus, while Van Seters' approach in some respects represents a radical revision of traditional compositional histories of the Pentateuch, his understanding of how Gen. 15 and 17 are related is fairly conventional.

153. J. Van Seters, *Prologue to History: The Yahwist as Historian in Genesis* (Louisville, KY: Westminster/John Knox Press, 1992), p. 251.

explained by the different historical circumstances of the respective writers; that is, the threat to the territory in the time of the exile, and threat to the Jewish population in the post-exilic period. According to Van Seters, therefore, 'it was natural to retain the close connection between land and covenant' in the Yahwist's account but merely summarize this in the Priestly tradition. Van Seters' thesis evidently hinges on a disputable premise; viz. that Genesis 17 is dependent upon Genesis 15, and not vice versa.[154] Regardless of the correctness of his historical reconstruction, however, Van Seters has pinpointed what is undoubtedly a most significant feature for any holistic reading of the divine–human covenant chapters in the Abraham narrative: the writer of Genesis 17 'take[s] for granted the emphasis on the land promise in Gen. 15.7-21 and merely summarize[s] it in 17.8 in his own way'.[155] In addition, like other traditio-historical critics Van Seters has highlighted several aspects of theological development reflected in Genesis 17 which serve to underline that each chapter serves a distinctive purpose.[156] If this was true in the pre-canonical stage, can it not equally be so in the final form of the text?

Unlike Van Seters, Coats adopts the more traditional source-critical analysis of the two chapters, maintaining that Genesis 15 is a combination of J and E material. Genesis 17 is identified as the Priestly version of the same tradition which 'in contrast to the parallel in Genesis 15 (JE) subordinates the promise of land to the promise for great

---

154. While until recently the direction of literary dependence has been assumed, this assumption has been challenged by T.C. Römer ('Genesis 15 und Genesis 17: Beobachtungen und Anfragen zu einem Dogma der "neueren" und "neuesten" Pentateuchkritik', *DBAT* 26 [1989–90], pp. 32-47). While Römer maintains that 'der Abrahamsbund in Gen 17 ist eine priesterliche Aufarbeitung von Gen 16 und 18', against the critical consensus he asserts that 'Gen 17 setzt allein den Kontext des Abraham- bzw. des Patriarchenzyklus voraus. Gen 15 hat hingegen den gesamten Pentateuch und damit auch Gen 17 im Blick' (p. 40). For a concise critique of Römer's argument 'daß der Verfasser von Gen 15 die priesterlichen Texte kannte' (p. 40), see Carr, *Reading the Fractures*, p. 85 n. 12.

155. *Abraham*, p. 289.

156. As well as noting five points of correspondence between Gen. 15 and 17 (which for Van Seters betrays literary dependence), Van Seters also notes the following: the extension of the promise of nationhood to a plurality of nations; Israel's distinct (royal) role among the nations; the inclusiveness reflected in the promises to and circumcision of Ishmael (and the other members of Abraham's household), pp. 282-93.

prosperity'.[157] He agrees, nevertheless, that 'the principal difference...
is that for P, covenant does not come to expression in a land promise...
the context of the covenant is an oath for descendants'.[158] This latter
promissory aspect (i.e. great posterity) is linked in Gen. 17.15-16 with
the promise of a son, Isaac, with whom a covenant will also be established. While Coats recognizes that the promissory focus of this latter
covenant (i.e. the covenant with Isaac, 17.17ff.) is not stated explicitly
in Genesis 17, he reasonably assumes that v. 19 links it directly with
the promise of numerous descendants.[159] Thus for Coats the two covenant pericopes, while reflecting different underlying traditions, have
distinctive promissory emphases. As the following chapters in this book
will illustrate, this is extremely significant for a synchronic reading of
the Abraham narrative.

Scullion likewise embraces a typical traditio-historical understanding
of Genesis 15 and 17. Thus the writer of Genesis 17

> is heir to the promise material in Israel and reworks the traditions at hand
> to him (12.1-3; 15; 18.1-15; traces of 16; 21)... It is very likely that the
> chapter was composed for and addressed to the post-exilic community to
> help it to find its identity by anchoring circumcision in the tradition of
> the covenant with Abraham.[160]

While Scullion betrays a reluctance to label the pericopes along typical
source-critical lines, he clearly has no reservations with the underlying
premise: the presence of two covenant chapters in the Abraham narrative can be explained by different underlying sources.

c. *Recent Reappraisals and Developments in the Historical-Critical
Approach*
The core documentary premise (i.e. that several continuous and originally independent literary strands are discernible in the final form of the
Pentateuch) has dominated the critical study of Genesis for over a
century. In the last three decades, however, this premise has been
increasingly challenged, not only by those opposed to its anti-super-
natural tenets,[161] but also by those who are simply dissatisfied with its

157. *Genesis*, p. 133.
158. *Genesis*, p. 134.
159. *Genesis*, p. 135.
160. J.J. Scullion, *Genesis: A Commentary for Students, Teachers and Preachers*
(Collegeville, MN: Liturgical Press, 1992), p. 145.
161. For example, Garrett, *Rethinking Genesis*.

results.[162] Chief among the antagonists are Thompson,[163] Van Seters,[164] Rendtorff,[165] Blum,[166] and Whybray.[167]

The modified documentary hypothesis of Van Seters has already been mentioned above.[168] The most significant dimension of his approach is the late date (exilic) which he gives the Yahwist (responsible for material traditionally labelled JE). This exilic Yahwist creatively borrowed not only from Second Isaiah (the Exodus theme), but also from the Deuteronomistic History, for which (according to Van Seters' thesis) he was compiling an introduction. Thus while Van Seters' analysis represents a significant mutation of the Documentary Hypothesis as traditionally conceived, it does not constitute a radical break from the basic source-critical tenets of the Wellhausenian school.

Unlike Van Seters, however, Rendtorff and Blum have abandoned

162. Earlier attempts had been made to provide an alternative source analysis by F.V. Winnett (*The Mosaic Tradition* [Toronto: Toronto University Press, 1949]) and his students, N.E. Wagner ('A Literary Analysis of Genesis 12–36' [PhD thesis, University of Toronto, 1965]) and D.B. Redford (*A Study of the Biblical Story of Joseph [Genesis 37–50]* [VTSup, 20; Leiden: E.J. Brill, 1970]). None of these reappraisals was as significant, however, as that offered by Van Seters, another of Winnett's protégés. Mention should also be made of F.R. Van Develder's study ('The Form and History of the Abrahamic Covenant Traditions' [PhD thesis, Drew University, Madison, NJ, 1967]) in which he suggests that Gen. 12.1-9 (excluding the Priestly material of vv. 4b-5) is 'the J-writer's equivalent to what is elsewhere (Gen. 15, 17) spoken of as God's *berîth* with Abraham' (p. 52). Van Develder rejects (p. 258) the traditional source-critical identification of a J core underlying Gen. 15.

163. T.L. Thompson, *The Historicity of the Patriarchal Narratives* (BZAW, 133; Berlin: W. de Gruyter, 1974); *idem*, *The Origin Tradition in Ancient Israel. I. The Literary Formation of Genesis and Exodus 1–23* (JSOTSup, 55; Sheffield: JSOT Press, 1987).

164. As well as his *Abraham in History and Tradition* and his *Prologue to History* see also *The Life of Moses: The Yahwist as Historian in Exodus–Numbers* (Kampen: Kok, 1994).

165. R. Rendtorff, *The Problem of the Process of Transmission in the Pentateuch* (trans. J.J. Scullion; JSOTSup, 89; Sheffield: JSOT Press, 1990) (originally published as *Das überlieferungsgeschichtliche Problem des Pentateuch* [BZAW, 147; Berlin: W. de Gruyter, 1977]).

166. E. Blum, *Die Komposition der Vätergeschichte* (WMANT, 57; Neukirchen–Vluyn: Neukirchener Verlag, 1984); *idem*, *Studien zur Komposition des Pentateuch* (BZAW, 189; Berlin: W. de Gruyter, 1990).

167. Whybray, *The Making of the Pentateuch*.

168. Cf. Section 4b.

the Documentary Hypothesis altogether and resurrected a form of sup-
plementary hypothesis, a theory first proposed by Ewald in the early
part of the nineteenth century.[169] Rendtorff dismisses the idea of independent and continuous J, E or even P documents on the grounds that it
is impossible to reconcile these with the presence within the Pentateuch
of a number of large and (allegedly) originally independent units.[170] For
Rendtorff, the Abraham stories were originally short, independent traditions, subsequently amalgamated by a process of inserting various
divine promises (i.e. descendants, land and blessing). The various stages
of composition are reflected in the different formulations of and sometimes quite minor variations in the promise speeches. Thus while Rendtorff adopts quite a radical view of the compositional process reflected
in the Abraham narrative, his explanation of the relationship between
Genesis 15 and 17 is not quite so revolutionary: Genesis 17 reflects a
different stage in the compositional process.[171]

Blum, one of Rendtorff's former pupils, further develops this supple-
mentary alternative to the Documentary Hypothesis. For Blum the first
part of the Patriarchal History to be composed (sometime after the division of the Solomonic kingdom) was the *Jakoberzählung* (25.9-34; chs.
27–33). This was later supplemented with the Joseph story to form the
Jakobgeschichte (a large amount of chs. 25–50). A Judaean author,
wishing to highlight Judah's importance, subsequently inserted ch. 34,
35.21-22a, chs. 38 and 49. Further expansion of the *Jakobgeschichte*,
through the introduction of the *Abraham-Lot-Erzählung* (chs. 13, 18–
19), took place after the collapse of the northern state of Israel. Thus
evolved the first *Vätergeschichte* (Vg[1]). Subsequent revision took place
during the Babylonian Exile (Vg[2]), with the focus on people, land and
blessing. Genesis 15, along with several other parts of Genesis 18–21,
was added during a post-exilic redaction by a Deuteronomistic editor,

169. H. Ewald, *Die Komposition der Genesis kritisch untersucht* (Braunschweig:
L. Lucius, 1923).

170. For example, the primaeval history, the patriarchal narratives, the Exodus
account, the revelation and covenant at Sinai. A concise critique of Rendtorff's
analysis is offered by Alexander, *Abraham in the Negev*, p. 24. A fuller critique is
offered by Nicholson (*The Pentateuch in the Twentieth Century*, pp. 95-131).

171. *The Problem of the Process of Transmission*, ch. 2. Rendtorff (p. 86) reads
Gen. 17 in terms of an extensive development (incorporating all the patriarchal
promises) of the covenant in Gen. 15 (which focused simply on the promise of
land).

whereas a further redaction by a Priestly writer provided the *tôl^edôt* framework and the inclusion of other texts such as Genesis 17.[172]

Even though Blum's reconstruction is significantly different from the traditional documentary analysis, his explanation of the relationship between Genesis 15 and 17 is much the same: Genesis 17 reflects a different and later stage in the process of compilation.[173]

Perhaps the most trenchant assault on the documentary and traditio-historical approaches to date is that offered by Whybray, who favours a form of fragmentary hypothesis. The author

> had at his disposal a mass of material, most of which may have been of quite recent origin and had not necessarily formed part of any Israelite tradition. Following the canons of the historiography of his time, he radically reworked this material, probably with substantial additions of his own invention, making no attempt to produce a smooth narrative free from inconsistencies, contradictions and unevenness.[174]

Whybray is extremely critical of the presuppositions and traditional criteria employed by source critics in their dissection of the text, and is even more critical of the purely hypothetical reconstructions of the traditio-critical approach. In Whybray's opinion 'there appears to be no reason why (allowing for the possibility of a few additions) the *first* edition of the Pentateuch as a comprehensive work should not also have been the *final* edition, a work composed by a single historian'.[175]

While Whybray offers no analysis of the relationship between Genesis 15 and 17 in his *Making of the Pentateuch*, his more recent

---

172. For a detailed appraisal of the traditio-historical approach advanced by Rendtorff and Blum, see D.J. Wynn-Williams, *The State of the Pentateuch: A Comparison of the Approaches of M. Noth and E. Blum* (BZAW, 249; Berlin: W. de Gruyter, 1997). As Wynn-Williams tellingly comments, 'it is clear that the "independent units", which are its starting point, come to light only when abstracted from the present canonical text, and that they are themselves no less hypothetical than the sources of the Documentary Hypothesis' (p. 250). Thus, rather than rendering the Documentary Hypothesis obsolete, 'the alternative approach proposed by Rendtorff and Blum cannot be said to be inherently superior or less problematical' (p. 251).

173. The same applies to Hagelia's analysis (H. Hagelia, *Numbering the Stars: A Phraseological Analysis of Genesis 15* [ConBOT, 39; Stockholm: Almquist & Wiksell, 1994]). Despite his late dating of Gen. 15, Hagelia accepts the traditional source-critical distinction between this account and the 'parallel tradition' of Gen. 17 (pp. 159-61).

174. Whybray, *The Making of the Pentateuch*, p. 242.

175. Whybray, *The Making of the Pentateuch*, pp. 232-33 (emphasis his).

Introduction to the Pentateuch discloses that he sees in them a single covenant.[176] Whybray does not fully develop his assertion that 'God made a covenant with Abraham and his descendants (15.18; ch. 17) which would remain in force for ever'. All he explicitly says is that 'the covenant, the blessing—which implies both material wealth and progeny, and the continuous divine protection—which preserved the existence of the family—may be said to have come into operation immediately'.[177] It would appear, however, that he thinks of Genesis 17 in terms of further elaboration and expansion of the concise statement of Gen. 15.18. Whybray approvingly cites Alter's observation that variations in content and form of the promissory passages such as Genesis 15 and 17 reflect the literary technique of biblical writers to repeat, adapt and alter their choice of language.[178] Thus Whybray represents a complete break from what was, and to a large extent still is, the consensus view; viz. that differences between passages like Genesis 15 and 17 provide clues regarding the gradual development of the Abraham narrative.

Garrett is extremely critical not only of the assumptions reflected in traditional source, form, and traditio-historical analyses of Genesis, but also of the more recent theories postulated by Thompson, Van Seters, Rendtorff and Whybray.[179] His alternative source analysis postulates a four-stage development of the Genesis text in relation to a number of *ancestor epics*:

> During the period of the initial recollection, the patriarchs recounted the stories of their life histories to their children. Also during this period, the patriarchs would have passed on to the next generation whatever written materials they possessed. In the second stage, the various stories would have been redacted into complex narrative structures and preserved in written form... The third stage, the Mosaic redaction, gave the book its present form and most of its present content. This stage may be properly called Urgenesis. The fourth stage, the post-Mosaic redaction(s), gave the work its present shape.[180]

176. R.N. Whybray, *An Introduction to the Pentateuch* (Grand Rapids: Eerdmans, 1995), p. 54.

177. Whybray, *Introduction to the Pentateuch*, p. 54.

178. Cf. R. Alter, *The Art of Biblical Narrative* (New York: Basic Books, 1981), pp. 88-113.

179. He does not mention Blum, but his criticisms of Rendtorff (e.g. *Rethinking Genesis*, pp. 246-47) clearly apply to Blum's analysis also.

180. Garrett, *Rethinking Genesis*, p. 91.

Garrett maintains that no 'ancestor epic' existed for Abraham on the grounds that 'unlike Jacob, Esau, or Ishmael, Abraham is not the ancestor of a single national group, and therefore no single, simple ancestor epic is possible for him as it is for Jacob...or Ishmael'.[181] After extracting what he identifies as 'extraneous pieces of material' from the Abraham cycle, Garrett concludes that one is left with 'a structurally and thematically unified piece in four sections'.[182] For Garrett this core Abraham material focuses primarily on the covenant established between the patriarch and God, and especially the promise of a son and heir.[183] Garrett tentatively suggests that this hypothetical source may originally have been much larger. He reluctantly concedes this, however, in order to explain the fact that what has been preserved in the present text of Genesis makes a number of rather telling assumptions (e.g. the separation of Lot, the birth of Ishmael, and the birth of Isaac).[184]

Garrett's understanding of the relationship between Genesis 15 and 17 is somewhat confused.[185] While his outline would appear to suggest that Genesis 15 and 17 reflect different dimensions/stages of the same covenant, he approvingly cites Alexander's observation that 'the covenant signified in circumcision is confirmed by an oath after the "sacrifice" of Isaac'.[186] Presumably Garrett either misunderstands or else disagrees with Alexander's interpretation of the significance of this observation for the covenant announced in Genesis 17.[187] Thus, unlike

---

181. Garrett, *Rethinking Genesis*, p. 159.

182. Garrett, *Rethinking Genesis*, p. 160. The four sections identified by Garrett as constituting the Abraham source (labelled by Garrett 'the Gospel of Abraham') are Gen. 12.1-9; 15.1-21; 17.1-27; and 22.1-19.

183. Garrett, *Rethinking Genesis*, p. 164.

184. Such a concession, however, seems rather to undermine his basic premise: that these four texts constitute a structural and thematic unity. One suspects that Garrett recognizes this, however, in that he immediately qualifies his observation by pointing out: 'it is not essential to assume that the original Gospel of Abraham, to which the present text witnesses, explicitly mentioned either the annunciation to Sarah or Isaac's birth. All that one need assume is that the community that heard the account knew that Isaac was born' (Garrett, *Rethinking Genesis*, p. 165). This is not very convincing in relation to Isaac. It is even less so in the case of Lot and Ishmael.

185. To some extent this is due to the paucity of direct comment.

186. Garrett, *Rethinking Genesis*, p. 160; cf. T.D. Alexander, 'Genesis 22 and the Covenant of Circumcision', *JSOT* 25 (1983), pp. 17-22.

187. See Section 5 below.

traditional source critics, Garrett appears to think of Genesis 15 and 17 in terms of separate covenant stages rather than separate covenant traditions.

While many advocates of Mosaic authorship will undoubtedly welcome Garrett's analysis, it is fundamentally flawed: his premise—that Genesis reflects distinctive, ancient literary forms—is too circular to be convincing.[188]

Summary and Assessment

Since the establishment of the source-critical method in the latter part of the nineteenth century it has become axiomatic to explain Genesis 15 and 17 in terms of covenant doublets, each deriving from independent literary sources. Even with refinements brought about through the extensive influence of form and traditio-historical criticism, this explanation has remained fundamentally unchanged: Genesis 17 reflects the Priestly account of the Abrahamic covenant, whereas Genesis 15 reflects a Yahwistic (or redacted Yahwistic-Elohistic) version of this significant episode in the Patriarchal tradition. While more recent developments have radically altered the way these chapters are dated and labelled, the vast majority of scholars still embrace the fundamental suggestion that the differences between the covenant-making accounts of Genesis 15 and 17 can be explained by the different origins of the underlying literary/editorial strands.

Although Pentateuchal studies are presently in a state of flux, it is unlikely that any new consensus on the composition of the Pentateuch will differ all that radically from the established explanation of Genesis 15 and 17 in terms of different literary or redactional strands in the process of compilation. To date, Whybray's suggestion of a single author for the entire Pentateuch has not won many supporters, and given the current interests in amalgamating diachronic and synchronic approaches,[189] it seems unlikely that Whybray's hypothesis will ever secure anything other than token acceptance. Unless convincing reasons are offered to the contrary, therefore, it is probable that the explanation of Genesis 15 and 17 within the Abraham narrative in terms of their different literary

188. For this and other incisive criticisms of Garrett's proposal, see Alexander, *Abraham in the Negev*, pp. 28-29.

189. For example, Boorer, 'A Diachronic Approach'; J.C. De Moor (ed.), *Synchronic or Diachronic? A Debate on Method in Old Testament Exegesis* (OTS, 34; Leiden: E.J. Brill, 1995); Carr, *Reading the Fractures*.

provenance will continue to be propounded for many years to come.

However, there are several major objections to the traditional documentary explanation of Genesis 15 and 17 as 'doublets'. The theory presupposes a somewhat piecemeal and incoherent process of final redaction. As traditionally conceived, the Documentary Hypothesis offers no convincing explanation for the rationale of the various redactors, most especially the redactor of JE(D)P: Why did the final redactor of the Abraham narrative not simply disguise or amalgamate the 'parallel' covenant accounts as the JE redactor allegedly did somewhat skilfully in Genesis 15? Even the more refined analysis of traditio-historical critics, who generally give more credence to the skilful artistry of redactors, betrays a similar selectivity in how the method is applied. For some reason the final editor is denied the literary finesse granted to earlier redactors of the tradition(s). Alleged redactional deference to one's sources,[190] in the final analysis, raises more difficulties than it solves.

The most fundamental criticism of the historical-critical partition of the Abraham narrative between different sources and traditions, however, is that this allocation of the material to different sources does not really explain the literary and theological function of a second covenantal chapter. Even if one assumes that deference to existing sources obligated the final redactor of Genesis to incorporate both covenant-making pericopes within the Abraham narrative, the question remains: what purpose within the final form of the narrative does Genesis 17 serve? Historical-critical analysis has suggested some interesting explanations for the existence and function of Genesis 17 as part of an independent source or tradition, but not as an intrinsic part of the final form of the Abraham account. The literary function of Genesis 17 within the final redaction of Genesis must surely be given greater attention, and this is arguably the necessary first step toward a coherent reading of the Abraham narrative.

---

190. As R.N. Whybray (*The Making of the Pentateuch*) points out, among source critics 'there was general agreement that conservatism was the reason why the documents as they succeeded one another did not simply supersede and consign to oblivion the earlier versions, but were combined with them to form new works. It was held that the earlier documents had acquired such an authoritative standing as "standard" accounts of national tradition that, even though they might be judged inadequate and in need of supplementation in a later age, there could be no question of their suppression' (p. 30).

5. *Different Promissory Foci and Functions*

As indicated above, Augustine was the first of the Church Fathers to discuss the relationship between Genesis 15 and 17 in any detail. Augustine distinguishes two core promises in the programmatic announcement of Gen. 12.1-3:

> the one, that his seed should possess the land of Canaan...but the other far more excellent, not the carnal but the spiritual seed, through which he is the father, not of the one Israelite nation, but of all nations who follow the footprints of his faith.[191]

Augustine interprets the covenant of Genesis 15 in terms of the first of these two core promises; viz. the possession of the land by Abraham's descendants.[192] Genesis 17, on the other hand, is interpreted by him in relation to the other basic promissory aspect, the dimension relating to Abraham's spiritual descendants:

> Here there are more distinct promises about the calling of the nations in Isaac, that is, in the son of the promise, by which grace is signified, and not nature... And because this was to be brought about, not by generation, but by regeneration, circumcision was enjoined now, when a son was promised to Sarah. And by ordering all, not only sons, but also home-born and purchased servants to be circumcised, he testifies that this grace pertains to all.[193]

For Augustine the two covenantal chapters in Genesis reflect quite distinct promissory foci: the first (Gen. 15) relates to Abraham's physical seed and their possession of the land of Canaan; the second (Gen. 17) relates to Abraham's spiritual seed and his fatherhood of all nations who follow in his footsteps of faith. While Augustine stops short of explicitly labelling Genesis 17 a covenant in its own right, this is nevertheless a logical corollary of the sharp dichotomy that he has drawn between the promissory focus of each chapter.

A somewhat different dichotomy is implied by the sixteenth-century

---

191. Augustine, *The City of God*, 16.16 (*NPNF*, First Series, II, p. 321). Augustine sees the same core promises reflected in Gen. 18.18 (*The City of God*, 16.29).
192. Augustine, *The City of God*, 16.24.
193. Augustine, *The City of God*, 16.26 (*NPNF*, First Series, II, p. 326).

reformer, Martin Luther.[194] Genesis 17 constitutes for Luther a covenant made with all the descendants of Isaac, as opposed to the covenant
of Genesis 15 which had been established with Abraham personally:

> But because it did not suit God to make a new covenant with each gener-
> ation and to confirm new promises—as He did to Abraham, Isaac, and
> Jacob—He gives all the descendants of Isaac a common revelation or
> seal by which they are not only to be distinguished from the rest of the
> nations but are also to be reminded as by a sacrament that they are the
> people of God and that God, in turn, will be a God to them.[195]

Thus Luther explicitly speaks of Genesis 15 and 17 as two quite distinct
covenants:

> Abraham hears that *both covenants* are being confirmed: the material one
> involving the land of Canaan and the spiritual one involving the eternal
> blessing... God confirms with a covenant that from the descendants of
> Abraham there will arise the church which is to have its home in the land
> of Canaan until Christ is born, in order that both the Gentiles and the
> Jews who will believe what Abraham had believed may be saved.[196]

Luther is clearly suggesting that Genesis 17 has a quite different
(though not altogether unrelated) focus to Genesis 15.

Interestingly Luther also distinguishes between two separate covenants in the context of Genesis 17; viz. the covenant of circumcision
(made with Abraham, but encompassing Ishmael and others) and the
covenant established with Isaac (which expressly excludes Ishmael):

> The covenant of circumcision is given for our performance...and is
> established for a definite people, in a definite land, and for a definite
> time... The covenant of Isaac, however, is not given for our perfor-
> mance; it is entirely free, without a name, without a time, and yet from
> the seed of Isaac, lest one look for the blessing from another place.[197]

For Luther three divine–human covenants are established in the Abrahamic narrative: a covenant established with Abraham personally (Gen.
15); a covenant established with Isaac and all his seed (Gen. 17); and a
covenant of circumcision, made with Abraham and all his family (also

194. See *ad loc.*, 'Lectures on Genesis Chapters 15–20', in J. Pelikan and H.T.
Lehmann (eds.), *Luther's Works* (56 vols.; Saint Louis: Concordia Publishing
House; Philadelphia: Fortress Press, 1955–72), III.
195. 'Lectures', p. 92.
196. 'Lectures', pp. 111-12, emphasis mine.
197. 'Lectures', p. 163.

Gen. 17). The precise demarcation of the latter two covenants in terms of the material in Genesis 17 is left rather ambiguous; Luther does not elaborate on precisely how the promissory material at the beginning of this pericope (Gen. 17.3-8) fits into the two covenants which he has identified within this chapter.[198]

In the twentieth century the first to suggest that Genesis 17 represents a distinct covenant was the Jewish commentator, Benno Jacob.[199] Jacob clearly understands that a covenant was established in Genesis 15, as is clear from his comments on v. 18: 'The epochal event is the covenant... A covenant is not a contract with mutual obligations as such are not mentioned on the part of Abraham.'[200] His interpretation of Genesis 17 is more equivocal, but he seems to be suggesting that here God establishes another covenant, 'a twofold covenant with Abraham, with him personally, and with his descendants; one covenant refers to all mankind, the other to this single people'.[201] Jacob also speaks of this 'special covenant' as 'a gift of divine grace [which] parallels the gift of the land',[202] and goes on to assert that 'circumcision shall be a covenant of God with Abraham and with all succeeding generations'.[203] Thus while he does not expressly address the question of the relationship between the covenants in Genesis 15 and 17, it is at least implicit that he interprets them as two distinct entities, each having a different focal point.

As indicated above,[204] while Westermann advocates a typical source-critical analysis (i.e. that Gen. 15 and 17 derive from different literary sources), he insists that a covenant is not introduced before the latter chapter. For Westermann Genesis 15 relates, not to the making of a 'covenant' between Yahweh and Abraham, but simply the making of a 'promise'. 'The text presents in narrative form God's solemn promise of the land, not Yahweh's striking of a covenant with Abraham'.[205]

198. Cf. 'Lectures', pp. 99-125; 144-64.
199. B. Jacob, *Das erste Buch der Tora: Genesis übersetzt und erklärt* (Berlin: Schocken Books, 1934) (abridged trans. E.I. and W. Jacob, *The First Book of the Bible: Genesis* [New York: Ktav Publishing House, 1974]).
200. Jacob, *The First Book of the Bible*, p. 102.
201. Jacob, *The First Book of the Bible*, p. 110.
202. Jacob, *The First Book of the Bible*, p. 110.
203. Jacob, *The First Book of the Bible*, p. 111.
204. Cf. Section 4a above.
205. Westermann, *Genesis 12–36*, p. 223. That is, Westermann defines the meaning of ברית in Gen. 15.18 in terms of its function there, whereas Jacob (*The First*

Westermann thus explains Gen. 15.18 in terms of a solemn assurance rather than a mutual contract. He sees the key term, ברית, being used also by P in this rather loose way up until Gen. 17.7. At this point, however, a covenant (in the strict sense of a mutual contract) is introduced. Therefore Westermann views the ברית of Gen. 15.18 and the ברית of Gen. 17.7 as two quite distinct entities: the former is a solemn oath focusing on the promise of land; the latter is a mutual pact governing an enduring divine–human relationship. He is adamant, moreover, that 'the institution of the covenant took place once only, and that with Abraham. This covenant continues on in Isaac, so that the הקמתי has here more the sense of an act of confirmation.'[206]

A growing interest in new literary approaches to the text prompted Clines to attempt a synchronic reading of the Pentateuch, in which he identified 'the partial fulfilment of the patriarchal promises of descendants, relationship and land' as the main theme.[207] Clines appears to understand the relationship between Genesis 15 and 17 not only in terms of expansive reaffirmation, but also in terms of a new development:

> As for the promise of divine relationship, its formulation in Genesis remains somewhat cryptic and its outworking variable and provisional. In 12.3 it is in terms of blessing, whether of Israel or of the nations or of both, and in terms of a patronage that operates against Israel's enemies as well as for its allies (cf. also 27.29). In ch. 17 it is a covenant, which, although it is linked with reiterated promises of progeny (17.2, 4ff.), is essentially a 'covenant to be God to you and to your descendants' (17.7). Yet what the covenant will entail beyond the practice of circumcision, which is properly only the 'sign' of the covenant (15.11) [*sic*], is undisclosed.[208]

Book of the Bible, p. 102) defines the biblical concept of covenant in terms of the nature of the ברית in Gen. 15.18.

206. *Genesis 12–36*, p. 269.

207. D.J.A. Clines, *The Theme of the Pentateuch* (JSOTSup, 10; Sheffield: JSOT Press, 1978). McKeown, in his analysis of Genesis ('Unifying Themes') basically agrees, albeit with a cosmetic change of label from 'descendants' to 'seed', and preferring to gather the concept of relationship under the more pervasive (i.e. in Genesis) rubric of 'blessing'.

208. Clines, *The Theme of the Pentateuch*, pp. 46-47. In the most recent edition of this book (Sheffield: Sheffield Academic Press, 2nd edn, 1997) Clines maintains his original thesis, adding only a qualifying *Afterword* (pp. 127-41) in which he offers some suggestions for how one might approach such a literary study in the changing intellectual climate of our postmodern age.

This recognition that Genesis 17, while in some sense a continuum with Genesis 15, also reintroduces a promissory theme last found in 12.3 and absent altogether from Genesis 15 is most significant for the relationship between the covenant pericopes.[209]

The doctoral dissertations presented by Alexander and Chew in the early 1980s offered quite novel synchronic readings of the Abraham narrative.[210] In a radical challenge to the traditional source-critical analysis of the Abraham narrative, Alexander rejects labelling Genesis 15 and 17 as doublets, arguing instead that these chapters relate to two altogether distinct covenants. He identifies these as a promissory covenant focusing on 'the divine gift of land to [Abraham's] descendants', and a conditional covenant focusing on 'the formation of a special relationship between God and Abraham which would extend to Abraham's descendants and be for all time'.[211] In an appendix Alexander makes an impressive case for seeing Genesis 17 merely as heralding this second Abrahamic covenant; it is not actually ratified by oath until the Akedah episode in Genesis 22.[212] Alexander finds 'no reason to assume that the covenant in chapter 17 was established immediately after it was revealed to Abraham'.[213] Thus for him, the first covenant was established by divine oath in Gen. 15.18, whereas a second and quite different covenant (announced in Gen. 17) was established by divine oath in Gen. 22.15-18.

More recently Alexander has refined his twin covenant approach.[214]

209. The implications of this fact will be explored in detail below; cf. esp. Chapter 6.

210. T.D. Alexander, 'A Literary Analysis of the Abraham Narrative in Genesis' (PhD thesis, The Queen's University of Belfast, 1982); Chew, '"Blessing for the Nations"'.

211. Alexander, 'Literary Analysis', p. 49; cf. pp. 160-82.

212. Alexander, 'Literary Analysis', Appendix III, subsequently published as 'Genesis 22 and the Covenant of Circumcision', *JSOT* 25 (1983), pp. 17-22. This is discussed in more detail in Chapters 6 and 7 below.

213. 'Genesis 22 and the Covenant', p. 19.

214. Cf. T.D. Alexander, 'Abraham Re-assessed Theologically: The Abraham Narrative and the New Testament Understanding of Justification by Faith', in R.S. Hess, G.J. Wenham and P.E. Satterthwaite (eds.), *He Swore an Oath: Biblical Themes from Genesis 12–50* (Carlisle: Paternoster Press, 2nd edn, 1994), pp. 7-28; *idem, From Paradise to the Promised Land: An Introduction to the Main Themes of the Pentateuch* (Carlisle: Paternoster Press, 1995), pp. 33-62; *idem, Abraham in the Negev*, pp. 77-89, 111-25.

The two covenants (that established in Gen. 15 and that announced in Gen. 17 and ratified in Gen. 22) each pick up one of the core promises enshrined in Gen. 12.1-3 (i.e. the promise of nationhood and the promise of Abraham's international significance as 'the father of many nations').[215] Thus for Alexander:

> In the light of the divine promises given in 12.1-3 it is clear that the covenants in chs. 15 and 17 complement each other. Whereas chapter 15 focuses on descendants and land, the emphasis in chapter 17 is upon Abraham as the one who imparts God's blessing to others; in this capacity he is the father of many nations. This understanding of the covenant of circumcision is later reflected in the divine oath of chapter 22 which establishes the covenant with Abraham.[216]

While Chew's synchronic reading of the material is not nearly so radical, he also acknowledges that in Genesis 17 'the domestic horizon of Gen. 15 is unexpectedly broadened to the widest possible horizon'.[217] Chew maintains that Genesis 17 serves to reiterate the universal horizon reflected initially in Gen. 12.1-7, but obscured by the nationalistic concerns of Genesis 15: 'This is done to re-focus Abraham's narrowing concern in Gen. 15 which could have been at the expense of his universal destiny first pronounced in Gen. 12'.[218] Like Alexander, therefore, Chew sees in Genesis 17 a strong allusion to the promise of blessing for all the families of the earth.[219] Significantly, like Alexander, Chew detects a link between Genesis 17 and 22, suggesting that:

---

215. Alexander, 'Abraham Re-assessed', p. 13 n. 11; cf. *idem, From Paradise to the Promised Land*, pp. 50-57; *idem, Abraham in the Negev*, p. 117.

216. Alexander, 'Abraham Re-assessed', p. 18.

217. Chew, ' "Blessing for the Nations" ', p. 96.

218. Chew, ' "Blessing for the Nations" ', p. 97. Chew likewise explains the 'juxtaposition' of Gen. 15 and 17 with the intrusion of Gen. 16: 'with the birth of Ishmael, Abraham's concern and vision has been seriously impaired and narrowed to such an extent that it needs a radical action on God's part to re-establish for Abraham the universal horizon of his destiny of 12.1-3. By the radical expansion and transformation of name, Abraham would then have to put in the forefront of his concern the horizon of his universal destiny and responsibility' (Chew, ' "Blessing for the Nations" ', p. 132).

219. He maintains that although the formula itself is absent in Gen. 17 it is nevertheless in view, reflected by the fact that 'the reference to the formula in 18.18 is in fact closely connected to the expansion and transformation of Abraham's destiny in Gen. 17' (Chew, ' "Blessing for the Nations" ', p. 98).

Gen. 22 is taking the very particularistic concern of Abraham in Gen. 15 which could prove to be an obstacle to his fulfilling his universal destiny, and is transforming and restoring it to Yahweh's universal purpose. The restored universal perspective in Gen. 17 is reaffirmed by Gen. 22.[220]

Thus within the narrative structure of Gen. 12.10–22.19 Chew identifies movement 'from an introverted, particularistic concern in 12.10 to 15.21 (displacing the initial universal destiny of 12.1-9) to an expanded, universal horizon in 17.1 to 22.19'.[221] This being so, Genesis 17 'really amounts to a reaffirmation of the initial call in 12.1-3, if not a new beginning altogether'.[222]

Although, as acknowledged above, McComiskey identifies the covenant introduced in Gen. 17.2-8 with that ratified in Genesis 15, he nevertheless suggests that a distinct covenant is introduced in Genesis 17; viz. the covenant of circumcision in 17.9-27.[223] This latter stipulatory covenant is quite unlike the promissory covenant. For McComiskey it serves a different role altogether, being, in McComiskey's terminology, an 'administrative' as opposed to a 'promissory' covenant, the former functioning 'to administer an aspect of obedience necessary for the maintenance of one's relationship to the promise'.[224] Thus although in McComiskey's opinion there is only one covenant in relation to the obligation God made to Abraham, there is nevertheless a second (and quite distinct) covenant reflected in Genesis 17.

As noted earlier, in his synchronic analysis of the Abraham corpus Rosenberg argues that the cycle's symmetrical structure first becomes visible with the second covenant episode, the first of several 'major narrative repetition[s]'.[225] While Rosenberg recognizes the two covenants as 'clearly parallel' in terms of the literary framework, he rejects the source-critical atomization of the text in favour of a 'different dichotomy' suggested by the *oracles* themselves;[226] that is, 'between

220. Chew, ' "Blessing for the Nations" ', p. 102.
221. Chew, ' "Blessing for the Nations" ', p. 133.
222. Chew, ' "Blessing for the Nations" ', p. 133.
223. See Section 3 (n. 87) above. On the basis of Acts 7.8 McComiskey concludes that the New Testament also treats circumcision as a covenant in its own right (*The Covenants of Promise*, p. 148).
224. McComiskey, *The Covenants of Promise*, p. 62.
225. Rosenberg, *King and Kin*, p. 88. (Rosenberg represents the Abraham cycle in chiastic symmetry on p. 84.)
226. So called by Rosenberg in view of their resemblance to prophetic call narratives (p. 88).

a conditional and an unconditional sense of Israel's tenure—and...
between a confederate and a royal polity'.[227] Thus in terms of their
literary framework, at least, Rosenberg thinks of these two covenants as
quite separate and distinct entities.[228]

　　While Abela's synchronic study of the Abraham narrative does not
address directly the issue of the precise relationship between the covenants in Genesis 15 and 17, his understanding of the distinct focus of
each chapter highlights a considerable degree of expansion and development.[229] Abela understands the promissory focus in Genesis 15 to be
in relation to Abraham's seed, whereas in Genesis 17 attention shifts to
the outworking of the promises in relation to Abraham himself. For
Abela, as the narrative progresses, the promise of a 'great nation' (12.2)
is more narrowly defined. The vague promise of innumerable descendants (13.16) becomes personalized in 15.4 through the promise of a
natural son whose descendants are—as implicit in the further elaboration of 15.13-16—to become a 'nation' in the land presently inhabited
by such 'nations'. Thus Genesis 15 is Yahweh's answer to Abraham's
acute crisis of faith (15.2), solemnly reiterating and better specifying
the divine promises concerning Abraham's descendants and land.
Genesis 17, on the other hand, 'defines Abraham's proper relationship
to his two sons' and spells out that the land would become 'an everlasting possession' only in the future.[230] Moreover, the promise to make
Abraham a father of a multitude of nations 'puts Abraham within a
universalistic perspective that gives the impression of going beyond the
physical and the genealogical to reach the spiritual'.[231] In addition,
however, the chapter serves to define further the son theme in that the

227. Rosenberg, *King and Kin*, p. 89.
　　228. It must be acknowledged, nevertheless, that despite labelling these chapters
respectively the 'covenant of sacrifice' and the 'covenant of circumcision', Rosenberg thinks in terms of 'the Abrahamic covenant', perhaps postulating some form of
two-stage interpretation of the covenant. However, since such an interpretation is
nowhere made explicit, and since he at least twice refers to 'covenants' in the plural
(Rosenberg, *King and Kin*, p. 89), it seems fairly acceptable to discuss his analysis
under this present section.
　　229. A. Abela, *The Themes of the Abraham Narrative* (Zabbar, Malta: Veritas,
1989).
　　230. Abela, *The Themes of the Abraham Narrative*, p. 123.
　　231. Abela, *The Themes of the Abraham Narrative*, p. 53. Abela defends this
statement on syntactical grounds (cf. pp. 53-54 n. 161).

promised heir will come through *Sarah*, and the covenant will be established with *Isaac*.

Abela detects a similar logical development of the themes of blessing and land within the Abraham narrative.[232] The former, according to Abela, does not come into view between Gen. 14.19-20 and Gen. 17.16. Consequently, this theme sheds less light on Abela's analysis of the relationship between the two covenant chapters.[233] The land theme, however, is brought into focus in both these pericopes. Chapter 15 explains why there will be a delay in the inheritance of the land (15.16).[234] Chapter 17 does not simply reiterate the promise of land, but makes it clear that 'for the patriarch, Canaan is meant to remain *'ereṣ megûrîm* (17.8)'.[235]

In his synchronic investigation of the plot of Genesis, Turner likewise notes that Genesis 17 'introduces several new elements in the unfolding of the promise'.[236] Specifically, Turner draws attention to the following: nations, kings, the divine–human relationship, and Sarah's maternity. In relation to the covenant introduced in Genesis 17, Turner broadly embraces Alexander's suggestion that this conditional covenant is merely announced at this point, not being established until after the conditions have been fulfilled by the Akedah incident in Genesis 22.[237]

Turner concludes that in the Abraham narrative (i.e. Gen. 12–25) 'the posterity promise provides much of its connective tissue'.[238] For him both covenant chapters address the crucial issue of Abraham's legitimate heir in relation to potential candidates; viz. Lot in Genesis 15 and Ishmael in Genesis 17.[239] Both chapters clarify significant aspects of the initial promissory announcement in Gen. 12.1-3: Genesis 15 clarifies

232. Cf. Abela, *The Themes of the Abraham Narrative*, pp. 32-33; pp. 121-25.

233. It is clear, however, that Abela understands that an important development in this theme does take place in Gen. 17; here 'the blessing theme is joined to the motif of multiplicity and fertility' (*The Themes of the Abraham Narrative*, p. 24).

234. A fact which for Abela is illustrated by the Abimelech episode in Gen. 20.4.

235. Abela, *The Themes of the Abraham Narrative*, p. 121. Cf. his detailed discussion on pp. 100-102.

236. L.A. Turner, *Announcements of Plot in Genesis* (JSOTSup, 96; Sheffield: JSOT Press, 1990), p. 76.

237. Turner, *Announcements of Plot*, pp. 91-92. Cf. n. 212 above.

238. Turner, *Announcements of Plot*, p. 94.

239. Turner, *Announcements of Plot*, pp. 73, 77. Turner interprets the enigmatic clauses in Gen. 15.2-3 as veiled references to Lot; see Chapter 3 Section 3a (n. 65) below.

not only that Abraham's numerous descendants will be traced through a physical son, but also that it is these descendants, rather than Abraham himself, who will possess the land—the boundaries of which are now shown to be larger than previously disclosed.[240] Genesis 17, by contrast, reveals that Sarah would play an essential role in the fulfilment of the promise of multitudinous posterity, for the promised son was not Ishmael, as Abraham had mistakenly assumed, but Isaac.

While Turner does not comment directly on the relationship between the covenants in Genesis 15 and 17, the fact that he adopts Alexander's premise (i.e. that Gen. 17 announces a covenant which is not established until Gen. 22) can only be understood as implicit acceptance of Alexander's conclusion that Genesis 15 and 17 relate to two quite separate covenants. This is borne out by his apparent adoption of a covenantal interpretation of the theophanic ritual in Genesis 15.[241] In any case, Turner clearly aligns himself with those who detect significant development and expansion in Genesis 17, certainly sufficient to warrant treating the two covenants as distinct entities.

Such is certainly the conclusion reached by Sailhamer, for whom the two covenants have an entirely different focus.[242] For Sailhamer the simplest solution to the otherwise incongruous *establishment* of a covenant in Genesis 17 (subsequent to Gen. 15) is to differentiate between the two covenants: the covenant between the pieces relates to the promise of land, whereas the covenant of circumcision relates to the promise of descendants.[243] By qualifying this, however, with the tentative admission that 'there may have been the need to *reestablish* the earlier covenant after that unsuccessful attempt [i.e. in Gen. 16] to take the promise into their own hands', Sailhamer seems to vacillate between the interpretation of Genesis 17 as a renewal of the covenant and the interpretation of it as a distinct covenant.[244] Even so, Sailhamer high-

240. Turner, *Announcements of Plot*, p. 101. To get round the awkward inclusion of Abraham in the promise of land in Gen. 17.8 Turner tentatively suggests a *waw explicativum*: 'And I will give you, *that is* to your descendants after you...' (Turner, *Announcements of Plot*, p. 102).

241. Turner, *Announcements of Plot*, p. 100.

242. J.H. Sailhamer, *The Pentateuch as Narrative: A Biblical-Theological Commentary* (Library of Biblical Interpretation; Grand Rapids: Zondervan, 1992).

243. Sailhamer, *The Pentateuch as Narrative*, p. 156.

244. Sailhamer, *The Pentateuch as Narrative*, p. 156 (emphasis mine). He suggests an analogous situation in the golden calf incident between the establishment and re-establishment of the Sinaitic covenant in Exod. 24 and 34.

lights a number of developments in Genesis 17 which suggest more than a reaffirmation of the covenant established in Genesis 15.[245]

Summary and Assessment
The recognition of fundamental differences between the nature and content of the covenants in Genesis 15 and 17 can be traced at least as far back as Augustine, although, admittedly, he stops short of identifying in Genesis 17 a distinct covenant. The sixteenth-century reformer Martin Luther is apparently the first to develop this important dichotomy between the two chapters to its logical conclusion; namely, that two distinguishable covenants are in view.

Such a distinction between the two chapters (Gen. 15 and 17) does not surface again until the twentieth century, in the commentary by B. Jacob. Westermann also sees in Genesis 17 the making of a covenant quite distinct from the ברית of Genesis 15, although for him the latter chapter recounts the making of a promise rather than an actual covenant.

With the development of new literary approaches since the early seventies, it is no surprise that there have been a growing number of attempts to explain the relationship between Genesis 15 and 17 within the final form of the Abraham narrative. What is significant, however, is that several such interpretations have explained these chapters in terms of two distinct covenants.

Alexander's proposal is undoubtedly the most novel, uniting the announcement of a second covenant in Genesis 17 with the solemn oath sworn after the Akedah incident in Genesis 22. Working independently, Chew shares with Alexander several key observations.[246]

The perspective of McComiskey is very different, although with Alexander he recognizes the same fundamental difference between the covenants in Genesis 15 and 17: one is purely promissory, whereas the other necessitates a human response.

Both Abela and Turner understand the second covenant chapter in

---

245. For example, the allusions to Gen. 1.29 and 9.1 which suggest that 'the covenant with Abraham was the means through which God's original blessing would again be channeled to all humankind' (p. 157); mediation of the blessing through a royal seed of *Abraham* (p. 157); the concept of eternality (p. 158); the identification of Sarah as the matriarch, and Isaac as the covenant heir (p. 159).

246. For instance, both identify in Gen. 17 the universalistic emphasis of Gen. 12.3; both identify a similar universalistic link between Gen. 17 and 22.

terms of elaboration and refinement of the promises made to Abraham in 12.1-3. While neither expressly mentions a second covenant in Genesis 17, such appears to be the implication of the sharp dichotomy their analyses suggest between the promissory foci of chs. 15 and 17.

Sailhamer, by contrast, is very explicit. For Sailhamer, Genesis 15 records the establishment of a covenant in relation to the promise of land, whereas in Genesis 17 a covenant is established concerning the promise of descendants.

The suggestion that Genesis 15 and 17 relate to two quite different covenants is certainly appealing.[247] Such an interpretation helps to answer some obvious questions which otherwise present the interpreter with serious problems:

1. Why has the covenant in ch. 17 become stipulatory, with certain ethical and ritual requirements being attached?
2. Why are additional promises of nations, kings and a divine–human relationship incorporated into ch. 17?
3. Why is an 'eternal' dimension introduced in ch. 17?
4. Why is the promise of land, a major focus of the covenant between the pieces, passed over almost casually in ch. 17?
5. Why is the promise of multitudinous seed so radically transformed in ch. 17?

Nevertheless, while the twin-covenant interpretation provides helpful answers to these questions, it raises a number of new ones:

1. Why, if the two covenants focus on different promises, is the promise of land reiterated in ch. 17?
2. What is the connection between the promise of innumerable seed in ch. 15 and the promise of multitudinous expansion in ch. 17?
3. What is the connection between the promise of nationhood (descendants and land) in ch. 15 and the promise concerning nations and kings in ch. 17?
4. Why are elements from both covenantal chapters brought together in the solemn oath of Gen. 22.16-18?[248]

247. A detailed examination of the differences between the two covenants is presented in the following chapter.

248. This last question is especially acute for Alexander's analysis in that, according to his interpretation, this oath signifies the establishment of the covenant merely announced in Gen. 17.

It is clear, therefore, that before embracing this interpretation of Genesis 15 and 17 as two quite separate and distinct covenants, these basic questions must be answered, and in a way that does full justice to both the continuity and the discontinuity between these central chapters in the Abraham narrative.

6. *Conclusion*

While there are clear and significant degrees of overlap, this review of the *status quaestionis* has illustrated that at least four identifiable interpretations of the relationship between Genesis 15 and 17 have been advocated. The two chapters may be seen to represent:

1. progressive stages in the establishment of the same covenant;
2. the making and renewal of a single covenant;
3. different oral or literary traditions about the establishment of the same covenant;
4. two separate covenants, each with its own particular emphasis.

As this synopsis has also illustrated, these interpretations all explain the presence of two divine–human covenant pericopes within the Abraham narrative by emphasizing elements either of continuity or discontinuity. Clearly the degree of continuity and discontinuity is important for determining the relationship between the two covenant pericopes. Therefore, before a detailed analysis of either Genesis 15 or 17 is undertaken, both covenant accounts will be carefully compared in order to establish not only the points they have in common, but also the areas of significant difference.

Chapter 3

THE COVENANTS IN GENESIS 15 AND 17
COMPARED AND CONTRASTED

1. *Introduction*

As is clear from the above discussion, diachronic studies—in contrast to synchronic explanations of the relationship between Genesis 15 and 17—assume that each account reflects a variant recounting of the same event. The detailed comparison of the two covenant pericopes that follows will show that it is difficult to reconcile this diachronic premise with their distinctive details and emphases.

One could argue, nevertheless, that while these two covenant accounts are not presented as variant forms of a single covenant in the final form of the text, this does not preclude them from being so originally (i.e. their present cohesiveness in the Abraham narrative has been artificially engineered by later redactors). It is necessary, therefore, before comparing the contents of the two covenant chapters synchronically, to show why diachronic analyses of the material contained in Genesis 15 and 17 are unconvincing.

2. *A Critique of Diachronic Analyses of Genesis 15 and 17*

As noted above, diachronic approaches to the Genesis text explain the presence of two different accounts of the institution of a divine covenant with Abraham in terms of underlying sources. Source analysts almost unanimously[1] accept Genesis 17 as P's account of the Abrahamic covenant—a later version than that which is traditionally understood as the older (non-P) account recorded in ch. 15.

---

1. As Wenham points out (*Genesis 16–50*, p. 18), there are a few dissenters: e.g. Jacob, *Das erste Buch der Tora*; S.R. Külling, *Zur Datierung der 'Genesis-P-Stücke': Namentlich des Kapitels Genesis 17* (Kampen: Kok, 1964); Alexander, 'Literary Analysis'.

Having detected features which suggest more than one underlying source, most source critics[2] have labelled Genesis 15 the composite JE account[3] of the institution of the Abrahamic covenant. The following features allegedly reflect the chapter's composite nature.[4]

1. There is an apparent time discrepancy: it is night-time in v. 5 but early evening in vv. 12 and 17.

2. Two different foci are evident, the prospect of posterity (vv. 1-6) and the promise of land (vv. 7-21).

3. There are parallel statements: Yahweh's self-introduction in vv. 1 and 7, and Abraham's responses in vv. 2-3 and 8.

4. There is the anomaly that in v. 6 Abraham expresses faith, whereas in v. 8 he reverts to doubt.

5. There is evidence of doublets within each of the two distinct sections (i.e. vv. 1-6 and vv. 7-21). Verses 2-3 allegedly combine two separate forms of the same statement.[5] Likewise, the promise of numerous offspring (v. 5) is distinct from, and additional to, the promise of a single natural heir in v. 4. In the second section (vv. 7-21) vv. 13-16 are identified as a doublet of vv. 18-21. The former verses are misplaced before the theophany of v. 17 and seem intrusive, not being directly relevant to Abraham's question of v. 8.

6. Verse 16 employs 'Amorites' as the comprehensive term for the indigenous population of Palestine (cf. vv. 19-21) rather than J's typical term of reference, 'Canaanites'.

While such observations have led many scholars to the conclusion that Genesis 15 is a composite narrative, no consensus has been reached among source analysts about how the passage should be divided up between the suggested J and E sources.[6] For Wellhausen[7] the two sources follow each other consecutively (vv. 1-6 = E; vv. 7-21 = J). For

---

2. See the discussion in the following paragraph.

3. The reasons for identifying J and E as the sources underpinning this chapter are discussed below.

4. Cf. Speiser, *Genesis*, pp. 114-115; Van Seters, *Abraham*, pp. 249-50.

5. Some scholars (e.g. Clements, *Abraham and David*, p. 18) prefer to see v. 3 as a gloss upon v. 2, thus not affecting the essential unity of vv. 1-6.

6. For a concise discussion, see Westermann, *Genesis 12–36*, pp. 214-17.

7. J. Wellhausen, *Die Composition des Hexateuchs und der historischen Bücher des Alten Testaments* (Berlin: W. de Gruyter, 4th edn, 1963), pp. 21-22.

Gunkel,[8] however, they are interwoven (E = vv. 1b, 3a, 5, 11, 12a, 13a, 14, 16; J = the rest), having been radically reworked by a JE redactor. Subsequent analysts have similarly disagreed over precisely how the verses should be assigned to the suggested literary sources,[9] several freely acknowledging the complexity of this particular chapter and the difficulties it presents for an entirely satisfactory source-critical analysis.[10]

Following Lohfink,[11] more recent source critics such as Van Seters[12] and Coats[13] have maintained that ch. 15 is almost entirely J's reworking of an earlier tradition. This growing tendency among source critics to merge the J and E sources has been further encouraged by the computer-assisted analysis of Radday and others,[14] whose research uncovered no significant difference in style between similar genres of material within J and E, strongly suggesting their unified origin—though

8. Gunkel, *Genesis*, pp. 176-77.

9. The following scholars follow Wellhausen's division: G. Hölscher, *Geschichtsschreibung in Israel: Untersuchungen zum Jahvisten und Elohisten* (Lund: C.W.K. Gleerup, 1952), pp. 278-280; O. Kaiser, 'Traditionsgeschichtliche Untersuchung von Genesis 15', *ZAW* 70 (1958), pp. 107-126; Clements, *Abraham and David*, pp. 15-22; von Rad, *Genesis*, pp. 182-190; Zimmerli, *1. Mose 12–25*, pp. 48-59; M. Anbar, 'Genesis 15: A Conflation of Two Deuteronomic Narratives', *JBL* 101 (1982), pp. 39-55; Westermann, *Genesis 12–36*, pp. 216-17. Among those who have adopted Gunkel's general approach are: Procksch, *Die Genesis*, pp. 107-12, 293-99; H. Cazelles, 'Connexions et structure de Gen., XV', *RB* 69 (1962), pp. 321-49 (347-49); R. Kilian, *Die vorpriesterlichen Abrahamsüberlieferungen, literarkritisch und traditionsgeschichtlich untersucht* (BBB, 24; Bonn: Peter Hanstein, 1966), pp. 54-66; H. Sebass, 'Landverheissung an die Väter', *EvT* 37 (1977), pp. 210-29 (217).

10. For example, Skinner, *Genesis*, p. 276; L.A. Snijders, 'Genesis XV. The Covenant with Abram', in P.A.H. De Boer (ed.), *Studies on the Book of Genesis* (OTS, 12; Leiden: E.J. Brill, 1958), p. 262; von Rad, *Genesis*, pp. 182-83; Noth, *A History of Pentateuchal Traditions*, p. 111; Clements, *Abraham and David*, p. 17; A.W. Jenks, *The Elohist and North Israelite Traditions*, pp. 33-34.

11. Lohfink, *Die Landverheissung*, pp. 35-44.

12. Van Seters, *Abraham*, pp. 260-63.

13. Coats, *Genesis*, p. 123.

14. Y.T. Radday, H. Shore, M.A. Pollatschek and D. Wickmann, 'Genesis, Wellhausen and the Computer', *ZAW* 94 (1982), pp. 467-81; Y.T. Radday and H. Shore, *Genesis: An Authorship Study in Computer-Assisted Statistical Linguistics* (AnBib, 103; Rome: Biblical Institute Press, 1985); cf. G.J. Wenham, 'Genesis: An Authorship Study and Current Pentateuchal Criticism', *JSOT* 42 (1988), pp. 3-18.

admittedly not proving this categorically.[15] At present, therefore, source analysts suggest that the material in Genesis 15 reflects the J source (or a redacted JE composite for those who still accept that a separate E source ever existed).

However Genesis 15 is apportioned, there is a general consensus among source analysts that the material in this chapter and in ch. 17 clearly reflects at least two different sources, J (or R^{JE}) and P respectively. The different underlying sources are betrayed, it is alleged, not only by the distinctive vocabulary and style of these two chapters, but also by the particular emphasis of each account. These features will be considered in detail below.[16] The inclusion of both passages in the canonical Genesis is seen to be due to the JEP redactor(s), who out of respect for their sources pursued a policy of minimal editorial interference and therefore incorporated both accounts into the narrative framework. So, as elsewhere, 'parallel' or 'duplicate' accounts were set into the framework as consecutive narratives, with little or no attempt being made to disguise the resulting inconsistencies.

The main arguments marshalled in support of the documentary analysis of Genesis 15 and 17 are as follows.

a. *Distinctive Vocabulary*
One of the most important arguments used by source critics is that which focuses on the allegedly distinctive vocabulary reflected by the various underlying sources. Most source analysts maintain that a careful examination of the text of Genesis 15 and 17 will disclose a clear distinction in the vocabulary each chapter uses, a fact which, it is suggested, points to at least two different underlying sources. Moreover, by comparison with other Pentateuchal material, source critics suggest that it is possible to identify which sources are reflected in each chapter. Therefore, on the basis of the vocabulary contained in Genesis 15 and 17, source analysts confidently assert that the former is derived from J or JE, whereas the latter is derived almost entirely from P.

---

15. The limitations of such computer-assisted analysis are underlined by S.L. Portnoy and D.L. Petersen, 'Genesis, Wellhausen and the Computer: A Response', *ZAW* 96 (1984), pp. 421-25. See also the more recent and trenchant critique by R.E. Friedman, 'Some Recent Non-Arguments Concerning the Documentary Hypothesis', in M.V. Fox *et al.* (eds.), *Texts, Temples and Traditions* (Festschrift M. Haran; Winona Lake, IN: Eisenbrauns, 1996), pp. 92-101.

16. See Section 3c.

The following vocabulary is said to betray the J and/or E sources underlying ch. 15:

1. The divine appellation יהוה is predominantly used.
2. The phrase אחר[י] הדברים האלה is frequent in E (22.1; 40.1; 48.1) and is also used by J (22.20; 39.7), but is not thought to have been used by P.[17]
3. The archaic covenant terminology, כרת ברית, is said to characterize the J and E sources, whereas P uses the phrase הקים ברית or sometimes נתן ברית.

Recently a number of scholars have questioned whether the distribution of divine names can legitimately be used as a criterion for a source-critical analysis of the text of Genesis. The value of the tetragrammaton as a criterion for distinguishing the J account in Genesis has been challenged by Wenham and Moberly,[18] both of whom contend that the presence of יהוה in Genesis is editorial, the name itself not having been disclosed to the patriarchs. Though initially appealing, a number of fundamental objections have been raised in relation to Wenham and Moberly's hypothesis,[19] the most acute of which is the fact that it fails to explain adequately the uneven distribution of the divine names in Genesis. Even if the presence of 'Yahweh' in Genesis is to be explained by redactional activity, the redactor's selectivity still calls for explanation.

---

17. This traditional source-critical labelling is reflected in the standard commentaries by Gunkel, Driver, Skinner and von Rad. Noth (*A History of Pentateuchal Traditions*, pp. 264-67) is in general agreement, although he labels Gen. 40.1 'J'.

18. G.J. Wenham, 'The Religion of the Patriarchs', in A.R. Millard and D.J. Wiseman (eds.), *Essays on the Patriarchal Narratives* (Leicester: InterVarsity Press, 1980), pp. 157-188; R.W.L. Moberly, *The Old Testament of the Old Testament: Patriarchal Narratives and Mosaic Yahwism* (OBT; Minneapolis: Fortress Press, 1992), pp. 36-78.

19. See the following critiques: L.M. Eslinger, 'Knowing Yahweh: Exod 6.3 in the Context of Genesis 1–Exodus 15', in L.J. de Regt, J. de Waard and J.P. Fokkelmann (eds.), *Literary Structure and Rhetorical Strategies in the Hebrew Bible* (Assen: Van Gorcum, 1996), pp. 191-98; Alexander, *Abraham in the Negev*, pp. 94-96; Nicholson, *The Pentateuch in the Twentieth Century*, pp. 230-31. While Eslinger's study and statistical charts are most interesting, his thesis—that before God's saving acts in Exodus Yahweh had not disclosed himself as such—seems to overlook some key events in Genesis; there are several divine interventions in the Abraham narrative alone!

Other scholars have pointed either to the fact that there is no reason why the Yahwist could not have used the common noun, Elohim,[20] or to the inadequacy of this criterion to distinguish the E from the P material—as Whybray astutely comments, 'The criterion of the divine names...can at best do no more than help to distinguish J from the rest of the material'.[21] But as Whybray further observes, it is doubtful whether it can even achieve this more modest goal very well:

> Since both the authors of E and P and their readers would themselves have been familiar with the name Yahweh, there is no reason why these writers should not from the very outset have used this proper name of God except when quoting the words of their characters... Some other explanation for the relatively frequent use of Elohim in Genesis as compared with the rest of the Pentateuch seems to be required.[22]

Thus, by itself, the divine name criterion provides no firm basis for labelling Genesis 17 'P' (as opposed to 'E' or even 'J'), for dividing the material in Genesis 15 between 'J' and 'E' (as source analysts have traditionally done), or even for identifying 'J' as one of the sources underlying Genesis 15. This criterion is therefore of limited value for the purpose of a source-critical analysis of Genesis 15 (allegedly reflecting non-J material to a greater or lesser extent) and Genesis 17 (P).

But perhaps the most serious criticism of this traditional criterion for source analysis is the fact that the divine name allegedly peculiar to one source is occasionally found in another stratum.[23] As Whybray correctly maintains, 'Once the possibility of...editorial alteration has been admitted, the case for the criterion is seriously weakened'.[24] Therefore

20. For example, Blum, *Vätergeschichte*, pp. 471-75; Garrett, *Rethinking Genesis*, p. 19. Indeed, as Alexander (*Abraham in the Negev*, pp. 91-92) observes, 'there are contexts which permit only the use of Elohim as a common noun meaning "deity"'. He offers the following examples in Genesis: 9.26; 17.7, 8; 24.3, 7, 12, 27, 42, 48; 26.24; 27.20; 28.13 (×2), 21; 31.5, 19, 29, 30, 32, 34, 35, 42 (×2), 53 (×2); 32.10 (×2); 33.20; 35.2, 4; 43.23 (×2); 46.1, 3; 50.17.

21. Whybray, *The Making of the Pentateuch*, p. 64.

22. Whybray, *The Making of the Pentateuch*, pp. 64-65.

23. The use of 'Yahweh' in Gen. 17.1 is one such example. Whybray also lists Gen. 15.1-6 as one of the passages 'where the divine names either do not "match" the documentary analysis or pose insoluble problems for it' (Whybray, *The Making of the Pentateuch*, p. 65).

24. Whybray, *The Making of the Pentateuch*, p. 65. In view of these criticisms it is not surprising that even those advocating the use of this criterion for source-

without other criteria, the traditional source analysis is clearly deficient.

In relation to the second argument based on distinctive vocabulary (i.e. the use of the phrase הדברים האלה [אחר]ין), the acknowledgment that this phrase is used by more than one postulated stratum in Genesis surely undermines its usefulness as a reliable criterion for accurate source analysis. Like the divine name criterion, by itself this phrase cannot be used to distinguish between the sources allegedly underlying Genesis 15. This, and the fact that it occurs so infrequently in the Pentateuch (all the occurrences are in Genesis and have been noted above), renders it rather inadequate for any comprehensive source-critical analysis of the text. It is surely unhelpful to reach any firm conclusions on the basis of a phrase that occurs in Genesis a mere six times, only half of which can be confidently identified with any particular source. Moreover, the fact that this phrase occurs in literature as late as Esther and Chronicles precludes denying it to 'P' on anachronistic grounds.[25] Therefore, on a purely linguistic level, the employment of this phrase to differentiate between alleged sources is highly dubious, and seems to be based on the *a priori* assumption that the 'P' source never uses it. Yet the burden of proof lies with those who maintain this premise. As the evidence from Esther and Chronicles suggests, there is really no reason why 'P' could not have employed this phrase.

The strongest argument for a source-critical analysis of these chapters (Gen. 15 and 17) in terms of their distinctive vocabulary relates to the covenant terminology that each pericope employs. Here source criticism has highlighted a significant fact: whereas the idiom of 'cutting a covenant' is deployed in Genesis 15, the terminology used in Genesis 17 is that of 'giving' and 'establishing' a covenant. Nevertheless, it is important to examine the precise connotations of the various verbs used in relation with ברית in these chapters. As noted in the previous chapter, some have challenged the premise that 'to cut a covenant' and 'to establish a covenant' (or 'to set a covenant in place') are semantically synonymous,[26] thus casting serious doubt on their value as *bona*

---

critical analysis of the text have warned against its mechanical application; see, for example, C. Westermann, *Genesis 1–11* (trans. J.J. Scullion; London: SPCK, 1984), p. 579; Nicholson, *The Pentateuch in the Twentieth Century*, p. 232.

25. Cf. Est. 2.1; 3.1; 2 Chron. 32.1. (The only other occurrences are Josh. 24.29; 1 Kgs. 17.17; 21.1.)

26. For example, Cassuto, *The Documentary Hypothesis*, pp. 47-48 (see preceding section); see also Dumbrell, *Covenant and Creation*, p. 25 (cf. Chapter 6

fide criteria for source-critical analysis. If a subtle distinction in the nuance of these verbs (consistent with their deployment in the Abraham narrative) can be sustained, or if the absence of כרת ברית in Genesis 17 can be otherwise explained, this difference in covenant terminology can no longer be used as a legitimate mechanism for distinguishing between underlying sources. Thus the source-critical arguments for detecting a distinctive vocabulary in Genesis 15 are not as strong as they may initially appear.

In contrast to Genesis 15, ch. 17 employs a number of key terms and phrases which are said to be characteristic of the P source.[27] This allegedly Priestly terminology includes:

1. The divine epithets אלהים, throughout (except v. 1b[28]), and אל שדי, v. 1c.
2. The verbs used in ch. 17 in relation to the covenant, נתן or הקים, vv. 2, 7, 19, 21.
3. The phrases במאד מאד, vv. 2, 6, 20; אתה וזרעך אחריך, vv. 7, 8, 9, 10, 19; לדרתם, vv. 7, 9, and לדרתיכם, v. 12; כל־זכר, vv. 10, 12, 23; ארץ כנען, v. 8; בן־נכר, vv. 12, 27; ונכרתה הנפש ההוא, v. 14; פרה ורבה, v. 20; היום בעצם הזה, vv. 23, 26.
4. The use of עולם in relation to the divine–human ברית, vv. 7, 13, 19; the use of מגריך with 'land', v. 8; אחזה in v. 8; מקנה in vv. 12, 13, 23, 27; an allegedly peculiar usage of עמים in v. 14, and presence of the terms נשיאם and הוליד in v. 20.

In response to this generally accepted suggestion that the words and phrases in Genesis 17 are characteristic of 'P', Alexander has made a number of pertinent observations,[29] which are outlined and supplemented in the following points.

Section 2b below). Though disagreeing with the precise nuances which both Cassuto and Dumbrell place on these terms, I concur that the phrases should not be treated as exact equivalents; cf. my discussion in Chapter 6 Section 2b below.

27. Cf. Gunkel, *Genesis*, p. 264; Driver, *The Book of Genesis*, pp. vii-ix; Skinner, *Genesis*, p. 289.

28. יהוה in v. 1 is conveniently dismissed by most source critics as either redactional or a scribal error on the basis that according to P—Exod. 6.3—the tetragrammaton was unknown before Moses.

29. Alexander, 'Literary Analysis', pp. 179-82.

1. Many of the expressions allegedly typical of the P source also occur in the account of the Noahic covenant (Gen. 6–9). Alexander illustrates this with the following table.[30]

Table 3.1. *Parallel expressions in the accounts of the Noahic and Abrahamic covenants* (from Alexander, 'Literary Analysis').

Expression	Noahic covenant	Abrahamic Covenant
הקים ברית	9.9, 11, 12, 17	17.2, 7, 19, 21
נתן ברית		
אתה וזרעך אטריך	9.9	17.7, 8, 9, 10, 19
במאד מאד	7.19	17.2, 6, 20
לדרתם	6.9; 9.12	17.7, 9, 12
ונכרתה הנפש ההוא	9.11	17.14
פרה ורבה	8.17; 9.1, 7	17.20
הוליד	6.10	. 17.20
בעצם היום הזה	7.13	17.23, 26
כל־זכר	6.19; 7.3, 9, 16	17.10, 12, 23

To explain such parallelism in terms of source critcism, one must postulate that while the Priestly Source had its own version of the Noahic covenant as well, the redactors interweaved their sources in Genesis 6–9, rather than isolating the P from the non-P material as they allegedly did in relation to the Abrahamic covenant. Apart from the difficulty of explaining why two different (if not antithetical) redactional strategies should have been adopted, not all literary analysts are convinced that the Flood Narrative is as disjointed as some suppose.[31]

However, even though it may still be argued that the similar

---

30. 'Literary Analysis', p. 179. To this table the phrase ברית עולם (cf. 9.16; 17.7, 13, 19) could also be added. This does not detract from, but further supports Alexander's suggestion (see below) that Gen. 17 is describing a particular kind of covenant.

31. See especially the helpful discourse between G.J. Wenham ('The Coherence of the Flood Narrative', *VT* 28 [1978], pp. 336-48; 'Method in Pentateuchal Source Criticism', *VT* 41 [1991], pp. 84-109) and J.A. Emerton ('An Examination of Some Recent Attempts to Defend the Unity of the Flood Narrative in Genesis: Part One', *VT* 37 [1987], pp. 401-20 and 'An Examination of Some Recent Attempts to Defend the Unity of the Flood Narrative in Genesis: Part Two', *VT* 38 [1988], pp. 1-21).

terminology (in Gen. 6–9 and 17) simply reflects the same underlying source, it is worth noting with Alexander that much of the allegedly P terminology occurs mostly within a covenant context. As Alexander contends:

> This suggests that [these expressions] may represent traditional covenant terminology unconnected to any particular source, and their subsequent inclusion in P possibly results from an incorrect assumption that such covenants are found solely in this source. Thus these expressions are typical not of any particular source, but of narratives recounting conditional covenants.[32]

Therefore the so-called Priestly terminology of Genesis 17 is open to a quite different explanation (and a more feasible one from a synchronic perspective) from that offered by source critics. The shared vocabulary is due to similarity of subject matter. Thus understood, much of the distinctive vocabulary in Genesis 17 is characteristic of the special theme of this chapter, rather than the specific source which lies behind it.

2. Several of the words which are said to reflect P in Genesis 17 recur throughout Genesis in passages which presuppose the account in ch. 17: the expressions אל שדי and פרה ורבה occur along with the promises of land and numerical increase in 28.3-4; 35.11-12; 48.3-4;[33] the terms מגרים and אחזה are also found in 28.4; 36.7; 37.1 and 23.4, 9, 20; 36.43; 47.11; 48.4; 49.30; 50.13 respectively. Two explanations are equally possible: either (i) all these passages have a single, underlying source,[34] or (ii) the passages in which the allegedly Priestly terminology recurs are alluding specifically to the details about the promise of land reflected in 17.8.[35] There is evident circularity of argument involved in identifying these other passages as P on the basis of their use

---

32. Alexander, 'Literary Analysis', pp. 179, 180.

33. Each of these passages relates to God's reiteration (to Jacob) of the promises given to Abraham in Genesis 17.

34. However, such an analysis is not supported entirely by Noth (*A History of Pentateuchal Traditions*, pp. 264-67), who labels 47.11 'E' and identifies 36.15-43 as 'an addition to P' (p. 266). Cf. Carr's reconstruction (*Reading the Fractures*, pp. 339-40), which accredits all these texts to P except for 23.1-20, which is attributed to a later redactor.

35. These texts can be separated into two groups: (a) those that focus on the promise of land directly (i.e. 28.4; 37.1; 48.4) and (b) those that focus on the promise of land indirectly (i.e. 23.4, 9, 20; 36.7, 43; 47.11; 49.30; 50.13).

of 'P terminology', therefore the use of this criterion for any confident source analysis is open to serious criticism. But more importantly, once again a synchronic alternative to the source-critical explanation is not only possible, but just as feasible.

The value of the terminology criterion is further undermined by the fact that several of these expressions allegedly typical of P are found in passages which are not unanimously accepted as belonging to the P strand. The phrase ארץ כנען occurs in Gen. 35.6; 42.5, 7, 13, 29, 32 and in 44.8, respectively assigned to E and J by Driver.[36] The expression כל־זכר is found related to the rite of circumcision (cf. Gen. 17) in Gen. 34.15, 22, 24, 25. Since there is no unanimity on the source analysis of this latter chapter[37] the employment of this phrase as a P criterion is seriously undermined. The same may be said of the term נשיא which is also found, among other places (23.6; 25.16), in ch. 34 (v. 2). Moreover, if with Noth this term is accepted as early, it cannot be used as a criterion for identifying P at all.[38] In any case, there seems to be a deliberate contrast in Genesis 17 between the 'kings' who will descend from Abraham through Isaac and the 'tribal leaders' who will descend from Ishmael.[39] Thus the single occurrence in Genesis 17 of a term which is not exclusively used by any one source, and which is apparently demanded by the context, is not a strong basis for labelling this chapter 'P'.

This leaves the expressions מעמיה, מקנת and בן־נכר. These, however, are so rare in Genesis—indeed in the entire Pentateuch—that their usefulness for identifying the underlying sources is open to serious doubt.[40] Moreover, the deployment of these unusual terms may just as

36. Driver, *The Book of Genesis*, pp. 16-17.

37. Cf. Driver, *The Book of Genesis*, p. 17; Skinner, *Genesis*, p. 418; Noth, *History of Pentateuchal Traditions*, pp. 30, 265; Speiser, *Genesis*, pp. 266-67; G. Fohrer, *Introduction to the Old Testament* (trans. D.E. Green; Nashville: Abingdon Press, 1968), p. 161.

38. M. Noth, *Exodus* (trans. J.S. Bowden; OTL; London: SCM Press, 1962), pp. 187-88. Admittedly, this argument loses force if one accepts a pre-exilic dating for P (cf. Friedman, 'Torah', pp. 614, 617).

39. See Chapter 5 Section 3c below.

40. Admittedly the term מעמיה is found elsewhere only in material associated with P (viz. Lev. 7 [×4]; 19.8; 23.9 and Num. 9.13—labelled respectively 'P', 'additions to P', 'additions to P', and 'P' by Noth); cf. his similar labelling of the four texts which use מעמיו: Exod. 30.33; 30.38 (both 'P'); Lev. 17.9; 21.14 (both 'additions to P'). Other than its twofold appearance in Gen. 17, בן־נכר occurs only

feasibly be explained in terms of context as by hypothetical sources. If the latter two terms are the most accurate way of describing precisely the type of purchase which the author had in mind, their deployment in Genesis 17 would be significant only if analogous material in 'parallel sources' used different terminology. The same principle applies to the use of מעמיה. If this relationship (i.e. a cutting off *from one's people*) were expressed in a parallel text using synonymous but different terminology (assuming that such existed), source criticism might indeed offer the most cogent explanation. But as such an expression is paralleled nowhere else in the entire book of Genesis, it is by no means self-evident that Gen. 17.14 derives from P.

A careful examination of the allegedly Priestly terminology in Genesis 17, then, reveals that much of it can be explained in terms of subject matter (i.e. a conditional covenant) and the rest is difficult to connect solely with the P source. Thus as Alexander suggests, 'the arguments from vocabulary are not as conclusive as they may at first appear'.[41]

From the above discussion one must conclude that source-critical arguments for differentiating between P and non-P sources on the basis of the terminology used in Genesis 15 and 17 are at most suggestive, and by no means conclusive. Indeed, since subject matter and context must always be determining factors in the use of vocabulary, terminology is inherently suspect as a foundation on which to build a source-critical analysis.

b. *Different Theological Emphases*
The major element in the covenant of Genesis 15 is that of inheritance, chiefly that of the Promised Land, whereas circumcision is undeniably a major emphasis in ch. 17. In contrast, the land element of the divine promise to Abraham is conspicuous by its relegation to the periphery in the latter chapter. Thus Westermann observes, 'it is mentioned only once and is consciously enclosed by the promise of the divine pres-

---

in Exod. 12.43; Lev. 22.25 and Ezek. 44.9; מקנת is found elsewhere only in Exod. 12.44 (although cf. the similar use of the noun in Gen. 23.18; Lev. 25.16, 51; 27.22; Jer. 32.11-16 and the related verb in Gen. 25.10; 33.19; 39.1; 47.19-23; 49.30; 50.13; Lev. 22.11; Josh. 24.32; Neh. 5.8—all of which refer to purchases of *slaves* or *fields*. Significantly, the other Hebrew word meaning 'to purchase' [שבר] is used of buying grain or food; cf. Gen. 41.56, 57; 42.2-7, 10; 43.2, 4, 20; Deut. 2.6, 28).

41. Alexander, 'Literary Analysis', pp. 181-82.

ence'.[42] The stress on the importance of circumcision as the essential proof of adherence to the covenant is considered late and characteristic of P. Von Rad typically comments:

> Because of the abolition of the great cultic regulations, the feasts, sacrifice, etc. which were binding on the national community, the individual and family were suddenly summoned to decision... since the Babylonians (like all eastern Semites) did not practice circumcision, the observance of this custom was a *status confessionis* for the exiles; i.e., it became a question of their witness to Yahweh and his guidance of history. The significance that circumcision thus received was unknown to ancient Israel. It was a rite which was practiced from earliest times, but it was not yet connected in such a way with the center of faith.[43]

Thus source critics see obvious theological development in ch. 17. The covenant of ch. 15 focusing on the issue of land has been reworked by P to encompass the new circumstances of his own day—ethnic distinctiveness rather than territorial claims.

If the antiquity of circumcision in Israel is assumed (and there is no reason why it should not be), then it must have had some significance before the Babylonian exile. In the absence of any indisputable alternative explanation to the introduction of circumcision in Israel,[44] the one offered in Genesis 17 deserves consideration and should certainly not be prejudged solely on account of its alleged lateness.

Moreover, if the theological basis for circumcision in Israel is not to be found in Genesis 17, where is it to be found? The fact that circumcision took on a greater significance during the exile is not in doubt; it certainly was a mark which distinguished the Israelites from their Babylonian overlords. Yet this does not rule out a theological significance for circumcision at an earlier period in Israel's history. Without Genesis 17, however, it is difficult to discern the function that this ancient rite may have served in Israel.

There does not seem to be any clear evidence that circumcision was ever merely a puberty rite in ancient Israel.[45] Texts that are suggestive

---

42. Westermann, *Genesis 12–36*, p. 255.

43. Von Rad, *Genesis*, p. 201; cf. Noth, *History of Pentateuchal Traditions*, pp. 231, 241; Clements, *Abraham and David*, p. 74; Westermann, *Genesis 12–36*, p. 265.

44. See the discussion in the next two paragraphs.

45. *Pace* Clements, *Abraham and David*, p. 73.

of a puberty ritual clearly deal with special circumstances.[46] It is surely invalid to explain the normal practice in the light of the exceptions.[47] However, it is equally mistaken to explain Israelite practice simply in terms of the practice of surrounding cultures. As Lewis and Armerding aver:

> There is no reason to affirm that circumcision arrived in Israel in a vacuum, but neither is there reason to deny its application to Abraham and his posterity in the form outlined by the text [i.e. Genesis 17]. The editor of the Genesis account has no interest in the ultimate origin of circumcision; he is, rather, concerned with its subsequent application and significance in Israel.[48]

It may well be that Zipporah used the term חתן (Exod. 4.25) in a sense akin to the Arabic cognate,[49] but her perception of the rite may have been influenced too much by her own non-Israelite culture. Significantly, this notoriously difficult text probably suggests that it was Zipporah's infant son who was actually circumcised; it evidently reflects a source which assumed infant circumcision. To resolve this difficulty Propp is forced to 'hypothesize that circumcision had already moved to childhood by the Yahwist's day'.[50] Once the validity of such a hypothesis is granted, however, the use of the rite of infant circumcision to distinguish the P source in Genesis becomes untenable.

Thus, while not denying the important emphasis placed on circumcision by Jewish exiles wishing to maintain their ethnic distinctiveness in Babylon, this is not sufficient grounds for dating the tradition in Genesis 17 to this period and identifying this chapter as part of the P source in Genesis.

But what about the other major distinguishing feature: the lack of emphasis on the territorial promise in Genesis 17? This does not indisputably point to a late Priestly writer either. The exilic and post-exilic writers clearly had not abandoned belief in this element of the Patriarchal promise.[51] Given that the territorial promise remained an

---

46. Gen. 34.13-24; Exod. 4.24-26; Josh. 5.2-8. Significantly, all three texts tacitly assume the existence of the tradition reflected in Gen. 17.

47. As W.H. Propp does in his article, 'That Bloody Bridegroom', *VT* 43 (1993), pp. 495-518.

48. T. Lewis and C.E. Armerding, 'Circumcision', *ISBE*, I, p. 700.

49. As argued by Propp, 'That Bloody Bridegroom', p. 507.

50. Propp, 'That Bloody Bridegroom', p. 508.

51. See, for example, Jer. 30.3; Ezek. 11.17; Zech. 10.6-7.

important issue in the post-exilic period, why should the Priestly
writer(s) downgrade it vis-à-vis the promise of numerical expansion?
Indeed, why, for that matter, should the Yahwist, in his covenant
account, ignore the prospect of royal descendants? It is as inconceivable
that P was deliberately playing down God's promise of land to Abra-
ham/Israel as to suggest that J was deliberately downgrading the promise of royal descendants in Genesis 15. Thus the fact that the land
element of the promise is not central in Genesis 17 must be given a
different interpretation; namely, that the covenant in ch. 17 is not dealing primarily with this aspect of the promise but rather has a radically
different focal point.

c. *Different Portrayals of Deity*

Chapter 17 supposedly reflects P's less anthropomorphic representation
of God—as elsewhere in P God 'appears' and 'goes up' from an individual, with no further description of his appearance being offered. This
is considered typical of P's non-graphic style (cf. the writer's attempt to
describe the theophany in Gen. 15).

It is difficult, however, to see how the portrayal of God in Genesis 17
is any less anthropomorphic or graphic than that contained in ch. 15.
The latter opens with the statement: 'After these things the word of the
LORD came to Abram *in a vision*' (NRSV, emphasis mine). In the subsequent dialogue—which is not significantly different from that contained in Genesis 17—there is nothing particularly anthropomorphic.
Indeed, most (and perhaps all) of the recorded divine speech is found in
the context of a trance-like state (cf. vv. 1, 12). The actual 'theophany'
(v. 17) is more a symbol than a manifestation of deity; if anything, it is
the narrative in Genesis 17 which is the more anthropomorphic of the
two accounts (cf. vv. 1 and 22). Even some source critics have recognized this anomaly in Genesis 17.[52] Therefore, given the lack of clear
distinction in the portrayal of the deity in these pericopes (Gen. 15 and
17), this seems to be a rather tenuous basis on which to argue that the
two chapters reflect the particular characteristics of their alleged
sources.

---

52. For example, Skinner (*Genesis*), who identifies this on the basis of vv. 1 and
22, and acknowledges the incongruity of such anthropomorphic language in allegedly P material.

d. *Different Styles and Frameworks*

It is further argued that the chronological data in Gen. 17.1, 17, 24, 25, as well as the broad style of the narrative, reflect the Priestly source—the only Pentateuchal source whose chronological framework is thought to have been preserved in the redacted text.

This argument based on the style and chronological framework of the P narrative is equally slender. Recent writers have been quite dismissive of alleged stylistic differences. Thus Whybray, for example, observes that ' "P", like the other supposed "documents", has no distinctive narrative style of its own'.[53] Furthermore, such a variable entity as style is surely a rather dubious criterion on which to construct a source analysis of any given text; it fails to take into consideration important factors such as the subject material, the mood of the author, the time-period over which the material was compiled, and perhaps most importantly, the subjective aesthetic judgments of the literary critic.[54]

The argument on the basis of chronological data in Genesis 17 is once again rather circular in nature—the chronological data must be P because P's chronological data have alone been preserved in the narrative! Wenham has justifiably questioned the validity of this latter premise that only chronological data from P have been preserved in Genesis.[55] Once it is conceded that chronological data from other sources may also have been incorporated into the composite narrative, the argument for distinguishing two different underlying sources in Genesis 15 and 17 on the basis of chronological information is seriously undermined.

e. *Literary Dependence*

Source critics generally accept that Genesis 17 is dependent upon Genesis 15—some (for instance, von Rad and Coats) suggesting

---

53. Whybray, *The Making of the Pentateuch*, p. 61.

54. Significantly, even while defending the stylistic criterion against its detractors, J. Tigay ('The Stylistic Criterion of Source Criticism', in *Empirical Models*, pp. 149-73) can only 'partially endorse' its use in source-critical analysis (p. 172).

55. Cf. Wenham, *Genesis 16–50*, p. 5. While employing chronological data in his attempt to isolate P material in Genesis, Carr (*Reading the Fractures*, pp. 48-113) also reflects a more cautious approach to the application of this premise, acknowledging that 'the present Genesis genealogical structure is formed out of a combination of P and non-P material' (p. 97).

dependence also on 18.4-15.[56] This dependence is seen as evidence of the relative lateness of the account in ch. 17 and also serves to explain its different emphasis.

On this question of alleged literary dependence of Genesis 17 on ch. 15 it should be noted with Wenham that the striking differences preclude the idea that ch. 17 is simply a reworking of ch. 15.[57] Furthermore, ch. 17 'both presupposes what precedes it and is presupposed by what follows'; thus, whatever its prehistory, this chapter 'has been carefully and thoroughly integrated into the present work'.[58] Wenham cogently argues (contra Westermann and others) that the editor responsible for this integration was J, thus explaining the presence of the tetragrammaton in v. 1 and an employment of the niphal ראה akin to other J texts. Further support for J redaction is found in the affinity of structure between ch. 17 and chs. 16, 18 and 19 (three chapters generally ascribed to J). This possibility of a J-like redaction of Genesis 17 exposes the inherent weakness of an explanation of the two covenant passages which rests on a straightforward division between distinct literary sources. Why did a J redactor of ch. 17 not amalgamate this material with the J account of the covenant—especially if they were understood simply as two variant accounts of the same covenant? In order to facilitate this (and maintain a policy of minimal interference) the order of Gen. 15.7-21 and 16 could simply have been inverted. This would have placed the covenant passages together in a way that would not have detracted from the particular emphasis of each account. The strong possibility that a J redactor of ch. 17 instead isolated these two covenant chapters from other J material would surely suggest that each should be understood as having a different function in the narrative structure.

As the close examination above has clearly illustrated, when the various supporting arguments for the standard diachronic analysis of Genesis 15 and 17 are carefully examined, it becomes increasingly clear that the cumulative chain forged by them has several weak links which seriously undermine the strength of the whole. Not only does the standard source-critical analysis fail to account adequately for the

56. Cf. Skinner, *Genesis*, p. 290; von Rad, *Genesis*, p. 202; McEvenue, *Narrative Style*, pp. 145-46; Westermann, *Genesis 12–36*, p. 255, Coats, *Genesis*, p. 136.
57. Wenham, *Genesis 16–50*, p. 19; cf. Section 3c below.
58. Wenham, *Genesis 16–50*, p. 18.

'distinctive vocabulary' used in these two chapters, but it is also possible to explain this phenomenon without recourse to diachronic presuppositions at all. The same applies to the different theological emphases reflected in these chapters. While the emphasis of each chapter is undeniably distinct, source criticism does not satisfactorily explain this significant difference. The different *Sitze im Leben* presupposed in diachronic analyses have, to date, not sufficiently accounted for the contrasting promissory emphases of these chapters. In relation to the other two criteria—the portrayal of God in each chapter and the differences in style and framework—source criticism is particularly unconvincing, reflecting a high degree of subjectivity and circular argumentation. Taken in isolation, each of the links in the source-critical argument is rather weak, and there is therefore no reason to suppose that together they form anything like an unbreakable chain.

However, even apart from the intrinsic weaknesses just highlighted, diachronic explanations of the divine–human covenant pericopes in the Abraham narrative face a much greater problem. As noted at the beginning of this chapter, it is difficult to reconcile the basic premise—that Genesis 15 and 17 are simply variant accounts of the same event—with the material contained in these two chapters, as the following analysis of their contents and emphases will illustrate.

3. *An Analysis of the Contents and Emphases of the Two Chapters*

There are various elements common to both Genesis 15 and 17. In both God is said to take the initiative (cf. 15.1a; 17.1a); in both passages God reveals a new dimension of his character (cf. 15.1b; 17.1b); in both the issue of a son or 'offspring' is addressed and resolved (cf. 15.3-5; 17.4, 15-21); in both Abraham's descendants are promised similar territory (cf. 15.18-19; 17.8);[59] in both Abraham questions God's intentions (cf. 15.3, 8; 17.17-18); in both Abraham faithfully carries out God's instructions (cf. 15.10; 17.23-27).

However, this similarity of content must be balanced by the striking differences in detail and emphasis between the two chapters—differences which weigh heavily against the contention that these are simply variant accounts of the same event (i.e. the inauguration of a single divine covenant with Abraham).

59. In ch. 17, nevertheless, there is less detail on the parameters of the Promised Land; cf. Section 3c.12 below.

a. *The Contents and Emphases of Chapter 15*

In ch. 15 Abraham's divine encounter is introduced in terms of prophetic inspiration—as a visionary experience (היה דבר־יהוה אל־אברם במחזה, v. 1). Not all of what follows records what happened while Abraham remained in this visionary state (cf. vv. 12 and 17), but some of this divine–human encounter clearly did.

Yahweh's self-introduction is in terms of his ability to provide adequate protection[60] and generous reward[61] for Abraham, apparently in response to Abraham's present trauma.[62] As the following two verses disclose, the trauma of Abraham implied by 15.1 evidently relates to the fact that he was still without an heir. The immediately preceding chapter does not shed much light on Abraham's anxiety. Perhaps Abraham's earlier hopes that Lot might be his heir had been further undermined by the latter's resettlement in Sodom after he had been rescued from the Eastern kings (ch. 14). This seems unlikely, however, in that, as several commentators point out, the opening phrase in Genesis 15 (אחר הדברים האלה) establishes only a rather loose connection with what precedes.[63] Sailhamer rather overstates the case, however, when he claims that Genesis 15 'opens by making a major break with the preceding chapter'.[64] Whatever the connection between the two episodes (i.e. Genesis 14 and 15), the only apprehension of Abraham

60. M. Dahood's proposal ('Ugaritic Lexicography', in *Mélanges Eugène Tisserant* [Studi e Testi, 231; Rome: Pontifical Biblical Institute, 1964], pp. 81-104 [94]) that מגן should be read as a participle and linked to the Ugaritic *mgn* = 'bestow' which, taking the following שכרך also as a participle, gives the reading: *I am your benefactor, who will reward you very greatly*, has not won general support.

61. The general meaning is unaffected whether the SP's 'I shall multiply' or the MT's 'great' is adopted.

62. Suggested by the use of the introductory אל־תירא formula. Though frequently introducing salvation oracles, elsewhere in Genesis it is introduced in the context of present trauma (cf. 21.17; 26.24; 35.17; 43.23; [46.3] 50.19, 21).

63. See, for example, Delitzsch, *A New Commentary on Genesis*, II, p. 3; Driver, *The Book of Genesis*, p. 174; Ryle, *The Book of Genesis*, p. 185; Skinner, *Genesis*, p. 278; Davidson, *Genesis 12–50*, p. 42; Gibson, *Genesis*, II, p. 49; Sarna, *Genesis*, p. 112; Sailhamer, *The Pentateuch as Narrative*, p. 150; Scullion, *Genesis*, p. 130.

64. Elsewhere in Genesis the phrase is admittedly used to indicate a break in the narrative (22.1, 20; 39.7; 40.1; 48.1). However, in all these other instances it is preceded by the idiomatic ויהי. Thus while the Targums (*Neofiti* and *Pseudo-Jonathan*) are mistaken to link Gen. 15 so closely with the aftermath of the episode recorded in Gen. 14, Sailhamer is perhaps equally mistaken to locate such a sharp syntactical break at this point in the narrative.

expressly mentioned is found in Genesis 15, and there it relates to the non-realization of God's promise of a son and heir.

Abraham verbally responds to God's revelation, addressing him as 'Lord Yahweh' and highlighting the main obstacle to the fulfilment of God's original promise (cf. 12.2a, 7; 13.15-17). The only heir apparent is his household slave, Eliezer of Damascus.[65] Therefore, Abraham's chief concern in ch. 15 is the fact that he is still childless—an axiomatic problem standing in the way of the promise's fulfilment.

Yahweh's word of reassurance to Abraham (vv. 4-5) addresses this fundamental obstacle directly—Abraham would indeed father an heir from whom innumerable 'offspring' (זֶרַע) would derive.

In response to this divine (salvation?) oracle Abraham 'trusted Yahweh',[66] apparently fully reassured. Whether the subsequent 'it' refers to Abraham's faith or Yahweh's reassurance is ambiguous on grammatical grounds alone, making equally uncertain just who is being credited with צְדָקָה. Nevertheless, as Hamilton contends, 'the traditional interpretation makes the most sense in the wider biblical context and is grammatically justifiable'.[67] In any case, what is crucial to the present discussion is simply the fact that, according to the narrator, Abraham responded in faith to Yahweh's promise of a son.

The second pericope in Genesis 15 clearly moves on to address (or expand upon) the question of the inheritance, rather than the inheritor. Once again it opens with an identification statement by Yahweh,[68]

---

65. The underlying Hebrew phrase is notoriously difficult. Modern commentators generally attempt to emend or reinterpret the text, perhaps the most novel of such efforts being that of Turner, who, by disregarding the 'unintelligible' altogether, is able to identify Lot as the only genuine contender to fit the clear part of the text; viz. בֶן־בֵּיתִי יוֹרֵשׁ אֹתִי (Turner, *Announcements of Plot*, pp. 70-72). So too (although more tentatively) D.J.A. Clines, *What Does Eve Do to Help? And Other Readerly Questions to the Old Testament* (JSOTSup, 94; Sheffield: JSOT Press, 1990), p. 73. Cf. M.F. Unger's less radical solution: 'Some Comments on the Text of Genesis 15.2,3', *JBL* 72 (1953), pp. 49-50.

66. This is the first occurrence of the root אמן in Genesis. The hiphil stem is used only here and in Gen. 42.20 and Gen. 45.26, a fact which has been offered several explanations (the causative connotation often associated with the hiphil is clearly excluded in 15.6 and 45.26), but the traditional explanation is still the most plausible; cf. Hamilton, *Genesis 1–17*, pp. 423-24.

67. Hamilton, *Genesis 1–17*, p. 425.

68. The fact that the covenant name (יהוה) is employed in the present covenantal context is hardly surprising.

which is followed this time by an implicit reminder of his unchanging purpose in relation to Abraham's inheritance of the Promised Land.

The reservations which Abraham expresses in v. 8 are not a reversal of his previous faith (v. 6), but relate to an entirely different element of the divine promise: his possession of territory. Consequently, it is unnecessary to play down Abraham's doubts on the basis that it conflicts with the faith expressed in v. 6.[69] Rather, as Ross observes, 'the mention of the *land* raised doubts in Abram's mind'.[70] So it is not surprising that the following verses record how Yahweh offered Abraham reassurance relating primarily to this aspect of the divine promise. Therefore, just as vv. 2-6 relate to the promised offspring, vv. 7-19 deal with the promised territory.

The reassurance requested by Abraham came both by word and sign, but God first demanded that a 'sacrificial' ritual be performed.[71] Significantly, this is the only obligation placed on Abraham in this present chapter.

With everything now in place, despite the temporary disruption caused by the carrion birds, Abraham fell into a deep sleep during which time Yahweh offered him more verbal reassurance, this time in relation to the promised territorial inheritance (vv. 12-16). This further revelation of Yahweh unequivocally answers Abraham's earlier reservations—as is clear from a comparison of Abraham's כי אדע במה (v. 8) with Yahweh's ידע תדע כי (v. 13). However, along with this

---

69. Contra Wenham, *Genesis 1–15*, p. 331; Hagelia, *Numbering the Stars*, pp. 88-89; Hamilton, *Genesis 1–17*, p. 429; Scullion, *Genesis*, p. 132. With Targumic and Midrashic interpreters (see L.M. Barth, 'Genesis 15 and the Problems of Abraham's Seventh Trial', *Maarav* 8 [1992], pp. 245-63 [258-62]), the following scholars acknowledge genuine doubt on Abraham's part: Gros Louis, 'Abraham I', p. 63; Nelson, 'Was Not Abraham Justified?', p. 260; Ross, *Creation and Blessing*, p. 310; Youngblood, *The Book of Genesis*, p. 162; Stek, 'Covenant "Overload"', p. 29; Anderson, *Contours*, p. 100.

70. Ross, *Creation and Blessing*, p. 310.

71. Abraham was literally to '*take for/to*' Yahweh the animals in question, but as Wenham observes, 'This very common word often introduces a ritual such as sacrifice, e.g. Lev 9.2,3' (*Genesis 1–15*, p. 331). Other features are also suggestive of sacrifice; for example, the list of animals covers all those species which could be offered in sacrifice (cf. Lev. 1); the thrice-repeated *three-year-old* (v. 9) echoes the language of an ordered rite; the non-dissection of the slaughtered birds is analogous to Lev. 1.6, 17; but there are also important distinctives (e.g. the arrangement of the animal pieces in two rows).

reassurance that his descendants would certainly take possession of the inheritance, it is here clearly stated that Abraham would not take possession of the Promised Land himself (vv. 15-16).[72] Thus the promise of land would remain unfulfilled in Abraham's lifetime, and indeed for several centuries.[73]

Finally, this verbal reassurance is symbolically affirmed by the theophanic fire passing between the arranged animal pieces. The significance of this unusual ritual is then explained by the narrator in terms of covenant ratification (v. 18). This particular ברית is explicitly connected with the promise of geographical territory which Abraham's descendants would eventually inherit and possess.

The emphasis of Genesis 15, therefore, is indisputably on the divine promise of nationhood: Yahweh solemnly promises to give Abraham descendants and land.

b. *The Content and Emphases of Chapter 17*

As noted above, Genesis 17 begins by giving Abraham's age as 'ninety-nine years' at the time of the ensuing encounter with Yahweh. There is no explicit indication that Abraham's experience was of a visionary nature; rather, all the indications in the text point to a theophany (cf. vv. 1 and 22).

Yahweh introduces himself as אל שדי,[74] and immediately proceeds

---

72. This was at least implicit from the beginning (cf. Gen. 12.7), and a close reading of Genesis may suggest that the Abraham narrative consistently maintains that the promise of land will not be realized within Abraham's lifetime, but only at a future time by his *descendants* (as observed, for example, by Gros Louis, 'Abraham I', p. 59). For more on this, see P.R. Williamson, 'Abraham, Israel and the Church', *EvQ* 72 (2000), pp. 99-118.

73. According to the figure in Gen. 15.13, this promise would remain unrealized for at least another four centuries. For the difficulty presented by the period(s) alluded to in Gen. 15.13 and 15.16, see Chapter 4 Section 3b.2.

74. The combination of these two terms as a divine epithet occurs mainly in Genesis; cf. Exod. 6.3 and Ezek. 10.5. Apparently this was the title by which the patriarchs knew God (Exod. 6.3), though the etymology of שדי—and therefore the meaning of the term—is somewhat obscure; see Westermann, *Genesis 12–36*, pp. 257-58 and Hamilton, *Genesis 1–17*, pp. 462-63, for concise treatments of the most prominent proposals. Occurring some 48 times in the Hebrew Bible (most frequently in Job, but without the accompanying אל), it is translated by the LXX as παντοκρατωρ which via the Vulgate's *omnipotens* has had an obvious influence upon the most common English translation of the term as 'almighty'. Wenham

to give Abraham the exhortation, 'Behave in an exemplary fashion so that I may establish my covenant with both you and your descendants, and greatly increase your numbers' (17.1b-2).[75] This exhortation would appear to place certain obligations on Abraham, the fulfilment of which is a prerequisite to the 'establishing' or 'giving'[76] of the anticipated ברית. Thus the covenant is introduced in Genesis 17, not as something already instituted, but as something yet to be established, the actual establishment of which is dependent upon Abraham's response to the divine requirement stated in Gen. 17.1. Moreover, the fact should not be overlooked that the promissory element of this statement concerns phenomenal numerical expansion, elucidated in the following verses in terms of Abraham's international significance.

Abraham's response (ויפל אברם על־פניו, v. 3a) to this encounter with Yahweh is also noteworthy. On this occasion there was no verbal response; only a physical response, according to the narrator, who continues by expanding on the divine communication which Abraham received (vv. 3b-16).

The divine speech in vv. 3b-16 is clearly composed of two literary units, each beginning with emphatic pronouns (cf. vv. 4a, 9b). In these two units the divine and human obligations involved in the aforementioned covenant are spelled out; those God places upon himself (vv. 4-8), and those God places upon Abraham and his descendants (vv. 9-14).

In vv. 4-8 God discloses what his purposes are in relation to Abraham and his descendants. These include the fatherhood of *many nations* (vv. 4-5)—here given symbolic bolstering by means of an actual

defends this traditional interpretation by observing that 'it is always used in connection with promises of descendants: Shaddai evokes the idea that God is able to make the barren fertile and to fulfil his promises' (Wenham, *Genesis 16–50*, p. 20).

75. My translation is influenced by Alexander's proposal ('Genesis 22 and the Covenant', p. 19) that here a cohortative following an imperative expresses the purpose or result of the imperative; see also Turner, *Announcements of Plot*, pp. 55, 58 and 76, and the following: GKC, §108d, p. 320; S.R. Driver, *A Treatise on the Use of the Tenses in Hebrew and other Syntactical Questions* (Oxford: Clarendon Press, 3rd edn, 1892), p. 64; M. Greenberg, *Introduction to Hebrew* (Englewood Cliffs, NJ; Prentice Hall, 1965), pp. 183-84; T.O. Lambdin, *Introduction to Biblical Hebrew* (London: Darton, Longman & Todd, 1973), p. 119; *IBHS*, pp. 577-78; Joüon, §116, pp. 381-86 (other possible interpretations are noted as well); J.C.L. Gibson, *Davidson's Introductory Hebrew Grammar—Syntax* (Edinburgh: T. & T. Clark, 4th edn, 1994), p. 106.

76. Hebrew: first common singular imperfect of נתן with waw conjunction.

change of name: from 'Abram' to 'Abraham'[77] (v. 5); the progenitor of *kings* (v. 6);[78] the establishing of an *everlasting* covenant with Abraham and his descendants (v. 7); the provision of the whole land of Canaan as their *everlasting possession* (v. 8); and the establishment of a divine–human relationship not only with Abraham himself, but also with Abraham's descendants (vv. 7b, 8).

In the subsequent verses (vv. 9-14) God expands upon the human obligations involved in this particular covenant. Both Abraham and his descendants are required to practise perpetually the rite of infant male circumcision as the sign of the covenant between God and themselves (vv. 10-12). This external mark in the flesh was clearly a crucial feature as far as inclusion in this particular covenant was concerned (vv. 13-14).

Now, for the first time in the canonical Abraham narrative, Sarah's role in the fulfilment of God's promise of descendants is made explicit (vv. 15-16). Like Abraham, her name is also changed—albeit not quite so radically—thus indicating that she, with her husband, has undergone some change in status.

Extraordinarily (for both her and her husband, though not for the narrator and reader) she would indeed be the progenitrix, the mother of Abraham's promised offspring. Moreover, not only would she be the progenitrix of a single nation but, as God had previously said in relation to Abraham, Sarah would 'give rise to *nations*; *kings* of *peoples* shall come from her' (v. 16, NRSV, emphasis mine).

God's comments concerning Sarah provoke Abraham's response of incredulity (vv. 17-18). Abraham appears to have taken everything up to this last aspect in his stride; he clearly finds this final idea absurd. Therefore Abraham's response to God's revelation on this occasion is

77. The biblical explanation of the new name is generally interpreted as a sound play (cf. *'ab-hamon*) rather than an exact etymology. Thus interpreted, the name 'Abraham' is probably a dialectal variant of 'Abram', with no appreciable difference in meaning. Aalders, however, challenges this consensus, arguing that there might possibly have been an ancient Hebrew cognate of the Arabic *ruehām* (copious number); cf. Aalders, *Genesis*, I, p. 306. Similarly N.M. Sarna ('Abraham', *EncJud*, II, col. 112) allows the possibility of 'father of multitudes' being the correct meaning of 'Abraham', and in his commentary (*Genesis*, p. 124) mentions favourably Ibn Ezra's suggestion that the consonants ABRHM were interpreted as an acronym for ABiR (mighty one) + Hamon (multitude) + goyiM (nations).

78. It is instructive that this aspect is again related to Abraham's international fatherhood; cf. the immediately preceding לגוים.

one of unbelief. This unbelief is in no way mellowed by his physical prostration or his plea on behalf of Ishmael (v. 18). The mention of Ishmael is akin to (but clearly not the same as) the mention of Eliezer in Genesis 15. While both are presented as potential surrogates for the improbable heir that God had promised, Abraham's attitude to each candidate is very different: Eliezer is presented as part of the problem, whereas Ishmael is presented as a possible solution (cf. 15.2; 17.18).

In the following section (vv. 19-22) God plainly rebukes Abraham's unbelief.[79] Contrary to Abraham's considered opinion, such an unusual birth was not in fact impossible; the elderly pair would indeed produce a male heir within a year whose name would be Isaac.[80] Furthermore, the prospect of this child meant that Abraham's hopes concerning Ishmael were misplaced—it was with Isaac that God's everlasting covenant would be maintained (v. 19).

Though in some sense excluded from the terms of the covenant,[81] Ishmael is nevertheless promised divine blessing in the form of numerical expansion, tribal significance and national acclaim (v. 20).

At this point in the narrative the theophany comes to an end (v. 22) and the narrator records Abraham's complete and immediate compliance with the divine instructions regarding the circumcision of every male in his household (vv. 21-27).[82]

c. *A Comparison of the Contents and Emphases of the Two Chapters*
Though a superficial reading might suggest that the emphasis of both chapters is the same (namely, a divine–human covenant confirming for Abraham God's promises of descendants and territory), a careful reading of the contents uncovers subtle differences in emphasis between the

---

79. As Wenham (*Genesis 16–50*, p. 26) observes, 'His doubt is emphatically contradicted by the opening אבל "indeed" instead of הנה "behold", which is more usual in an announcement scene'.

80. Various etymologies have been proposed; cf. Wenham, *Genesis 16–50*, p. 26; Hamilton, *Genesis 1–17*, p. 478. However, wherever the name Isaac is discussed in Genesis, it is associated with the verb צחק and reflects either the sceptical laughter of both his parents when his birth was announced (cf. 17.17; 18.12-15), the joyous laughter of Sarah and others at Isaac's birth (21.3-6), or Ishmael's mocking (laughter?) in Gen. 21.9.

81. This is implicit in the contrast between Isaac and Ishmael in vv. 20, 21.

82. It is a most interesting fact that despite the apparent exclusion of Ishmael (vv. 20-21) he nevertheless receives the covenant sign of circumcision. For further discussion, see Chapter 5 Section 1c below.

two chapters. The major differences between the two passages are as follows:

1. *The Covenant Ritual Commanded.* It is true that a ritual of cutting is commanded by God in both chapters, yet this ritual is not only completely different, but also serves an entirely different purpose. In Genesis 15 Abraham is instructed to perform a ritual cutting of animals for the purpose of covenant ratification. In Genesis 17 the cutting of the foreskin is portrayed as a mark or sign of the covenant, but there is no explicit association with covenant ratification.[83] These striking differences cannot simply be ignored by those wishing to treat these as parallel accounts. One account is absolutely silent on the archaic covenant ratification rite, whereas the other is equally silent on the distinguishing covenant mark or seal in human flesh.[84]

2. *The Obligation Placed on Abraham.* The covenant in ch. 17, unlike that in ch. 15, is clearly conditional. The covenant recorded in ch. 15 appears to be solely promissory. This is emphasized especially by the fact that only the theophanic fire passed between the animal pieces.[85]

---

83. *Pace* Sheriffs (*The Friendship of the Lord*, pp. 42-43), who suggests that circumcision is the covenant-cutting oath in Gen. 17 (i.e. circumcision is the human corollary to the divine self-malediction rite of ch. 15). See also Kline, *By Oath Consigned*, pp. 43-49, and Stek, '"Covenant" Overload', p. 30. Apart from the fact that such an interpretation of the ritual of passing between the dismembered animals is by no means certain (see following discussion), the author of Gen. 17 never applies the key verb (כרת) to the rite of circumcision.

84. Postulating two (or more) underlying sources does not really provide a solution to this enigma for source analysts, in that it does not address the question of why the compiler or editor chose to separate them as he did by the account of Ishmael's birth (Gen. 15.7-21 could have been inverted with Gen. 16 without any radical change to the plot). Why then did the compiler so arrange these chapters? There seem to be two possible options: either he intended to portray two different aspects of a single covenant, or else he is describing two different covenants altogether. The cumulative evidence which follows suggests the reasonableness of the latter alternative.

85. Few scholars have followed *Targ. Neof.* (which has Abraham also passing between the pieces) or adopted an interpretation such as that advocated by Janzen (viz. that the 'smoking fire pot' and the 'flaming torch' represent Yahweh and Abraham respectively [*Genesis 12–50*, p. 40]). In contrast, Van Develder makes an impressive case ('Abrahamic Covenant Traditions', pp. 248-53) for interpreting the

The usual custom in such a rite of covenant ratification was apparently for both parties to pass between the pieces, so obligating themselves to the terms of the agreement (cf. Jer. 34.17-18). While convincingly challenging the idea that Genesis 15 describes a rite of self-curse or self-imprecation (cf. Jer. 34.18-19),[86] Hasel nevertheless maintains the consensus view of the ritual as a ratification of the covenant.[87] Similarly Wenham, while offering a different interpretation of the details,[88] is in complete agreement with Hasel's basic premise that Genesis 15 records a ratification rite and not a self-imprecatory curse. More recently Hess, on the basis of suggested Alalakh parallels, has likewise maintained that the animal sacrifice in Genesis 15 is best understood in terms of a ratification rite and not a self-imprecatory curse.[89]

imagery in Genesis 15 not so much as a veiled reference to Yahweh, but one which, through the cultic and Sinaitic associations, would have been readily understood.

86. The best case for understanding the ritual as a self-imprecatory curse is made by Van Develder, 'Abrahamic Covenant Traditions', pp. 244-46, 255-61; see also Hillers, *Covenant*, p. 41; M. Weinfeld, 'The Covenant of Grant in the Old Testament and in the Ancient Near East', *JAOS* 90 (1970), pp. 184-203 (196) (also *idem*, 'The Loyalty Oath in the Ancient Near East', *UF* 8 [1976], pp. 379-414 [400]); D.J. McCarthy, *Treaty and Covenant: A Study in the Form in the Ancient Oriental Documents and in the Old Testament* (AnBib, 21a; Rome: Biblical Institute Press, 1978), p. 94; Kline, *By Oath Consigned*, pp. 16-17; J.L. Townsend, 'Fulfillment of the Land Promise in the Old Testament', *BSac* 142 (1985), pp. 320-37 (322); C.T. Begg, 'Doves and Treaty-Making: Another Possible Reference', *BN* 48 (1989), pp. 8-11 (11).

87. G.F. Hasel, 'The Meaning of the Animal Rite in Genesis 15', *JSOT* 19 (1981), pp. 61-78.

88. G.J. Wenham, 'The Symbolism of the Animal Rite in Genesis 15: A Response to G.F. Hasel', *JSOT* 22 (1982), pp. 134-37. The clean animals symbolize Israel, the carrion birds Israel's enemies, and the theophanic fire is a symbol of Yahweh's presence among his people. Cf. Van Develder's interpretation of the birds as part of the imagery of a self-imprecatory curse ('Abrahamic Covenant Traditions', p. 246).

89. R.S. Hess, 'The Slaughter of the Animals in Genesis 15: Genesis 15.8-21 and its Ancient Near Eastern Context', in Hess, Wenham and Satterthwaite (eds.), *He Swore an Oath*, pp. 55-65. So too A. Pagolu, *The Religion of the Patriarchs* (JSOTSup, 277; Sheffield: Sheffield Academic Press, 1998), pp. 62-65. The antiquity of the Alalakh material clearly makes it better comparative evidence than turn-of-the-century voodoo practices among Bedouin tribes to which some previous scholars looked for interpretative insight; cf. P.J. Henninger, 'Was bedeutet die rituelle Teilung eines Tieres in zwei Hälften? Zur Deutung von Gen. 15,9ff', *Bib* 34 (1953), pp. 344-53.

Regardless of how the precise details of the animal rite in Genesis 15 and its significance are understood, scholars agree that the obligation of keeping this covenant is placed solely on God. No obligations, either implicitly or explicitly, are placed upon Abraham as far as this covenant is concerned. By passing between the pieces, God (represented by the smoking fire pot and flaming torch) obligates himself to keep this covenant. In contrast, Abraham is presented in this passage as little more than a passive spectator to this rite of covenant ratification.

The covenant spoken of in ch. 17 differs in that it is plainly obligatory,[90] depending on Abraham's continuing obedience to God. This conditional aspect is reflected both in how the covenant is introduced in ch. 17, 'Behave in an exemplary fashion so that I may establish my covenant with both you and your descendants, and greatly increase your numbers' (17.1, 2, my translation), [91] and in the emphasis within this chapter on the duty of circumcision as the means by which Abraham and his 'seed' were instructed to *keep* this covenant (cf. vv. 9-14, 23-27).

This emphasis on human obligation in ch. 17 marks an important distinction between the two covenants. The covenant in ch. 15 relates to promises which ostensibly would be fulfilled unconditionally. In contrast, the covenant in ch. 17 relates to promises which apparently would not be fulfilled unconditionally or automatically, but required human activity and response.[92]

---

90. The conditional nature of the covenant is clear not only in the text here (cf. vv. 9-10), but also in other texts in the Pentateuch; cf. Lev. 26.33-35; Deut. 4.26-28; 28.63-68 as well as the Prophetic Literature; cf. Hos. 9.17; Amos 9.9.

91. *Pace* Rendsburg, cf. Section 4c (n. 128); Section 3b (n. 75).

92. Those who attempt to reconcile the accounts on source-critical grounds again face the insuperable difficulty of why the compiler or a later editor chose not to conflate the two accounts (as has allegedly been done elsewhere, for instance in the Flood Narrative). Such a conflation would have avoided the enigma of a divine–human covenant into which only one party (God) had fully entered for the first fourteen years of its existence. If this time-lapse was introduced by the redactor(s), it was obviously his (their) intention somehow to harmonize the two discordant accounts of J (or JE) and P. Such a harmonization will be exactly how the canonical narrative is meant to be understood; therefore, by over-emphasis on the different underlying sources, documentary critics have overlooked this important issue of the theological relationship between these two chapters within the final composition of Genesis. This question of how the final editor(s) understood the relationship is of paramount importance for a synchronic analysis, and so cannot simply be ignored.

3. *The Change of Names*. One of the most obvious aspects distinguishing the two covenant chapters is the introduction of new names for both Abraham and Sarah in ch. 17. It is significant that not only are these name-changes unmentioned in Genesis 15, but also that their non-usage prior to Genesis 17 is perfectly matched by the consistency of their usage after their introduction in the latter chapter.

In that these new names are given covenantal significance in ch. 17, their non-introduction in ch. 15 would imply that the covenant recorded there served a different purpose—or at least had a distinct emphasis. Again, this inference is confirmed by a careful analysis of each chapter.[93] Genesis 15 stresses Abraham's role as the progenitor of a single nation who would inherit the Promised Land, whereas Genesis 17 stresses Abraham's role as the 'father' of a multitude of nations who would inherit the promised blessing (cf. 17.4-6, 16). Thus the name-changes in ch. 17 subtly alert the reader to the fact that the scope of the two covenant passages in the Abrahamic narrative is not the same.

4. *The Emphases of the Promise*. Following on from the last point, the promise of Genesis 15 has a domestic horizon, whereas Genesis 17 has a universalistic horizon.[94] These chapters concentrate respectively on God's promise to make Abraham into a great nation and God's promise to make Abraham the father of a multitude of nations. In the former chapter the promises that relate to Abraham's physical descendants are chiefly in focus. In the latter chapter attention is no longer on just domestic or even national affairs; rather, the fourfold mention of 'nations' gives ch. 17 an international dimension nowhere evident in ch. 15.[95]

Moreover, as observed above, the promise of land, predominant in ch. 15, is almost relegated to the periphery in ch. 17. This would suggest that the land element of the promise is the focal point of the covenant in ch. 15, whereas it has only secondary importance in the covenant of ch. 17.

If these passages were somehow harmonized in the mind of the editor(s), unlocking such a harmonization must surely be the objective of the modern interpreter.

93. See Chapters 4 and 5 of this book.

94. This has been ably demonstrated by Chew, '"Blessing for the Nations"', pp. 95-110.

95. This international aspect is probably reflected in the name change to Abraham. The etymology implicit in the text (v. 5) certainly suggests this.

Unlike that of Genesis 15, the covenant referred to in ch. 17 explicitly involves a special relationship with God. This is reflected in the covenant formula—*to be your...their God.*[96] This unique relationship with God which Abraham and his descendants were to enjoy may be implicit in the Genesis 15 account, but it is not until ch. 17 that it is explicitly disclosed. Moreover, as Hamilton has perceptively commented, 'the end of this particular promise...focuses on Abraham's progeny, not on himself'.[97] This further emphasizes the difference in the role of Abraham's descendants in chs.15 and 17: in the former chapter they are primarily covenant beneficiaries; in ch. 17 they are covenant partners.

It might be objected that the standard corollary of the covenant formula (namely, '*you/they shall be my people*') is not included in Gen. 17.8. However, following Westermann this omission may be seen as deliberate, stressing that the establishment of the covenant is solely an act of God.[98] If this is correct, the relationship between Genesis 15 and 17 cannot be explained simply in terms of the divine initiative and human obligations inherent in the covenantal relationship between God and Abraham. Both chapters emphasize the divine initiative. The fact that ch. 17 alone mentions human obligations may again point to the distinctive partnership element of the covenant it unfolds.

For the first time Sarah is explicitly mentioned in relation to the divine promise, though the narrator has obviously implied that she is to be the nation's progenitrix. As Turner has keenly perceived, Abraham's behaviour thus far clearly demonstrates that he considered her expendable.[99] It would not appear that Abraham considered Sarah to have the role God intended her to have in the fulfilment of the promise of nationhood and international blessing. Though in one sense this ties the two chapters together, in another sense it distinguishes them, given that the promises contained in the latter chapter (both concerning Abraham and

96. For von Rad this element does not belong originally to the ancient patriarchal promise (which consisted only of posterity and land), but is rather an antedating of the Sinaitic covenant. His argument is rather circular in nature, however, presupposing on *a priori* grounds that the Gen. 15 material alone reflects 'the two really old patriarchal promises' (von Rad, *Genesis*, p. 200).

97. Hamilton, *Genesis 1–17*, p. 466.

98. Westermann, *Genesis 12–36*, p. 262.

99. Turner, *Announcements of Plot*, pp. 65-66.

Sarah) have a more personal dimension (the promise of ch. 15 relates exclusively to Abraham's seed, whereas the promises of ch. 17 relate not only to the future nation, but also to Abraham and Sarah themselves).

5. *The Surrogate Heir Suggested.* While both passages record the fact that in response to God's promise Abraham suggested a surrogate heir, there are fundamental differences which must not be overlooked. As mentioned above,[100] an obvious example is the difference in Abraham's attitude toward each potential surrogate: while Abraham is favourably disposed towards Ishmael's candidature as his heir, he is clearly less so in the case of Eliezer.

Another striking difference is the distinctive promissory context of each chapter. In Genesis 15 the promise evoking Abraham's remarks about Eliezer is the rather general divine promise of protection and reward, whereas in Genesis 17 Abraham 'nominates' Ishmael in the light of a very specific promise of a male heir by his wife Sarah. In addition there is the more transparent difference in the actual surrogate suggested in each chapter. In Genesis 15 the suggested surrogate is the enigmatic household servant, Eliezer of Damascus. In Genesis 17 the only surrogate heir suggested by Abraham is Ishmael, the son of his Egyptian slave. Thus Genesis 15 makes no mention of Ishmael and Genesis 17 makes no mention of Eliezer.[101] In that an identification of these two seems impossible, there are only two explanations:

1. Genesis 15 (and thus the alleged author of the underlying JE account) knows nothing of Ishmael's birth.[102]

---

100. Cf. Section 3b above.

101. This in no way detracts from S.D. Kunin's observation that the rejection of Ishmael and Eliezer in these two chapters makes them 'structurally equivalent' ('The Death of Isaac: Structuralist Analysis of Genesis 22', *JSOT* 64 [1994], pp. 57-81 [61]). Equivalent, yes; identical, no!

102. This is assuming the literary unity of the Genesis 15 account; admittedly, if the chapter is divided between J and E the most one could conclude from Abraham's suggestion of Eliezer as surrogate is that the writer of J (or whoever was responsible for Gen. 15.1-6) knew nothing of a covenant prior to Ishmael's birth. However, given the clear parallelism between the two main sections in Genesis 15 (see my analysis of structure, Section 4 below), such an arbitrary dissection of this chapter seems unjustifiable.

2. The covenant of Genesis 15 was established before Ishmael was born, whereas the covenant referred to in Genesis 17 post-dated this event.

However, as the first option is excluded by the traditional source analysis—in that Genesis 16 is allegedly composed of material derived mainly from J—it must be concluded that two quite distinct (at least chronologically distinct) covenants are being portrayed in these two chapters.

In addition to these major differences a number of subsidiary points are also pertinent.

6. *The Nature of God's Revelation to Abraham.* In Genesis 15 Abraham's experience is plainly visionary (at least in its initial and final parts, cf. 15.1, 12, 17), whereas in Genesis 17 it is portrayed more in the nature of a theophany (cf. 17.1, 22).[103] In that the final editor of the Genesis text undeniably presents Abraham's experience in these quite distinct ways, it seems reasonable to conclude that the reader is intended to understand these two accounts in terms of two quite different revelations which Abraham received.[104] This would appear to be confirmed by the other distinguishing features of the two chapters.

7. *The Introductory Self-Description by God.* While the use of 'Yahweh' in the first verse is common to both passages,[105] Yahweh's self-introduction is very different. In ch. 15 Abraham is reminded of God's protection, whereas in ch. 17 he is reminded of God's power.[106] Since such self-descriptions in announcement oracles are presumably of some contextual significance,[107] it may be anticipated that the thrust of the

103. *Pace* J.J. Niehaus (*God at Sinai: Covenant and Theophany in the Bible and Ancient Near East* [SOTBT; Carlisle: Paternoster Press, 1995]), who interprets Gen. 15 as a 'glory-theophany'. While I do not disagree that God gloriously revealed himself to Abraham during a supernatural sleep on the occasion narrated in Gen. 15, this is not what is normally understood by the term 'theophany'. Gen. 15 is implicitly set in a visionary context, whereas Gen. 17 is not.
104. It must be conceded that the Gen. 15 passage may itself recount two different revelations which were separated by an unspecified time-period, but this in no way detracts from the fact that the divine–human encounter of Gen. 17 is depicted in a markedly different fashion.
105. Although see n. 28 above.
106. See n. 74 above.
107. Cf. Gen. 26.24; 28.13; 35.11.

ensuing announcement will be likewise distinct—which is indeed the case.[108] Thus the fact that the passages begin with two quite different divine self-descriptions may be designed to alert the astute reader to expect two different underlying themes.

8. *Abraham's Implied Psychological State.* As observed above, Yahweh's revelation(s) in Genesis 15 appear to address Abraham in a traumatic state (cf. 15.1, 12, 13). There is no hint of any such trauma in Genesis 17. It is surely significant that whereas in Genesis 15 Abraham expresses deep concern over his childlessness (apparently the main cause of his 'fear'), in Genesis 17 absolutely no concern is expressed in relation to this particular matter. Clearly in this and other details Genesis 17 assumes knowledge of the events recounted in Genesis 16; viz. that a physical heir, Ishmael, had been fathered by Abraham. This alone explains the apparent absence of any concern Abraham might otherwise have had prior to the unfolding revelation of Genesis 17. It appears most likely, therefore, that the events of Genesis 16 best account for the absence of anxiety at the start of Genesis 17 (cf. the presence of it at the start of Gen. 15). Thus the final editor clearly suggests that the covenant of Genesis 15 was established prior to Ishmael's birth, whereas the Genesis 17 revelation evidently post-dated this event.

This is further confirmed by the apparent age difference in the two passages (cf. 12.4; 16.3—suggesting Abraham was approximately 85 in Genesis 15;[109] Gen. 17.1, 24 recording the patriarch's age as 99).

9. *Abraham's Response to God's Revelation.* Abraham's response to God's revelation is quite distinct in both chapters. In Genesis 15 Abraham initially responds verbally and negatively (15.2, 3); by contrast, in Genesis 17 Abraham responds physically and positively[110] (17.3). Abraham's subsequent response to God's expanded revelation is likewise distinct in each chapter. In relation to the specific promise of a son, Abraham responds in faith in Gen. 15.6, but with unbelief and reservations in Gen. 17.17-18. As Blum observes, 'Whereas in Gen 15

108. Cf. Section 3c.4 above.
109. This assumes reading the contents of ch. 15 in their present literary context.
110. This is admittedly inferred from the fact that there is nothing in the text to suggest otherwise, but such an inference does seem wholly plausible in that such physical prostration usually signified reverent submission; cf. 1 Sam. 20.41; 25.23; Est. 8.3; Job 1.20.

(KD) Abraham believes the promise of increase and this is credited to him "as righteousness", in Gen 17 he responds to the promise of a son with unbelieving laughter and doubt'.[111] These differences in Abraham's response again suggest a difference in underlying circumstances. The precise nature of this change of circumstances is explained in Genesis 16. Whereas before the revelation of Genesis 15 Abraham had no physical offspring at all (making Yahweh's promise of reward sound rather hollow), before the revelation of Genesis 17 Abraham had a son (Ishmael), through whom he apparently thought God's promises could be fulfilled (Gen. 17.18). In view of this difference in Abraham's circumstances, his differing responses in the two chapters are very understandable. On the first occasion there was nothing to bolster his confidence in God's promises; on the second occasion there was at least tangible evidence, albeit self-engineered, which lent rationality to what God had promised to do for him.

The fact that both chapters portray a very different reaction on the part of Abraham is another indication that these two chapters must not be understood as doublets or parallel accounts of the same event.

10. *The Institution and Duration of the Covenant(s)*. As noted above,[112] the two chapters use quite different vocabulary in relation to the term ברית. Genesis 15 employs the verb כרת, whereas Genesis 17 uses both the verb נתן and the hiphil of the verb קום. This difference in vocabulary has been explained diachronically in terms of the usage of the various source authors/editors and synchronically in terms of covenant renewal. This difference in vocabulary usage, however, is open to an alternative interpretation,[113] and it is plausible to argue from this that, rather than preserving duplicate accounts or two separate stages of one covenant, the compiler is describing two quite distinct covenants.

This conclusion is also supported by the fact that, in contrast to the covenant in Genesis 15, the covenant in ch. 17 is explicitly given a permanent dimension. It is described as 'an *everlasting* covenant'.[114] It must be acknowledged that the Hebrew term עולם does not necessarily denote 'eternal' or 'permanent' (cf. its use in 17.8), but here (17.7) it

111. Blum, *Studien*, p. 236.
112. See Section 2a.
113. See Chapter 6 Section 2a below.
114. Cf. Gen. 9.16; Exod. 31.16; Lev. 24.8; 2 Sam. 23.5; Isa. 55.3; 61.8; Jer. 32.40; 50.5; Ezek. 16.60; 37.26; Ps. 105.10; 1 Chron. 16.17.

must certainly convey the enduring nature of the covenant relationship. This would again seem to distinguish it markedly from the covenant described in ch. 15. The latter appears to have been much more temporal in its focus, being completed or fulfilled as soon as the promise of nationhood and possession of the land was realized.

11. *The Future of Abraham and his Descendants.* The future of Abraham and his descendants is very different in the two chapters. Whereas Genesis 15 anticipates the death of the patriarch prior to the inheritance of the Promised Land, there is no allusion whatsoever to this in Genesis 17. Here, rather, the land is explicitly promised 'to *you*, and to your offspring after you' (v. 8, NRSV, emphasis mine).

Moreover, according to Genesis 15, Abraham's descendants can anticipate a prolonged period of expatriation, servitude and oppression, tempered only by the promise that these unfavourable circumstances will eventually be reversed (vv. 13-16). In Genesis 17, however, a much brighter future is expected, with no mention whatsoever of the darker aspects reflected in Genesis 15. Rather, Genesis 17 announces a much more positive future for Abraham's descendants: the patriarch is associated with nations and kings (vv. 4-6). Furthermore, there is no thought of either Abraham or his descendants 'forfeiting' the land, albeit temporarily, for it will be a 'perpetual holding' (v. 8, NRSV).

12. *The Specific Details regarding the Extent of the Land.* Although both chapters reiterate the promise of land, there are differences in the detail regarding the extent of this territory. In Gen. 15.18b-21 the parameters are delineated in terms of two of its borders (north-east and south-west) and its indigenous inhabitants: the territory would extend from the Euphrates to the river of Egypt,[115] and incorporate the land occupied by the Kenites, Kenizzites, Kadmonites, Hittites, Perizzites, Rephaim, Canaanites, Girgashites and Jebusites. In Genesis 17 the parameters are more generally and less grandiosely described as 'the

---

115. That is, not the Nile, but the 'Brook of Egypt' (*Wâdi el-'Arîsh*), which enters the Mediterranean 87 kilometres south-west of Gaza (so E.A. Martens, *God's Design: A Focus on Old Testament Theology* [Leicester: InterVarsity Press, 2nd edn, 1994], p. 40; see also C.G. Libolt, 'Canaan', *ISBE*, I, p. 586, and W.C. Kaiser, 'The Promised Land: A Biblical-Historical View', *BSac* 138 [1981], pp. 302-11 [303]). Cf. D.J. Wiseman, 'Abraham in History and Tradition. Part II: Abraham the Prince', *BSac* 134 (1977), pp. 228-37 [229 n. 9]; Townsend, 'Fulfillment of the Land Promise', p. 335 n. 17.

land where you are now an alien, all the land of Canaan' (v. 8, NRSV). Thus, of the two chapters, the description of the allotted territory in Genesis 15 is rather more precise.

A careful examination of the contents and emphases of the two chapters, therefore, indicates that the promises encapsulated by the covenants referred to are certainly not identical, and may arguably be quite distinct. This has important ramifications for the covenants themselves. If they relate to different promises, they can no longer be seen as simply variant accounts derived from two or more different sources. They must be viewed either as reflecting two stages of a single divine covenant with Abraham, or two different covenants between God and Abraham.

4. *An Analysis of the Structure of Genesis 15 and 17*

A close examination of the structure of the two chapters further suggests that rather than being a 'reworking' of ch. 15, ch. 17 serves an entirely different purpose in the mind of the compiler. Chapter 15 is structured around the promise of nationhood (descendants and land) sealed by an unconditional covenant given to believing Abraham. In contrast, ch. 17 is arranged around the themes of Abraham's 'progeny' and the covenant sign of circumcision.

a. *The Structure of Chapter 15*

The limits of this pericope are clearly demarcated: the opening phrase, 'After these things', introduces into the story a new episode which reaches its climax in vv. 18-21. The chapter divides into two scenes which generally run in close parallel:

The fact that each section (vv. 6, 18) incorporates an important observation by the narrator should not be missed.[116] Nor should the implicit link between the two statements forged by the structure of the passage be overlooked. The structure of the two parts of the chapter would suggest that the covenant guarantee and Abraham's faith-righteousness were intimately related.

---

116. As Alexander ('Abraham Reassessed', p. 14) observes, 'The rarity in Genesis of such comments by the narrator makes them all the more important when they occur'.

	Scene 1		Scene 2	
A. *Yahweh's word*	v. 1	Promise (reward)	v. 7	Promise (land)
B. *Abraham's response*	vv. 2-3	Reassurance sought (about heir)	v. 8	Reassurance sought (about land)
C. *Yahweh's reassurance in word and by sign*	vv. 4-5	Amplification (own body/stars)	vv. 9-21	Amplification (seed and land/firepot and torch)
D. *Narrator's comment*	v. 6	Abraham's faith	v. 18	God's covenant

b. *The Structure of Chapter 17*

As with ch. 15, this pericope is clearly demarcated (cf. 16.16; 17.1, 23). Once again the account begins with a divine–human encounter, this time presented as a theophany (cf. both the way it is described [17.1b, 22] and how Abraham reacts to it [17.3, 17]). The chapter may be set out as follows:

1. Introduction and preamble (vv. 1-3)
2. God's covenant with Abraham (vv. 4-14)
   a) The divine obligations (vv. 4-8)
   b) The human obligations (vv. 9-14)
3. God's promises relating to Sarah (vv. 15-16, 19a)
4. God's promises relating to Isaac and Ishmael (vv. 17-21)
5. Conclusion and epilogue (vv. 22-27)

Some recent commentators have emphasized the passage's artistic symmetry. McEvenue, for example, has detected the following palistrophic arrangement:[117]

A	Abraham 99 years of age (v. 1a)
B	Yahweh appears to Abraham (v. 1b$_a$)
C	God speaks (v. 1b$_b$)
D	First speech (vv. 1b$_c$-2)
E	Abraham falls on his face (v. 3a)
F	Second speech (name-change, nations, kings) (vv. 4-8)
G	THIRD SPEECH (vv. 9-14)
F'	Fourth speech (name-change, nations, kings) (vv. 15-16)
E'	Abraham falls on his face (etc.) (vv. 17-18)
D'	Fifth speech (vv. 19-21)
C'	God ceases speaking (v. 22a)
B'	God goes up from him (v. 22b)
A'	Abraham 99 years of age (and Ishmael 13) (vv. 24-25)

---

117. McEvenue, *Narrative Style*, pp. 157-58. McEvenue identifies the essential feature of a 'palistrophe' as 'return'. Thus a palistrophe is a textual unit which reflects a symmetric pattern in which the elements in the latter half form a mirror-image of those in the first part of the unit.

In addition to this palistrophe McEvenue has also identified the following two parallel panels within the chapter: [118]

A   Yahweh's intention to make an oath about progeny (vv. 1-2)
B   Abraham falls on his face (v. 3a)
C   Abraham father of nations (vv. 4b-6)
D   God will carry out his oath forever (v. 7)
E   The sign of the oath (vv. 9-14)

A'   God's intention to bless Sarah with a son (v. 16)
B'   Abraham falls on his face (etc.) (vv. 17-18)
C'   Sarah mother of a son, Isaac (v. 19)
D'   God will carry out his oath forever (vv. 18b-21a)
E'   The sign of the oath (vv. 23-27)

While equally convinced that 'the division of the chapter is carefully thought out right down to the finest detail', Westermann appears to detect a somewhat different 'artistic composition'.[119] For him the basic structure is as follows:[120]

A   Genealogical note (v. 1aα)
B   God's appearance (v. 1aβ)
C   God's speech (vv. 1c-21)
D   God's withdrawal (v. 22)
E   Conclusion—Abraham's obedience and genealogical note (vv. 23-27)

The main section, God's speech, is divided by Westermann into two component parts, the preamble (vv. 1b-3a) and the divine speech (vv. 3b-21). The latter is further sub-divided into three parts:

A   Promise to Abraham and name change (vv. 3b-8)
B   Command and penalty (vv. 9-14)
C   Promise to Sarah and name change (vv. 15-21)

For Westermann, the arrangement of this central section 'is meant to tell us that the promise is dominant and all-embracing in what God says... the command rests on the promise'.[121] Hamilton likewise

---

118. McEvenue, *Narrative Style*, pp. 158-59. In addition to the symmetric compositions detected in Gen. 17, McEvenue recognizes the logical development, the pericope consistently moving 'from intention to fact, and from vague to specific' (*Narrative Style*, p. 156). Thus the literary arrangement McEvenue postulates for this chapter is a most intricate one.

119. Westermann, *Genesis 12–36*, p. 255.

120. Unfortunately, Westermann does not illustrate his suggested structure diagrammatically, but it is nevertheless clear that his structural analysis is quite different from McEvenue's.

121. Westermann, *Genesis 12–36*, p. 255.

observes that 'the major speech by God to Abraham about Abraham's
need to take appropriate action (vv. 9-14) is ringed by speeches of
God's promises to Abraham (vv. 3-8 and 15-21), showing that the
demands of God must be interpreted within the context of the promises
of God'.[122] While such observations are certainly valid, there is perhaps
a danger of allowing them to lessen the significance of human obligation upon which this chapter (Gen. 17) unquestionably places considerable emphasis.[123]

c. *A Comparison of the Structure of Genesis 15 and 17*

A comparison of the structure of the two chapters reveals a further
significant difference between these two covenant pericopes. In Genesis
15 there are two 'parallel' sections (vv. 1-6, 7-21), each of which
focuses on a different (albeit related) promissory aspect; viz. seed and
land. In each of these parallel sections in Genesis 15 God assures
Abraham with a promise, Abraham asks for further reassurance, God
amplifies the promise visually and verbally (in both sections this
reassurance involves some physical activity on Abraham's part), and
the narrator offers a concluding observation.

The structure of Genesis 17 is rather different. Here there are three
main 'panels' (vv. 4-14, 15-16, 17-21) bracketed by an introduction
(vv. 1-3) and a conclusion (vv. 22-27). The first of these three panels
(vv. 4-14) divides into two parts, in which the covenant obligations of
both divine (vv. 4-8) and human (vv. 9-14) partners are set out.

Unlike the two sections in Genesis 15, each of the three main panels
in Genesis 17 is linked by the promissory theme of nations and kings.
'Nations' and 'kings' are explicitly mentioned in the case of Abraham
(17.4-6) and Sarah (v. 16), and strongly alluded to in the discussion
concerning the future of Isaac and Ishmael.[124]

---

122. Hamilton, *Genesis 1–17*, p. 459.

123. Westermann appears almost to downplay the significance of circumcision in
this pericope by placing emphasis on the promissory elements of the covenant
(*Genesis 12–36*, p. 255). The compiler of Gen. 17 seems, however, to have emphasized the obligatory aspects. For a fuller critique of Westermann and McEvenue's
analyses, see Chapter 5 Section 2 below.

124. This is one of the promissory aspects which seems to distinguish between
Isaac's role as covenant heir and Ishmael's rather more enigmatic relationship to the
covenant. While Ishmael is promised 'a great nation' and princes, the promise
relating to 'nations' and 'kings' exclusively belongs to the son of Abraham and
Sarah.

Thus a close comparison of the structure of Genesis 15 and 17 is most revealing. Despite a number of verbal and thematic links, these two chapters are not structurally parallel.

Recently it has been argued, however, that a case can be made for a degree of parallelism between the two chapters in terms of the order of action, ideas and motifs.[125] Building on a proposal of Cassuto,[126] Rendsburg contends that the two chapters—which he labels Ea and E'a—form the centre (along with Gen. 16.1-16 ['Eb'] and Gen. 18.1-16 ['E'b']) of a larger chiasmus which expands over the entire Abraham narrative.[127]

Comparing chs. 15 and 17, the 'parallels' suggested by Rendsburg are as follows:

1. Each scene opens with a divine appearance to Abraham (15.1a; 17.1a).
2. Both commence with a reassurance of divine protection.[128]
3. Both accounts continue with God speaking of reward and increase (15.1; 17.2).
4. The promise of multitudinous offspring (17.4) is the corollary to Abraham's complaint about having no offspring (15.3).
5. Also, the מִמְּךָ יֵצֵאוּ (17.6) reiterates the יֵצֵא מִמֵּעֶיךָ of 15.4.
6. Both chapters then include mention of the Promised Land (15.7; 17.8).
7. This is followed in each pericope by a description of a cere-monial ritual (15.9-11; 17.10-14).
8. Both then have the beginning of a second divine communica-tion (15.13; 17.15), which in each case deals further with the promised offspring (15.13-16; 17.15-22).

---

125. Rendsburg, *The Redaction of Genesis*, pp. 41-52.

126. U. Cassuto, *A Commentary on the Book of Genesis*. II. *From Noah to Abraham* (trans. I. Abrahams; Jerusalem: Magnes Press, 1964).

127. Rendsburg, *The Redaction of Genesis*, pp. 28-29. As noted above, several other scholars (e.g. Chew, Alexander, Wenham) have also detected chiastic struc-tures in the Abraham narrative (Gen. 12.1–22.19), which likewise place the two covenant chapters in juxtaposition.

128. Following Jacob (*Das erste Buch der Tora*) and allegedly Davidson (*Genesis 12–50*), Rendsburg understands הִתְהַלֵּךְ לְפָנַי (17.1) to have this connotation. My own reading of Davidson's comment is very different; cf. p. 57 of his commen-tary.

9.   Both episodes conclude with the completion of the ceremony
      described earlier (15.17; 17.23-27).

However, a closer examination of this suggested parallelism between
sequences of thought, language, speech and action discloses that it is of
a rather superficial nature and does not adequately address the major
points of dissimilarity noted above.

The suggested parallel introduction (i.e. a divine appearance to Abraham) is less exact than Rendsburg alleges. As he himself acknowledges, in Genesis 15 the experience is explicitly a visionary one (מחזה,
v. 1); in contrast, a theophany is certainly implied in ch. 17 (cf. וירא,
v. 1 and וירא, v. 22). In any case, the fact that each chapter should begin
with a divine–human encounter is neither surprising nor unique (cf.
18.1).

The contention that the phrase התהלך לפני (17.1) has the connotation suggested by Rendsburg is disputable. A more straightforward
interpretation of the phrase is to read it simply as an imperative, con-
veying not divine reassurance but rather divine instruction. In contrast
with ch. 15, rather than beginning with a word of encouragement, ch.
17 opens with a word of advice or command.

Admittedly both chapters portray God speaking to Abraham of
numerical increase. However, there is a subtle difference in the way
this is referred to in each. In ch. 15 the numerical increase relates to
Abraham's fatherhood of a single nation; in ch. 17 it relates to his
fatherhood of many nations. It is therefore spurious to find in ch. 17's
mention of 'many nations' the corollary to Abraham's complaint about
'no offspring' in ch. 15. God had already addressed and resolved this
complaint of Abraham's in the earlier chapter. Rather than reiterating
the earlier promise that Abraham would become a national progenitor,
ch. 17 speaks of him becoming an international 'father'.[129]

Although the promise of land is reiterated in ch. 17, the fact that it is
relegated to the periphery surely demarcates the two chapters, as has
been argued above.[130] In his analysis Rendsburg clearly fails to take
account of this major distinction. The same holds true for the suggested
semantic parallel of 15.4 and 17.6.

While ceremonial rituals are present in both chapters, they are very

129. The ramifications of this description will be explored more thoroughly in
Chapter 5 Section 3a below.
130. See Section 3c.4 above.

clearly distinct both in content and sequence. One involves the 'sacrificial' cutting of animal flesh; the other the symbolic cutting of human flesh. Further, the former 'cutting' was part of a rite through which the covenant was ratified, whereas the latter 'cutting' was a symbolic sign through which the covenant was to be maintained by Abraham and his descendants.[131]

The suggested parallel between the second divine communication in both chapters is again inexact. In ch. 15 the focus is on the promised inheritance of the aforementioned 'offspring' (the Promised Land is more clearly delineated and explained). The expansion in the latter half of ch. 17, conversely, concentrates primarily on the role of Sarah, Isaac and Ishmael in relation to the aforementioned promises of nations and kings. Therefore ch. 15 enlarges on the promise of nationhood, whereas ch. 17 enlarges on the promise regarding nations and kings. These distinctive emphases have not been taken into account in Rendsburg's analysis.

Rendsburg, therefore, achieves his 'parallelism' between chs. 15 and 17 by relinquishing attention to detail. When close attention is given to the latter, the suggested parallelism in the structure and contents of the two chapters is less than convincing.

Nevertheless, the over-arching chiastic structure detected by Rendsburg and others does suggest a carefully composed artistic symmetry in the Abraham cycle. This certainly militates against the idea that the Abraham narrative is a loose collection of sagas brought together in an *ad hoc* fashion. On the contrary, this is another feature which suggests that the redactor(s) intended each pericope to serve a specific function within the wider Abrahamic canvas. Accepting this to be the case, the question must again be asked: What purpose did each of these two covenant passages serve in the overall narrative framework?

5. *Conclusion*

It has been shown that the two covenant chapters in the Abraham cycle contrast markedly in both major points and peripheral details.[132] Surely

---

131. *Pace* Sheriffs, *The Friendship of the Lord*, p. 42.

132. This is not to deny the points of theological and linguistic contact between these two chapters outlined respectively by Skinner (*Genesis*, p. 290) and Römer ('Genesis 15 und Genesis 17', pp. 39-40). Such similarities, however, are surely outweighed by the differences listed above and some are not surprising in that a

to have incorporated two such strikingly different passages into the narrative the editor must have seen no intrinsic conflict between them. Indeed, arguably he saw each as having a specific and distinctive purpose in its present literary context. Thus it would seem that the final editor (at least) understood and so presented them as describing two different episodes in the Abraham narrative rather than reflecting two different accounts of the same event.

Accepting this to be the case, the question of the precise nature of their relationship must obviously be reassessed. Are these two aspects of one divine covenant made with Abraham (as traditionally understood by scholars adopting a synchronic approach), or do they in fact refer to two distinguishable covenants which have quite different foci?

It is of key importance, therefore, that the focal point of the covenant in these two chapters is precisely identified. Does each chapter focus on different aspects of a two-stage divine covenant with Abraham? Or do the two chapters focus on two distinct elements of the divine promise to Abraham? The close examination of each account in the following two chapters will demonstrate the plausibility of the latter alternative.

covenant is the focus of both chapters (e.g. self-introduction of deity, Abraham's incredulity, and use of the terms ברית, נתתי and זרעך).

Chapter 4

THE PROMISSORY FOCUS OF THE 'COVENANT BETWEEN THE PIECES'

1. *Introduction*

The fundamental differences between the two chapters in the Abraham cycle which explicitly mention a divine–human covenant raise questions about their promissory focus and literary function within the overall narrative framework.[1] In this chapter the promissory focus of Genesis 15 will be carefully analysed in order to examine further the obvious differences in contents and emphases between this chapter and Genesis 17.[2]

In relation to the promissory focus of Genesis 15, a number of pertinent questions must be asked of the text:

1. To what divine promise(s) does the covenant explicitly mentioned in v. 18 relate?
2. Are the promises of land and descendants in this chapter depicted as interrelated or as independent elements of the divine promises?
3. What promissory elements in the Abraham narrative are and are not incorporated in Genesis 15?
4. How is the selectivity reflected in Genesis 15 to be explained? Why does this pericope focus only on certain aspects of the divine promises to Abraham and not others? Does it reflect a different literary source? Is it the first stage of a two-part covenant? Or does it describe the first of two distinct covenants established between God and Abraham?

---

1.   The question of focus in relation to Gen. 17 is explored in Chapter 5 of this book, and the question of the literary function of these chapters within the Abraham cycle is addressed in Chapters 6 and 7.

2.   As outlined in section Chapter 3 Section 3c above.

2. A Structural Analysis of Genesis 15

The generally accepted twofold division of this chapter has been set out
succinctly above.[3] There it was observed that the two narrative segments (vv. 1-6, 7-21) are broadly parallel, the first focusing on the
promise of descendants and the second on the promise of possession of
land. This twofold literary structure of the chapter will now be examined in more detail through a careful analysis of the statements and
actions of the two main characters in the plot, Yahweh and Abraham.[4]

In the first section Yahweh makes three statements (vv. 1b, 4 and 5b),
the latter two resulting from Abraham's negative response (vv. 2-3) to
Yahweh's opening pledge (v. 1). In the second section Yahweh again
makes three statements (vv. 7, 13-16 and 18b-21) and once more the
latter two are responses to Abraham's negative rejoinder (v. 8)[5] to

3.   Cf. Chapter 3 Section 4a. For the related source-critical analyses, see Chapter 3 Section 1. A fairly detailed comparison of the literary source divisions proposed from Gunkel (*Genesis*) to Anbar ('Genesis 15: A Conflation', pp. 39-55) is
presented in tabular form in J. Ha, *Genesis 15: A Theological Compendium of Pentateuchal History* (BZAW, 181; Berlin: W de Gruyter, 1989), p. 30. The equally
conflicting positions resulting from traditio-historical studies of the chapter are also
succinctly sketched by Ha, *Genesis 15*, pp. 31-33.

4.   As Ha (*Genesis 15*, pp. 59-62) observes, such a person-based literary analysis is certainly the most straightforward. Ha's own analysis identifies two main sections (vv. 1-5 and vv. 7-21) linked together by v. 6, but this inexplicably fails to
take into consideration the fact that v. 18a clearly constitutes the narrator's concluding comment on the second scene, and is thus in literary parallel to v. 6. In the
following analysis these concluding comments of the narrator will therefore be kept
separate from the speeches/actions of the two key personages around which Gen. 15
revolves.

5.   While Abraham's response in v. 8 is not nearly so negative as that reflected
in vv. 2-3, it certainly falls somewhat short of the faith referred to in v. 6. Even
when Abraham's response in v. 8 is interpreted in terms of requesting a confirmatory sign (so Wenham, *Genesis 1–15*, p. 331; Ha, *Genesis 15*, pp. 49-50), it is difficult to exclude at least some degree of doubt on Abraham's part. In three of the
examples cited by Ha (i.e. Gen. 24.14; 42.33; Exod. 7.17) the requests are not
strictly parallel with the situation reflected in Gen. 15.8: Abraham's servant is
requesting a means of specific guidance; Joseph is demanding evidence of truthful-
ness from his brothers, not God; Moses is offering Pharaoh an unsolicited sign from
Yahweh. Ha's fourth example (Exod. 33.16), and Wenham's two examples (Judg.
6.36-40; 2 Kgs 20.8-11) are much more analogous, but in all these instances an
element of doubt is at least implicit. It is therefore unconvincing to deny any ele-

Yahweh's opening pledge (v. 7). The oral and visual assurance of v. 5b is facilitated by the instruction and action in v. 5a:

ויוצא אתו החוצה ויאמר הבט־נא השמימה וספר הכוכבים אם־תוכל
לספר אתם

Similarly, the oral and visual assurance of vv. 17-21 is facilitated by the instruction and action in vv. 9-11:

ויאמר אליו קחה לי עגלה משלשת ועז משלשת ואיל משלש ותר וגוזל:
ויקח־לו את־כל־אלה ויבתר אתם בתוך ויתן איש־בתרו לקראת רעהו
ואת־הצפר לא בתר: וירד העיט על־הפגרים וישב אתם אברם:

Thus, while vv. 9-11 are to be interpreted within the framework of Yahweh's response to Abraham's request in v. 8, the actual reply of Yahweh does not materialize until v. 16, as a comparison of the במה אדע in v. 8 with the ידע תדע in v. 13 strongly suggests. Therefore, rather than being Yahweh's answer to Abraham's request for reassurance, vv. 9-11 merely paint the canvas for the audio-visual assurance of vv. 17-21.

In each section the narrator makes a concluding observation; in the first on Abraham's faith (v. 6) and in the second on Yahweh's covenantal oath (v. 18). Thus the symmetry between these two sections in Genesis 15 may be set out in tabular form (Table 4.1, below).

The effect of this symmetry between the two distinct units of the chapter is to bind the promise of seed and the promise of land together in such a way that the fulfilment of the latter is absolutely dependent on the fulfilment of the former. The promise of land applies primarily to Abraham's descendants; it is not Abraham himself who will inherit the land of Canaan (v. 15), but rather his descendants (vv. 13, 18b-21). For this to be so, Abraham first must have a son and heir (v. 4); indeed he must be the progenitor of a great nation (vv. 5, 14).

Therefore, the two sections of Genesis 15, while focusing on two different promissory elements, are nevertheless interrelated. The first section addresses the question of the inheritor; the second the question of the inheritance. Consequently, the covenant spoken of in Gen. 15.18, while strictly referring only to the promise of land for Abraham's descendants, assumes at the same time that Abraham will actually have descendants and thus encompasses the promise of 'seed' as well.

---

ment of doubt in Gen. 15.8. Early Jewish exegetes plainly acknowledged doubt on Abraham's part, as is illustrated by L.M. Barth ('Genesis 15', pp. 258-62).

Table 4.1. *Symmetry between Gen. 15.1-6 and Gen 15.7-21.*

	First section, vv. 1-6 (Promise of heir)	Second section, vv. 7-21 (Promise of inheritance)
Yahweh's first promissory statement	self-revelation and promise of great reward (v. 1)	self-revelation and promise of land inheritance (v. 7)
Abraham's negative reaction	promise of reward questioned on grounds of childlessness and thus no seed to inherit (vv. 2-3)	assurance of personal possession of the Promised Land requested (v. 8)
Yahweh's second promissory statement	complaint answered—with the promise of a genuine son/heir (v. 4)	request answered—with the assurance that the descendants of Abraham would eventually inherit (vv. 13-16)
Yahweh's third promissory statement	promise reinforced with the oral and visual assurance of innumerable seed to inherit (v. 5b) —facilitated by Abraham's compliance with Yahweh's instruction to look up at the stars (v. 5a)	promise reinforced with the oral and visual assurance of land to be inherited (vv. 17-21)—facilitated by Abraham's compliance with Yahweh's instruction to prepare animals for ritual (vv. 9-11)
Narrator's comment	Abraham's faith (v. 6)	Yahweh's covenant (v. 18a)

Thus the structure of Genesis 15 points to the thematic unity of the chapter. Whatever their pre-canonical history, the two narrative segments (vv. 1-6 and vv. 7-21) within Genesis 15 have been carefully crafted into a coherent, thematic whole, focusing on the issue of Abraham's inheritors and inheritance.[6]

3. A Literary Analysis of Genesis 15

A detailed literary analysis of the chapter suggests that, following a number of contemporary scholars,[7] Genesis 15 may be treated as a

---

6.   As is cogently argued by A. Abela ('Genesis 15: A Non-Genetic Approach', *MelT* 37.2 [1986], pp. 9-40).

7.   Ha (*Genesis 15*, pp. 33-36) lists the following examples: P. Heinisch, *Das*

literary, and not simply a redactional, unity. The former has been questioned by many source and traditio-historical critics,[8] chiefly because of the structural features of the text.

a. *The Structural Complexity of Genesis 15*
The following structural features, as helpfully collated by Ha,[9] have been traditionally interpreted by literary critics as betraying the composite nature of the chapter:

1. *Repetition.* The chapter contains several 'redundant' words and/or expressions: two-word advent formulae in vv. 1 and 4; two successive uses of ויאמר אברם to introduce the same concept (childlessness) in vv. 2 and 3; a similar recurrence of ויאמר in v. 5 to introduce a single utterance of Yahweh; two promises of land donation in vv. 7 and 18; two almost identical notices at the start of vv. 12 and 17; redundant repetitions relating to the landlessness of Abraham's descendants (v. 13), their enslavement (v. 13), Abraham's death (v. 15) and the extent of the land (vv. 18b and 19-21).

2. *Discrepancies.* The chapter contains two chronological 'discrepancies': the first relates to the time of day when Abraham experienced the various divine revelations, and the second arises from the predicted duration of the oppression of Abraham's descendants in a foreign land.

Buch Genesis übersetzt und erklärt (HSAT; Bonn: Peter Hanstein, 1930), pp. 229-34; J. Hoftijzer, *Die Verheissung an die drei Erväter* (Leiden: E.J. Brill, 1956), pp. 17-55; Snijders, 'Genesis XV', pp. 261-79; Van Seters, *Abraham*, pp. 249-78; H.H. Schmid, *Der sogennante Jahwist: Beobachtungen und Fragen zur Pentateuchforschung* (Zürich: Theologischer Verlag, 1976), pp. 119-43; R. Rendtorff, 'Genesis 15 im Rahmen der theologischen Bearbeitung der Vätergeschichten', in R. Albertz, H.P. Müller, H.W. Wolff and W. Zimmerli (eds.), *Werden und Wirken des Alten Testaments* (Festschrift C. Westermann; Göttingen: Vandenhoeck & Ruprecht, 1980), pp. 74-81; Westermann, *Genesis 12–36*, pp. 216-31. More recent examples include, as well as Ha's own work (pp. 39-62), Blum, *Vätergeschichte*, pp. 362-83; *idem, Studien*, p. 103 and *passim*; Wenham, *Genesis 1–15*, p. 326; Van Seters, *Prologue to History*, pp. 248-51. The substantial unity of the chapter is supported by Lohfink (*Die Landverheissung*, pp. 47-49), whose analysis is followed by McEvenue (*Narrative Style*, p. 149) and Vawter (*On Genesis*, pp. 203-204).

8.   For details, see Chapter 3 above. Cf. Ha's helpful survey, *Genesis 15*, pp. 30-37.

9.   Ha, *Genesis 15*, pp. 39-42.

In relation to the former, in at least two verses a night scene is pre-supposed (vv. 5 and 17) for Abraham's encounter with Yahweh, where-as v. 12 suggests sunset. In relation to the time of the exodus of Abra-ham's descendants from the land of oppression, a relatively long period (four hundred years) is suggested in v. 13, but a much shorter period (the fourth generation) is implied in v. 16.

As well as these discrepancies relating to time it is further observed that the chapter reflects both 'archaic' elements (e.g. אליעזר in v. 2; the passing between the pieces rite of vv. 9-10, 17) and relatively late, Deuteronomistic elements (e.g. the stars metaphor in v. 5; the prophetic 'Yahweh's word came to...' in vv. 1, 4; the gentilic list in vv. 19-21).

3. *Antitheses*. The chapter contains a number of antitheses, some of which could be seen as internal contradictions. For example, in v. 7 Abraham is to be given the land (לתת לך), whereas in v. 18b it is to be given to Abraham's descendants (לזרעך נתתי); Abraham's descendants will be oppressed as slaves in a foreign land (v. 13a), yet will come out with 'great possessions' (v. 14b).

4. *Discontinuity*. The narrative thread is 'broken' in a number of places by the non-use of the waw-consecutive: the conjunctive hiphil perfect וְהֶאֱמִן at the start of v. 6; the avoidance of waw-perfects in vv. 14-16 (cf. use of waw-perfects in v. 13); and the complete absence of waw in the opening temporal phrase, ביום ההוא (v. 18). Further 'breaks' in the narrative are occasioned by the introduction of a 'disconnected' idea: the tension between the promise of progeny in vv. 1-6 and the promise of land in vv. 7-21; Abraham's excursion 'outside' without any indica-tion of having been 'inside' in v. 5; the expression of doubt (v. 8) fol-lowing hard on the heels of an affirmation of Abraham's faith (v. 6); the interruption of the covenant rite (vv. 9-10, 17) by the birds of prey (v. 11) and the intrusive prophecy contained in vv. 12-16; a prophecy concerning Abraham's demise (v. 15) within a divine speech that focus-es otherwise on the future of Abraham's descendants.

b. *The Compositional Unity of Genesis 15*
In response to these arguments,[10] the compositional unity of Genesis 15 has been cogently defended by Ha, who has interpreted the same

---

10. As set out in points 1–4 in Section 3a.

literary features in terms of artistic devices consciously employed to produce 'a coherent and closely-knit whole, whose unity has been remarkably worked out by its author'.[11] Thus Ha contends that:

1. The repetitions are not in fact redundant, but reflect progression of thought—Ha prefers the term 'progressive doublets'.
2. The discrepancies are more apparent than real.
3. The antitheses are not in fact contradictions; rather, like the repetitions, they reflect progression in thought (from thesis to antithesis).
4. There is no real break of continuity; an unbroken thread unifies all the verses and themes into a coherent whole. [12]

Ha attempts to demonstrate the validity of these conclusions through a close reading of the text itself,[13] the salient points of which will now be set out and then critically examined.

1. Ha's Defence of the Compositional Unity of Genesis 15. For Ha, vv. 1-6 are held together by the theme of Abraham's great reward, initially reinforced by the promise of a genuine heir. The fourth verse provides the specific content for the general and rather elastic 'Heilswort' in v. 1. The latter is queried in vv. 2-3, verses which themselves reflect not mere repetition, but progression of thought.[14] The cosmic sign presented in v. 5 complements the oral assurance in v. 4. The concluding verse of this pericope (v. 6), with its non-sequential waw-perfect, reflects on all that has been said from v. 1 and underlines Abraham's disposal to accept future promises with equal confidence. The thematic unity of the pericope is reinforced to some extent by the stylistic pattern of the double dialogue in vv. 1-4: Yahweh speaks—Abraham responds; Abraham speaks—Yahweh responds.

Ha also submits that the theme of Abraham's 'great reward' is further developed in the second part of the chapter (vv. 7-21). Verse 7, while undoubtedly opening a new section in the chapter, certainly alludes to the initial divine word in v. 1, and gives direct specification to the query of vv. 2-3 (cf. the use of the verb נתן in both vv. 2-3 and in

11. Ha, *Genesis 15*, p. 58.
12. Ha, *Genesis 15*, p. 39.
13. Ha, *Genesis 15*, pp. 43-58.
14. A similar synchronic reading of these two verses (vv. 2-3) is defended by Abela, 'Genesis 15: A Non-Genetic Approach', pp. 28-31.

v. 7). Furthermore, through the use of ירש this verse (v. 7) reiterates the promise of an heir in v. 4. Moreover, Yahweh's self-identification not only recalls that of v. 1, but also provides a theological continuum through its use of the hiphil of the verb יצא.

Verse 8, while appearing to create a tension with the declaration of Abraham's faith in v. 6, is interpreted much more positively by Ha: rather than expressing doubt in God's promise, Abraham is merely requesting a confirmatory sign.[15]

The ויאמר אליו of v. 9 indicates that the rite of vv. 9-10 was intend-ed as an answer to Abraham's request. The intrusion into the ritual by the birds of prey (v. 11) constitutes a potential 'foreign threat' to Abra-ham, thus linking up with the somewhat similar threat presented in vv. 2-4.

Verses 13-16 partially express the confirmation that Abraham had requested in v. 8. The prophecy about the fate of Abraham's זרע pro-vides another link with the promise of such a זרע in v. 5. The antithesis between Abraham and his descendants serves to unite rather than divide the verses within the chapter; Abraham's exodus from his homeland to a foreign land (v. 7) finds a chiastic parallel in his descendants' exodus from a foreign land (v. 13) to their homeland. The double blessing for Abraham's descendants alluded to in v. 14 and v. 16 mirrors the double 'curse' anticipated in vv. 2-3. The repetitions in vv. 13-16 are not superfluous; rather, the information about Abraham's descendants being 'strangers in a land which is not their own' (v. 13) serves as a subtle reaffirmation of the two different aspects which unite the chapter as a whole.[16]

---

15. In support Ha cites the following texts which employ a similar formula: Gen. 24.14; 42.33; Exod. 7.17; 33.16. However, see Section 2 (n. 5) above and my critique below.

16. Abela, ('Genesis 15: A Non-Genetic Approach', p. 39) likewise maintains that vv. 13-16 are an integral part of Gen. 15: 'Before performing in front of Abraham the oath rite (v. 17) in order to confirm his intention of giving "this land" as Abraham's possession (v. 7), *Yhwh* explains how this land is going to pass on into the patriarch's hand. Abraham has asked how *he* was going to inherit the land (v. 8). *Yhwh* combines in his oracle Abraham's future to [sic] that of his descen-dants: he also places Abraham himself as a parable of how this future is meant to evolve. Abraham is going to inherit this land "in his descendants", so that *Yhwh*'s oath of giving this land *to Abraham* is actually fulfilled even though this fulfilment is meant to remain a strictly future event.'

The theophanic symbols passing between the pieces (v. 17) bring to completion the entire ceremony that began in vv. 9-10, and thus function as the sign which Abraham had requested in v. 8; these particular phenomena also serve as symbols of God's destructive-salvific qualities,[17] thus tying in theologically with the prediction about liberation and judgment in vv. 13-16.

Despite the absence of a connecting waw in v. 18, this verse is clearly connected with the preceding promises and thus serves as their climax.[18] There is therefore clear progression from v. 1 to vv. 18-21, with both the concept of Yahweh serving as Abraham's 'shield' and the grounds for the divine assurance אל־תירא being gradually unfolded in the ensuing verses.

Ha is equally sceptical about the perceived difficulties in relation to the chronology of Genesis 15. On the basis of several texts, especially in Jeremiah,[19] he sees 'no reason to take *bammaḥᵃzeh* as secondary'.[20] The perceived difficulty arising from the opening clause of v. 5 is resolved by postulating a theological rather than a local connotation for the hiphil form of יצא and the adverb החוצה; thus Abraham is to look 'outside' of himself.

The chronological sequence is explained as follows: the time discrepancy between the sunset of v. 12 and the night scene of v. 5 may be resolved by postulating two separate evenings, between which Abraham brought, ritually slaughtered and arranged the animals specified by Yahweh. There is a subtle time difference between v. 12 and v. 17, the latter bringing the reader fully into a night as opposed to merely a sunset environment.[21]

The discrepancy between the 'four hundred years' of v. 13 and the 'four generations' of v. 16 is best solved for Ha by Caquot's suggestion that two different periods are involved: the 'four hundred years' refer-

---

17. Ha cites a number of texts that amply illustrate this point.

18. For example, the mention of Abraham's זרע alludes to v. 5 and vv. 13-16; הארץ הזאת refers back to v. 7 and v. 16; the ideal depiction of the land's borders, implying the innumerability of Abraham's descendants, offers final specification to the 'very great reward' promised in v. 1.

19. Jer. 1.13; 13.3; 28.12; 33.1; 34.12; 36.27; 43.8, all of which have a word or an entire clause before the infinitive construct, לאמר.

20. Ha, *Genesis 15*, p. 43.

21. For a similar reading, see Abela, 'Genesis 15: A Non-Genetic Approach', pp. 24-27.

ring to the sojourn in Egypt, and the 'fourth generation' to the period between the exodus and David's conquest of Jerusalem.[22]

2. *Assessment of Ha's Arguments for the Compositional Unity of Genesis 15.* While generally presenting a convincing case, there are several points at which Ha's arguments seem to be built upon a rather tenuous premise. One example is his presupposition with regard to v. 8. A negative interpretation of v. 8 does not necessarily conflict with the statement about Abraham's faith in v. 6. The non-sequential waw-perfect in v. 6 may imply that the narrator is pointing out that 'Abram had believed...', rather than that 'Abram *now* believed'.[23] Thus the narrator at this point may merely be reminding his readers of Abraham's status as a believer in a context where Abraham's faith is being stretched by Yahweh's promise. In any case, genuine faith is not immune from doubts and sometimes seeks reassurance.[24] Moreover, a different dimension of God's promise is in focus in v. 8. The focus is now on the possession of land rather than on the prospect of progeny; thus Abraham could conceivably have embraced the latter promise while retaining reservations in relation to the former.

Ha's theological re-reading of v. 5 (i.e. Abraham looking 'outside himself') is completely unconvincing. Were such a hermeneutic consistently applied, texts could easily be taken to mean whatever the interpreter wanted them to say. A similar grammatical construction is found in Gen. 19.17, where the sense is obviously local. Indeed, as Ha himself recognizes, the same hiphil verb used in Gen. 15.7 has a patently local connotation. Thus Ha's interpretation of v. 5 is at least highly questionable, if not altogether absurd. It seems to be quite unnecessary in any case. In such a succinct narrative there is no compelling argument against an implicit tent-setting for Abraham's 'vision' (v. 1). Admittedly there is no explicit mention of a tent in Genesis 15, but there is no reason why the author and readers could not simply assume that such

22. A. Caquot, 'L'alliance avec Abram (Genèse 15)', *Sem* 12 (1962), pp. 51-66 (63, 65).

23. So, for example, Ross, *Creation and Blessing*, pp. 309-10; cf., however, W.C. Kaiser, 'Salvation in the Old Testament: With Special Emphasis on the Object and Content of Personal Belief', *Jian Dao* 2 (1994), pp. 1-18 (10-11).

24. Cf. Caquot ('L'alliance avec Abram', p. 59) who approvingly cites the 'analogous' requests of Gideon and Hezekiah suggested by Dillmann and others to illustrate that 'la foi n'exclut pas la demande d'un signe'.

was the locale for at least the first stage of this particular divine–human encounter. Furthermore, if the experience of v. 5 is still part of Abraham's vision, Abraham's physical location is quite irrelevant; the vision ostensibly presupposes an internal setting up until v. 5.[25]

Ha's suggested link between the birds of prey and Eliezer seems to be equally contrived. The underlying premise again appears to be without foundation; in what sense can the 'birds of prey' be dubbed 'foreign'? They certainly cannot be foreigners in the same sense as Eliezer, even if one allows the MT to stand and translates the disputed words as 'and the usurper of my house—he is a Damascene—is Eliezer'.[26] However, even if Eliezer was indeed from Damascus and thus in some sense a 'foreigner' (was not Abraham as well?), there is nothing in the text that portrays him as a 'threat'; at least, not in the same sense as the birds of prey which, by their behaviour, were *actively* placing the theophany in jeopardy.[27] Thus if a parallel exists at all between the problem posed by Abraham's steward and that posed by the scavenging birds, it must surely be antithetical. Other, less problematic parallels can at any rate be drawn: in the first pericope (vv. 1-6) God's promise of personal blessing (great reward, v. 1) is apparently jeopardized by Abraham's circumstances (childlessness, vv. 2-3). In the second pericope (v. 7-21) God's promise of national blessing (great possessions, v. 14) is apparently jeopardized by Israel's circumstances

25. Admittedly, it is unclear where the visionary experience ends and terrestrial experience resumes in Gen. 15. Does the visionary experience end at v. 4, v. 5, v. 9—or is the entire episode recorded in Genesis 15 to be so understood?

26. So Ha, *Genesis 15*, p. 15. For a concise discussion of this notoriously difficult text that undermines an explicit 'foreign' connotation, see H.L. Ginsberg, 'Abram's "Damascene" Steward', *BASOR* 200 (1970), pp. 31-32. Whatever the actual meaning, it certainly seems to be a rather tenuous place upon which to erect any compelling argument.

27. *Pace* Snijders ('Genesis XV', p. 270), who associates מֶשֶׁק in Gen. 15.2 with the hapax form כְּמַשַּׁק in Isa. 33.4, to which he attaches the connotation of 'attacking'. Thus Eliezer is 'the attacker, the man who forces himself upon a person'. While the connotation given to the form in Isa. 33.4 is not impossible (though by no means certain), the methodology of interpreting one hapax legomenon in the light of an almost equally obscure word is surely defective. Snijders' association of Eliezer with Damascus on the grounds that the name of a Damascene king, Hadadezer (1 Kgs 11.24) contains a similar ending is as convincing as locating Ebenezer in Syria on the same grounds! Snijders' argument is certainly ingenious, but unconvincing.

(subjugation, v. 13). The latter threat is typified in the action of the birds
of prey, and the removal of this threat is typified by Abraham's expulsion of these birds. In response to Hasel's article, Wenham has proposed that 'Abram's experience in a sense foreshadows that of his
descendants. He sees them under attack from foreign powers but pro-
tected and enjoying the immediate presence of God'.[28] While such a
general explanation of the birds of prey is certainly not excluded, the
very definite nature of the threat alluded to in Gen. 15.13 surely warrants a more specific interpretation for the birds of prey in v. 11.[29]

The question of the relationship between the 'four hundred years' of
v. 13 and the 'fourth generation' of v. 16 deserves further investigation.
Despite what Ha suggests, Caquot's solution is not the only explanation
that preserves the literary unity of the chapter. Following Albright,[30]
who reasons on the premise that דור in Gen. 15.16 means 'lifetime'
rather than 'generation', Kidner and Hamilton maintain that the figure
of four hundred years (i.e. four lifetimes according to patriarchal
reckoning) and the fourth lifetime (v. 16) are in fact synonymous.[31] A
similar equation of the two periods has been suggested by others.[32]
However, as Skinner has correctly observed, the conclusion that 'the
generation was reckoned as 100 years...cannot be held unless vv. 13-16
are a unity'.[33] Thus to affirm the compositional unity of Genesis 15 on
the basis that the figures reflected in vv. 13 and 16 are synonymous
would in fact be circular reasoning. Nevertheless, the fact that these
two verses may indeed be reflecting the same period of time fundamentally negates their use as evidence that the passage is composite.
Therefore, the compositional unity of Genesis 15 is certainly not dis-
lodged by the allegedly conflicting periods of time reflected in vv. 13
and 16.

Unquestionably the most serious problem with Ha's case, however, is

28. 'The Symbolism of the Animal Rite in Genesis 15', p. 136.
29. I concur with Anbar ('Genesis 15: A Conflation', p. 47) that 'presumably
the appearance of the birds of prey is the omen that is interpreted in vv. 13-16'.
30. W.F. Albright, 'Abram the Hebrew: A New Archaeological Interpretation',
BASOR 163 (1961), pp. 36-54.
31. Kidner, *Genesis*, p. 125; Hamilton, *Genesis 1–17*, p. 436.
32. For instance, Dillmann, *Genesis*, II, p. 64; Driver, *The Book of Genesis*,
p. 177; R.R. Rickards, 'Genesis 15: An Exercise in Translation Principles', *BT* 28
(1977), pp. 213-20 (218); Wenham, *Genesis 1–15*, p. 332; Youngblood, *The Book
of Genesis*, p. 163.
33. Skinner, *Genesis*, p. 292.

that it is suggestive rather than conclusive. Overall Ha has certainly presented a strong case for the thematic and structural unity of Genesis 15 in its final form. But this does not rule out the work of a skilled redactor. Ha's analysis does not demand the explanation that a single author was responsible for this text in its entirety; pre-existing strands could well have been woven together by the final editor to form the present compositional unit. However, while Ha's observations do not exclude the hand of a skilful redactor per se, they certainly do constitute a strong cumulative case for treating the chapter as much more than a redactional unity. Thus as Hoftijzer formerly concluded, 'it is quite unnecessary to ascribe the promise of posterity of v. 5 and the promise of land of vv. 7ff to different strata'.[34]

4. *The Relationship between the Promises of 'Land' and 'Descendants'*

As the structure of the chapter suggests, a close relationship exists between the promissory aspects of 'seed' and 'land'. In fact they are integrated elements of the divine promise. Both must be read in conjunction with the other, rather than in isolation from one another. Neither of these two aspects of the patriarchal promise stands on its own. As Snijders maintains, 'in the stories of the patriarchs the promises of numerous descendants and the possession of the land of Canaan are connected'.[35]

On the one hand, without 'seed', the prospect of land was worthless. Thus Abraham questions the value of the 'great reward' assured to him by Yahweh in Gen. 15.2. If, as the unfolding chapter implies, the patriarch's reservations related primarily to the promise of land, Abraham's initial difficulty was with the significance of such a reward if he had no descendants to inherit it. For the 'reward' of v. 1 to be of lasting value, it was imperative that Abraham produce physical heirs. It was for this reason that Abraham challenged Yahweh's reassurance in Gen. 15.1.[36]

---

34. Hoftijzer, *Die Verheissungen an die drei Erväter*, p. 23. Abela's judgment ('Genesis 15: A Non-Genetic Approach', p. 14) is rather more guarded, but is in substantial agreement: 'One may concede that behind Gen 15 there subsists various promise traditions (Lohfink) and that we have here the amalgamation of two narratives (Westermann); yet the text as it stands has clearly been conceived as a unity'.

35. Snijders, 'Genesis XV', p. 265.

36. I concur with Hamilton that 'it is not necessarily a fact that Abraham interprets Yahweh's promise of a reward as a promise of a child' (*Genesis 1–17*,

As Brueggemann observes, 'the reward of land requires having heirs. Land is never for one generation. The capacity to transmit land for long generations to come is required. So the large [*sic*] promise depends upon the quite concrete matter of an heir'.[37]

On the other hand, without land the promise of seed was meaningless. Regardless of how numerous his descendants would become, they would never constitute a גוי גדול without territory that they could claim as their own.[38] Admittedly, the Old Testament nowhere explicitly states what constitutes Israel's becoming a גוי. However, it is no more explicit as regards this matter with respect to the other nations (most of whom did have their own territory); moreover, the usage of this noun vis-à-vis עם indicates that generally it denotes a territorial and political entity.[39] That the two nouns (עם and גוי) are sometimes used synonymously (e.g. Exod. 33.13; Deut. 4.6) is not in doubt; nevertheless, the territorial-political connotation is certainly more prominent in the case of גוי. An illustration of the latter is found in Ezek. 35.10, where the basis for Israel's division into two גוים is their territorial separation from one another. Thus while the concept of racial affiliation can certainly not be excluded, the concept of a גוי as reflected in the Hebrew Bible seems to be 'the counterpart of what in the modern world would be regarded as a nation'.[40]

p. 420). Rather, Abraham perceived that a reward that could not be transmitted served no useful or lasting purpose. Cf. Rickards, 'Genesis 15: An Exercise in Translation Principles', p. 215.

37. Brueggemann, *Genesis*, p. 142.

38. See further, Chapter 7 Section 3c below.

39. *Pace* Z. Weisman ('National Consciousness in the Patriarchal Narratives', *JSOT* 31 [1985], pp. 55-73 [66]), who asserts that גוי in the patriarchal promises does not presuppose possession of a land'. Admittedly Ishmael's case presents something of an anomaly, but at least two observations are apposite: the concept of land may not be totally foreign to the promise concerning Ishmael, cf. Gen. 25.18; in any case, this possible exception does not detract from the general usage. Cf. E.A. Speiser, '"People" and "Nation" of Israel', *JBL* 79 (1960), pp. 157-63; L. Rost (ed.), *Das kleine Credo und andere Studien zum Alten Testament* (Heidelberg: Quelle & Meyer, 1965), pp. 86-101; S.E. Loewenstamm, 'גוי', in *Encyclopaedia Biblica* (8 vols.; Jerusalem: Bialik Institute, 1965), II, col. 457 (Hebrew); R.E. Clements, 'גוי *gôy*', *TDOT*, II, pp. 426-33; *HALOT*, I, pp. 182-83 and II, pp. 837-39; A.R. Hulst, 'גוי/עם *ʿam/gôy* people', *TLOT*, II, p. 913.

40. Clements, 'גוי', p. 429. So too Speiser, '"People" and "Nation"', p. 160. As Speiser observes (p. 158), "*ām* is something subjective and personal, *gôy* objective and impersonal'.

This being so, the prospect of numerous descendants automatically evoked the question of dwelling-place. On several occasions in the patriarchal narratives peaceful coexistence in the same territory is depicted as being fraught with difficulty.[41] The idea of innumerable descendants who would become a 'great nation' (Gen. 12.2) would have been quite inconceivable, even absurd, in isolation from the obvious corollary, a geographical location in which this nation would reside and over which it would have inheritance rights. The concept of numerous progeny implied the prospect of national territory. So for the promise of Gen. 12.2 to be fulfilled, it was essential that Abraham's descendants inherit the land as promised explicitly in Gen. 12.7.[42] Without land of their own, Abraham's descendants might multiply into numerous tribes, but they would never constitute a 'great nation'. Together these two aspects (numerous descendants and land) frame the promise of national greatness in Genesis 12. It is only if and when both these expectations are realized that this aspect of the patriarchal promise can be said to have been fulfilled.

It comes therefore as no surprise that both these elements (i.e. descendants and land) should be brought together in Genesis 15. Nor is it at all surprising that the verb uniting both aspects within the chapter is ירשׁ. From beginning to end the focus in Genesis 15 is Abraham's inheritance. The two parts of the chapter deal respectively with Abraham's heirs and with Abraham's inheritance. Together these constitute the 'great reward' promised to the patriarch at the beginning of the chapter.

5. *The Nature of the Covenant in Genesis 15*

Genesis 15 is presented as the formal ratification of a covenant between God and Abraham; of this there can be no doubt. However the precise details and symbolic significance of the theophanic 'passing between

---

41. Cf. the crises involving Abraham and Lot, Gen. 13 [esp. v. 6]; Isaac and Abimelech, Gen. 26; Jacob and Laban, Gen. 30–31; Jacob and Esau, Gen. 36.7. I am indebted to Snijders for this judicious observation.

42. Speiser aptly concludes: 'to carry out God's purpose, as that purpose is expressed by the Bible as a whole, the *'ām* was not enough; what was needed was the added status and stability of nationhood in a land specifically designated for that purpose' ('"People" and "Nation"', p. 163).

the pieces' are to be understood,[43] the final editor of Genesis clearly understood it to be ratifying a divine–human covenant (Gen. 15.18). However, the precise nature, scope and purpose of the covenant ratified on this occasion are less obvious, giving rise to a number of pertinent questions which must be addressed: is the covenant ratified in Genesis 15 conditional or unconditional? Does this covenant embrace all or only some of the programmatic divine promises in Gen. 12.1-3, 7 (cf. Gen. 22.16-18) to Abraham? How does the covenant spoken of here in Genesis 15 function within its present literary framework? As the latter two questions are examined in detail below,[44] only the first of these important issues will be discussed at this point: Is the covenant ratified in Genesis 15 unconditional or provisional; does the writer present this covenant as unilateral or reciprocal?

Since there are no conditions explicitly imposed upon Abraham in Genesis 15, it is possible to interpret the covenant described in this chapter as purely promissory.[45] Such an interpretation has been adopted by Alexander:

> Nowhere is it indicated that the fulfilment of the covenant is dependent upon the actions of either Abraham or his descendants; God covenants unreservedly to fulfil his promise that Abraham's descendants will possess the land of Canaan. For this reason it may be designated an unconditional, promissory covenant.[46]

Bright also understands the Abrahamic covenant to be unconditional, but does not differentiate, as do both Alexander and McComiskey (albeit in different ways), between the covenant ratified in Genesis 15 and that spoken of in Genesis 17:

---

43. Cf. the discussion of this in Chapter 3 Section 3c.2 above.

44. The question of the scope of the covenant in Gen. 15 is taken up in Section 6 below; the function of Gen. 15 within its present literary framework is considered in Chapter 7.

45. So, for example, McComiskey, *The Covenants of Promise*, pp. 139-44.

46. Alexander, 'Abraham Reassessed', p. 15. See also E. Kutsch ('Gottes Zuspruch und Anspruch. *bᵉrît* in der alttestamentlichen Theologie', in C. Brekelmans [ed.], *Questions disputées d'Ancien Testament: Méthode et théologie* [Leuven: Leuven University Press, 2nd edn, 1989], pp. 71-90), who observes: 'Subjekt der *bᵉrît* ist—allein—Jahwe; er ist es, der die *bᵉrît* "festsetzt". Er—Jahwe—setzt für eine Verpflichtung fest. Abraham auf der anderen Seite ist nur der Empfänger der *bᵉrît*' (p. 79).

> It is to be noted that this covenant is depicted simply as a binding promise—or better, a promissory oath—on the part of God. No particular conditions are attached to it. True, it is assumed that Abraham would continue to trust God and walk before him in righteousness and obedience... But the giving of the promise itself is not made subject to conditions. There is no list of commandments that Abraham must obey, or obligations that he must fulfil, if it is to be made good. In fact, in the covenant ceremony (15.7-12, 17) Abraham is depicted as passive... The patriarchal covenant thus rests in God's unconditional promises for the future, and it asks of the recipient only that he trust.[47]

However, such an interpretation has not gone unchallenged. Youngblood, for example, has contested Bright's suggestion that the covenant initiated in Genesis 15 is depicted simply as a promissory oath on the grounds that obligations in a ברית do not necessarily have to be spelt out.[48] Rather, as Eichrodt observed, 'the relationship which grows out of the nature of the *berith* could very well include the obligation also of the receiver, without its being expressly mentioned, if it were simply presumed as well known'.[49]

Youngblood further argues that this relationship aspect of a covenant is inherent in the Hebrew word, ברית. He rejects the commonly suggested etymological connection between *bᵉrît* and the Akkadian noun *birītu* ('bond' or 'fetter'), suggesting that a link with the Akkadian word *birīt* ('between') is more plausible etymologically and can be illustrated by a comparative study of a number of ancient Near Eastern texts from Mari. In these texts

> the Akkadian *birīt* occurs...precisely where we find the Hebrew word *bên*, 'between', in similar (including, of course, covenant) contexts... The Akkadian preposition *birīt*, then, stressing the 'between-ness' that is the essence of the covenant relationship, would via Mari...have been substantivized and adopted into Hebrew by the Israelites as their specific word for 'covenant'.[50]

The fact that one of the Mari texts cited by Youngblood has some similarities with the initiation rite depicted in Genesis 15 certainly

---

47. Bright, *Covenant and Promise*, pp. 25-26.

48. R.F. Youngblood, 'The Abrahamic Covenant: Conditional or Unconditional?', in M. Inch and R.F. Youngblood (eds.), *The Living and Active Word of God* (Festschrift S.J. Schultz; Winona Lake, IN: Eisenbrauns, 1983), pp. 31-46.

49. W. Eichrodt, 'Covenant and Law: Thoughts on Recent Discussion', *Int* 20 (1966), pp. 302-21 (305).

50. Youngblood, 'The Abrahamic Covenant', p. 35.

corroborates the etymological connection suggested between the Hebrew term for covenant and the Akkadian preposition meaning 'between'. Nevertheless, this does not inexorably support Youngblood's conclusion that such an inter-party treaty must of necessity impose obligations on each covenant partner. At most it merely establishes that in Hebrew thought a ברית was understood as sealing or formalizing a relationship between two or more parties. Thus, even if Youngblood's suggested etymology is accepted, it no more implies the presence of bilateral *obligations* than does the use of the English preposition 'between' when used with reference to a relationship between two or more parties.

In the same way, it is far from clear that the use of the preposition את in Gen. 15.18 'assumes bilateral agreement rather than unilateral imposition, and this in turn assumes the presence of conditions'.[51] How else could the making of a covenant between two parties have been expressed? The use of the preposition את does not, in itself, detract from the unilateral nature of the covenant ratified in Genesis 15, any more than the use of the English preposition 'with' implies that bilateral obligations have been imposed on those it unites.

More significant, however, is the fact that the unilateral dimension of the covenant ratified in Genesis 15 is at least implicit in the text itself. Not only are human obligations altogether absent in this chapter, in marked contrast to the other chapter which explicitly refers to a covenant between God and Abraham (cf. Gen. 17.1, and 17.9-14), but in addition, the actual ratification ritual of passing between the *disjecta membra* is solely the action of God in Gen. 15.17.[52] While admittedly there is no evidence in the extant second millennium BCE literature of either treaty party or indeed of both of them passing between the dissected carcasses,[53] the very fact that only God performed this rite in Genesis 15 is clearly indicative of the unilateral nature of the covenant thus ratified. 'God alone passed between the pieces, because He alone had something to promise.'[54] In a somewhat similar vein Ha concludes,

51. Youngblood, 'The Abrahamic Covenant', p. 35.

52. Prompting Van Develder's comment: 'It would be difficult to conceive of a more dramatic and daring way to depict the completely unilateral character of the agreement which Yahweh here makes with Abraham' ('Abrahamic Covenant Traditions', p. 259).

53. So Hasel, 'The Meaning of the Animal Rite', p. 68; Ha, *Genesis 15*, p. 72.

54. Dillmann, *Genesis*, II, p. 65.

in Gen 15 the author's concern is YHWH'S part, not Abraham's. This is why apart from making the necessary preparations for the animal rite Abraham had no part to play in the chapter. All for him was YHWH'S grace manifested in His unilateral oath of land donation to him.[55]

For Snijders, who likewise concludes that 'in Gen 15 the covenant is quite onesided',[56] this event (i.e. Yahweh's symbolic passing between the pieces) is in fact the source of the 'oath' tradition subsequently and frequently mentioned in relation to God's promises of land and people.[57] On the surface this appears to be a most plausible suggestion, especially given that the focal point of the divine oath is primarily the promise of land. This is certainly so in the majority of the texts which explicitly draw attention to the solemn nature of the divine promise to the Patriarchs.[58] Against Snijders' suggestion, however, is the fact that Gen. 22.16 is the only text within the Abraham narrative that explicitly describes Yahweh making an oath to Abraham. Moreover, in Gen. 26.3, where Yahweh expressly reiterates the oath which had been made to Abraham, there is obvious allusion to the oath-making event recorded in Gen. 22.16-18. As well as the content and sequences of the promises being essentially the same, the reference in both chapters to 'Abraham's obedience' as the catalyst for Yahweh's oath ties the two passages inseparably together: The oath alluded to in Gen. 26.3 cannot be other than the oath sworn in Gen. 22.16-18. This is not to suggest, however, that Snijders' hypothesis is fundamentally flawed. Indeed, just as Gen. 26.3 most plausibly alludes to Gen. 22.16-18, Gen. 24.7 may indeed relate back to Gen. 15.17-21.[59] If this is indeed the case, the implication must surely be that Yahweh is presented by the narrator as having made two separate oaths to Abraham, or, at least, as having

---

55. Ha, *Genesis 15*, p. 167.

56. Snijders, 'Genesis XV', p. 278.

57. Cf. Snijders, 'Genesis XV', pp. 274-75.

58. Snijders lists ('Genesis XV', p. 275 n. 29) the following texts: Gen. 22.7; 50.24; Exod. 13.5; Num. 14.16, 23, 30; Deut. 1.8, 35; 6.10, 18, 23; Josh. 1.6; 5.6; Mic. 7.20; Ps. 105.9. In addition to these texts specifically cited by Snijders, other examples abound; most of these, not surprisingly, are found in the book of Deuteronomy, but not exclusively so; cf. Exod. 13.11; 33.1; Num. 32.11; Josh. 21.43.

59. The most appealing alternative within the Abraham narrative is Gen. 12.7. On this occasion, however, there is nothing in the text suggesting anything like a solemn oath; rather this text records a straightforward promissory statement made by Yahweh to Abraham; cf. Gen. 13.15; 17.8.

made an oath to Abraham on two separate occasions, the first on the occasion reflected in Genesis 15, and the second on the occasion reflected in Genesis 22. The ramifications of this certainly warrant careful investigation.

6. *Promissory Selectivity in Genesis 15*

a. *The Absence of the International Dimension of the Divine Promise*
As reflected by both the structure and the contents of Genesis 15, the promissory emphases in this chapter are clearly 'seed' and 'land'. These two prospects, descendants and land, are at least implicit in the initial promise of nationhood in Gen. 12.2 (ואעשׂך לגוי גדול).[60]

This national dimension of the patriarchal promise is taken up twice in the narrative between Gen. 12.2 and ch. 15. On Abraham's arrival at Shechem, Yahweh promises the land to Abraham's 'seed' (Gen. 12.7); again, after Abraham and Lot's separation Yahweh reiterates the promise of land to Abraham's 'seed', on this occasion adding that the gift was to be perpetual and that the seed would be innumerable (Gen. 13.15-17).

In Genesis 15 these same dimensions of the original promise are picked up and expanded upon: Abraham will produce a physical heir and he will also be the progenitor of innumerable descendants (vv. 4-5); Abraham's descendants will indeed inherit the Promised Land, if only after a protracted period of enslavement in a foreign land (Gen. 15.13-16). It is these two dimensions, descendants and land, to which the covenantal assurance of Gen. 15.18 relates. Noticeably absent is the wider dimension of the promise contained in Gen. 12.2-3: the blessing mediated to כל משׁפחת האדמה through Abraham. Admittedly, the concept of 'cursing those who curse Abraham' (Gen. 12.3b) could be inferred from Gen. 15.14a, where God promises to 'punish the nation they serve as slaves', but other than this debatable allusion, the broader, international dimension of the patriarchal promise finds no echo whatsoever in ch. 15. There is certainly no hint of blessing being mediated through Abraham to any of the foreign nations mentioned implicitly or explicitly. It seems reasonable, therefore, to conclude that Genesis 15 picks up on only one dimension of the patriarchal promise; viz. the promise of nationhood.

---

60. Cf. Chapter 7 Section 3c below.

This observation and its significance, however, seem largely to have escaped the attention of most commentators on Genesis. The narrow, national focus of Genesis 15 surely warrants some explanation, especially since the international dimension of the initial promise (Gen. 12.1-3) is implicit in the other 'covenantal' chapter (cf. Gen. 17.4-6, 16),[61] and comes to prominence in the two reiterations of the patriarchal promise that follow in the Abraham narrative (Gen. 18.18; 22.17-18).[62] In that these subsequent passages highlight the broader dimension of the patriarchal promise, the fact that it is bypassed altogether in Genesis 15 is all the more striking and significant. Moreover, the fact that it has a prominent place in each of the speeches which together occupy such a significant place in the overall narrative framework[63] clearly indicates its importance in the thought of the final editor. Why, then, does this important aspect of God's original promise to Abraham receive no mention in such a theologically significant chapter as Genesis 15? Why is this international element of the promise not incorporated into the covenant ratified by divine oath in Gen. 15.18-21? If, as the subsequent passages (i.e. Gen. 17.4-7, 16; 18.18; 22.17-18) suggest, international blessing was an integral part of God's promise to Abraham, why is it entirely ignored in the first place where God's promises were ratified by a special covenant assurance?

b. *Reasons for Such a Glaring Omission*
There are at least two ways to explain why such a prominent aspect of the divine promise to Abraham should be completely omitted in Genesis 15:

1. The dimension of international blessing was unknown to the author or compiler of Genesis 15. The author or compiler of Genesis 15 was working in the period before the promise of international blessing

---

61. This point will be defended in Chapter 5 below.

62. Gen. 24.7, like Gen. 15, explicitly mentions only the national element of the divine promise. It should be noted, however, that this is not a reiteration of the promise to Abraham by Yahweh, but the reported speech of Abraham to his chief servant. Moreover, the context (i.e. finding a bride for Isaac to ensure the distinctiveness of Abraham's seed in the land of Canaan) renders the promise of international blessing less relevant here. It is primarily the national dimension of the divine promise that will be jeopardized if a suitable bride is not found for Isaac.

63. Gen. 12.1-3 and Gen. 22.16-18. For more on the function of these speeches within the Abraham narrative, see Chapter 7 Section 2 below.

through Abraham was incorporated into the patriarchal traditions, and therefore he could not include it in his own material.

However, while such a hypothesis might explain why an alleged source would not have included the international aspect of the patriarchal promise, it must assume that Genesis 15 predates Gen. 12.1-3 and must postulate a rather haphazard and piecemeal compilation on the part of the final editor(s) of the Pentateuch; neither of these *a priori* assumptions can claim any consensus in current Pentateuchal criticism. If, as is generally accepted among source critics, Gen. 12.1-3 and ch. 15 reflect the J source at least to some extent, then, regardless of the antiquity of J, the compiler of Genesis 15 must have been familiar with the promise of international blessing through Abraham. In any case, if, as much recent scholarship acknowledges, the compilation by the final editors of the Pentateuch was not as slipshod as earlier scholarship supposed, the omission of any reference to the international dimension of the patriarchal promise in Genesis 15 must be seen as quite deliberate and in keeping with the theological objectives of the literary whole. Thus, rather than explaining this significant omission in Genesis 15, the source-critical 'solution' simply evades the crux of the matter: what is the significance of this omission here in the final compilation of Genesis?

2. The second way to explain the absence of international blessing in Genesis 15 is by suggesting that this prospect lies outside the scope of the promises being ratified here. Thus there is no mention of the nations in Genesis 15 because this aspect of the patriarchal promise is not included in the 'covenant between the pieces'. The covenants in Genesis 15 and 17 reflect two quite distinct foci. The omission of any reference to international blessing through Abraham in Genesis 15 is explained by the special focus and distinct emphasis of the covenant recorded in this particular chapter.

As noted above, Alexander contends that Genesis 15 focuses exclusively on the national aspect of the patriarchal promise, whereas the covenant heralded in Genesis 17 relates primarily to the international dimension.[64] Sailhamer, on the other hand, while also interpreting the two chapters in terms of two distinct covenants, suggests that the focus of the covenant in ch. 15 is the promise of land (15.18-21), whereas the

---

64. Alexander, 'Abraham Reassessed', pp. 14-18; *idem, From Paradise to the Promised Land*, pp. 48-57.

focus of ch. 17 is the promise of abundant descendants (17.2).[65]

While Alexander has correctly identified the particular focus of the covenant in Genesis 15, his distinction between chs. 15 and 17 is drawn rather too sharply. Admittedly Genesis 17 focuses much more upon the nations who will trace their origin to Abraham and Sarah, but the promissory aspect of land-inheritance is certainly not lost to view completely (cf. Gen. 17.8). Thus while Alexander's thesis explains why the international aspect of the patriarchal promise should be altogether ignored in Genesis 15, it does so at the expense of introducing an insuperable problem into the Genesis 17 passage: why should a covenant relating primarily to the second dimension of the patriarchal promise (i.e. international blessing) incorporate elements clearly belonging to the national aspect (the land gift of Canaan)?[66]

Rather than having an altogether different emphasis, Genesis 17 has a more comprehensive or inclusive emphasis, encompassing both dimensions of the patriarchal promise; that is, blessing on a national and on an international scale. Alexander's sharp dichotomy between the covenant of Genesis 15 and the covenant announced in Genesis 17 is too simplified and, as observed above, in view of Gen. 17.8 (and indeed Gen. 22.17) is not sustainable. Instead of being so sharply differentiated, the 'covenant between the pieces' and the 'covenant of circumcision' should be understood in terms of distinct, but related covenants. In Genesis 17 there is both a broadening and a narrowing of the promissory focus of Genesis 15.[67]

However, the fact that Genesis 17 is more encompassing than Genesis 15 does not negate nor detract from Alexander's basic premise (i.e. that the covenant in Gen. 15 focuses primarily on the national dimension of the patriarchal promise). As Alexander has pointed out, this is the simplest explanation as to why, in the final compilation of Genesis, ch. 15 makes no mention of the blessing mediated through Abraham to the nations. Only the promises of descendants and land are being

---

65. Sailhamer, *The Pentateuch as Narrative*, p. 156.

66. This criticism applies equally to Sailhamer's distinction between a covenant relating to land (Gen. 15) and a covenant relating to numerous descendants (Gen. 17). The inclusion of the promise of land in Gen. 17.8, albeit with a connotation of permanence not explicit in Gen. 15, cannot be accommodated by a rigid differentiation between the focus of Gen. 15 and that of ch. 17.

67. This is elaborated upon in Chapter 6 Section 4 below.

ratified by covenant in Genesis 15, and therefore no mention is made at this stage of the broader dimension of international blessing.

7. Conclusion

Having addressed the key questions in the light of the text, it has become increasingly clear that the final editor of Genesis 15 presents this pericope with a carefully defined covenantal focus: rather than developing the divine promises to Abraham in a general or comprehensive manner, the covenant recorded in this chapter specifically focuses on one particular aspect of God's promissory agenda for Abraham,[68] that of nationhood (incorporating both the prospects of seed and land). Given this specific focus in Genesis 15, the announcement of a second covenant in Genesis 17 is not nearly so anomalous as would otherwise be the case. If God's initial covenant with Abraham (i.e. as recorded in Gen. 15) has picked up on only the first of two major elements in the promissory agenda of 12.1-3,[69] astute readers should therefore anticipate the establishment of a second divine covenant which would encompass the promissory element(s) omitted in the first. Thus a close reading of Genesis 15 vis-à-vis Gen. 12.1-3 may lead one to expect a further covenantal oath within the Abraham narrative.

Rather than finding the obvious differences between chs. 15 and 17 somewhat incongruous, the differences in emphases between these two covenantal passages are precisely what the reader should have expected. Just as Genesis 15 expands upon the programmatic promise of nationhood, so (the reader might reasonably anticipate) Genesis 17 will primarily expand upon the dimension of international blessing. We turn our attention now, therefore, to examine whether or not the material included within Genesis 17 supports such a conclusion.

---

68. For the programmatic nature of the divine speech of Gen. 12.1-3, see Chapter 7 Section 3 below.

69. For a detailed discussion, see Chapter 7 below.

Chapter 5

THE PROMISSORY FOCUS OF THE 'COVENANT OF CIRCUMCISION'

1. *Introduction*

The mention of a prospective covenant in Gen. 17.2 must immediately capture the attention of the observant reader. The fact that this particular covenant, rather than simply some aspect of the divine promises, is spoken of in the future tense ('I *will* give my *covenant*', Gen. 17.2) is surely significant. This covenant is apparently being presented, in the final form of Genesis at least, as a different one from that which has been depicted in Genesis 15. The NIV avoids the force of this observation by translating the verb נתן in Gen. 17.2 as 'confirm'. A number of other English versions opt for a more neutral interpretation with translations such as 'establish' (NASB),[1] 'set' (NEB), 'give' (REB) and 'grant' (NJB). Other translations, however, make no attempt to soften the anomaly, rendering the verb 'make' (KJV; RV; ASB; RSV; JB; TEB; NKJV; NRSV; NLT). In view of the nature of the theophany and the narrator's comment in Gen. 15.17-18, the question naturally arises: How can the 'giving' or 'making' of a covenant between God and Abraham be spoken of here in ch. 17 in the future tense?

On the premise that this anomaly between Gen. 15.18 and Gen. 17.2, 7 is evidence of a different source underlying the narrative at this point, it has become axiomatic for source critics to ascribe this account of the institution of the Abrahamic covenant to the Priestly strand.[2] It is telling, however, that in the compilation or editorial process no effort was apparently made to remove or even to disguise the divergences

---

1. The same English verb is used by the NASB in 17.7 to translate the Hebrew causative verb, הקים. Here the KJV; RV; ASB; RSV; NKJV; NRSV also use 'establish'; the NEB translates 'fulfil'; the REB and NJB, 'maintain'; TEV, 'keep'; and the NLT renders the verb 'continue'.
2. See the discussion in Chapters 2 and 3 above.

between the two accounts.[3] The most likely explanation of this editorial feature is that the redactor(s) saw no intrinsic conflict between the two passages. Rather, in the opinion of the redactor(s) the two chapters reflected, if not different covenants, at least distinctive emphases.[4] The contents of Genesis 17 must therefore be examined in order to determine the precise focus of this chapter within the Abraham narrative, and the relationship between it and the national dimension of the divine promise which already has been solemnly ratified by covenant in ch. 15.

2. *The Contents and Structure of Genesis 17*

As highlighted in the earlier comparison between these chapters,[5] Genesis 17 is radically different from Genesis 15 in terms of both contents and structure.

Instead of a clear twofold division as in ch. 15, the structure of Genesis 17 is much more complex. At the most basic level the chapter records further directives and promises given by God to Abraham. The report of these divine utterances is briefly interrupted by Abraham's initial prostration (v. 3) and by his verbal interjection (vv. 17-18), and it is concluded with an account of how Abraham carried out God's command to circumcise himself and his household (vv. 23-27).

The divine communiqué can be broken down into at least five component parts. The initial speech (vv. 1-2) includes the divine self-introduction and a provisional promise.[6] After Abraham's initial response (prostration), the divine speech continues with an expansion of the promissory statement in v. 2. The demarcation of this part of the address from the next is facilitated by the use of the personal pronouns in vv. 4 and 9, a literary feature highlighted by some English translations (e.g. NASB; NIV, 'As for me, ...as for you...') and noted by

---

3. For details, see Chapter 3 Section 3c above.

4. The traditional interpretation takes the sense of both נתן in Gen. 17.2 and the causative of קום in Gen. 17.7 to be 'confirm', thus suggesting that the two chapters address different aspects of the same covenant. The fallacy of such an interpretation, however, is demonstrated in Chapter 6 below.

5. See Chapter 3 Section 3c above.

6. Cf. Chapter 3 Section 3b (n. 75) above. The NEB and REB read a resultative sense here, as is also suggested by several grammarians and commentators: e.g. GKC, §108d; Westermann, *Genesis 12–36*, p. 253; Hamilton, *Genesis 1–17*, p. 458; *IBHS*, pp. 577-78; Janzen, *Genesis 12–50*, p. 48; Wenham, *Genesis 16–50*, p. 15.

numerous commentators since Rashi.[7] Having set forth the promissory aspects in vv. 4-8, the compiler explains the human obligations (in terms of the rite of circumcision) in vv. 9-14. A fourth stage of the divine announcement is introduced in vv. 15-16 where, for the first time, Sarah is explicitly included within the divine promises made to Abraham and is named as the progenitrix of the 'nations' and 'kings' promised to Abraham (v. 6).[8] After Abraham's brief interjection (vv. 17-18), the final part of the divine communiqué (vv. 19-21) confirms the promise made with regard to Sarah, and includes further promises relating both to Isaac and Ishmael. The dialogue ends at this point (v. 22), and the account concludes with Abraham's immediate compliance with the divine instruction regarding circumcision (vv. 23-27).

As noted previously,[9] several different symmetrical structures have been suggested for this pericope. Although McEvenue's structural and stylistic analysis has been embraced by others,[10] it is certainly debatable whether 'one could not accept the possibility that it [i.e. his palistrophe] was unintended' and whether 'this parallelism is clearly there'.[11] Admittedly, like many of the artistic structures detected by modern readers in the Hebrew Bible, McEvenue's palistrophe and parallel panels are initially impressive. However, as the following critique of McEvenue's stylistic analyses of Genesis 17 will underline, it is prudent to embrace postulated literary patterns with cautious reserve.

The very dissimilarity of the literary frameworks which McEvenue has detected within the same textual unit is a case in point. While such complex literary arrangements (linear development, palistrophic pattern and parallel panels) may reflect the deliberate design of the author or

---

7.   See, for example, S.R. Hirsch, *The Pentateuch Translated and Explained by Samuel Raphael Hirsch* (trans. I. Levy; New York: Judaica Press, 2nd edn, 1971), I, p. 298; Delitzsch, *A New Commentary on Genesis*, II, p. 33; Dillmann, *Genesis*, II, p. 82; Skinner, *Genesis*, p. 293; M.V. Fox, 'The Sign of the Covenant: Circumcision in the Light of the Priestly *'ôt* Etiologies', *RB* 81 (1974), pp. 557-96 (588); Zimmerli, *1. Mose 12–25*, p. 67; Westermann, *Genesis 12–36*, p. 255; Sarna, *Genesis*, p. 125; Hamilton, *Genesis 1–17*, p. 468; Hays, 'The Abrahamic Covenant', p. 49; Wenham, *Genesis 16–50*, p. 15.

8.   The name changes recorded in both texts also suggest that the author/editor intended such a connection to be drawn between vv. 4-6 and vv. 15-16. The significance of these name changes is examined below (Section 3a).

9.   See Chapter 3 Section 4b above.

10.   For example, Wenham, *Genesis 16–50*, pp. 17-18.

11.   McEvenue, *Narrative Style*, pp. 158-59.

compiler of this pericope, the presence of one seems to cast serious doubt over the existence of the others. It is difficult to conceive of the author or compiler, however skilful, sustaining three structures which are not consistently built on the same individual units within the pericope.

More serious, however, is the fact that at least some of the elements in the patterns suggested by McEvenue appear to be somewhat artificial, and are thus less than convincing. For instance, in McEvenue's suggested 'parallel' arrangement, his A is apparently delineated under the influence of his A'. Thus he 'creates' the analogy; it does not arise naturally out of the text. Likewise, in his palistrophic arrangement, C (God speaks) seems to be overly influenced by his C' (God ceases from speaking); the verb דבר (v. 22) is not used in the clause which introduces God's speech (וירא יהוה אל־אברם ויאמר אליו), nor does the latter sentence contain any verb corresponding to כלה in v. 22. Similarly, in both patterns proposed by McEvenue, the material in v. 3a and vv. 17-18 is not strictly matching; the connection is made only by inexplicably ignoring most of v. 17 and all of v. 18.[12] The same criticism can be levelled against his treatment of the final verses (vv. 23-27), of which only vv. 24-25 are mentioned in his palistrophic structure. Is this because the rest of the material does not quite fit? One must clearly be sensitive to the fact that complex stylistic analyses may reflect more on the literary finesse of the contemporary critic than on the artistic endeavours of the compiler responsible for the material's present arrangement and canonical shape.

While Westermann's structure is admittedly more straightforward,[13] his consignment of vv. 1b-3a to 'preamble', thus isolating them from the 'promise–command–promise' pattern of the central section, could be challenged. While it is true that 'the elements of vv. 1b-3a are unfolded in God's speech in vv. 3b-21',[14] the analogous break between vv. 4-16 and vv. 19-21 would surely make 'epilogue' a fitting caption for the final part of the chapter (i.e. vv. 19-27). One suspects that Westermann, like McEvenue, struggles to find a place for the concluding verses (vv. 23-27) in his suggested structure. He is clearly forced to break up the verses in a non-symmetrical, indeed almost clumsy

---

12. It will surely not suffice simply to dismiss this incongruity by incorporating the rogue material within a bracketed 'etc.'.

13. See Chapter 3 Section 4b above.

14. Westermann, *Genesis 12–36*, p. 255.

fashion. Thus while Westermann's proposed structure is less engineered than the symmetry suggested by McEvenue, it is probably preferable to look for a structure in the pericope which is both less complex and more apparent from the present arrangement of the material.

The following structure is uncomplicated and presents itself naturally from the text. The pericope's description of the divine–human encounter divides into three distinct speeches of God and three distinct responses of Abraham:

> A God's appearance to Abraham and his promissory stipulation (vv. 1-2)
> A′ Abraham's initial response—prostration (v. 3a)
> B God's elaboration in terms of a) promise (vv. 3b-8)
>   b) command (vv. 9-14)
>   a′) promise (vv. 15-16)
> B′ Abraham's intermediate response—prostration and appeal (vv. 17-18)
> C God's affirmation and his withdrawal from Abraham (vv. 19-22)
> C′ Abraham's third response—submission to circumcision (vv. 23-27)

Alternatively, the structure of the pericope could be set out in terms of the people mentioned. Hence:

> 1. Introduction and preamble (vv. 1-3)
> 2. God's covenant with Abraham (vv. 4-14)
>   a) The divine obligations (vv. 4-8)
>   b) The human obligations (vv. 9-14)
> 3. God's promises relating to Sarah (vv. 15-16, 19a)
> 4. God's promises relating to Isaac and Ishmael (vv. 17-21)
> 5. Conclusion and epilogue (vv. 22-27)

However the pericope's structure is understood, one fact seems to stand out plainly: the central focus in this text is the connection between the covenant promise(s) and the covenant obligations imposed upon Abraham by God, especially the requirement of circumcision.[15] Rather than diminishing the significance of the human obligation, the fact that the ritual stipulation is bracketed by divine promises serves to highlight its importance at this particular juncture in the Abraham narrative. Moreover, the emphasis on human obligation in Genesis 17 is further

---

15. This is reflected in each of the suggested structures set out above, as well as in those of McEvenue and Westermann set out in Chapter 3 Section 4b above; cf. McEvenue's G (in his palistrophic arrangement), panels E and E′ (in his parallel structure), and the promise–command–promise section in Westermann's structure and my own.

reflected in both the opening verses (vv. 1-2) and the closing section (vv. 23-27); both at the beginning and at the conclusion of this pericope the human obligations laid upon Abraham are in focus. Thus the structure and contents of Genesis 17 seem to highlight the obligatory aspects of the divine–human covenant of which this chapter speaks.

This conclusion is further supported by the deployment of the term ברית in Genesis 17. The noun occurs 13 times in this chapter; thus its identification as a *Leitwort* within this pericope is beyond dispute. Its distribution throughout the material not only reflects the literary artistry of the compiler, but also verifies that vv. 9-14 form the heart of the passage: in vv. 3b-8 ברית occurs three times; in vv. 9-14 it occurs six times; and in vv. 19-21 it occurs three times.[16] The literary kernel, vv. 9-14, focuses most sharply on the covenant, expressly relating it to the human obligation of circumcision. Furthermore, in the initial speech (vv. 1-2) the prospect of a ברית is expressly dependent upon Abraham's compliance with the divine stipulation of v. 1b. The non-occurrence of the term ברית in the final section (vv. 23-27) is remarkable. If, as it would appear, circumcision is being presented as an important aspect of the obligation(s) inherent in this covenant (i.e. the obligations upon which the divine disclosure insisted at the outset, v. 1b), one would anticipate an explicit reference to its covenantal significance in these final verses; in that case circumcision is the tangible expression of acceptance by the vassal (Abraham and his descendants) of the cove- nant obligations (an irreproachable lifestyle) imposed by the suzerain (God). An explanation of the covenantal ramifications of the rite is even more appropriate if circumcision is presented here as the rite through which this covenant was ratified. Given the announcement in Gen. 17.2 of a prospective covenant, and the fact that no explicit mention is made of such a covenant in these final verses of Genesis 17, there is reason to question whether or not such a covenant was ratified at this point.[17]

From the organization and contents of Genesis 17 it is reasonable to conclude that unlike Genesis 15, this chapter is alluding to a covenant between God and Abraham which is plainly bilateral, involving not only divine promises but also human obligations, and which is perpetu- ated from one generation to the next through the rite of circumcision.

16. While these three passages are not precisely the same length, they are close enough to detect literary significance in the preponderance of occurrences in vv. 9- 14.

17. This will be explored more fully in the following two chapters of this book.

These differences alone suggest that the promissory focus of Genesis 17 must be thoroughly investigated, and that the relationship between Genesis 15 and 17 should be examined more critically than has been traditionally the case.

3. *The Promissory Elements of the Covenant Described in Genesis 17*

As noted in the above discussion of this pericope's structure, the promissory elements (i.e. the covenantal commitment of the deity) and the obligatory elements (i.e. the covenantal responsibilities of the human partners) are clearly demarcated by use of the personal pronouns in v. 4 and v. 9. Thus the promissory elements of this covenant are the focus of vv. 4-8 (which expand on the divine announcement in v. 2), and the obligatory dimension is brought into focus in vv. 9-14 (which seem to expand on the divine injunction in v. 1).

The two clauses of Gen. 17.2 would appear to be related to one another in one of two ways: either the second clause expresses action simultaneous with the first (thus, 'so that I may give my covenant between me and you and cause you to be extremely numerous'), or else the second clause expresses the purpose or result of the first (thus, 'so that I may give my covenant between me and you in order to make you extremely numerous').[18] In either case, the second clause would appear to be refining or offering concrete explanation to the first. Thus the second clause in Gen. 17.2 explicates the essence of the anticipated covenant.

This explanatory statement in Gen. 17.2 (וארבה אותך במאד מאד) suggests that the covenant spoken of in this chapter will principally relate to Abraham's social status and/or his numerical increase. The hiphil of רבה may convey either 'make great' (cf. 2 Sam. 22.36 and the SP's ארבה of Gen. 15.1) or 'multiply' (e.g. Gen. 3.16; 16.10; 22.17; 41.49). The latter meaning of the hiphil stem is indisputably the more common, and certainly fits well with both MT usage elsewhere in Genesis and with how this particular guarantee is developed in the rest of Genesis 17. Admittedly, if the SP's reading in Gen. 15.1 is accepted,[19] the parallel between the preliminary divine announcement in chs. 15 and 17 provides some grounds for not restricting the sense in the latter chapter to just numerical increase. Nevertheless, while there is some

18. Cf. Joüon, §120 (p. 408).
19. As is tentatively suggested by Westermann, *Genesis 12–36*, p. 213 n. 1d.

allusion in the Genesis 17 pericope to Abraham's social status (cf. the royal descendants mentioned in vv. 6c, 16c), the initial divine announcement of Gen. 17.2 seems to be developed primarily in terms of Abraham's numerical multiplication. As Scullion has observed:

> The promise of increase or a multitude of descendants dominates and is distributed throughout the divine speech: 'I will multiply you very greatly' (vv. 2b, 20a); 'I will make you very fruitful' (vv. 6a, 20a); 'you will be the father of a great number of nations' (vv. 4b, 5b); 'kings shall come from you' (vv. 6b, 16b, 20b); 'I will bless her (him) and make her (him) fruitful' (vv. 16b, 20a); 'I will make him a great nation' (v. 20b).[20]

Two further features in the text suggest that the verb רבה conveys here the idea of numerical growth: the presence of the double adverb, במאד מאד, and the occurrence of the verb פרה in association with רבה in 17.6. In the other occurrences in Genesis 17 of the double adverb, the context strongly favours the numerical nuance.[21] Moreover, the fact that the idea of abundance is reflected in all but two of the occurrences of this rare double adverb outside Genesis 17 further strengthens the numerical interpretation.[22]

Where the verbs פרה and רבה are found in close association in the Hebrew Bible, the sense is exclusively that of numerical increase.[23] Thus the fact that the verb פרה is used in Gen. 17.6 to expand on the promissory statement employing רבה in v. 2 immediately suggests the idea of numerical expansion. This would appear to be confirmed by their deployment together in v. 20; once more the idea of numerical growth best fits the context. Thus the idea of numerical increase would seem to figure largely in the covenant on which Genesis 17 focuses our attention.

20. Scullion, *Genesis*, pp. 145-46.
21. Cf. vv. 6, 20.
22. In addition to Gen. 17, this precise phrase occurs in three other texts, Exod. 1.7; Ezek. 9.9; 16.13. Without the prefixed preposition the phrase occurs a further six times: Gen. 7.19; 30.43; Num. 14.7; 1 Kgs 7.47; 2 Kgs 10.4; Ezek. 37.10. In every instance it conveys a superlative sense. Only in 2 Kgs 10.4 and Ezek. 16.13 is there no idea of abundance or quantity. In Ezek. 9.9 the volume of iniquity is probably in view as well as its reprehensible nature (cf. the use of the verb מלא in the following explanatory clauses).
23. The two verbs are deployed together in the following texts: Gen. 1.22, 28; 8.17; 9.1, 7; 17.20; 28.3; 35.11; 47.27; 48.4; Exod. 1.7; Lev. 26.9; Jer. 3.16; 23.3; 29.6; Ezek. 36.11.

Such numerical increase is apparently a concrete expression of what it means to be 'blessed' by God (cf. vv. 4-6; 16; 18-20). The verses in Genesis 17 which speak explicitly of 'blessing' imply that the nature of the promised blessing is primarily related to the question of progeny. In v. 16, where the object of the blessing is Sarah, the tangible promise is that she will give birth to Abraham's son, will share Abraham's special relationship to 'nations' and will be the progenitrix of the 'kings' who, according to God's promise, will be generated from Abraham (vv. 3-6).[24] In v. 18, where Abraham wishes God's blessing for Ishmael, the immediate context points once more to progeny. In v. 20, in which Ishmael is to be the recipient of God's blessing, the promise is again expanded in terms of numerical increase. While subtle differences are discernible between the blessing promised to Sarah and that promised to Ishmael,[25] it is significant that in each case the promised blessing is expressly related to numerical growth. Thus the dominance of the numerical increase theme in Genesis 17 is beyond dispute. This would seem to confirm that, as frequently elsewhere in the Hebrew Bible, Yahweh's promised blessing would materialize primarily in terms of numerical growth.[26] This inference finds further support in Gen. 12.2, where a similar link is apparently drawn between numerical increase and blessing: 'I will make you into a great nation and bless you'.

The occurrence in v. 1 of the enigmatic אֵל שַׁדַּי further suggests that the emphasis in Genesis 17 is on numerical proliferation. While neither the etymology nor the contextual meaning of this divine appellation has been established with certainty,[27] within the patriarchal narratives the name always occurs in the context of the promise of blessing and

---

24. Even if one rejects the reading reflected in the MT in preference for the masculine suffixes suggested by the ancient versions (as suggested, for example, by the BHS editors), the basic point remains unaffected: whether the recipient of the blessing is Sarah, Isaac, or both, the 'blessing' promised is inextricably bound up with the prospect of progeny.

25. See below, Section 3a.

26. As von Rad observes, 'The substance of Yahweh's blessing in the Old Testament is predominantly a material increase in life, especially in the sense of physical fruitfulness' (*Genesis*, p. 160). Cf. A. Murtonen, 'The Use and Meaning of the Words *lᵉbārek* and *berākāh* in the Old Testament', *VT* 9 (1959), pp. 158-77; G. Wehmeier, *Der Segen im Alten Testament: Eine Semasiologische Untersuchung der Wurzel brk* (Theological Dissertation, 6; Basel: Friedrich Reinhardt, 1970), pp. 70-96.

27. See Chapter 3 Section 3b (n. 74).

fertility (cf. Gen. 17.1; 28.3; 35.11; 48.3). Hays is surely correct, therefore, in his tentative suggestion that 'El Shaddai seems to reflect the
character of the one who brings about blessing and increase of posterity'.[28]

The initial promissory clauses in this pericope, therefore, lead one to
anticipate that the covenant of which it speaks relates primarily to
Abraham's exceptionally large numerical growth. Such a conclusion
finds strong support from the promissory material in vv. 4-6, in which
the initial statement of v. 2 is elaborated upon in terms of Abraham's
international significance, his phenomenal expansion and his royal
progeny, each of which will now be examined.

a. *International Significance*

וְהָיִיתָ לְאַב הֲמוֹן גּוֹיִם וְלֹא־יִקָּרֵא עוֹד אֶת־שִׁמְךָ אַבְרָם וְהָיָה שִׁמְךָ
אַבְרָהָם כִּי אַב־הֲמוֹן גּוֹיִם נְתַתִּיךָ (vv. 4b-5)

Unarguably this is a key exposition of the initial promissory statement
contained in v. 2. This is apparent not only from the way this promise is
repeated here,[29] but also from the fact that this promise introduces
Abraham's new name and subsequently offers an explanation of its
significance. God's promise to make Abraham extremely numerous is
explained in terms of his international significance, the latter being
encapsulated in the new name which the patriarch is given here.

The theological importance of this latter development in Genesis 17
has largely been overlooked by scholarship. Surely, however, the reason for the name change at this particular juncture in the Abraham
narrative and its precise connection with the introduction of 'nations'
(and 'kings') needs to be given careful consideration.

Regardless of the etymological nuance,[30] the alteration in Abraham's

---

28. Hays, 'The Abrahamic Covenant', pp. 38-39. For a similar conclusion, see
Westermann, *Genesis 12–36*, p. 258 and Wenham, *Genesis 16–50*, p. 20.

29. Abraham's relationship to these 'nations' is mentioned three times within
the relatively short compass of vv. 4-5.

30. Etymologically, there are two main explanations for אַבְרָהָם: (1) If, with the
overwhelming majority of scholars, רהם is identified as no more than a dialectal
variant of the root, רום, the meaning is 'the father is exalted'. Whether the father in
question is human or divine is a moot question: West Semitic influence would
suggest a reference to human ancestry, whereas there is some Ugaritic evidence to
support a reference to deity. (2) If, however, רהם is associated with the Arabic noun
ruhāmun (multitude), the etymology implied in the text itself is entirely feasible. In

name is clearly designed to emphasize the magnitude of the divine promise in relation to Abraham's role as אב המון גוים. Abraham's new name underscores the fact that he will indeed enjoy a special relationship to a 'multitude of nations'. As Janzen has correctly noted:

> Whatever historical linguists may rightly decide about the origins and meaning of the name 'Abraham', a proper understanding of the name in the context of this story depends on our willingness to allow the name to be redefined by the narrative in which it is introduced.[31]

The latter clearly defines the meaning of the new name in terms of Abraham's multinational significance (vv. 4-5). Notably, the same is true in relation to Sarah's new name (vv. 15-16). In contrast with Abraham's name change, no attempt is made to explain the linguistic significance of Sarah's new epithet, whether by 'popular etymology' or otherwise. Although it is commonly understood, as with Abraham's name change, to reflect nothing more than a dialectal variant, the two names of the matriarch may possibly be unrelated—the old name may be derived from a verb meaning 'to strive, persist' (שׂרה), and the new from a verb meaning 'to rule' (שׂרר).[32] In any case, Sarah's new name clearly has overtones of royalty.[33] Nevertheless, the primary rationale for Sarah's name change is located in her international significance. This would appear to be the climactic aspect of the divine promises made in relation to Sarah in v. 16. As in v. 6 there is a clear syntactical break before the final phrase relating to 'kings coming out from her'.[34] Thus, whatever the exact meaning of the patriarchal couple's new names, they were clearly meant to express some facet(s) of their special status and international significance.

It is most important that these new names should be conferred on the patriarchal couple by God himself, given the fact that in the cultural context reflected in the Hebrew Bible personal names were more than

---

this case the אב element relates to the Patriarch himself, in contradistinction to its reference to deity in his former name. Cf. Chapter 3 Section 3b (n. 77).

31. Janzen, *Genesis 12–50*, p. 49.

32. Ross, *Creation and Blessing*, p. 334. Ross acknowledges, however, that this distinction may have been conjured up by the LXX translator.

33. The possibility of such regal overtones in Abraham's new name is discussed below.

34. It is plain, not only from their close association here in Gen. 17, but also from the similar association reflected in Gen. 35.11, that this promise of 'kings' relates in some way to both Abraham and Sarah's international significance.

identifying labels, but rather expressed a person's character and destiny. Thus God's renaming of Abraham (and Sarah) constituted 'a divinely guaranteed statement about Abraham's identity and future destiny. His very name guarantees that he will father many nations.'[35] The role of God in this aspect of Abraham's destiny is further emphasized in the next verse, in which the hiphil of פָּרָה 'suggests that Abraham will be given divine power to achieve this fertility'.[36] Thus their new names were a perpetual reminder for Abraham and Sarah of the extent to which God would fulfil his promise of blessing.

These name changes, however, were probably much more than perpetual reminders of God's promise. The changing of a name was more significant in the culture of the ancient Near East than in our own—such a name change implied a change in the bearer's status or circumstances.[37] As Sarna observes:

> a change of name is of major significance and symbolizes the transformation of character and destiny... a name was not merely a convenient means of identification but was intimately bound up with the very essence of being and inextricably intertwined with personality.[38]

Thus by changing the names of Abraham and Sarah, God was apparently heralding a change in their covenantal status. Abraham was no longer to be simply the father of one nation, albeit one that would be 'great' (Gen. 12.2) and 'numerous' (Gen. 13.16; 15.5); rather he and Sarah (cf. Gen. 17.16) would be the ancestors of 'a multitude of nations' (17.4). Therefore this important transition or change in Abraham and Sarah's status clearly marks out the 'covenant of circumcision' as a new development in God's covenantal dealings with Abraham. Since this new aspect was neither explicitly stated nor implicitly present in the former covenant, this surely militates against identifying

35. Wenham, *Genesis 16–50*, p. 21.
36. Wenham, *Genesis 16–50*, p. 22.
37. Cf. Gen. 32.28; 35.10; 41.45; Num. 13.16; 2 Kgs 23.34; 24.17. As E. Fox (*In the Beginning: A New English Rendition of the Book of Genesis* [New York: Schocken Books, 1983], p. 63) observes, 'This act [i.e. name changing] is of the utmost significance in the biblical world. Since a person's name was indicative of personality and fate, the receiving of a new one signified a new life or a new stage in life'.
38. Sarna, *Genesis*, p. 124. Sarna cites the extra-biblical example of the Egyptian king, Amen-hotep IV, whose adoption of the name Akh-en-aten signalled the revolutionary nature of his state policy.

the covenant of Genesis 17 with, or relating it too closely to, the covenant of Genesis 15.

In what sense, then, was Abraham to be לאב המון גוים? Some combination of the nations physically related to Abraham is suggested by a number of scholars.[39] Yet, as Dumbrell insists, 'This reference cannot refer to general Abrahamic descent (i.e. Edomites, Midianites, Ishmaelites etc.) since this promissory aspect is repeated to Sarah (v. 16)'.[40] Von Rad similarly asserts:

> One does not grasp the meaning of this promise if one thinks primarily of the Ishmaelites, Edomites, and sons of Keturah...for the descendants about whom these words speak are not to be sought among those who are outside God's covenant, even less since later the same promise is made to Sarah (v. 16).[41]

Von Rad insists on expressly excluding Ishmael from the covenant, but it is difficult to reconcile this with the fact that Ishmael received the covenant sign of circumcision.[42] The text of Genesis 17 isolates Ishmael only from covenantal lineage (vv. 19-21) rather than from all the blessings enshrined in the promises made to Abraham.[43] Yet whatever the precise nature of Ishmael's covenantal status, it is clear from the reference to Sarah in Gen. 17.16 that this international dimension of Abraham's fatherhood should not be connected to the Ishmaelite offspring of the patriarch.

Moreover, as observed by Alexander,[44] since only the Israelites and

---

39. For example, Driver, *The Book of Genesis*, p. 186; Skinner, *Genesis*, pp. 291-92 (Skinner qualifies his interpretation with his comment on Gen. 28.3, where he relates the 'nations' to the promise of Gen. 12.3 and tentatively suggests a messianic connotation); Kidner, *Genesis*, p. 129; Willis, *Genesis*, p. 247; Gunkel, *Genesis*, p. 264.

40. Dumbrell, *Covenant and Creation*, p. 73.

41. Von Rad, *Genesis*, p. 200. Others make substantially the same observation; e.g. Keil, 'The Pentateuch', pp. 225-26; Leupold, *Genesis*, p. 526; Fox, 'The Sign of the Covenant', p. 590.

42. Unless it is argued that Abraham was wrong to circumcise Ishmael and the other members of his household. Gunkel transfers the 'error' (with regard to Ishmael's circumcision) from Abraham himself to the Priestly compiler (*Genesis*, p. 267), but this, in effect, has P contradicting himself in the space of a few short verses.

43. This is a useful distinction made by a number of commentators; e.g. Leupold, *Genesis*, p. 531; Fretheim, 'The Book of Genesis', p. 459.

44. Alexander, 'Abraham Reassessed', p. 17.

Edomites could trace their physical lineage to Abraham and Sarah, the concept of fatherhood here must surely be much wider than mere physical descent.[45] Alexander contends, rather, that the 'fatherhood' of Abraham here is akin to Joseph's being 'a father to Pharaoh' (Gen. 45.8), a phrase which Alexander understands to mean a mediator of divine blessing.[46] The fact that such a non-biological nuance of the Hebrew term אב is also reflected elsewhere in the Hebrew Bible strongly supports Alexander's proposal in principle.

In addition to Gen. 45.8, a number of other texts in the Hebrew Bible similarly attach a non-physical nuance to אב: in some places the idea of a counsellor, protector or benefactor is suggested;[47] texts which speak of the fatherhood of God likewise use the term in a non-literal manner;[48] a further example is where the word is employed as a respectful term of address.[49] This metaphorical usage of the term אב in the Hebrew Bible certainly illustrates that there is no *a priori* reason to restrict the international community associated with Abraham to those who are able to trace their genealogical lineage back to the patriarch himself.[50]

There may, however, be a further clue in the opening verses of Genesis 17 to the precise nuance that אב has here, for the Hebrew

45. As Keil ('The Pentateuch', pp. 225-26) further observes, since Esau received no part of the covenant promise, one is restricted to the descendants of Jacob for a lineal posterity. Thus this promise, as presented in Genesis, must of necessity embrace more than Abraham's physical descendants.

46. Alexander, 'Abraham Reassessed', p. 17.

47. Cf. Judg. 17.10; 18.19 (Micah's personal Levite priest who, as well as being Micah's 'father', is also said to have become as one of his 'sons'. The latter apparently refers to the Levite's dependency on Micah, thus suggesting the interdependency of their relationship: the Levite was 'father' to Micah in the metaphorical sense of being his spiritual adviser; Micah, it is implied, was 'father' to the Levite in terms of being his physical benefactor. In either case, a non-literal fatherhood is in view.); Isa. 9.5 (the messianic 'Everlasting Father'); Job 29.16 (Job being a 'father to the needy'; cf. Sir. 4.10 'Be a father to the fatherless'). Cf. C.J.H. Wright, 'אָב', *NIDOTE*, I, pp. 219-23.

48. Cf. Deut. 32.6; Isa. 63.16; Jer. 3.4, 19; Mal. 2.10 (Israel); Ps. 68.6 (the destitute); Ps. 89.27; 1 Chron. 22.10 (Solomon).

49. Cf. 1 Sam. 24.12 (David to Saul); 2 Kgs 2.12 (Elisha to Elijah); 2 Kgs 5.13 (MT) (Namaan's servants to Namaan); 2 Kgs 6.21; 13.14 (Israelite king to Elisha).

50. Wiseman's observations ('Abraham in History: The Prince', pp. 234-37) in relation to analogies between a 'provincial governor' (*abu bîtim* = father of the house) and Abraham's representation in Genesis are also suggestive in this respect.

syntax is somewhat unusual. This is one of relatively few texts in which the inseparable preposition לְ is attached to an indeterminate form of the noun אָב.[51] The inseparable preposition לְ commonly serves to express 'direction' (for instance, to identify a noun as the indirect object of the clause in which it is found), to identify the accusative, or to indicate the idea of possession.[52] Here in Gen. 17.4, however, the preposition appears to serve none of these functions: rather, לְ is apparently deployed here in a 'resultative' sense.[53] In every other instance where the preposition is so joined with אָב, a metaphorical concept of fatherhood is undeniably in view.[54] Moreover, on each occasion it is implied that the אָב has special duties and authority: Joseph has significant governmental authority and duties to carry out on Pharaoh's behalf; the Levite's duties involve priestly authority over Micah and, subsequently, the Danites; God has 'parental' responsibilities, with authority over Solomon and Israel; Eliakim is to be given governmental responsibilities and authority over Jerusalem and the house of Judah. As an אָב, each has special status and each has particular responsibilities to discharge. Could this be what is conveyed through the promise of Abraham's international fatherhood? Is Abraham to be considered a 'father' not in the sense of becoming the physical progenitor of these multitudinous nations, but rather through the special status that he will enjoy in relation to them, and the particular responsibilities that he will discharge to their benefit? At the very least, such an interpretation is feasible, both linguistically and contextually.

It is also possible that attention is deliberately drawn by the compiler(s) to this special sense of Abraham's 'fatherhood'. Interestingly, the vocalization of the noun is quite peculiar to Genesis 17; in the entire MT, this is the only chapter in which אָב is vocalized with a patah. Elsewhere the construct form is consistently rendered אֲבִי.[55] While

---

51. Cf. Gen. 45.8; Judg. 17.10; 18.19; 2 Sam. 7.14; Isa. 22.21; 45.10; Jer. 31.9; Ezek. 44.25; Prov. 30.17; 1 Chron. 17.13; 22.10; 28.6.

52. Cf. Joüon, pp. 473-74, 487-88.

53. Cf. GKC, 119*t*; cf. Gibson's somewhat similar description (*Davidson's Introductory Hebrew Grammar—Syntax*, p. 150) as 'alternative to the obj. complement'. Unfortunately this text is not included in the *DCH* לְ entry; presumably it is understood in the same way as Gen. 17.6 (i.e. 'as' or 'into', IV, p. 481 §3a).

54. Cf. Gen. 45.8; Judg. 17.10; 18.19; 2 Sam. 7.14; Isa. 22.21; Jer. 31.9; 1 Chron. 17.13; 22.10; 28.6.

55. The only other instances are in names compounded with אָב, but even the vast majority of these employ the normal construct form.

some scholars attempt to explain this extraordinary spelling in Genesis 17 simply in terms of the patriarch's renaming,[56] it may in fact reflect a deliberate attempt to underline that Abraham's 'fatherhood' has indeed a somewhat unusual connotation here. Nevertheless, whatever the significance of the vocalization, it is clearly quite legitimate to look for Abraham's multitudinous and international progeny beyond the parameters of his physical descendants. It is at least conceivable that Abraham will be לאב המון גוים not in any physical sense at all, but rather in a metaphorical sense: as their spiritual benefactor, the mediator of God's blessing to them.[57]

Further evidence that this is indeed the case is found by Keil in the fact that even in Genesis 17 the covenant sign of circumcision was not confined to Abraham's physical offspring, but extended to his entire household;[58] that is, 'his son Ishmael and all the slaves born in his house or bought with his money, every male among the men of Abraham's house' (v. 23, NRSV).[59] Such an application of the sign of God's covenant to these other members of Abraham's household suggests that, like Ishmael, they enjoyed some sort of covenantal status; in some sense they too were included within the focus of this particular covenant. Such a concept of covenantal inclusion is implicit also in the incident recorded in Genesis 34; while Jacob's sons had ulterior motives, the success of their ruse clearly depended on a shared understanding that the act of circumcision would form a 'kinship' between the parties involved (cf. vv. 16, 23).

This raises the rather complex issue of Ishmael's status in relation to this covenant. Ishmael, whose covenantal status is deliberately con-

---

56. For example GKC, §96 (p. 282), followed by Wenham (*Genesis 16–50*, p. 15 n. 4c).

57. Sarna, while allowing for the narrow, physical sense, prefers 'a more general application in that a larger segment of humanity looks upon Abraham as its spiritual father' (*Genesis*, p. 124). In a similar vein von Rad concedes that 'the hope of a universal extension of God's salvation beyond the limits of Israel' is reflected here in Gen. 17 (*Genesis*, p. 200). Beecher (*Prophets and the Promise*) is even more categorical; while accepting that nations will descend from Abraham, he insists: 'but his being a father of a multitude of nations is parallel with all the nations being blessed in him, and not with his being the progenitor of numerous descendants' (p. 201 n. 1).

58. 'The Pentateuch', I, p. 226.

59. 'Every male among the men of Abraham's house' is probably an all-embracing catch-phrase, rather than identifying a further group.

trasted with that of Isaac in Gen. 17.20-21, nevertheless receives the covenant sign of circumcision (Gen. 17.23, 26). Yet, if the covenant applied particularly to Isaac (Gen. 17.19, 21), why was Ishmael circumcised, along with all Abraham's household? In view of his circumcision, it is difficult to avoid the implication that Ishmael is as much embraced by the covenant as any other person within Abraham's household, including Isaac. This being so, perhaps the question we should ask is not, 'In what sense was Ishmael excluded from the covenant?' but rather, 'In what sense did this covenant relate uniquely to Isaac?'

The significant feature which is applied exclusively to Isaac is the perpetuity of the covenant. The narrator seems to lay great emphasis on this particular point, employing the rather tautologous phrase זרעך אחריך no less than six times within the pericope,[60] and the apparently redundant חדרתם or לדרתיכם three times.[61] Prior to Genesis 17 the preposition אחרי is used in this relational sense (i.e. referring to posterity) only once; viz. Gen. 9.9 (where again the concept in view is that of a *perpetual* covenant; cf. 9.16). Moreover, the idea of perpetuity looms large in subsequent texts that deploy אחרי in this manner.[62] Perpetuity is also the dominant idea in other texts where לדרתם or לדרתיכם is deployed.[63] This suggests, therefore, that the aspect of this covenant that applied uniquely to Isaac was its perpetuity.

This would also explain the deployment of הקים in association with the establishment of this particular covenant. This eternal covenant will

---

60. In vv. 7 (×2), 8, 9, 10, 19.

61. In vv. 7, 9, and 12.

62. אחרי is deployed in this relational sense in connection with (a) perpetual covenants: Gen. 9.9; 17.7-10, 19; Num. 25.13; 2 Sam. 7.12 ‖ 1 Chron. 17.11; 1 Kgs 15.4; (b) perpetual inheritance of land: Gen. 35.12; 48.4; Deut. 1.8; 1 Chron. 28.8; (c) perpetual ordinances: Exod. 28.43; 29.29; 30.21; (d) perpetual possession of slaves: Lev. 25.46; (e) perpetual well-being: Deut. 4.40; 12.25, 28; Jer. 32.39; (f) perpetual love: Deut. 4.37; 10.15; (g) perpetual witness: Josh. 22.27; (h) perpetual loss: 1 Sam. 24.21; Job 21.21; (i) perpetual punishment: Jer. 32.18; (j) perpetual integrity: Gen. 18.19; Prov. 20.7. The only other occurrence is in 1 Chron. 27.7, where the emphasis is strictly chronological (i.e. Zebadiah took charge after [the death of] Asahel). Cf. also Ps. 109.13.

63. Exod. 12.14, 17, 42; 16.32, 33; 27.21; 29.42; 30.8, 10, 21, 31; 31.13, 16; 40.15; Lev. 3.17; 6.11; 7.36; 10.9; 17.7; 21.17; 22.3; 23.14, 21, 31, 41; 24.3; Num. 9.10; 10.8; 15.14, 15, 21, 23, 38; 18.23; 35.29. See also Gen. 9.12 (which uses לדרת in the same sense).

be set up (i.e. perpetuated) not through Abraham's descendants generally, but through the line of Isaac exclusively. Whereas Ishmael, as
part of Abraham's family, was himself included within the covenant
community, this covenantal status was not explicitly extended to his
progeny, as is clearly so in the case of Isaac (Gen. 17.19). Thus this
eternal covenant was to be perpetuated exclusively through Isaac's
'seed'. It was in and through them (i.e. the special Abrahamic line of
descent, beginning with Isaac) that the promissory aspects of this
covenant would find fulfilment. Therefore, while Ishmael and Isaac
were both included within the parameters of this covenant, Isaac stood
in special relationship to the covenant since it would be perpetuated
exclusively through his זרע.[64]

Nevertheless, the fact that the sign of the covenant was applied to all
Abraham's household, and not restricted to his physical offspring, hints
at the fact that Abraham will fulfil the role of אב to a much wider circle
than those who are his biological descendants. How Abraham will be
transformed into this internationally significant figure is elaborated
upon in vv. 6-8, which focus on Abraham's phenomenal expansion,
royal progeny and special relationship with God.

b. *Phenomenal Expansion*

והפרתי אתך במאד מאד ונתתיך לגוים (v. 6a)

The very fact that the promissory element of expansion is reiterated in
Genesis 17 (cf. vv. 2 and 6) immediately calls attention to its significance for the chapter as a whole.[65] Its climactic location in the opening
promissory statement in vv. 1-2 already suggests its relative importance. This is confirmed by the fact that it constitutes the unifying

64. This special line of Abrahamic descent is further refined as the patriarchal
story unfolds. For example, it is Jacob through whom the special line of Abrahamic
descent will be traced (cf. Gen. 28.3-4, 13-15; 35.9-12). Even though physically
descended from Abraham and Sarah, Esau is excluded from the 'special seed' in
and through whom the divine promises will materialize.

65. Although two different verbs are used, the meaning is substantially the
same: God promises to make Abraham extremely numerous (v. 2). Consequently,
God must make him extremely fertile. The former is a result of the latter. The latter
is a prerequisite for the former. Thus for all practical purposes, they amount to one
and the same promise. This link is further underlined by the fact that the roots are
regularly paired with one another in Genesis (cf. Gen. 1.28; 8.17; 9.1,7) in a
synonymous fashion.

thread that binds together the other promissory clauses in vv. 4-8. Each of the promissory clauses in Genesis 17 relates either directly or indirectly to the prospect of Abraham's progeny: they will incorporate nations (v. 4c-5, 6b); they will include kings (v. 6c); and they will perpetually inherit the covenant blessings of land and a special relationship with God (vv. 7-8).[66] It is reasonable, therefore, to conclude that this promise of phenomenal expansion is the central promissory thrust of the covenant that makes the material in this chapter a unified whole. As Westermann correctly observes, 'the promise of increase runs like a thread through the whole chapter: vv. 2b, 4b, 6a, 16b, 20aβb... It is clear then that the promise of increase has a dominating role in ch. 17.'[67]

The hiphil conjugation is surely significant here, especially given the ages and circumstances of the patriarchal couple.[68] Moreover, the thinly veiled allusion to God's primaeval imperative to humankind, פרו ורבו (Gen. 1.28; cf. 9.1), will not be lost on the careful reader.[69] What Adam and Noah were commanded to do, Abraham will be divinely enabled to do; the creational command here becomes a divine promise. Thus this covenant with Abraham will be 'the means through which God's original blessing would again be channelled to all mankind'.[70]

The next clause, ונתתיך לגוים (v. 6b), appears to elaborate further on the prospect of Abraham's phenomenal expansion.[71] At least two translations are possible for this clause: it is traditionally understood in the sense of 'I will make you into nations', but it could equally be

---

66. Coats perceptively comments, 'the context of the covenant is an oath for descendants. The land enters the picture only as a place for the descendants to dwell' (*Genesis*, p. 134).

67. Westermann, *Genesis 12–36*, pp. 260-61.

68. The implication of Abraham's mental reservations in Gen. 17.17 is surely that both Sarah and he were now incapable of producing children naturally.

69. This allusion to the creation and flood narratives is especially significant in that these stories represent respectively the beginning of and a new beginning in the *Heilsgeschichte*. The covenant with Abraham in Gen. 17 represents a further significant development in the Old Testament story of salvation.

70. J. Sailhamer, 'Genesis', in F.E. Gaebelein (ed.), *The Expositor's Bible Commentary* (12 vols.; Grand Rapids: Zondervan, 1990), II, p. 138.

71. The consecutive waw strongly suggests that the two phrases are closely related. Cf. the disjunctive waw of the following clause.

rendered 'I will give you to/for nations'.[72] Even though the latter reflects the predominant usage in the Hebrew Bible, the fact that a similar clause is employed in v. 20 seems to lend some weight to the traditional interpretation; it is difficult to conceive of Ishmael being 'given to/for a great nation'. Admittedly, the idea of Abraham being 'given to/for nations' (i.e. as their spiritual benefactor) is not nearly so strange in the immediate context, especially if the above interpretation of Abraham's 'fatherhood' of the nations is correct. Nevertheless, it seems improbable that this clause would be deployed in the same pericope with two quite different connotations. Thus this promise would appear to reaffirm that Abraham's descendants will so expand as to become not one nation, but many.

Prior to Genesis 17 the divine promise to Abraham had related to a single nation. According to Gen. 12.2 Yahweh had promised, among other things, to make Abraham into a 'great nation' (ואעשׂך לגוי גדול). Likewise, in Gen. 18.18 Yahweh speaks of a single nation stemming from the patriarch (ואברהם היו יהיה לגוי). Ishmael also is to become the father of a 'great nation' (Gen. 17.20; cf. Gen. 21.13, 18), but there is no anticipation before Genesis 17 that Abraham will expand into anything other than a single nation, albeit one that would be 'great' (Gen. 12.2) and 'innumerable' (Gen. 16.10). Nowhere in the antecedent narrative has there been any hint that more than one nation would trace its ancestry back to the patriarch, but now this intriguing element is incorporated within the promises communicated to both Abraham and Sarah. What is more, the term המון is twice employed in this context with reference to these 'nations' (vv. 4-5), suggesting not only their plurality but also their multiplicity.[73] Such a description is hardly fitting if only the physical descendants of Abraham are in view. The descendants of Ishmael and Isaac might legitimately be described as 'nations',

72. The preposition ל in conjunction with an object suffix on the verb נתן is used in three main ways: (1) to mark an infinitive construct; e.g. Gen. 20.6; Josh. 10.19; Judg. 1.34; 1 Sam. 18.2; 24.8. (2) to mark the indirect object; e.g. Gen. 23.11; 38.26; Num. 18.8; Deut. 26.13; 29.7; Judg. 15.2, 6; 1 Sam. 15.28; 18.4; 28.17; 1 Kgs 8.46; 11.11; 17.23; 2 Kgs 18.16; 22.5; Jer. 27.5; Ezek. 3.17; 12.6; 16.19; 25.10; 28.17; 29.5; 33.7, 27; 39.4; Est. 3.10; 2 Chron. 20.7. (3) to mark the copula (an implicit 'to be'); e.g. Gen. 17.20; 48.4; Isa. 42.6; (49.6); 49.8; Jer. 15.4; 24.9; 29.18; 51.25; Ezek. 5.14; 26.14, 18; 2 Chron. 7.20; 29.8; 30.7; 35.25.

73. The noun המון has the connotation of abundance, with particular emphasis on unrest, turbulence, or noise. So A. Baumann, 'המה *hāmāh*', *TDOT*, III, pp. 414-18; see also W.R. Domeris, 'המה', *NIDOTE*, I, pp. 1041-43.

but to describe them as a 'multitude of nations' would surely constitute a gross exaggeration. Given that this would have been so throughout the time-span reflected in the Hebrew Bible, this is a most interesting element in the Abraham narrative, certainly warranting careful investigation.

This promise relating to nations is surely significant, not only because it introduces a somewhat unexpected aspect into the narrative plot, but also because of the plain contrast it draws between the covenantal status of Abraham's two sons.[74] Since this promissory element is exclusively applied to the patriarchal couple (vv. 4-6, 16) and does not incorporate all Abraham's posterity (vv. 17-21), one may reasonably anticipate its fulfilment exclusively through the promised 'seed'. Indeed, if in Gen. 17.16 the masculine reading is preferred over against the MT's feminine ending,[75] the point is made even more emphatically: these international descendants of Abraham will be traced exclusively through the promised son.

Gen. 21.12 (בְיִצְחָק יִקָּרֵא לְךָ זָרַע) would appear to confirm that Abraham's promised descendants will indeed be traced in a particular sense through Sarah's son. The general sense of this rather enigmatic clause is clear: Abraham's line of promise will be continued exclusively through Isaac. A somewhat similar phrase (וְיִקָּרֵא בָהֶם שְׁמִי) is found in Gen. 48.16, where the idea is that of perpetuating the family name.[76] Gen. 21.12 seems to convey a similar idea; viz. that Isaac will perpetuate the special זָרַע promised to Abraham. This זָרַע has generally been interpreted solely in terms of Israel, Abraham's national descendants through Isaac.[77] In view of Gen. 17.16, however, there is surely no compelling reason to preclude the international expansion so conspicuous in Genesis 17.[78] This is all the more so if it can be

74. Another difference between the promises to Isaac and Ishmael relates to the prospect of land; there is no explicit mention of territory or land in the promise made concerning Ishmael, whereas the covenant with Isaac clearly incorporated this important dimension—as reflected in v. 8.

75. See Section 3 (n. 24) above.

76. It is probably significant that 'in his [Joseph's] career the promises to Abraham of universal blessing to all nations began to see fulfilment' (Wenham, *Genesis 16–50*, p. 493).

77. So, for example, Dillmann, *Genesis*, II, p. 130; Procksch, *Die Genesis*, p. 311; Skinner, *Genesis*, p. 322; Westermann, *Genesis 12–36*, p. 340.

78. While Rendtorff (*The Problem of the Process of Transmission*, p. 79) correctly notes that Gen. 21.12 makes no explicit mention of numerous progeny, he is

demonstrated that the term זרע may sometimes reflect both nuances (i.e. biological and metaphorical).

How is this international dimension of God's promise to be understood? If, as is apparently the case, the promise of international expansion is to find its fulfilment exclusively through the promised line of Isaac, a literal fulfilment (in the sense of physical nations) is ruled out: the Israelites (descended from Jacob) and the Edomites (descended from Esau) hardly constituted a המון גוים. It is at least reasonable, therefore, to allow for a metaphorical sense, in keeping with the above interpretation of Abraham's international fatherhood. Thus, Abraham's multinational descendants should not be restricted to those able to trace their biological lineage to Abraham.

So who are these 'nations' into which Abraham will expand (and for whose benefit Abraham will discharge special responsibilities and for whom Abraham will have special status)? Could Dumbrell be correct in his tentative claim that this text 'has the final company of nations in view'?[79] As well as enjoying the support of apostolic exegesis,[80] this suggestion finds considerable support in the Abraham narrative itself: the climactic promise to Abraham was, after all, that all the families/ nations of the ground/earth would be blessed in him and his 'seed' (cf. Gen. 12.3; 18.18; 22.18).[81] Understood in this light, the 'nations' of Genesis 17 incorporate all those to whom divine blessing is imparted through Abraham's זרע.

In summary, therefore, the central promise in Genesis 17 closely relates to Abraham's phenomenal expansion in a multinational sphere. Abraham will be a 'father' to this international company, not in the sense of being their progenitor, but rather through his special status and the particular responsibilities that he will discharge on their behalf.

---

wrong to imply that such an omission can simply be explained by the contrast in the text between Isaac and Ishmael. Gen. 17 nowhere suggests that the promise of innumerable progeny will be fulfilled via Ishmael. Indeed, if anything, the text suggests the opposite.

79. Dumbrell, *Covenant and Creation*, p. 73. So too Keil, 'The Pentateuch', I, p. 226.

80. For example, Acts 3.25; Rom. 4.16-24; Gal. 3.6-9, 16, 29; cf. Williamson, 'Abraham, Israel and the Church'.

81. Significantly this aspect of the divine promise is interpreted in the New Testament in terms of Abraham's fatherhood of the international community of faith (cf. Rom. 4.16-17).

c. *Royal Descendants*

ומלכים ממך יצאו (v. 6c)

Like the plurality of nations, the promise of royal progeny is another feature that points to a significant difference between the covenantal status of Abraham's two sons, Isaac and Ishmael. Whereas 'kings' would descend from the former, only 'princes' would descend from the latter (cf. Gen. 17.16, 19-21). This subtle distinction accentuates the fact that, while some of the promises made by God to Abraham will be realized in Ishmael,[82] unlike Isaac he is not included in Abraham's royal lineage; the royal progeny of the patriarch will come exclusively through Isaac's descendants. Thus a strong link is established between the special זרע promised to Abraham and these מלכים who will descend from him.

Along with the prospect of multinational descendants, this promise of royal progeny is first explicitly introduced into the Abraham narrative in Genesis 17. Admittedly, it is possible to see kingship already implicit in the promissory aspects relating to nationhood in Gen. 12.2.[83] Nevertheless, as Clements correctly points out:

> although it was normal that, for a people to be constituted as a *goy*, it should have a *melekh* at its head, there is nothing to indicate that this was the only form of government that could lead to such recognition. Israel certainly regarded itself as having formed a *goy* before it possessed a monarchy.[84]

Two additional factors seem to confirm that the promise of royal progeny is indeed a new element in the Abraham narrative: (i) it is not alluded to in Genesis 15, a chapter which (as has been illustrated above) is primarily concerned with the national dimension of the divine promises; (ii) it is explicitly mentioned twice in Genesis 17 (vv. 6, 16), the latter time in connection with Sarah, whose specific absence from

---

82. The other promissory elements extended to Ishmael are divine blessing, fertility and numerical increase, and great nationhood. The fact that there is such a close correspondence between these and those promised to Abraham in Gen. 17.2-6 makes the substitution of 'princes' for 'kings' all the more striking.

83. This is especially true of the promise to make Abraham into a 'great nation' and the related promise of a 'great name'.

84. R.E. Clements, 'גוי *gôy*', *TDOT*, II, p. 428.

the patriarchal promises up until this point is well known, and subsequently in a text (Gen. 35.11) which clearly alludes to the promises made by God to Abraham in Genesis 17.[85]

Gen. 35.11 is especially interesting. Here a subtle distinction is implied between national and multinational descendants: גוי וקהל גוים יהיה ממך (a nation and a company of nations shall come from you).[86] If such a distinction is indeed intended, and this clause incorporates both a national and an international dimension, one must ask, 'To which of these facets does the subsequent promise of royal descendants relate: Abraham's national descendants or his multinational descendants?' In all three Genesis texts that explicitly mention this latter promissory aspect (Gen. 17.6, 16; 35.11), the promise of 'kings' immediately, but disjunctively, follows mention of a plurality of 'nations'. This would suggest that, while Abraham's royal descendants relate in some way to the international community that will spring from the patriarch, the two prospects must not be identified too closely. Moreover, in Gen. 35.11 these 'kings' are explicitly said to come out מחלציך, an expression that can only be understood in some physical sense. This means that these promised 'kings' would be descended directly from Jacob. Thus Genesis 17 and 35 both imply that the royal descendants of Abraham relate to both Abraham's national and his international descendants; this prospect of royal descendants somehow links what appear to be the two major promissory themes within the Abraham narrative: the patriarch's national expansion and the patriarch's international significance. Unfortunately, Genesis 17 does not elaborate on the role of Abraham's royal progeny in relation to either theme. Rather, the promise of royal descendants is disjunctively followed by the promise of specific territory for the patriarch's 'seed after

85. Gen. 35.9-13 contains several echoes of Gen. 17: the use of the divine appellation, El Shaddai; the divinely imposed change of the patriarch's name; the mention of a plurality of nations and royal progeny; promise of land to him and his descendants; a similar introductory and concluding formula for the divine revelation.

86. This distinction is maintained by Alexander, 'Abraham Reassessed', pp. 17-18. Others understand the second phrase as in some way expanding on or qualifying the promise of nationhood; so Sarna, *Genesis*, p. 242; V.P. Hamilton, *The Book of Genesis, Chapters 18–50* (NICOT; Grand Rapids: Eerdmans, 1995), p. 381; Alter, *Genesis*, p. 197.

him' (Gen. 17.7-8). Interestingly the same is true in Genesis 35, where the prospect of royal progeny is immediately followed by the promise of specific territory for Jacob's 'seed after him' (Gen. 35.12). The text sheds no further light on the royal progeny; nothing more is said about these kings or the precise nature of their role in the fulfilment of the patriarchal promises.

There is, however, at least one text elsewhere in the Hebrew Bible that appears to bring both aspects together; viz. Psalm 72. This 'royal psalm' envisages, among other things, a monarch 'in whom all the nations will be blessed/bless themselves' (v. 17), a clear allusion to Yahweh's promise to Abraham (Gen. 12.3; 22.18; cf. 26.4). The grandiose nature of this monarch's reign depicted throughout the psalm suggests that the king in question will far surpass anything accomplished under the reign of Solomon, with whom the title associates this poem. The ideal Davidic ruler about whom this psalm speaks will achieve universal dominion and establish international שלום (cf. vv. 4-14). What is especially interesting for our present discussion is the way in which Ps. 72.17 links the international dimension of the patriarchal promise with the role of this ideal Davidic king. This royal figure is clearly depicted as the mediator of the Abrahamic blessing; the role formerly associated with Abraham is assumed by the author of Ps. 72.17 to have been inherited by this Davidic king. As Anderson correctly observes:

> This verse seems to be an allusion to Yahweh's promise to Abraham (Gen 12.2f., 22.18), and the intention may have been to stress the fact that the divine promise to the patriarch has been fulfilled in the house of David.[87]

Commenting on Ps. 72.17 Blaising is much more categorical:

> This is the language of the Abrahamic covenant. The descendants of Abraham have been restructured politically so that the function of mediating blessing rests chiefly with the king. It is through him and his rule that the Abrahamic covenant promise to bless all nations will be fulfilled.[88]

---

87. A.A. Anderson, *Psalms 1–72* (NCBC; London: Marshall, Morgan & Scott, 1972), p. 526; cf. Clements, *Abraham and David*, p. 59.

88. C.A. Blaising and D.L. Bock, *Progressive Dispensationalism* (Wheaton: Victor, 1993), p. 168. See also R.A. Pyne, 'The "Seed", the Spirit, and the Blessing of Abraham', *BSac* 152 (1995), pp. 211-22 (213).

A further interesting observation is made by Alexander:

> The similarity between Genesis 22.18a and Psalm 72.17b is striking and
> supports the idea that the 'seed' mentioned in Genesis 22.17b-18a does
> not refer to all Abraham's descendants, but rather to a single individual.
> While Genesis 22 does not directly indicate that this 'seed' will be of
> royal standing, it is noteworthy that Genesis 17 anticipates that kings
> will come from Abraham and Sarah through Isaac (Gn. 17.6, 16).[89]

Thus Ps. 72.17 provides at least one insight into how the national and
international dimensions of the patriarchal promises may be linked by
the theme of Abraham's royal progeny. Through one of Abraham's
royal progeny, the blessing of Abraham will be mediated to the nations
mentioned in Gen. 17.4-6, 16 and Gen. 35.11.

In Genesis 17, however, the promise of royal progeny seems to be
augmented by the promise of a perpetual covenant (incorporating the
prospect of both a divine–human relationship and territorial inheritance) between God and Abraham's זרע.[90] Thus a further link is established between Abraham's royal progeny and the 'special seed' with
whom the covenant will be perpetuated.[91] Somehow these two promissory aspects are interrelated. So the question naturally arises: What is
the precise relationship between Abraham's 'special seed' and his royal
progeny, and what light is thrown on this by what is apparently the
climactic promise of these verses (vv. 4-8), the promise of an abiding
relationship? It is to the latter issue that we turn our attention first.

d. *Abiding Relationship*

והקמתי את־בריתי ביני ובינך ובין זרעך אחריך לדרתם לברית עולם
להיות לך לאלהים ולזרעך אחריך: ונתתי לך ולזרעך אחריך את
ארץ מגריך את כל־ארץ כנען לאחזת עולם והייתי להם לאלהים:

(vv. 7a-8b)

As with the promises relating to Abraham's international significance
and royal progeny, the prospect of an abiding relationship is something
that is noticeably absent in Genesis 15. In the latter chapter such a
relationship between God and Abraham may be implicit, but it is

---

89. Alexander, 'Further Observations', pp. 365-66.

90. Gen. 17.7 appears to continue on from what is said in the previous verse
with a waw consecutive; it is certainly not so sharp a division as that reflected in
Gen. 35.12.

91. See discussion at the beginning of this section.

certainly nowhere made explicit, and no promise is extended to Abraham's descendants other than the prospect of inheriting the land. Thus
the concept of a special divine–human relationship, a relationship that
will be maintained not only with Abraham himself, but also with his
posterity, appears to be introduced into the Abraham narrative for the
first time in Gen. 17.7.[92] Moreover, the fact that it is linked directly to a
covenant yet to be 'established' (hiphil waw consecutive perfect of the
verb, קוּם) is of particular significance. As in Gen. 17.2, the covenant
explicitly referred to in v. 7 is something that has not yet been ratified.

In contrast with v. 2, however, the emphasis initially appears to be
quite different: this verse (v. 7) speaks neither of phenomenal expansion nor international significance, but rather of a divine–human relationship: 'I will establish my covenant as an everlasting covenant
between me, you and future generations of your descendants, to be your
and your future descendants' God' (my translation).

However, the emphasis placed on Abraham's זֶרַע, underlined by the
recurring phrase וּלְזַרְעֲךָ אַחֲרֶיךָ (cf. vv. 7-8), suggests that it is to this
aspect that the writer is especially drawing our attention. Apparently
the significant point to grasp in relation to these two verses is that
Abraham's covenant status is being transmitted to his זֶרַע. The latter
will enjoy the same special divine–human relationship experienced by
Abraham, and consequently, they will also retain permanently the same
territorial inheritance.

This latter promissory aspect is of particular interest, because it
appears to reflect an important dimension of the covenant ratified in
Genesis 15. The promise of land, so prominent in the covenant of
Genesis 15, is only briefly mentioned in Genesis 17 (v. 8a), with
attention being drawn both to its geographical extent (כָּל־אֶרֶץ כְּנַעַן)
and its permanent possession (לַאֲחֻזַּת עוֹלָם). Admittedly, as Hamilton
acknowledges,[93] the thought in Gen. 13.15 is not fundamentally dis-
similar. However, the following observation of Sailhamer is pertinent:

> The focus of verses 7 and 8 lies in the repetition of the term *everlasting*.
> The covenant promised is an 'everlasting covenant' (v. 7a) and the
> possession of the land an 'everlasting possession' (v. 8). The promises
> contained in these verses are not given here for the first time (cf. 13.14-
> 15; 15.18-21), but the everlasting nature of the covenant—that which is

92. Cf. von Rad, *Genesis*, p. 200.
93. *Genesis 1–17*, p. 466 n. 19.

to assure the fulfilment of the promises—is new... when the covenant
was granted in chapter 15, there was no mention of its being 'eternal'.[94]

While nothing in Genesis 15 suggests that such a status pertained to the
covenant ratified there, it must be acknowledged that the term 'eternal'
was used earlier in the Abraham narrative (Gen. 13.15) in connection
with the gift of land. Even so, here in Gen. 17.7 it is used of the
covenant itself; the covenant, and by implication, the special relationship established by it, is said to be 'everlasting'. Thus it would appear
that this is another feature which is expressly applied to the actual
covenant between God and Abraham (and not simply to a promissory
element of it) for the first time in Genesis 17.

The connection that is made in v. 8 between this promise of land and
the prospect of a divine–human relationship is of particular importance.
This is the first time that a link between the promise of land and the
prospect of a divine–human relationship is made explicit. Moreover, the
symmetry discernible in vv. 7-8 suggests that it is the relationship
factor which binds these two promises (i.e. an 'everlasting covenant'
and an 'everlasting inheritance') together:

A   Promise to Abraham and all his descendants (v. 7a)
B   of an everlasting covenant (v. 7b)
C   forging a special relationship (v. 7c)
A' Promise to Abraham and all his descendants (v. 8a)
B'   of an everlasting inheritance (v. 8b)
C'   forging a special relationship (v. 8c)

Plainly the prospect of a special relationship is the climactic element
of each of the divine promises reflected in these verses. It would seem,
therefore, that the promise of land is subsumed in Genesis 17 by the
promise of a divine–human relationship. The former (everlasting possession of land) is an aspect of the latter (divine–human relationship).
The perpetual possession of the land serves as a tangible expression of
the enduring nature of the divine–human relationship. Thus, while
mentioned in Genesis 17, the promise of land is clearly not the central
focus in this pericope. The main emphasis, certainly in vv. 7-8, is on the
establishment of an enduring relationship between God and Abraham's
זרע.

As with the promise of 'kings', the two promissory elements reflected
in Gen. 17.7-8 are noticeably absent in the promises applied in v. 20 to

94. Sailhamer, *The Pentateuch as Narrative*, p. 158.

Ishmael. Significantly, it is the eternal and perpetual dimension of the covenant that is stressed in relation to Isaac (v. 19). It would follow from these observations that the perpetual aspects of the covenant referred to in vv. 19-20 belong exclusively to Abraham's זרע through the promised line of Isaac.

From the above discussion, then, it is clear that certain promises in this pericope (Gen. 17) apply solely to Abraham's זרע through Isaac: the promise of international significance; the promise of kings; the promise of a special divine–human relationship; and the promise of a permanent inheritance. The precise connection between these four promissory aspects, however, has yet to be established. This brings us back to the clear disjunction in v. 6 noted previously.[95] It is clear that this syntactical break is deliberate, given that it is found in each of the three texts explicitly holding out the prospect of a royal progeny.[96] It is imperative, therefore, to examine why this promissory element has been isolated from the preceding aspects and to investigate its precise relationship with what follows in Gen. 17.7-8.

There are thus at least three identifiable groups in Gen. 17.4-8: Abraham's multitudinous nations (vv. 4-6b); Abraham's royal progeny (v. 6c); and Abraham's physical seed (vv. 7-8). What is the relationship between these groups? How are Abraham's multitudinous nations, his royal progeny, and his 'seed after him' all linked?

Since it is clear that both the royal progeny and the 'seed after him' are physically related to Abraham through Isaac (and subsequently Jacob; cf. Gen. 35.11), it is logical to deduce that the former (royal seed) is a further refinement of the latter (the physical descendants of Abraham through Isaac and Jacob). Thus understood, the narrator sharpens the focus in Genesis 17 to a royal line of Abraham's 'seed' with whom God will perpetuate this eternal covenant.[97] Abraham's phenomenal expansion will result from the ברית עולם that will be established (i.e. perpetuated) between God and Abraham's royal 'seed'. As a result of this covenant a special and perpetual relationship between God and Abraham's royal 'seed' will be maintained (vv. 6-7), and

---

95. See Section 3a above.

96. Gen. 17.6, 16 and 35.11.

97. This would also account for the fact that there is no disjunction between the promise of royal progeny in v. 6c and the promises relating to Abraham's 'seed after him' in vv. 7-8.

through this royal 'seed' the promise of Abraham being לאב המון גוים (i.e. their spiritual benefactor) will be fulfilled.

4. *The Obligatory Aspects of this Covenant*

More significant than the differences in promissory foci between Genesis 15 and 17 is the different status that the writer ascribes to these two covenants. The prospects encapsulated within the covenant spoken of in Genesis 17 are not presented simply as unconditional promises of the deity, but rather as divine promises which are related to and are contingent upon a human response. The conditional nature of this particular covenant is emphasized throughout the pericope: the provisional promise with which the divine speech opens in vv. 1-2;[98] the deliberate comparison between what God will do and what Abraham and his descendants must do in vv. 4-14; the emphasis on the importance of submitting to the rite of circumcision for inclusion within the covenant (vv. 10, 14); the emphatic account of Abraham's spontaneous and total compliance with the divine instruction with which the pericope is brought to a conclusion (vv. 23-27). Therefore, unlike the covenant depicted in Genesis 15, that spoken of in Genesis 17 is patently conditional.

An explicit connection is made in Genesis 17 between the covenant announced and two distinctive human obligations, one ethical (the moral responsibility to 'walk before God and be blameless', v. 1) and the other ritual (the physical act of circumcision, vv. 9-14). Without the former, the covenant cannot be established; without the latter, the benefits of the covenant cannot be enjoyed. Each obligation and its covenantal significance must be examined carefully in order to determine how these obligations are related to one another.

a. *The Ethical Obligation: Moral Blamelessness*
The ethical obligation has two interrelated aspects, loyal service (התהלך לפני) and blameless behaviour (והיה תמים). It is interesting that the same terminology is used in the description of Noah in Gen. 6.9. This is possibly significant, in that this description is recorded prior to the ratification of the divine covenant with Noah and his seed (cf. Gen. 9.9), who are in some sense representative of all creation (cf. vv. 10-16). Is Abraham, therefore, being required to meet the same divine

98. Cf. Section 2 n. 6 above; also Chapter 3 Section 3b n. 75.

prerequisite for a special relationship with God; viz. a blameless walk before God? The idiom of 'walking before someone' primarily suggests the idea of loyalty and devotion.[99] Helfmeyer's suggestion that the expression is used by the JE sources (and in certain Psalms) in an altogether different theological sense (i.e. 'as the experience of God's benevolent presence') is less than convincing.[100] As well as failing to demonstrate that the phrase carries such a benevolent connotation, Helfmeyer provides no evidence for excluding the connotation of ethical and religious integrity in the texts which he cites.[101] Furthermore, as Helfmeyer's own examination of the general usage of this phrase illustrates, the primary connotation of 'walking before someone' is loyal devotion, such as that of a subject to his king.[102]

The second part of this imperative, והיה תמים, seems to enlarge on the first.[103] This is how God expects Abraham to express his loyal devotion; Abraham is to 'be whole (complete)'.[104] Contrary to Westermann's assertion,[105] however, תמים does seem to have clear cultic associations in the Hebrew Bible,[106] an association which may serve to

99. See nn. 102 and 109 below. Whereas von Rad (*Genesis*, p. 126) discerns a difference in nuance reflected in the preposition used in association with הלך, Wenham's assertion (*Genesis 16–50*, p. 20) that 'it is doubtful whether the different preposition [i.e. ב or לפני; cf. 5.22, 24; 6.9; 24.40; 48.15] makes much difference' has more to commend it; the prepositions do seem to be deployed interchangeably.

100. F.J. Helfmeyer, 'הלך *hālakh*', *TDOT*, III, p. 403.

101. *TDOT*, III, p. 403. Helfmeyer cites Gen. 24.40 (J); 48.15 (E); Pss. 56.14; 116.9.

102. Hamilton (*Genesis 1–17*, p. 461) selects the following texts as illustrations of this particular nuance: 1 Kgs 1.2; 10.8; Jer. 52.12 (expressing loyalty to human kings); and Gen. 5.22, 24; 6.9; 24.40; 48.15; Deut. 10.8; 18.7; Judg. 20.28; Ezek. 44.15 (expressing loyalty to the divine king). Cf. n. 109 below.

103. On the analogy with Gen. 12.2d it is preferable to retain the imperative mood rather than translating as a consequence from the first imperative; cf. Chapter 7 Section 3a below.

104. So Westermann, who maintains that neither Luther's 'be pious' nor contemporary translators' 'be without fault' accurately translates the term תמים (*Genesis 12–36*, p. 259).

105. Westermann asserts that the Hebrew word 'has neither moral nor religious echo, but is consciously secular' (*Genesis 12–36*, p. 259). However, as Sheriffs (*The Friendship of the Lord*, p. 39) observes, 'why this has no moral resonance is unexplained'. The same is true in relation to the cultic nuance ruled out by Westermann.

106. The cultic connection is suggested by the fact that the term is employed

link the ethical and the ritual imperatives in this particular pericope.[107]
Thus Wenham suggests:

> the rite of circumcision...is the sign of the covenant, which reminds its
> possessor of his obligation to walk before God and be perfect.
> Submission to it expresses submission to God and humility before him...
> the rite itself expressed faith and obedience to God.[108]

Whatever the precise nature of the relationship between circumcision
and the injunction of Gen. 17.1, it is clear from the semantic parallels in
extra-biblical ancient Near Eastern treaties that Abraham is here being
enjoined to offer unswerving loyalty in royal service.[109] As Sarna suggests, the biblical nuance means (in practical terms) 'to condition the
entire range of human experience by the awareness of His [God's] presence and in response to His demands'.[110]

It would seem, therefore, as is implicit in the allusions to Noah noted
above, that the ethical obligation imposed here upon Abraham should
be understood as the moral prerequisite for a divine–human relationship. Abraham is expected to emulate Noah's ethical perfection, prior
to the perpetual covenant that God would make with him and with his
'seed'. On such a prerequisite the establishment of God's eternal covenant with Abraham and his 'seed' was dependent.

b. *The Ritual Obligation: Physical Circumcision*

Circumcision is presented in Genesis 17 as mandatory for inclusion
within the covenant (vv. 10, 14). Its function seems to have been at
least threefold: it was the אות of the promised covenant between God

---

most frequently to describe blemish-free sacrificial animals; for this reason the
following scholars plausibly suggest a cultic allusion in Gen. 17.1 also: Wenham,
Genesis 1–15, p. 170; Hamilton, *Genesis 1–17*, p. 461; Janzen, *Genesis 12–50*,
p. 48.

107. Rabbinic tradition (*Gen. R.* 46.1) connects the term תמים with the following
law of circumcision.

108. Wenham, *Genesis 16–50*, p. 31. Cf. also Stek, '"Covenant" Overload',
p. 30.

109. So Sarna (*Genesis*, p. 123), who notes that the corresponding Akkadian
phrase *ina maḫrīya ittallak* seems to have been a technical term for absolute loyalty
to a king. Cf. Sheriffs (*The Friendship of the Lord*, pp. 43-45), who likewise
observes the analogous concept of 'walking properly before the deity' in several
Akkadian texts.

110. Sarna, *Genesis*, p. 123.

and the family of Abraham (v. 11); it was the medium for perpetuating the covenant from one generation of Abraham's descendants to the next (vv. 10-12a); it was the method of incorporating within the covenant others who were not physically related to Abraham at all (vv. 12b-13). All three functions warrant comment.

1. *Circumcision as the 'Sign' of the Covenant.* Circumcision is explicitly said in Gen. 17.11 to be instituted 'as a/the sign of a/the covenant' (לאת ברית).[111] In precisely what sense is the term אות applied to the rite of circumcision? In order to establish this, the use and meaning of this term elsewhere in the Hebrew Bible must first be explored.

Following McCullough's broad definition of אות as 'a mark, symbol, or portent, serving to convey a particular idea or meaning',[112] Fox identifies three main categories of אות: (1) proof signs, (2) symbol signs, and (3) cognition signs (subdivided into identity signs and mnemonic signs).[113] Fox's analysis is clearly embraced by Wenham, who likewise states that

> there are three kinds of signs (אות) in the OT. First, proof signs that convince the observer about something... Second, certain acts, e.g., acted prophecies, are signs in that they resemble the situation announced (e.g., Ezek 4.3). Third, certain signs are mnemonic in that they are reminders of something.[114]

Helfmeyer's categorization is not essentially different,[115] even though it is a little more nuanced; for example, he identifies three different types of 'proof signs': epistemic, faith and confirmation, and he treats 'covenant signs' as a special category of 'mnemonic signs'. Thus Fox's threefold categorization of the term אות in the Hebrew Bible seems to provide a generally acceptable framework from which to establish the connotation of the term in Genesis 17.

The context in Genesis 17 seems to rule out the thought of a con-

---

111. Most translations make both 'sign' and 'covenant' definite. Wenham inexplicably renders Gen. 9.13 'a sign of the covenant' and exactly the same clause in Gen. 17.11 'a sign of a covenant'. Grammatically the latter is quite correct, although in the present context the former ('a/the sign of the covenant') is perhaps the more appropriate.

112. W.S. McCullough, 'Sign in the OT', *IDB*, IV, p. 345.

113. Fox, 'The Sign of the Covenant', p. 562.

114. Wenham, *Genesis 16–50*, p. 23.

115. F.J. Helfmeyer, 'אות *'ôth'*, *TDOT*, I, pp. 167-88.

vincing proof; the sign of circumcision does not prove anything in Genesis 17. No more suitable in this pericope is the idea of a symbol sign, for according to both Fox and Helfmeyer, symbol signs are customarily followed by an appropriate interpretation, and such is notably absent in Genesis 17. However, the third of Fox's categories, cognition signs, is eminently suitable in the context of Genesis 17, for circumcision may be seen to function here either as an identity mark or else as a mnemonic device.

A major objection to the former, however, is that circumcision was not a particularly useful identity sign (at least, as far as non-Israelites were concerned). Its inadequacy as a mark of identity is suggested not only by the fact that circumcision would have gone unnoticed by others, but also by the observation that it did not distinguish the Israelites from all their neighbours, many of whom likewise practised circumcision. Hamilton appositely comments, 'Circumcision does not identify Israelites *qua* Israelites to non-Israelites, for many non-Israelites already practised the same rite... Also, how would one identify an Israelite via circumcision when clothing concealed it?'[116] Moreover, as Fox correctly observes (contra Gunkel), 'there is no point in referring the custom to a time when people went naked, for that custom is certainly not relevant for P, and even in earliest times Israelites did not go naked'.[117]

Nevertheless, while circumcision was inappropriate as a sign to outsiders, a cognitive function as a reminder of covenantal status cannot be eliminated. Indeed, circumcision is altogether appropriate as a mnemonic device for the benefit of the one circumcised, designed to renew cognizance in him. Thus every time he looks at his body he is reminded of the promissory and obligatory aspects of this particular covenant between God and Abraham.

For whom, therefore, we must ask, did circumcision serve as such a mnemonic device? Was its function to remind Abraham and his descendants (cf. the Sabbath of the Mosaic/Sinaitic covenant) of the covenant promises—especially 'seed'—and obligations? Or was it a 'sign' for God (cf. the rainbow of the Noahic covenant), who will see the circumcised penis of the Israelite at the time of sexual intercourse and then 'remember' his promise of a 'seed' through whom his blessing would come?[118]

---

116. Hamilton, *Genesis 1–17*, p. 470.
117. Fox, 'The Sign of the Covenant', p. 595.
118. H. Eilberg-Schwartz (*The Savage in Judaism: An Anthropology of Israelite*

On the premise that 'this covenant requires nothing of Israel other than circumcision', it is Fox's contention that 'we cannot suppose that it [the sign of circumcision] is a reminder to the Israelites to fulfill some duty'.[119] From this, and on the basis of suggested parallels between Genesis 17 and the Noahic covenant,[120] Fox concludes that circumcision, like the rainbow in Genesis 9, functions as a reminder to God, not humankind. However, while parallels between Genesis 17 and the Noahic covenant are undeniable,[121] the following objections raised by Wenham cast serious doubt over the validity of Fox's interpretation.

Fox overlooks at least one obvious difference: unlike the rainbow, circumcision is not explicitly said to remind God of his promises. Moreover, as Wenham astutely observes:

> though the covenant with Abraham does have many parallels with that made with Noah, in other respects circumcision is much closer to the other cultic obligations placed on Israel, such as passover and the sabbath, which clearly were intended *to remind Israel of its status* as the Lord's people and their *obligations* to keep the law.[122]

However, the most serious difficulty with Fox's argument relates to his assertion that

> this covenant requires nothing of Israel other than circumcision, and circumcision cannot be a reminder of itself. If the purpose of circumcision is to remind man to perform some action, the reader could have no idea what is meant, since nothing of the sort is hinted at in this chapter.[123]

This is clearly not the case, however; Fox has inexplicably ignored the duties imposed upon Abraham with which the pericope begins (v. 1b), obligations which, as has been demonstrated above,[124] were prerequi-

---

Religion and Ancient Judaism [Bloomington: Indiana University Press, 1990]) makes the interesting suggestion that as a symbol (אות) of the covenant circumcision was not arbitrarily chosen, but 'symbolised the fertility of the initiate as well as his entrance into and ability to perpetuate a lineage of male descendants' (p. 143); cf. E.C. McAfee, 'The Patriarch's Longed-For Son: Biological and Social Reproduction in Ugaritic and Hebrew Epic' (PhD thesis, Harvard University, Cambridge, MA, 1996), pp. 259-62.

119. Fox, 'The Sign of the Covenant', p. 595.
120. Fox, 'The Sign of the Covenant', pp. 569-85.
121. Cf. Table 7.1, below.
122. Wenham, *Genesis 16–50*, p. 24 (emphasis mine).
123. Fox, 'The Sign of the Covenant', pp. 595-96.
124. Cf. discussion at the beginning of Section 4.

sites for the establishment of this covenant (and by implication, for the fulfilment of the promises enshrined within it). Thus (contra Fox) circumcision could well have the purpose of reminding the covenant community of their intrinsic duty to lead a blameless life before God.[125] Indeed, this connection between the covenant sign of circumcision and the covenant obligation of an irreproachable lifestyle is reinforced, as Wenham tentatively suggests, by the fact that such a link 'may well have prompted prophetic criticism of Israelites as uncircumcised in heart and ears'.[126] If this is granted, then circumcision served to remind Israel not only of God's covenant promises, but also of their covenant obligations; viz. to walk blamelessly with God.[127]

However, while the אות of circumcision was primarily manward, a Godward aspect cannot be altogether excluded. As Wenham wisely acknowledges, 'This [i.e. the manward function of the sign of circumcision] does not exclude the notion that circumcision may also have reminded God of his promises'.[128] While emphasizing this Godward aspect, however, Fox appears to have overstated his case. For Fox, it is the impropriety of spelling out this Godward aspect that alone explains the absence here in Genesis 17 of any explicit explanation for the function and purpose of this cognitive sign.[129] The strength of Fox's argument is recognized by Hamilton, who admits that 'in other instances where a sign is given to the Israelites, the function or purpose of that sign is also given'.[130] The fatal flaw in Fox's interpretation, however, is

125. As E.B. Smick ('מוּל *mûl*', *TWOT*, I, p. 494) observes, 'To those in the OT who took its meaning seriously, it was the mark of submission to the sovereign will of God'.

126. Wenham, *Genesis 16–50*, p. 24. Wenham cites Jer. 6.10 and Jer. 9.24-25 as prophetic texts in which such a connection is implicit.

127. As R.W. Klein ('The Message of P', in J. Jeremias and L. Perlitt [eds.], *Die Botschaft und die Boten* [Festschrift H.W. Wolff; Neukirchen–Vluyn: Neukirchener Verlag, 1981], p. 64) concludes, 'Prompt circumcision is part of Abraham's perfect obedience'. Klein further observes (pp. 64-65) that when such signs 'serve a cognitive function for God, deliverance is the result (pascal blood/rainbow). When they serve a cognitive function for Israel, obedience is the result (Sabbath, fringe, altar covering, Aaron's rod, circumcision).'

128. Wenham, *Genesis 16–50*, p. 24. So too Klein, 'The Message of P', pp. 64-65.

129. Fox, 'The Sign of the Covenant', p. 595.

130. Hamilton, *Genesis 1–17*, p. 471. Hamilton cites the following illustrations: The Feast of Unleavened Bread (Exod. 13.3-10); the consecration of the firstborn

that 'it is unable to explain why the kareth ("cut off") penalty is invoked (v. 14) for failure to circumcise. If the sign is solely for God, why is the ultimatum for man?'[131] An exclusively Godward sign is thus apparently ruled out. However, in that this sign was a reminder of the promises and not just the obligations enshrined in this covenant, and given the inexplicable absence of an explanation of the function and purpose of this sign if it were exclusively intended for the human party's benefit, it would seem that the sign of circumcision was bi-directional. It reminded both God and the Abrahamic community of the promises and the obligations of this particular covenant. Thus the rite of circumcision had a mnemonic purpose,[132] serving as a physical reminder of the covenant reality into which one had entered.

2. *Circumcision as the Means of Perpetuating the Covenant to Future Generations.* The rite of circumcision, like the covenant for which it was a mnemonic sign, was not confined to Abraham's time. Not only was it a permanent sign for the individual; it was also a perpetual sign for the generations that followed. Both the permanency of the sign and the continuity of its practice underlined the eternal nature of this covenant.

The preponderance of second person plural forms and the references to 'your future descendants' (זרעך אחריך) and 'throughout your/their generations' in this section (Gen. 17.9-14) serve to emphasize that 'the prescriptions covered in these verses are to become legally incumbent upon all generations. God is speaking to those who are not yet born.'[133] Unlike Genesis 15, in which promises made to Abraham individually were solemnly ratified by the covenant, the covenant announced in Genesis 17 extends God's promises to Abraham's future descendants. Thus the rite of circumcision transfers the divine promises to succeeding generations, and so perpetuates the eternal covenant spoken of in Genesis 17.

However, it is not only the promises that are transferred to succeeding generations of Abraham's 'seed', but also the obligations of the

(Exod. 13.1-16); the Sabbath (Exod. 31.12-17); the bronze censers for the altar (Exod. 17.1-5); Aaron's rod (Exod. 16.25); the placing of the phylacteries (Deut. 6.8; 11.18); the monument of stones (Josh. 4.1-24).
    131. Hamilton, *Genesis 1–17*, p. 471.
    132. As cogently argued by Fox, 'The Sign of the Covenant', pp. 557-96.
    133. Hamilton, *Genesis 1–17*, p. 468.

covenant. This is reflected in the severe penalty imposed for non-circumcision (17.14). Failure to conform to this ritual requirement was considered a breach of the covenant, resulting in the offending party being 'cut off from his people'. Whether understood in terms of human or divine judgment, the כרת penalty underlines the seriousness with which Abraham's 'seed' were to take this covenant obligation.

While it is nowhere explicitly stated in Genesis 17, it is apparent from Gen. 18.18-19 that the ethical obligations of this covenant were likewise transferred to succeeding generations. Significantly, in the context of God's judgment on the city-states of Sodom and Gomorrah, Abraham is reminded of God's promise that 'in him all the nations of the earth will be blessed'. This will be realized, according to v. 19, by means of Abraham's progeny keeping (שׁמר) 'the way of Yahweh by doing what is right and just'. As Hamilton correctly observes, 'Implicit in this charge is the fidelity of Abraham and his offspring in meeting their covenant responsibilities. To that end, Gen 18.19 is much like 17.1, 9-14 before it, and 22.15-18; 26.2-5 after it.'[134] Thus while the duty of circumcision is the only obligation placed explicitly on Abraham's descendants in Gen. 17.11, it is clear from Gen. 18.19 that more than a physical ritual was required. Rather, not only Abraham himself, but his progeny also were under obligation to meet the requirement of Gen. 17.1, an obligation which was symbolized in the act of physical circumcision.[135]

3. *Circumcision as the Means of Extending the Covenant to Others.* In the context of a covenant which is specifically related to Isaac and his descendants after him, this is by far the most significant function of circumcision. Clearly this covenant cannot be viewed in an exclusively nationalistic sense. Rather than envisaging the inclusion of just one nation, the covenant in Genesis 17 encompasses those from other nations also. It is not just the physical descendants of Abraham who will be incorporated within this covenant, but all to whom the sign of the covenant is applied. Thus the multitudinous numbers envisaged in Gen. 17.2 will include more than Abraham's physical descendants; the numerical increase will apparently come about through all who will align themselves with Abraham by submitting to the conditions of the

---

134. Hamilton, *Genesis 18–50*, p. 19.
135. Cf. n. 124 above.

covenant, primarily expressed through circumcision. While the application of circumcision to the Hivites (Gen. 34) was a deceitful ploy, this incident illustrates (cf. vv. 16, 23), nevertheless, that circumcision was a mechanism through which non-Israelites could become part of the covenant community.[136]

It is clear from Gen. 18.19 that the same obligations applied to non-biological members of the covenant community (i.e. those who were not physically related to Abraham). Not only Abraham's 'children', but his entire 'household' (presumably including those 'bought with [your] money [from a foreigner]', Gen. 17.12-13), were to fulfil these covenant responsibilities. Thus by receiving the covenant sign of circumcision non-Israelites were obligating themselves to the covenant responsibility of irreproachable behaviour.

5. *The Anomalies and their Resolution*

If it is granted that Genesis 17 introduces a second covenant into the Abrahamic narrative, a conditional covenant involving an irreproachable lifestyle symbolized by the physical sign of circumcision, a number of important questions remain to be answered: At what stage and by what means was this second covenant between God and Abraham actually established?[137] What is the precise relationship between the rite of circumcision and the ratification of the covenant (vv. 10-11, 13)? If this particular covenant is in fact conditional, in what sense can it be described as 'everlasting'?

a. *The Connection between the Rite of Circumcision and Covenant Ratification*
In v. 13b, in which God speaks of 'my covenant in your flesh', the rite of circumcision is almost equated with the concept of the covenant. This close identification between covenant and circumcision is also a logical inference from the statement recorded in v. 10, 'This is my

---

136. Contra Hamilton (*Genesis 18–50*, p. 363), for whom circumcision here has nothing to do with the emphasis of Gen. 17, but has rather 'the primitive significance of initiation into marriage and into the communal life of a tribe'. While the latter may indeed be true (and is presumably how the Hivites understood the requirement), it does not exclude an allusion to Gen. 17. For the latter, see Wenham, *Genesis 16–50*, p. 308.

137. The question of when this covenant was established is discussed in detail in the following chapter of this book.

covenant which you must keep... you must all be circumcised'. Nevertheless, the text falls short of defining circumcision as the covenant itself. Rather, 'careful examination...demonstrates that the biblical sources note the rite as a means, *i.e.*, a token or sign marking the Covenant but they do not define circumcision as the Covenant itself'.[138]

As Hamilton plausibly infers, 'The designation of circumcision itself as a covenant is a synecdoche for covenantal obligation: "this is [the aspect of] my covenant you must keep"'.[139] Thus 'keeping' God's covenant (vv. 9-10) and submitting to the rite of circumcision were entirely synonymous. In order, therefore, to appreciate fully the relationship between the rite of circumcision and the establishing of this particular covenant, the meaning of 'keeping' the covenant (vv. 9-10) must first be ascertained.

For Hartley 'the basic idea of the root שמר is "to exercise great care over"'.[140] He goes on to note several semantic nuances:[141] in combination with other verbs שמר conveys the idea of 'doing something carefully or diligently'; frequently the connotation is of meticulous observation (i.e. implementation) of 'the obligations of a covenant, of laws, of statutes'; a third sense is 'to take care of' in the sense of guarding or protecting; a fourth nuance is 'showing respect for' or 'paying attention to' something or someone; and a fifth is 'safeguarding or storing up'. In what sense, we must therefore ask, is the verb used here in Gen. 17.9-10? Given the non-appearance of another finite verb the emphatic connotation appears to be ruled out. The absence of any explicit threat to the covenant in the immediate context militates against both the idea of 'protecting' and the idea of 'safeguarding' the covenant. Thus the context of this pericope, and especially the fact that it is God's ברית which is to be 'kept' in each verse, suggests that here שמר conveys either the idea of observing (i.e. implementing) the obligation(s) of the covenant, or else the closely related connotation of showing respect for the covenant (which, for all practical purposes, amounts to the same thing). In either case, therefore, to 'keep' God's covenant is to submit to its inherent obligation(s). Now given that in vv. 9-14 the only obligation explicitly mentioned, and repeatedly underlined, is that of

---

138. S.B. Hoenig, 'Circumcision: The Covenant of Abraham', *JQR* 53 (1962–63), pp. 322-34 (322).

139. Hamilton, *Genesis 1–17*, p. 470 (brackets his).

140. J.E. Hartley, 'שמר (shāmar)', *TWOT*, II, p. 939.

141. *TWOT*, II, pp. 939, 940.

physical circumcision, there can be little doubt that the compiler of Genesis 17 is presenting this rite as a most basic obligatory element of this particular covenant. Thus submission to the terms of the covenant was signified through the physical rite of circumcision.

Since v. 14 excludes from the terms of the covenant any male who, for whatever reason, has not been circumcised, it is evident that submission to the rite is presented in Genesis 17 as absolutely essential for every male member of the Abrahamic household or community. Any uncircumcised male was automatically in breach of the covenant and consequently excluded from the special divine–human relationship intrinsic to it. However, it is unlikely that the physical sign per se implied that one was a member of the covenant community, given that circumcision was practised so widely in the ancient Near East. Furthermore, as well as being hopelessly inadequate to identify publicly the male members of the covenant family or community, circumcision apparently left the female members with no identifying label at all. Together these facts make it difficult to interpret circumcision in Genesis 17 either as a badge of identification or an initiation or ratification rite. The first makes the covenant too broad; the latter makes it too narrow.

It seems best, therefore, to understand the act of circumcision simply as a mnemonic device through which both covenant partners (God and Abraham/Israel) would be perpetually reminded of the divine promises concerning Abraham's 'seed' and the human obligation of unswerving loyalty. Thus the rite of circumcision did not establish the covenant; rather, through this rite the substance of the covenant was maintained from one generation to the next.

b. *The Description of this Conditional Covenant as 'Everlasting'*
Three times in Genesis 17 (vv. 7, 13, 19) the term עולם is applied to this particular covenant. In addition, v. 8 applies the same term to promised possession of the land of Canaan. However, how could this covenant be 'eternal' if, as has been established above, it incorporates certain provisional aspects? In what sense is this covenant 'eternal' or 'everlasting'?

While it is true that the Hebrew term עולם does not always mean eternal or permanent,[142] it does carry the connotation of a long period of

---

142. As A.A. MacRae ('עלם ['lm]', *TWOT*, II, p. 673) states, 'That neither the Hebrew nor the Greek word (αἰώνιον) in itself contains the idea of endlessness is shown both by the fact that they sometimes refer to events or conditions that

time. Moreover, the use in Genesis 17 of phrases such as וזרעך אחריך לדרתם (vv. 7, 9, cf. v. 12) surely suggests that עולם carries the connotation here of this covenant's enduring nature. Thus, while it may be wrong to press the time-period encompassed by this ברית עולם into the unlimited dimensions of endlessness, the idea of perpetuity is undeniably present. At the very least the promises of the covenant heralded in Genesis 17, unlike the covenant depicted in Genesis 15, are to endure for a very long time. Furthermore, the conditional elements of this covenant, rather than detracting from its enduring nature, actually amplify it. The covenantal obligation of circumcision is explicitly applied to Abraham and to 'his seed after him *for generations to come*'. This, in itself, points to a very long time.

However, if—as has been suggested in the above discussion—this covenant has a much wider compass than the physical descendants of Abraham, and encompasses the 'nations' to whom blessing is mediated through Abraham's royal 'seed', then it is in the fullest sense a ברית עולם. This, apparently, was what the Psalmist anticipated in Ps. 72.[143] Moreover, this was certainly how the authors of the New Testament understood this covenant's fulfilment in the person and mission of Jesus Christ.[144]

6. *Summary and Appraisal*

As with Genesis 15, Genesis 17 picks up more than one of the promises in Gen. 12.1-3. Significantly, however, the two chapters do not emphasize the same promissory elements. In Genesis 15 the two particulars stressed and solemnly ratified are descendants and land.[145] While Genesis 17 certainly incorporates both these characteristics of the nationhood aspect of the promissory agenda, this chapter gives more emphasis to other promissory facets under which the dimension of nationhood

occurred at a definite point in the past, and also by the fact that sometimes it is thought desirable to repeat the word, not merely saying "forever", but "forever and ever"'.

143. The enduring nature of this idealized king's reign and attendant blessings is at least implicit in the following verses: v. 5 (LXX's 'May he prolong' [καὶ συμπαραμενεῖ = ויאריך] makes better sense than the MT's 'May they fear you' [ייראוך] in the immediate context), v. 7, and v. 17.

144. Cf. Acts 3.25; Rom. 4.16-24; Gal. 3.6-9, 16, 29.

145. This has been established in Chapter 4 above.

is apparently subsumed. The promise of phenomenal expansion is no longer envisaged on merely a national, but on an international scale (vv. 2-6). The promise of land is no longer the central focus of the promise, but is glossed over in a mere verse (v. 8). Other elements come to the fore in Genesis 17: the prospect of Abraham's international significance; the assurance that kings will be descended from his and Sarah's progeny (vv. 6, 16); the promise of an enduring divine–human relationship; and the establishment of an 'everlasting covenant' (v. 7). These pledges in Genesis 17, and the particular emphases reflected in this chapter, are of tremendous importance for assessing the literary and theological relationship between chs. 15 and 17 in the final form of Genesis.

It has been established, therefore, that the covenant spoken of in Genesis 17 differs from that depicted in Genesis 15 in at least three important respects: (1) it incorporates different foci; viz. promises of international significance, royal descendants, and a divine–human relationship; (2) it involves human as well as divine obligations; viz. the ethical obligation of moral blamelessness and the ritual obligation of circumcision; (3) it is of a more permanent character; viz. it is described as 'everlasting'. For these reasons alone one should be most reluctant to equate the two covenants of which the chapters speak. In terms of promissory focus, the author and/or final editor of Genesis clearly distinguishes them.

Chapter 6

THE COVENANTAL SIGNIFICANCE OF GENESIS 17

1. *Introduction*

It has been demonstrated that Genesis 17 is not simply an elegant variation (by 'P') on the covenant recorded in Genesis 15 ('JE').[1] In this chapter, therefore, the function of Genesis 17 within its present literary context will be explored more fully. Holistic readings of the Abraham narrative have thus far offered two quite distinct explanations:

1. Genesis 17 is merely a reaffirmation or amplification of the earlier 'covenant between the pieces'. In the following critique particular attention will be given to features which suggest to some scholars that this is indeed the case (for instance, its description as 'my covenant', the utilization of the verbs נתן and הקים, and the complete absence of the verb כרת).[2] It will be argued that none of these features demands that a previous covenant is being reiterated and/or elaborated upon; rather, some of them may actually support the suggestion that the covenant of circumcision is to be understood as a distinctively new development within the Abraham narrative.

2. Genesis 17 serves to introduce a covenant quite distinct from the one ratified in Genesis 15. Essentially two different propositions have been advanced in recent years: one proposes a different focus for each covenant,[3] whereas the other understands the difference in terms of

---

1. Cf. the third chapter of this book.

2. Dumbrell (*Covenant and Creation*) appears to offer the most comprehensively argued case for reading Gen. 17 in terms of a reaffirmation of the covenant that was established in Gen. 15. Thus in the following discussion I will interact primarily with the exegetical arguments put forward by Dumbrell.

3. So Alexander ('Literary Analysis') and Sailhamer (*The Pentateuch as Narrative*).

their distinctive function.[4] In this chapter it will be argued that, while the premise of these interpretations is essentially correct (viz. that Gen. 15 and 17 relate to two distinct covenants established between God and Abraham), the relationship between these pericopes is rather more complex than any of these 'solutions' has allowed.

Since none of these explanations does justice to all the material in Genesis 15 and 17, the case will be made for interpreting Genesis 17 as announcing the establishment of a covenant that is different from, while at the same time continuous with, the covenant already established in Genesis 15. It will be shown that the second covenant in the Abraham narrative not only encompasses the first, but also transcends it by both broadening and narrowing the promissory focus. Thus Genesis 17 is more than a mere reaffirmation of the promises guaranteed in the 'covenant between the pieces'. Rather, the 'covenant of circumcision' takes us beyond Abraham's national inheritance to his international significance.

2. *Genesis 17 as the Reaffirmation of the Covenant in Genesis 15*

As demonstrated above,[5] the noun ברית is clearly one of the key words in Genesis 17, occurring thirteen times (cf. the single occurrence in ch. 15).[6] Although, as J.J. Mitchell has observed,[7] this (i.e. ch. 17) is the first instance of God using the term ברית in direct speech to Abraham, the latter would presumably have comprehended the covenantal significance of the experience that is recorded in 15.17. Admittedly the term itself is not used in the reported speech. Thus the covenantal nature of the relationship is explicitly stated to Abraham only in ch. 17. Nevertheless, in view of the antiquity of the covenant initiation rite reflected in ch. 15, it may safely be assumed that the significance of the 'ceremony' was not lost on the patriarch. Moreover, given that an explanatory statement is included in ch. 15 (v. 18), it is equally unnecessary to insist that the term ברית is used in ch. 17 in order to emphasize to the *reader* the significance of the animal ritual described in the earlier

4.   So McComiskey, *The Covenants of Promise*.
5.   See Chapter 5 Section 2 above.
6.   Gen. 15.18 actually contains the only other explicit reference to a divine–human ברית in the entire Abraham narrative.
7.   J.J. Mitchell, 'Abram's Understanding of the Lord's Covenant', *WTJ* 32 (1969), pp. 24-48 (24).

chapter. In any case, the emphasis in ch. 17 falls not on the covenantal
nature of God's promises, but on the promises and obligations involved
in this particular covenant (whether perceived in terms of that inaugurated in ch. 15 or as a second covenant, the establishment of which is
announced in ch. 17). Therefore the introduction and usage of the term
ברית in the reported speech in ch. 17 cannot be explained merely in
terms of making the covenantal nature of the divine promises explicit—
this would have been quite clear already, to both Abraham and the
reader of the canonical Genesis.

What initially appears to be more significant, however, is the related
fact that the noun ברית attracts a first person singular pronominal suffix
several times in Genesis 17. It is to this feature, therefore, that attention
is now focused.

a. The First Person Singular Pronominal Suffix on ברית
In over half of its occurrences in ch. 17 (including its first occurrence in
the pericope) ברית has a first person singular possessive pronoun
attached (vv. 2, 4, 7, 10, 13, 19, and 21). It has been inferred, on the
basis that the covenant is so introduced in this chapter, that 'my covenant' is to be identified with the covenant previously mentioned in ch.
15.[8] This inference, however, does not bear up under close scrutiny. A
number of telling criticisms can be levelled against it.

The fact that the Noahic covenant (cf. Gen. 6.18; 9.8-17) is also
enigmatically (so McEvenue) introduced in the same manner (i.e.
בריתי) seriously undermines the suggestion that the pronominal suffix
points to an already established covenant. By analogy the 'covenant'
referred to in Gen. 6.18 must also be a reaffirmation of an already
established covenant. However, prior to this there is not even a hint of a

---

8.   Dumbrell, commenting on the parallel description in Gen. 6.18 and Gen.
9.8-17, contends that 'the most natural interpretation...is that an existing arrangement to be preserved is referred to, to which no more specific appeal is required
than the denomination of it as "my covenant"' (*Covenant and Creation*, p. 24). He
clearly assumes that the same argument holds for Gen. 17; cf. *Covenant and
Creation*, p. 25. P.A.H. De Boer similarly reasons that 'le pronom possessif, *bᵉrîti,
ma bᵉrît*, confirme la thèse du maintien d'une relation existante' ('Quelques
remarques sur l'Arc dans la Nuée', in C. Brekelmans (ed.), *Questions disputées
d'Ancien Testament: Méthode et théologie* [Leuven: Leuven University Press, 2nd
edn, 1989], p. 108). See also L. Dequeker's affirmation of De Boer's remarks
('Noah and Israel: The Everlasting Divine Covenant with Mankind', in Brekelmans
(ed.), *Questions disputées*, pp. 128-29).

covenant being established in the book of Genesis. The reference to ברית in Gen. 6.18 reflects not just the first occurrence of the noun in the flood narrative, but the first explicit reference to covenant in the Pentateuch as a whole. Thus to what pre-existing covenant could Gen. 6.18 possibly allude?

Dumbrell's conjecture, that the allusion in Gen. 6.18 is to an original covenant with creation, allegedly reflected in the opening chapters of Genesis, lacks firm exegetical support and therefore remains unconvincing.[9] While Dumbrell is undoubtedly correct in recognizing several clear echoes of the creation narrative in the Noahic covenant, his conclusion—that Genesis 1–3 must accordingly portray an antediluvian covenantal relationship—is a *non sequitur*. These echoes suggest merely that God intended, through Noah, to fulfil his original creative intent; they do not necessarily presuppose the existence of a covenant between God and inanimate creation. References in Jer. 33.20, 25 to a covenant with inanimate created things seem to allude more to dimensions of the Noahic covenant reflected in Gen. 8.22–9.13 (esp. Gen. 8.22) than to an antediluvian 'covenant with creation' for which there is absolutely no evidence in Genesis 1–3.[10] Although, as Thompson correctly observes,[11] 'the regular succession of day and night was established at creation',

9. Dumbrell claims that such a covenant is implicit in Gen. 1–3; see his *Covenant and Creation*, pp. 11-43 (esp. pp. 33-43). Cf. Stek's rebuttal ('"Covenant Overload"', pp. 23-24).

10. *Pace* Vogels who, on the basis of Jer. 33.20-25, maintains that 'besides all of the different covenants which are concluded in favour of the elected people, there is yet another one, which could be called natural; with natural laws for creation' (W. Vogels, *God's Universal Covenant: A Biblical Study* [Ottawa: University of Ottawa Press, 1979], p. 34). Several commentators understand the allusion in Jeremiah as being to the promise of Gen. 8.22 (e.g. C.L. Feinberg, 'Jeremiah', in F.E. Gaebelein [ed.], *The Expositor's Bible Commentary* [12 vols.; Grand Rapids: Zondervan, 1986], VI, p. 592; D.R. Jones, *Jeremiah* [NCBC; Grand Rapids: Eerdmans, 1992], p. 424; Scalise in G.L. Keown, P. Scalise and T.G. Smothers, *Jeremiah 26–52* [WBC, 27, Dallas: Word Books, 1995], pp. 174-75). R.P. Carroll, on the other hand, connects this ברית to creation itself, but understands the term to signify 'a fixed obligation rather than an agreement between two parties' (*Jeremiah* [OTL; London: SCM Press, 1986], p. 638). While the somewhat similar analogy drawn in Jer. 31.35-37 may indeed allude to the fixed order established at creation, significantly there is no mention here (Jer. 31.35-37) of a divine covenant. However, cf. Niehaus, *God at Sinai*, pp. 143-47.

11. J.A. Thompson, *The Book of Jeremiah* (NICOT; Grand Rapids: Eerdmans, 1980), p. 603.

there is no suggestion either here or elsewhere that the creative order of
Gen. 1.5 was ratified by divine covenant prior to Gen. 8.22. Moreover,
it is feasible to read Jer. 33.26 in precisely this way; both the cycle of
day and night and the other cosmic ordinances established at creation
were subsequently ratified by the Noahic covenant.

The only explicit mention of an antediluvian covenant in the Hebrew
Bible is the contested reference in Hos. 6.7. While reformed theologi-
ans have maintained that this text offers textual support for their
concept of a 'covenant of works' (i.e. a pre-fall covenant between God
and Adam),[12] the translation of Hos. 6.7 is open to several interpretations. The *crux interpretum* centres on how to understand the phrase
והמה כאדם עברו ברית. Several translations and commentators take
כאדם to mean 'like Adam'.[13] However, most interpreters prefer to
emend the key word to read באדם (in/at Adam), and take the proper
noun in a geographical sense, referring to the first town Israel reached
after crossing into the Promised Land (Josh. 3.16).[14] The NEB and REB
render the place name 'Admah', but clearly with the majority of interpreters understand the proper noun as a geographical site. Further
support for this geographical understanding is found in the reference to
Gilead (Hos. 6.8) and Shechem (Hos. 6.9) in the same context, and in
the deployment of the locative שם (there) immediately after ברית in
Hos. 6.7. Alternatively, the consonantal text could also be rendered
'like Edom they have transgressed a covenant', although the locative
שם clearly militates against this interpretation also. The Septuagint
understands כאדם in a generic sense: ὡς ἄνθρωπος (like a person),[15]

---

12. For example, L. Berkhof, *Systematic Theology* (Grand Rapids: Eerdmans,
1941), pp. 214-15; H. Hoeksema, *Reformed Dogmatics* (Grand Rapids: Reformed
Free Publishing Association, 1966), pp. 220-21; W. Grudem, *Systematic Theology:
An Introduction to Biblical Doctrine* (Leicester: InterVarsity Press, 1994), p. 516.

13. For example, KJV; ASV; NASB; NIV; C.F. Keil, 'The Minor Prophets', in
C.F. Keil and F. Delitzsch, *Biblical Commentary on the Old Testament* (10 vols.;
repr., Grand Rapids: Eerdmans, 1976–77), X, p. 100; Vogels, *God's Universal
Covenant*, p. 33; McComiskey, *The Covenants of Promise*, pp. 214-15.

14. For example, RSV; JB; TEV; NRSV; H.W. Wolff, *Hosea* (Hermeneia; Phila-
delphia: Fortress Press, 1974), pp. 121-22; J.L. Mays, *Hosea* (OTL; London: SCM
Press, 1969), p. 100; F.I. Andersen and N. Freedman, *Hosea* (AB; New York:
Doubleday, 1980), pp. 435-36; J. Day, 'Pre-Deuteronomic Allusions to the Cove-
nant in Hosea and Psalm LXXVIII', *VT* 36 (1986), pp. 1-12 (2-6); D.A. Hubbard,
Hosea (TOTC, Leicester: InterVarsity Press, 1989), p. 128.

15. Cf. J. Calvin, *Commentaries on the Minor Prophets* (Edinburgh: Calvin

although this singular subject does not agree with the plural verb in Hebrew. Both Dumbrell and Robertson are uncertain as to whether אדם should be understood in an individual or in a generic sense, but they reject any allusion to a geographical town.[16] A radically different interpretation, initially proposed by Dahood,[17] is adopted by Stuart,[18] who renders the verse 'But look—they have walked on my covenant like it was dirt, see they have betrayed me!', reading אדם as a variant of אדמה, עבר as 'walks on', and שם as 'see'. The fact that this particular text is open to such diverse interpretations clearly undermines its viability as an exegetical basis for a hypothetical Adamic covenant, still less the 'covenant with creation' suggested by Dumbrell. Nevertheless, on this text the whole concept of an antediluvian covenant stands or falls; without Hos. 6.7 there is absolutely no textual support for any covenant between God and humanity made prior to the announcement in Gen. 6.18. Moreover (*pace* Dumbrell) the latter text provides no real basis for such a covenant either. As Dumbrell himself admits, Gen. 6.18 clearly anticipates the covenant arrangements elucidated in 9.8-17.[19] Thus to some extent at least, the 'my covenant' of Gen. 6.18 heralds a new development in the primaeval narrative. Again, without Dumbrell's *a priori* assumption that a covenant between God and creation is implicit in Genesis 1–3, a straightforward reading of the text would lead one to conclude that Gen. 6.18 heralds the formal inauguration of the Noahic covenant set out in Gen. 8.20–9.17.[20]

Translation Society, 1846), pp. 233-35; W.R. Harper, *Amos and Hosea* (ICC; Edinburgh: T. & T. Clark, 1905), p. 288.

16. Dumbrell, *Covenant and Creation*, pp. 45-46, 169; Robertson, *The Christ of the Covenants*, pp. 22-25.

17. M. Dahood, 'Zacharia 9,1, *'ên 'ādām'*, *CBQ* 25 (1963), pp. 123-24; see also D.J. McCarthy, *'bᵉrît* in Old Testament History and Theology', *Bib* 53 (1972), pp. 110-21 (113).

18. D. Stuart, *Hosea–Jonah* (WBC, 31; Waco, TX: Word Books, 1987), pp. 98-99, 111. For a critique of McCarthy's original translation, see Day, 'Pre-Deuteronomic Allusions', pp. 2-3.

19. Dumbrell, *Covenant and Creation*, p. 24.

20. Admittedly, a major factor affecting the force of this argument is the precise connotation of the verb הקים. If, as Dumbrell insists, this verb is used exclusively for perpetuating a pre-existing relationship, one must concede that Gen. 6.18 must refer to a covenant which had been inaugurated some time prior to this. However, a detailed examination of the occurrences of הקים will amply demonstrate the fallacy of Dumbrell's premise. See the discussion below, Section 2b.

A second objection to the suggestion that the pronominal suffix on
ברית implies an element of continuity with a pre-existing covenant is
that Gen. 6.18 is not unique in this respect. In a similar fashion Exod.
19.5 plainly heralds the formal inauguration of the Sinaitic covenant
(cf. Exod. 24.8), but once more the first person singular possessive
pronoun is used. In keeping with his earlier suggestion, Dumbrell again
suggests that an element of continuity is reflected here by the pronominal suffix: 'The phrase "my covenant" contains the same unilateral implications as are suggested by references such as Gen 6.18; 9.9ff.,
hinting thus that the Sinai revelation may in fact be further specification
only of an already existing relationship'.[21] In this Dumbrell seems to
have fallen into the trap of circularity, uncritically assuming that the
Noahic covenant must be understood as an expansion of his postulated
'covenant with creation'. If, however, this latter premise is incorrect,
Dumbrell's conclusion with respect to the Sinaitic covenant is equally
suspect. There is, however, a more fundamental objection to Dumbrell's logic; viz. the fact that the Sinaitic covenant is presented as a
new development in the Pentateuchal narrative. Indeed, given the use of
the verb כרת in Exod. 24.8, this is something that even Dumbrell himself must surely concede.[22]

Thirdly, and most importantly, another explanation for the pronominal suffix on ברית is at least as feasible as that proposed by Dumbrell.
For Gunkel, the suffix simply underlines the *unilateral* aspect of these
divine–human covenants: 'The suffix...expresses the notion that God
grants Noah this covenant of his own free will, in free grace'.[23]
Motyer's explanation, albeit in another context (Isa. 59.21) is along
similar lines: 'It [בריתי] is the Lord's because it is his idea that there
should be a covenanted relationship and because it contains nothing,
whether promises or stipulations, except what is his'.[24] Indeed Dumbrell himself seems to recognize such a connotation for the pronominal

21. Dumbrell, *Covenant and Creation*, pp. 80-81.

22. Dumbrell maintains that כרת is the verb deployed in the context of an
initiation of a new covenant; cf. Section 2b below.

23. Gunkel, *Genesis*, p. 145. For a similar conclusion, see Wenham, *Genesis 1–
15*, p. 175.

24. J.A. Motyer, *The Prophecy of Isaiah* (Downers Grove: InterVarsity Press,
1993), p. 493.

suffix in Exod. 19.5,[25] and it is surely a fitting explanation for the identical usage of בריתי in the book of Genesis.

Therefore the use of בריתי in Genesis 17 (especially v. 2) cannot be said to prove per se that the covenant spoken of in this chapter is simply a reiteration or an expansion of the covenant already recounted in ch. 15. Rather, the pronoun may simply emphasize the divine prerogative in every aspect of a covenant so described.

b. *The Use and Nuances of the Verbs* כרת *and* הקים

Another argument used to support reading Genesis 17 as a reaffirmation of the covenant ratified in Genesis 15 focuses on the different verbs that are used in each chapter.[26] In Genesis 17 two verbs, נתן and הקים, are used with reference to the noun ברית: נתן in v. 2 and הקים in vv. 7, 19 and 21. In ch. 15 the verb used in association with ברית is כרת—the verb most commonly associated with the initiation or ratification of a divine–human covenant in the Hebrew Bible (cf. the Sinaitic covenant, Exod. 24.8; the Davidic covenant, Ps. 89.3; the new covenant, Jer. 31.31). Dumbrell asserts that the ratification of secular covenants reflected in the Old Testament is likewise described by this same verb and that none of the analogous verbs used in association with ברית is strictly synonymous with כרת. Such verbs, he maintains, are not deployed with reference to a covenant's actual initiation (i.e. the point of entry), but are consistently used in relation to covenants that have been established previously.[27]

Weinfeld offers a more comprehensive list of relevant biblical texts and therefore provides a better basis on which to evaluate Dumbrell's

25. Cf. the statement quoted above, and his telling comments in relation to Gen. 6.18: 'We may probably now surmise that what is being referred to in Gen. 6.18 is some existing arrangement *presumably imposed by God without human concurrence, since it is referred to as "my covenant"*' (Dumbrell, *Covenant and Creation*, p. 26, emphasis mine).

26. Cf. Dumbrell, *Covenant and Creation*, pp. 25-26, 73; Wenham, *Genesis 1–15*, p. 175; J.G. McConville, 'בְּרִית', *NIDOTE*, I, pp. 748-49 (the latter only applies the logic in the case of the Noahic covenant).

27. Dumbrell, *Covenant and Creation*, p. 25. Again De Boer reasons similarly: 'la bᵉrît entre Elohim et Noé n'est nullement, à mon avis, quelque chose de nouveau, mais le maintien d'une relation existante. La traduction de Genèse 6, 18 par "établir" ou "conclure une alliance" me paraît fautive' ('Quelques remarques', p. 106).

assertion.[28] In several of the texts cited by Weinfeld the key verbs do indeed refer back to a covenant that has already been established.[29] Nevertheless, this is by no means uniformly the case. Rather, as will be demonstrated below, a retrospective sense is difficult to maintain for the following texts: Gen. 6.18; 9.9, 11; 17.2, 7, 19; Num. 25.12; Deut. 29.11 and 2 Chron. 15.12. Thus Dumbrell's contention that 'outside the Book of Genesis the terminology of covenant entry appears to have been consistently maintained' deserves careful scrutiny.[30]

Dumbrell himself notes the exception of Ezek. 16.8 ('I spread the edge of my cloak over you, and covered your nakedness: I pledged myself to you and entered [בוא] into a covenant with you, says the Lord GOD, and you became mine' [NRSV]), suggesting that the legal formula might have been considered inappropriate in this context of a 'marriage' between Yahweh and Israel.[31] However, it must be acknowledged that the prophets—including Ezekiel—reflect no such reluctance to use legal metaphor in relation to God's relationship with his people elsewhere. Moreover, the metaphor is surely no less 'inappropriate' in the absence of the exact legal formula.

The fact that the traditional terminology for covenant entry (i.e. כרת ברית) is completely absent in the Noahic covenant is explained by Dumbrell by his postulated 'covenant with creation' which according to him is being perpetuated, not instituted, in Genesis 6–9.[32] If the

---

28. M. Weinfeld, ' בְּרִית *bʳrîth*', *TDOT*, II, p. 260.
29. The following synonyms are suggested by Weinfeld (*TDOT*, II, p. 260): שׂים (2 Sam. 23.5; Ps. 83.6 [*sic*—this verse uses the traditional verb כרת]); נתן (Gen. 9.12; 17.2; Num. 25.12); עדך (2 Sam. 23.5); הקים (Gen. 6.18; 9.9, 11; 17.7,10[?],19; Exod. 6.4; Lev. 26.9; Deut. 8.18; 2 Kgs. 23.3; Jer. 34.18); the hiphil or hophal of עמד (Ezek. 17.14; Ps. 105.10); בוא (1 Sam. 20.8; Jer. 34.10; Ezek. 16.8; 17.13; 20.37; 2 Chron. 15.12); עבר (Deut. 29.12).
30. Dumbrell, *Covenant and Creation*, p. 25.
31. Dumbrell, *Covenant and Creation*, p. 25 n. 17.
32. R.T. Beckwith ('The Unity and Diversity of God's Covenants', *TynBul* 38 [1987], p. 99 n. 23) suggests that Dumbrell is following O.P. Robertson (*The Christ of the Covenants*) with respect to this alleged covenant with creation. While admittedly there are similarities, for Dumbrell this alleged covenant was made with creation generally ('There could...be no question of two parties involved in any basic arrangement which is entered into by God *by virtue of creation itself*' [*Covenant and Creation*, p. 32, emphasis mine]), whereas for Robertson it was established with humanity in particular ('By the very act of creating *man* in his own image,

existence of a hypothetical 'creation' covenant is rejected, however, the use of the verb הקים rather than כרת in relation to the Noahic covenant clearly illustrates that the former verb may indeed be used of covenant establishment (or at least in anticipation of such). As demonstrated above, the exegetical basis for an antediluvian covenant is rather dubious, casting serious doubt over its very existence. If the concept of a divine covenant is introduced for the first time in Gen. 6.18, the fact that הקים is deployed in relation to its initial establishment (*pace* Dumbrell) weighs heavily against the contention that this verb is only used in relation to covenants that have already been ratified.

The deployment of הקים in Genesis 17 is similarly understood by Dumbrell (i.e. he understands this verb to be referring back to the covenant instituted or 'cut' in ch. 15). Once again, however, he is clearly forming his conclusion on questionable *a priori* grounds (i.e. he is assuming that the 'covenant' of ch. 17 is simply an expansion of that recorded in ch. 15, and therefore arguing that the verbs in ch. 17 assume an already existing covenant). The circularity of such reasoning obviously weakens his case. Without Dumbrell's presupposition that chs. 15 and 17 certainly refer to the same covenant, it could plausibly be argued that the verbs used in relation to covenant in ch. 17 are either practically synonymous with כרת, or else are actually being employed *prospectively* (i.e. anticipating the ratification of the covenant to which they are referring).

While the causative verb הקים may be understood as 'to confirm/maintain', it has a wide range of nuances in the Old Testament:

1. 'Maintaining' or 'confirming' or 'fulfilling' something which already existed: vows or promises;[33] predicted events and divine plans;[34] legislative stipulations.[35]
2. The restoration of something or someone to their previous position.[36]

God established a unique relationship between himself and creation' [*The Christ of the Covenants*, p. 67, emphasis mine]).

33. For example, Gen. 26.3; Lev. 26.9; Num. 23.19; 30.14, 15; Deut. 8.18; 9.5; 2 Sam. 7.25; 1 Kgs 6.12; 9.5; Isa. 44.26; Jer. 11.5; 29.10; 33.14; 44.25; Ezek. 34.29; Ps. 119.38; Dan. 9.12; Neh. 9.8; 2 Chron. 6.10.

34. For example, 1 Sam. 3.12; 1 Kgs 12.15; Jer. 28.6; 2 Chron. 10.15.

35. For example, Gen. 38.8; Deut. 27.26; 1 Sam. 15.13; 2 Kgs 23.24; Isa. 44.26; Jer. 23.20; 30.24; 34.18; 35.14; Neh. 5.13.

36. Deut. 22.4 (animals); 2 Sam. 12.17 (David); Isa. 49.6 (tribes of Jacob);

3.   The setting up of something new.[37]
4.   The establishment or renewal of a covenantal relationship.[38]
5.   The perpetuation of a name, tribe or dynasty.[39]
6.   The raising up of a person, nation or group.[40]
7.   Physical or metaphorical raising.[41]

In the light of the occurrences elsewhere, Dumbrell concludes that it is 'more likely that in contexts where *hēqîm bᵉrît* stands (Gen. 6.18; 9.9, 11, 17; 17.7, 19, 21; Exod. 6.4; Lev. 26.9; Deut. 8.18; 2 Kgs 23.3) the institution of a covenant is not being referred to but rather its perpetuation'.[42] However, as a close examination of the relevant texts will demonstrate, such a conclusion is open to several serious objections and a good case can be made in support of a covenant being instituted and not just renewed. The context alone must determine the meaning attached to הקים in any given text. Dumbrell is mistaken simply to infer from the use of this verb that an already existing covenant is being maintained. Rather, as Mitchell observes, הקים may equally suggest the initial establishment of a covenant, and either meaning is appropriate here (in Gen. 17).[43] Fixing the precise nuance must therefore be

Isa. 49.8 (land); Hos. 6.2 (people of God); Amos 9.11 (Davidic dynasty); Ps. 40.3 (feet); Eccl. 4.10 (fallen friend).

37.   Jer. 10.20 (tent); Exod. 26.30; 40.2, 17, 18, 33; Num. 1.51; 7.1; 9.15; 10.21 (tabernacle); Deut. 27.2, 4; Josh. 4.9, 20; 7.26; 8.29; 24.26 (witness heap); 1 Kgs 7.21; ‖ 2 Chron. 3.17 (pillars); Lev. 26.1; Judg. 18.30 (idols); 2 Sam. 24.18; 1 Kgs 16.32; (2 Kgs 9.2 [Jehu's dynasty]); 2 Kgs 21.3; 1 Chron. 21.18; 2 Chron. 33.3 (altar); 2 Sam. 3.10 (dynasty); Isa. 23.13; 29.3; Ezek. 26.8 (siege works); Prov. 30.4 (ends of earth); 2 Sam. 12.11 (calamity); Judg. 7.19 (change of guards); Ps. 78.5 (statutes).

38.   Exod. 6.4 (and arguably the texts in Genesis); Deut. 29.12 (cf. NIV and NRSV); 1 Sam. 22.8; 2 Kgs 23.3, Ezek. 16.60, 62.

39.   Deut. 25.7; Josh. 5.7; 1 Sam. 2.35; 2 Sam. 7.12; 1 Kgs 15.4; Jer. 30.9; (Ps. 89.44); Ruth 4.5, 10; 1 Chron. 17.11; 2 Chron. 7.18.

40.   Amos 6.14; Hab. 1.6 (Babylonians); (Judg. 7.19); Jer. 6.17; 51.12 (watchmen); Jer. 23.4; Ezek. 34.23; Mic. 5.4; Zech. 11.16 (shepherd[s]); Jer. 23.5 (righteous branch); 1 Kgs 11.14, 23 (adversary); Judg. 2.16, 18; 3.9, 15 (judges); Deut. 18.15, 18; Jer. 29.15; Amos 2.11 (prophets); Deut. 28.36; 1 Kgs 14.14 (king); 2 Sam. 23.1 (David); Deut. 28.9 (holy people).

41.   Gen. 49.9; Num. 24.9; 1 Sam. 2.8; Isa. 14.9; Jer. 50.32; Amos 5.2; Pss. 41.11; (107.29); 113.7; Job 4.4; 16.12.

42.   Dumbrell, *Covenant and Creation*, p. 26.

43.   Mitchell, 'Abram's Understanding', p. 34 n. 25.

determined by the function of Genesis 17 within its literary context. It cannot be established by linguistics alone.

As Beckwith observes, the deployment of הקים in Exod. 6.4 illustrates that this verb does not necessarily suggest the confirmation or perpetuation of a pre-existing covenant.[44] This latter text is of particular significance for a number of reasons. Although three patriarchs are alluded to, the covenant is spoken of in the singular. There is only one feasible explanation for this: God did not establish three different covenants, one with each patriarch, but made a singular commitment or covenant (i.e. solemn promise), initially to Abraham, but subsequently to Isaac and Jacob. It would appear from Exod. 6.4 that the commitment or promise in question relates essentially to the question of territory; only the promissory aspect relating to nationhood is picked up here; there is neither mention of nor allusion to the international dimensions of the promise that are reflected in Gen. 12.3; 17 and 22.18. It is reasonable to conclude, therefore, that the covenant referred to in Exod. 6.4 is that solemnly established by divine oath in Gen. 15.18. If this is indeed the case, the fact that the verb הקים should be applied in Exod. 6.4 to the establishment of the 'covenant between the pieces' is most significant; as Beckwith asserts, this would appear to confirm that this verb does not relate exclusively to the confirmation of a pre-existing covenant. While the latter interpretation of הקים could be said to fit in the case of Isaac and Jacob, it is rather strange in the case of Abraham; prior to Genesis 15 there was no pre-existing covenant to be 'confirmed'.

Admittedly, other explanations for the application of הקים to Abraham may be suggested. For example, since the promise of specific territory was made prior to Genesis 15 (cf. Gen. 12.7; 13.15, 17), one might reasonably contend that the oath recorded in Gen. 15.18 does in fact represent a confirmation of the territorial promise. The major problem with this, however, is that the 'wrong' verb is deployed in Genesis 15; if the oath there is intended merely to reaffirm the promise(s) of Genesis 12, rather than establish a covenant, the logic of this argument (if consistently applied) demands that הקים rather than כרת ought to have been deployed in Gen. 15.18. Alternatively, it may be argued that the allusion in Exod. 6.4 (in the case of Abraham) is actually to Gen. 17.8, an explicit confirmation of the covenant/promise ratified formally

44. Beckwith, 'The Unity and Diversity of God's Covenants', p. 99 n. 23.

in Gen. 15.18. However, this patently fails to take adequate account of the particularly striking allusions to Genesis 15 in the sixth chapter of Exodus.[45] Moreover, while both these arguments might ostensibly account for the use of הקים in relation to all three patriarchs, they do so at the expense of removing any allusion in Exod. 6.4 to the actual establishment of this particular covenant or promise.

The significance of Num. 25.12 is not discussed by Dumbrell, but he appears to understand it as an aspect of the Sinaitic covenant.[46] However, if with Beckwith this covenant between God and Phinehas is actually distinguished from the Sinaitic covenant,[47] this text can indeed be used to illustrate the establishing of a covenant by a verb other than כרת. Indirect evidence supporting this differentiation between the covenant with Phinehas and the Sinaitic covenant is found in Jer. 33.21, Mal. 2.1-8, and Neh. 13.29; in these texts the covenant with the Levitical Priesthood is portrayed not simply as an aspect of the Sinaitic covenant, but as a covenant in its own right. If the covenant with Phinehas is likewise a distinct entity, Num. 25.12 provides indisputable proof that verbs other than כרת are used in the Hebrew Bible in relation to the establishment of a divine–human ברית. If this is granted, Num. 25.12 might possibly parallel the prospective reference of Gen. 17.2 suggested above, for in both texts the covenant is anticipated, but not actually said to have been ratified.

Dumbrell argues that the covenant entered into in Deut. 29.11 refers to the people's adoption of the already existing Mosaic covenant. As he previously acknowledges,[48] however, the traditional terminology (כרת ברית) is also employed in this context (Dumbrell overlooks the use of כרת in vv. 11b and 24, noting only its deployment in v. 13). The use of כרת in this context, however, is surely more significant than Dumbrell admits. Indeed, on his own definition, its presence indicates that a covenant is being instituted on this occasion. If this is accepted, then it is difficult to see how the verb עבר, clearly used in parallel with כרת in v. 11, is being used retrospectively here. Rather, such usage suggests that כרת is not the only verb used in association with covenant initiation.

The final problematic text (i.e. 2 Chron. 15.12) is again explained by

45. Compare Exod. 6.5-8 with Gen. 15.13-16.
46. Cf. Dumbrell, *Covenant and Creation*, p. 94.
47. Beckwith, 'The Unity and Diversity of God's Covenants', p. 100.
48. Cf. Dumbrell, *Covenant and Creation*, p. 23.

Dumbrell in terms of the renewal of a formerly existing covenant—
between Northern and Southern tribes—on the basis that the definite
article is attached to ברית. It could surely be argued, however, that the
covenant referred to on this occasion is implicitly referred to in the
previous verse by the mention of animal sacrifice. If such is the
significance of the sacrifices mentioned in this context, then this verb
surely refers to a covenant being initiated.

Therefore a close examination of the texts that do not obviously harmonize with Dumbrell's contention (i.e. his insistence that a consistent
covenant-initiation formula is employed outside the book of Genesis)
would suggest that his conclusion is fatally flawed. Rather, as Weinfeld
acknowledges,[49] several verbs may be used to reflect the institution or
ratification of a ברית, one of which is הקים. This certainly leaves open
the possibility that Genesis 17 refers to a covenant other than that
recorded in Genesis 15. Moreover, if Weinfeld is correct in his assertion that 'in *heqim* the idea of "establishing" is dominant' (as opposed
to 'fulfilling'),[50] such a possibility is transformed into a probability.

It must be asked, nevertheless, why the terminology most closely
associated with covenant institution (i.e. the archaic expression כרת
ברית) is not employed here in Genesis 17? Is it, as Alexander suggests,[51] because the covenant ritual associated with the terminology (i.e.
a sacrificial rite) did not take place until Genesis 22, or is it rather
because ch. 17 is presenting an affirmation and expansion of the covenant already ratified by sacrificial ritual in ch. 15 (as assumed by Dumbrell)? In relation to these questions a comparison between the Abrahamic covenant and the Noahic covenant is deeply instructive.

At a purely linguistic level it is interesting to observe how the verbs
deployed in Genesis 17 are used in association with the Noahic Covenant (הקים in 6.18; 9.9, 11, 17 and נתן in 9.12).[52] Though the use of the
active participle of נתן in 9.12 is inconclusive in that it could be taken
in the sense that God is 'confirming' with Noah a covenant which had
previously been established, the inflections of the verb הקים in both

49. Weinfeld, *TDOT*, II, p. 260.
50. *TDOT*, II, p. 260.
51. See Section 3a below.
52. Wenham's note (*Genesis 16–50*, p. 20) that נתן is used only in Gen. 17.2
and Num. 25.12 with the object 'covenant' is slightly misleading—the participle of
נתן in Gen. 9.12 surely refers to the covenant being made rather than, as in the
following verse, to the sign being given.

chs. 6 and 9 are probably significant. When the covenant is announced in Gen. 6.18, a 'converted' perfect is used;[53] when the covenant is apparently instituted, an active participle (Gen. 9.9) is deployed.[54] Again, when its establishment is recalled in Gen. 9.17, a perfect is used. The pattern of these verbal inflections (converted perfect, active participle and perfect) is entirely consistent with the premise that the concept of a divine–human covenant is being introduced for the first time at this point in the Genesis narrative: advance notice is given in Gen. 6.18; the actual ratification of the covenant is spoken of in Gen. 9.9; and it may be inferred from Gen. 9.17 that this covenant is now a divine *fait accompli.*

Turning to Genesis 17 we discover that the inflections of הקים are again consistent with the introduction of a new covenant. The narrative has a converted perfect in vv. 7 and 19, and an imperfect in v. 21, which may suggest that a new covenant is being heralded at this point. Moreover, the fact that throughout this chapter the covenant is spoken of in the future tense cannot be ignored.

Of further significance is the stress on Abraham's obedience in Gen. 17.23-27, given the analogous stress on Noah's obedience in Gen. 6.22. In each case, immediately after the divine announcement of a covenant and related stipulations, there was a response of implicit obedience. The analogy, however, does not stop there, but can be drawn even more closely.[55] Subsequent to initial compliance of each human partner with the divine requirements, further stipulations are given, and in each case these further stipulations relate to sacrifice (Gen. 7.2-3; Gen. 22.2).[56] Once again the narrator emphasizes the model response of obedience (Gen. 7.5, 9, 16; Gen. 22.18). Moreover, in both cases God's solemn promise follows not only the human partner's obedient response, but

---

53. Admittedly, Gen. 9.11 begins with an identical inflection of הקים. Here, however, it may convey a present tense (so most English versions) or else anticipates the sealing of the covenant with the sign announced in the verses that follow (vv. 12-17).

54. Cf. the active participle of נתן in Gen. 9.12 and the implied copula in Gen. 9.15 ('the covenant which *is* between me and you').

55. As originally suggested by Alexander, 'Genesis 22 and the Covenant', pp. 17-22.

56. Admittedly the connection between the divine imperative and sacrifice is not made explicit in Gen. 7.2-3; the purpose of these seven additional pairs of clean animals and birds becomes clear only after the flood (cf. Gen. 8.20).

also the making of a burnt offering (cf. Gen. 8.20; 22.13-14).[57] Read in
this way, the verb הקים serves in Genesis 17 to *introduce* a covenant
that was not actually ratified until after the incident recorded in Genesis
22. In addition to providing a rationale for the future tenses in Genesis
17, this may also provide an explanation for the absence of the verb
כרת (in association with ברית); the sacrifice associated with the classic
idiom for making a covenant (כרת ברית) did not actually take place
until Genesis 22. Admittedly the customary phrase (כרת ברית) is not
found in Genesis 22 either. Nevertheless, the divine promises are there
introduced in an equally solemn (perhaps even synonymous) fashion
(כי נשבעתי).[58]

c. *The Tense and Significance of the Verb* נתן

If one understands Genesis 17 in terms of a reaffirmation of the covenant formally ratified in Genesis 15, the deployment in Gen. 17.2 of the
imperfect inflection of the verb נתן is rather puzzling. As Wenham
tellingly admits, 'it is not immediately obvious in what sense God
needs to give a covenant to Abraham, as it has already been inaugurated
(כרת "cut") in 15.18'.[59] Wenham resolves this difficulty by resorting to
the most popular synchronic interpretation, suggesting that here (Gen.
17) the concern is the confirmation or ratification of the covenant with
stress on the human response (summed up in the phrase 'walk before
me and be blameless', and explicated in the demand to circumcise
every male) rather than merely on the divine initiative. The difficulty of
the long delay (c. 14 years) between the covenant's establishment by
God and the stress on its inherent obligations on man has already been
underlined.[60] The reason why the obligatory aspects were not clarified
much earlier is somewhat obscure; if these two passages simply
describe two aspects/stages of the one covenant, why did God wait so
long to elaborate upon the human partner's responsibilities? Surely the
theological effect would have been the same had Genesis 15 already
alluded to the intrinsic responsibilities on Abraham's part? If, on the
other hand, a redactor is blamed for this literary enigma, the rationale
for separating two such intimately related passages has not been
adequately explained. Surely the redactor could have incorporated the

57. The term עלה is found in Genesis only in 8.20 and ch. 22.
58. Gen. 22.15.
59. Wenham, *Genesis 16–50*, p. 20.
60. See Chapter 3 of this book.

Hagar episode into the narrative at a more suitable place—for example, before the latter half of ch. 15—and amalgamated the J and P accounts of the covenant's institution?[61] Thus the anticipated 'giving' of the covenant in Genesis 17 does not sit easily with either the standard synchronic or diachronic explanations; the former offers no rationale for the unnecessary delay in revealing the covenant's obligatory aspects, whereas the latter challenges the literary competence of the redactor(s).

Dumbrell understands the sense of נתן (in 17.2) to be 'setting the covenant in operation'.[62] By this he means the realization of the covenant of Genesis 15 in the form of activated promises. Thus Gen. 17.2 should presumably be understood: '...so that I may set in motion my covenant between me and you and greatly increase your numbers'.[63] Such a translation is certainly supported by Labuschagne's lexical study of נתן; he contends that the basic connotation of the verb is the act through which an object or matter is set in motion.[64] Further support for this interpretation is found in the fact that נתן, when used in association with promised covenant blessings, heralds their realization or fulfilment.[65] Fulfilment of the gift of 'land' is heralded in 12.7; 13.15, 17; 15.7, 18; 17.8, and implicitly in 15.2. In 17.5, 6 and 20 the verb relates to the promise of international (or in Ishmael's case, national) significance. The focus in 17.16 is the promised son. This leaves 17.2, which in the context seems to relate to the promise of Abraham's phenomenal expansion (17.2b; cf. 12.2; 13.16; 15.5); this, as we have seen,[66] is undoubtedly a major theme in Genesis 17. Thus נתן in Gen. 17.2 may suggest the setting in motion of the covenant promise(s) in

---

61. This has the advantage of retaining the basic plot but avoiding any possible confusion through the inclusion of two variant accounts of the one event.

62. Dumbrell, *Covenant and Creation*, p. 73.

63. The only other text in the Hebrew Bible in which נתן is used with reference to a ברית is Gen. 9.12. Here the translation 'set in motion' is equally feasible; it can be argued that what is being set in motion is the temporal and material blessings promised in 8.22.

64. C.J. Labuschagne, 'נתן *ntn* to give', *TLOT*, II, p. 776. Labuschagne is followed by M.A. Grisanti, 'נתן', *NIDOTE*, III, pp. 205-206. Several other theological dictionaries suggest three primary meanings for נתן: give; set/set up/put; make/do; cf. *HALOT*, pp. 733-35; M.C. Fisher, 'נָתַן (*nātan*) give', *TWOT*, II, pp. 608-609; *HAHAT*, pp. 529-31.

65. The verb נתן is closely associated with covenantal blessings both in Gen. 17 and elsewhere (17.5, 6, 8, 16, [20?]; cf. 9.3; 12.7; 13.15, 17; 15.2, 7, 18; Isa. 49.8).

66. See Chapter 5 Section 3b above.

question; viz. Abraham's phenomenal expansion (as the latter half of the verse seems to imply).

However, even if it is correct to interpret the verb נתן as heralding the implementation or fulfilment of covenant promises, the legitimacy of identifying the covenant announced in Genesis 17 with the covenant already inaugurated in ch. 15 cannot simply be assumed. This still fails to take adequate cognisance of the different promissory emphases of the two chapters. The promissory focus of the covenant established in ch. 15 is the inheritance of the land by Abraham's innumerable off-spring—an aspect of the promissory programme which, though reiterated in the context of ch. 17 (v. 8), was certainly not implemented until very much later (and after at least one additional divine–human covenant; viz. the Sinaitic). However, the *primary* focus of the covenant 'set in motion' in Genesis 17 does not appear to be Abraham's national inheritance, but rather his international significance. Thus the fact that the prospect of nationhood appears to assume a rather subsidiary position in ch. 17 seriously weakens the case for understanding the 'covenant of circumcision' as *merely* another step towards the implementation of the covenant promises recorded in ch. 15. At the very least there is a difference in emphasis in these two chapters which any attempt to correlate the two records must take into account and seek to explain.

However, it is possible that, though overstating his case, Dumbrell is correct to see a continuum between Genesis 15 and 17; the emphasis in ch. 17 on Abraham's descendants clearly provides a literary and theological lynchpin. This pericope leaves the reader in no doubt that Abraham's international significance must not be isolated entirely from the prospect of his national inheritance. Both expectations are related in some way; indeed, given the order both here and elsewhere,[67] Abraham's international significance appears to be somehow contingent upon the prospect of nationhood having first been realized.

It is surely significant that upon fulfilling the ritual obligation of circumcision (Gen. 17.23-27), the covenant promise relating to Abraham's offspring is indeed set in motion (Gen. 18.1-15). This, and the fact that the subsequent narrative reintroduces both major facets of the divine promise to Abraham,[68] would appear to confirm the correctness of

---

67. Cf. Gen. 18.18; 35.11, which reflect the same sequence as Gen. 15 and 17.

68. Gen. 18.16-19 provides a twofold rationale for God's revelation to Abraham regarding the fate of Sodom and Gomorrah; viz. the patriarch's national and international significance.

understanding Gen. 17.2 as picking up the promissory threads of Genesis 15, while at the same time transcending them.

d. *The Difficulties in Reading Genesis 17 as Merely a Reaffirmation of Genesis 15*

Several major difficulties arise when the covenant in Genesis 17 is read simply as a reaffirmation of the covenant established in Genesis 15, some of which have been alluded to already.

1. If the covenant announced in ch. 17 merely reaffirms the covenant 'cut' in ch. 15, it is most unclear why its establishment should be consistently spoken of in the future tense in ch. 17 (cf. vv. 2, 4-8). How can a covenant already ratified be presented as the prize for future obedience (Gen. 17.1-2)? Why is the reaffirmation anticipated throughout Genesis 17, and not actualized, especially if the imperative of v. 1 relates chiefly to submitting to the rite of circumcision?[69] Is this future tense not better explained in terms of a covenant distinct from that of Genesis 15, which is yet to be formally established with Abraham and his 'seed'?

2. If the covenant promised in ch. 17 were little more than a reaffirmation and qualification of that described in ch. 15, one would surely expect the thematic link between them to be much more pronounced. One would certainly anticipate that land should be a more prominent theme in ch. 17; the fact that the promise of land is of relatively minor or secondary importance in ch. 17 is surely telling. Conversely, one searches in vain in Genesis 15 for the theme of international significance, clearly a major theme in Genesis 17. By identifying these covenants too closely, previous scholarship has failed to pay sufficient attention to and offer convincing explanations for their distinctive emphases.

3. No convincing theological or literary explanation has yet been offered for the allegedly two-phase nature of this particular covenant. The strange gap between the unilateral ratification of the covenant in Genesis 15 and the introduction of bilateral obligations in Genesis 17 does not seem to serve any theological or literary purpose. Any attempted parallel with the Sinaitic covenant is inexact,[70] for there is a clear breach of the covenant stipulations between Exodus 24 and 34. No

---

69. It seems more reasonable to conclude that this prerequisite involves something other than physical circumcision. See Chapter 5 Section 4a above.

70. Such as that drawn by Sailhamer in *The Pentateuch as Narrative*, p. 156.

such breach is found, or indeed is possible, between Genesis 15 and 17; prior to ch. 17 no covenant obligations were apparent. Admittedly Abraham was gravely mistaken in taking matters into his own hands (Gen. 16), but this can hardly be construed as a breach of covenant obligations.

e. *Assessment*
It is evident from the above discussion that there are serious exegetical, literary and theological objections to interpreting Genesis 17 as merely a reaffirmation and/or qualification of the covenant established in Genesis 15. Such an interpretation not only imposes itself upon the text, but builds on a disturbing number of premises and assumptions, which themselves do not stand up under close scrutiny. It fails to account for several significant facets in the pericope (for instance the future tense) and completely overlooks the subtle (and sometimes not so subtle) differences in content and emphases between these two chapters in the Abraham narrative. Most fundamentally, however, it fails to provide any compelling explanation for the existence of a gap (whether understood as a chronological fact or a literary device) between the initial establishment of the covenant in Genesis 15 and the somewhat abrupt and belated introduction of human obligations in Genesis 17.

3. *Genesis 17 as the Introduction of an Entirely New Covenant*

In recent years at least three scholars operating within a synchronic framework have clearly articulated the most straightforward solution to the apparent incoherence of Genesis 17 with the preceding narrative: God established not one covenant, but rather two different covenants with Abraham.[71]

a. *A Covenant of International as Opposed to National Significance*
For Alexander the covenant in Genesis 15 exclusively relates to the divine promises that centre on nationhood (i.e. the promises of physical descendants and national territory). By contrast, the covenant anticipated in Genesis 17 picks up the divine promise of blessing for the nations (Gen. 12.3).[72] In contrast to those who connect chs. 15 and 17,

71. Alexander, 'Literary Analysis'; McComiskey, *The Covenants of Promise*; Sailhamer, *The Pentateuch as Narrative*.
72. Although Chew (' *"Blessing for the Nations"* ', pp. 95-97) similarly main-

Alexander relates the 'giving' of the covenant in ch. 17 to the divine oath recorded in ch. 22. He argues that 'the account of the covenant of circumcision in Genesis 17 is merely the promise of such a covenant being established, not its actual ratification'.[73] The ratification of this covenant takes place in 22.15-18.[74] Alexander finds support for his suggestion in the account of the covenant with Noah, in which he identifies six important similarities: both covenants are described as 'everlasting' (cf. 9.16; 17.7, 13, 19); both are accompanied by an appropriate sign; both are described in terms of $h\bar{e}q\hat{i}m/n\bar{a}tan\ b^e r\hat{i}t$ (cf. 9.9, 11, 17; 17.7, 19, 21); both covenants are highly personal—'between me (i.e. God) and you' (cf. 9.12, 15; 17.2, 7)—yet each encompasses descendants also; the benefit for those included within both covenants is that they shall not be cut off (cf. 9.11; 17.14); the obligation placed on Abraham to be 'blameless' (17.1) closely resembles Noah's description as such (6.9). In addition to these similarities in content, Alexander detects a similarity in structure (taking chs. 17 and 22 together). Alexander finds in this alleged relationship the interpretative key for several of the problematic aspects of Genesis 22 and 26 (such as why God tested Abraham at all; why a sacrifice was required; why the fulfilment of the promise is related to Abraham's obedience). Thus the conditional covenant promised in ch. 17 explains the reason for the divine test of Abraham's faith, the necessity for the sacrificial ram, and accounts for the fact that Abraham merits the divine guarantee by his obedience. If this premise is correct (i.e. that chs. 17 and 22 are intimately related), then the covenant 'given' or 'established' in ch. 17 is a new and distinctive covenant, related but by no means identical to the covenant of ch. 15.

Alexander's thesis is most ingenious, explaining some of the otherwise enigmatic features in the Abraham story.[75] It does so, however, by introducing too sharp a distinction between the two covenants in ques-

---

tains this distinction in focus between Gen. 15 and 17, he does not distinguish the covenants themselves quite so sharply; rather, Chew suggests that 'the effect and function of Genesis 17 as a re-expansion and re-focussing of the narrow interest of Genesis 15 is to hold in check the narrowing of horizon by reaffirming or reiterating the initial universalistic horizon of Gen. 12.1-9' (pp. 96-97).

73. Alexander, 'Genesis 22 and the Covenant', p. 17.

74. Alexander, 'Genesis 22 and the Covenant', p. 20.

75. Alexander's hypothesis will be explored more fully in the following chapter of this book.

tion. As will be demonstrated in the following chapter, the absolute dichotomy suggested by Alexander is not supported by all the exegetical evidence. Thus, while Alexander has certainly shed valuable light on the literary and theological complexity of the Abraham narrative, his distinction between a national and an international covenant seems rather too neat.

b. *An 'Administrative' as Opposed to a 'Promissory' Covenant*
McComiskey contends that Genesis 15 represents a promissory covenant, whereas the 'covenant of circumcision' (Gen. 17.9-27) is to be understood in terms of an administrative covenant.[76] He explains this functional distinction (and his underlying thesis) as follows:

> the major redemptive covenants are structured bicovenantly. The promise covenant, made with Abraham and his offspring, is an eternal covenant that never loses its force or integrity. Its elements are explicated in several covenants, called in this work administrative covenants. These covenants govern human obedience. Both types of covenant must function together for the successful administration of the inheritance.[77]

For McComiskey, Genesis 15 and 17 reflect two different types of covenant. The 'covenant between the pieces' served to affirm the programmatic promises of Genesis 12 by placing them in the formal structure of a divine–human ברית, whereas the function of the 'covenant of circumcision' was to 'administer an aspect of obedience necessary for the maintenance of one's relationship to the promise'.[78] Although maintaining this functional distinction between them, McComiskey nevertheless views the two covenants as inextricably related; despite having separate covenantal status, circumcision served as the sign of the promissory covenant of Genesis 15.[79]

If, as has been suggested above, Alexander draws too sharp a distinction between the covenants of Genesis 15 and 17, McComiskey seems to err on the other side: elements of discontinuity are not given sufficient weight by him. Thus, while acknowledging that other promissory aspects are included along with the promise of land in Genesis 17, McComiskey offers no explanation for their complete absence in Gen-

---

76. For McComiskey (*The Covenants of Promise*, p. 61), Gen. 17.1-8 is a reaffirmation and elaboration of the covenant ratified in ch. 15.
77. McComiskey, *The Covenants of Promise*, p. 10.
78. McComiskey, *The Covenants of Promise*, p. 62.
79. McComiskey, *The Covenants of Promise*, pp. 144-50.

esis 15. He is undoubtedly correct in seeing the promise of offspring
included in the affirmation of Gen. 15.18. However, the fact that other
aspects of the divine promise are omitted altogether in this chapter, yet
included in Genesis 17, strongly suggests that McComiskey's deline-
ation between a covenant that is purely promissory and one that is
purely administrative is somewhat naïve. It is certainly misleading to
assert that 'the *běrît* of circumcision is not promissory, it is stipulatory.
There is no exposition of the promise in the context.'[80] As demonstrated in the previous chapter (and as McComiskey himself recognizes), promissory aspects not encapsulated in the covenant of Genesis
15 come into very sharp focus in Genesis 17. If, however, Genesis 17
serves primarily to administer the promises ratified by covenant in
Genesis 15, it is most unclear why at this point (and not previously) the
additional promissory material should be specifically mentioned. If, as
McComiskey asserts, 'the *běrît* of circumcision functions to administer
an aspect of obedience necessary for the maintenance of one's relationship to the promise',[81] it must surely be the promissory dimensions
elucidated in Genesis 17 itself.[82] Yet these, as we have seen in the previous chapter, are rather different from those that are the focus of the
covenant in Genesis 15.

Furthermore, if McComiskey's differentiation between the two covenants is correct, two features which distinguish Genesis 15 and 17 are
especially puzzling: the subordinate role of the promise of land in
Genesis 17;[83] and the description of the 'administrative' (rather than the
'promissory') covenant as 'eternal' (Gen. 17.7, 13, 19).[84]

McComiskey's explanation of the relationship between Genesis 15
and 17 thus raises as many questions as it answers, and notably fails to
offer any explanation of the most significant difference between the two
chapters; viz. their promissory focus.

---

80. McComiskey, *The Covenants of Promise*, p. 147.

81. McComiskey, *The Covenants of Promise*, p. 62.

82. McComiskey's distinction between the material in vv. 1-8 and that in vv. 9-
27 strangely misses the point!

83. In Gen. 17 the promise of land is almost entirely subsumed by the promises
of international significance and special relationship.

84. On McComiskey's premise one would surely have expected the reverse: it
is the 'promissory' rather than the 'administrative' covenant that is perpetual, thus
the absence of עולם in Gen. 15 must, for McComiskey, be as embarrassing as its
presence in Gen. 17.

c. *A Covenant Focusing on 'Seed' as Opposed to 'Land'*
Sailhamer's explanation of the relationship between Genesis 15 and 17 is the least complex. He too understands these chapters in terms of two distinct covenants, but for him the covenant of Genesis 15 relates to the promise of land, whereas the covenant of Genesis 17 has to do with the promise of descendants.[85]

Such a neat distinction is initially appealing, but in order to justify it Sailhamer is forced to be rather selective in his use of the text. He thus restricts the making of a covenant in Genesis 15 to vv. 18-21. While the land element is undeniably the prominent element in this covenant, the promise loses all significance without the related theme of descendants to inherit it.[86] Moreover, these heirs are certainly incorporated within the focus of this covenant; not only are they explicitly mentioned in Gen. 15.18, but the rest of the chapter makes their inclusion imperative.[87]

An even more rudimentary objection to Sailhamer's distinction, however, is that the promises reflected in Genesis 17 encompass much more than the promise of numerous descendants. As noted in the previous chapter, the promises in Genesis 17 include the promise of international significance, royal descendants, land, and a divine–human relationship. This suggests a complexity rather difficult to tie in with Sailhamer's overly simplistic dichotomy between 'a covenant made in regard to the promise of the land (15.18-21) and a covenant made in regard to the promise of a great abundance of descendants (17.2)'.[88]

These attempts, therefore, to explain the apparent incoherence between Genesis 15 and 17 in terms of two distinct covenants, while offering plausible explanations of some of the details, fail to do justice to all of the material in each chapter.

How, then, are we to understand the relationship between these two covenant chapters in the Abraham narrative? In the above discussion

85. Such a distinction in focus is alluded to by others also; for instance, Skinner, *Genesis*, pp. 276, 282; R.W. Klein, 'Call, Covenant and Community: The Story of Abraham and Sarah', *CurTM* 15 (1988), pp. 120-27 (123); Youngblood, *The Book of Genesis*, p. 169. This does not, however, automatically oblige them to treat Gen. 15 and 17 as two separate covenants, or indeed, as two distinct events in the life of Abraham.

86. See Chapter 4 Section 4 above.

87. Again, see Chapter 4 Section 4 above.

88. Sailhamer, *The Pentateuch as Narrative*, p. 156.

elements of discontinuity have been underlined, as well as other features that suggest a degree of continuity. Any satisfactory synchronic explanation of the literary and theological relationship between Genesis 15 and 17 must encompass both these facets. This can be achieved only by understanding the 'covenant between the pieces' and the 'covenant of circumcision' as two distinct, but related covenants.

4. *Genesis 15 and 17 as Distinct, but Related Covenants*

Understood in this way, the two chapters focus on two quite different covenants which are nevertheless united by common promissory threads; viz. Abraham's numerical proliferation (15.5; 17.2) and his territorial inheritance (15.18-21; 17.8). The covenant ratified in Genesis 15 solemnly guarantees that Abraham will indeed have 'descendants' (12.7; 13.16; 15.4-5, 13, 18), and that they will inherit the land that Yahweh had promised to Abraham and his 'seed' (cf. 12.7; 13.15; 15.7, 16, 18-21). The covenant announced in Genesis 17 transcends this guarantee of 'seed' and 'land' by both broadening and narrowing the promissory focus. The promissory focus is broadened in Genesis 17 in terms of Abraham's international significance. Abraham is no longer simply the progenitor of a single nation, however great and innumerable. He is the 'father of multitudinous nations' (i.e. their spiritual benefactor). The prospect of numerical proliferation is not restricted to a national entity that will trace its ancestral roots back to the patriarch (i.e. Abraham's physical descendants). Genesis 17 shows that God's promise of numerical proliferation (cf. 13.16; 15.5; 17.2) encompasses more than just one nation. It incorporates 'nations' (17.6, 16), indeed, 'a multitude of nations' (17.4-5), to whom Abraham will be 'father' in a metaphorical sense (i.e. their spiritual benefactor). Thus in Genesis 17 the promissory horizon is no longer national, but international. Abraham will be significant not just for one nation, but for 'multitudinous nations'.

However, as well as this broadening of promissory focus in Genesis 17, there is also a narrowing of it in relation to Abraham's physical 'seed'. Indeed, this feature best accounts for the introduction of the second covenant pericope after the birth of Ishmael and before the birth of Isaac. While the benefits and obligations apply to all those associated with Abraham and his 'seed' (cf. 17.7-8, 12-14), this covenant will be established (i.e. perpetuated), not with Abraham's 'seed' generally, but with a particular line of 'seed'. This line will commence with *Isaac*

(vv. 16-21) and continue through Jacob (Gen. 35.11-12). From this line of 'seed' will come 'kings' (cf. 17.16; 35.11) through whom this eternal covenant—guaranteeing Abraham's phenomenal increase (17.2), international significance (17.4-6), and perpetual inheritance (17.8)—will be maintained.[89] While the precise role of these royal descendants of Abraham through Isaac (vv. 6, 16) is nowhere spelt out in Genesis 17, the fact that they are mentioned in association with 'nations' each time (cf. also 35.11) strongly suggests that these 'kings' are directly linked to Abraham's international significance.[90] Abraham and Sarah's royal progeny provides the theological lynchpin between God's promise to make Abraham a 'great nation' (12.2) and his promise to make Abraham the 'father of multitudinous nations'. Thus the two covenants are not as unrelated as their respective promissory foci might initially suggest. Rather, the promise concerning the nations is entirely dependent upon the promise concerning nationhood. Without the establishment of the nation, there would be no kings through whom to perpetuate the covenant encompassing the nations. Consequently, the covenant introduced in Genesis 17 is contingent upon the fulfilment of the promises divinely guaranteed by covenant in Genesis 15. The latter is the foundation upon which the subsequent divine promises relating to Abraham's royal descendants and his international significance are built. This explains why the national dimension of the divine promise is not expunged altogether from Genesis 17, even though it clearly assumes a subsidiary role.

Therefore, in relation to the covenant in Genesis 15, the covenant announced in Genesis 17 is both broader and narrower in focus. It relates to Abraham's international, and not just his national, significance. But it will be established (i.e. perpetuated) not with Abraham's descendants generally, but with a particular line of his descendants: kings whose ancestry will be traced back to Abraham through Jacob and Isaac. It is this latter dimension which ties the two covenants together. These royal descendants of Abraham will rule over the nation guaranteed by covenant in Genesis 15. And through these royal

89. Admittedly, it is not explicitly stated in Genesis that God will perpetuate this covenant through the 'kings' who will descend from Abraham. However, such an inference is a logical one to draw, given that the context of each of the three texts that highlight these royal descendants (i.e. Gen. 17.6, 16; 35.11) is the transfer of covenant promises from one generation to the next (cf. 17.7-8, 17-21; 35.12).

90. This is discussed more fully in Chapter 5 Section 3c above.

descendants God's promise to make Abraham the 'father [i.e. bene-factor] of multitudinous nations' will be fulfilled.

5. The Ratification of the Eternal Covenant in Genesis 17?

Perhaps the most important question with regard to the literary function of Genesis 17 is whether a second covenant with Abraham is actually ratified in this chapter, or merely announced. The latter is suggested, not only by the inflection of the verbs נתן and הקים, but also by the absence of any sacrificial ritual or solemn oath.

For scholars who understand the 'covenant of circumcision' simply in terms of a reaffirmation of the 'covenant between the pieces', the absence of any ratification formula in Genesis 17 is to be expected; both the covenant's ratification by ritual and the associated oath had already been recorded in Genesis 15. However, as the above discussion has demonstrated, such a simplistic reading of the Abraham narrative overlooks the significant differences in the promissory foci reflected in these two chapters. Nor does it account for the fact that the actual establishment of the covenant depicted in Genesis 17 is repeatedly projected into the future; this makes no sense at all if the covenant has already been established in Genesis 15. To resolve this by suggesting that both נתן and הקים must respectively mean 'fulfil' and 'maintain' is not only circular reasoning, but also indefensibly empties the 'covenant of circumcision' of any significant promissory contribution; its chief purpose is simply to qualify the divine assurances given in Genesis 15.

This also introduces a theological conundrum into the narrative by implying that the solemn assurances that God had already given to Abraham in Genesis 15 were somehow deficient. Rather than being un-conditional guarantees, the fulfilment of these earlier promises becomes entirely contingent upon Abraham's subsequent behaviour. Only if Abraham fulfils the newly disclosed prerequisites will the 'covenant between the pieces' have any real significance. This makes the cove-nant in Genesis 15 both rather pointless and potentially misleading. It would seem, therefore, that if Genesis 17 is read as a reaffirmation and qualification of Genesis 15, the contribution of each passage to the overall narrative is severely undermined.[91]

91. By contrast, if understood in terms of two different (albeit related) cove-nants, each chapter makes a distinctive contribution to the development of the basic plot. Gen. 15 ratifies by covenant God's promises to make Abraham nationally

If, on the other hand, the covenants in Genesis 15 and 17 are distinguished, the actual establishment or ratification of the latter covenant must be located within the Abraham narrative. Thus the question arises, 'Was the second covenant ratified in Genesis 17 itself, or at some subsequent point in the Abraham narrative?'

There are several objections to locating the ratification of the second covenant within Genesis 17. Perhaps the most telling objection is the fact that throughout this chapter the establishment of this particular covenant is projected into the future (cf. the verbal inflections in vv. 2, 7, 19, and 21).[92] Significantly, nowhere in this pericope is the ratification of the covenant referred to as an established fact. Nor is there anything in Genesis 17 analogous to the narrator's comment and the solemn oath of Gen. 15.17-21. Interestingly, the narrator's concluding comments relate solely to Abraham's compliance with one of the covenant's requirements—the physical obligation of circumcision.[93] Together this leads one to suspect that while a second covenant between God and Abraham is announced in Genesis 17, it is not in fact ratified at this point in the narrative. For this we must look elsewhere.[94]

6. *Conclusion*

It would appear, therefore, that the function of Genesis 17 within its present literary context is much more complex than scholars of all shades of the theological spectrum have thus far imagined. The differences in emphasis between this pericope and Genesis 15 raise serious questions, not only for the traditional source-critical analysis, but also for standard synchronic interpretations. While Alexander, McComiskey and Sailhamer have all highlighted some of these differences, their recent attempts to resolve the problems raised by the inclusion of two

significant, whereas Gen. 17 heralds a similar ratification of the promise to make Abraham internationally significant.

92. The last two references relate to Isaac, with whom the establishment of the covenant must clearly be projected into the future. While it is possible to understand הקים as 'maintain' in all four verses, it is equally possible to read 'establish' in the sense of 'to ratify'.

93. Admittedly it could be argued that Abraham's ready submission to the rite of circumcision constituted his fulfilment of the moral obligation set out in Gen. 17.1.

94. Alexander's hypothesis—that this second covenant is ratified after the Akedah in Gen. 22—will be fully set out and critiqued in the following chapter.

covenant pericopes within the Abraham narrative fail to incorporate adequately the elements of continuity and discontinuity. Any holistic attempt to provide a coherent reading of the Abraham narrative must not only provide some sort of rationale for the differences in the promissory emphasis of Genesis 15 and 17, but also offer some explanation for the following features: the elements of continuity and discontinuity in the two pericopes; the literary gap between the 'covenant between the pieces' (Gen. 15) and the 'covenant of circumcision' (Gen. 17); the establishment of a covenant in Genesis 15 and the allusions to the future establishment of a covenant in Genesis 17; the unconditional nature of the covenant in Genesis 15 and the obligatory nature of the covenant in Genesis 17.

In the next chapter such a holistic reading is offered, demonstrating that one can make good literary sense of the Abrahamic narrative, while at the same time taking full cognizance of what are perhaps its most enigmatic features.

Chapter 7

THE COVENANTS OF GENESIS 15 AND 17 IN THEIR PRESENT
LITERARY CONTEXT

1. *Introduction*

In this chapter the relationship between the covenants in Genesis 15 and
17 and the rest of the Abraham narrative will be set out, especially in
relation to the promise of Gen. 12.1-3 and the ratification oath of Gen.
22.15-18. It will be shown that, in their present literary context, Genesis
15 and 17 describe two distinct, yet related covenants which reinforce
the divine promises of Gen. 12.1-3. The covenant recorded in Genesis
15, focusing primarily on the promise of nationhood, will be understood
as affirming the first dimension of the divine promise reflected in Gen.
12.2-3, whereas the covenant announced in Genesis 17, with its main
emphasis on Abraham's international significance (cf. vv. 4-6, 16), will
be interpreted in the light of the second promissory element reflected in
the original divine promise. It will be demonstrated further that the
latter covenant is not actually ratified until the episode recorded in
Genesis 22, when Yahweh reaffirms by solemn oath and reiterates both
dimensions of his original promise to bless Abraham.

2. *Genesis 12.1-9 and 22.1-19 as the Inclusio around the Main Abraham Narrative*

The striking similarities between Gen. 12.1-9 and 22.1-19 have suggested to several commentators that they function as an inclusio for the
major part of the Abraham cycle.[1] Both episodes commence with the

---

1.   See, for instance, N.M. Sarna, *Understanding Genesis: The Heritage of Biblical Israel* (New York: Schocken Books, 1970), pp. 160-163 (also *idem*, *Genesis*,
p. 150); G.W. Coats, 'Abraham's Sacrifice of Faith: A Form-Critical Study of Genesis 22', *Int* 27 (1973), pp. 389-400 (395-97); J.L. Crenshaw, 'Journey Into Oblivion: A Structural Analysis of Gen. 22.1-19', *Soundings* 58 (1975), pp. 243-56 (245)

rare phrase לְךָ לְךָ which in each case is heightened by the expansion which follows (cf. 'your land, your clan and your father's house', Gen. 12.1; 'your son, your only son Isaac, whom you love', Gen. 22.2). The immediate objective of the command in both instances is similarly vague (cf. 'to the land that I will disclose to you', Gen. 12.2; 'to…one of the mountains which I will tell you', Gen. 22.2). In both chapters the divine instructions carry an element of promise (cf. 12.2-3; 22.15-18) and are met with Abraham's immediate compliance (cf. 12.4a; 22.3), although the order of these two features is noticeably inverted: in Genesis 12 the order is command, promise, obedience, whereas in Genesis 22 it is command, obedience, oath.[2] Such an inversion of order is surely significant; it implies that Abraham's obedience was a prerequisite for the divine oath, an observation confirmed by the emphasis on his obedience both in Genesis 22 itself (vv. 16b, 18b) and elsewhere.[3] In any case, Chew is correct to conclude that 'the two speeches encasing the Abraham narratives constitute a literary frame'.[4]

As well as these assonances in content, there are at least two other factors which suggest that Gen. 12.1-9 and 22.1-19 function as an inclusio in the Abraham narrative. The first is the fact that they record respectively the first and last divine self-disclosure to Abraham, which

(also *idem, A Whirlpool of Torment* [OBT; Philadelphia: Fortress Press, 1984], p. 15); W. McKane, *Studies in the Patriarchal Narratives* (Edinburgh: Handsel Press, 1979), p. 233; W. Yarchin, 'Imperative and Promise in Genesis 12.1-3', *StudBT* 10 (1980), pp. 164-78 (173); Chew, '"Blessing for the Nations"', pp. 103-104; Magonet, 'Abraham and God', pp. 160-70 (also *idem, Bible Lives*, pp. 24-27); J.B. Moster, 'The Testing of Abraham', *Dor Le Dor* 17 (1988–89), pp. 237-42 (238-39); Abela, *The Themes of the Abraham Narrative*, p. 26 n. 61; Garrett, *Rethinking Genesis*, pp. 160-63; J. Doukhan, 'The Centre of the Aqedah: A Study of the Literary Structure of Genesis 22.1-19', *AUSS* 31.1 (1993), pp. 17-28 (21-22); Stek, '"Covenant" Overload', p. 30 n. 63; K.A. Deurloo, 'The Way of Abraham', in M. Kessler (ed. and trans.), *Voices From Amsterdam* (Atlanta: Scholars Press, 1994), pp. 96, 109; Alexander, 'Abraham Reassessed', pp. 9, 18 (also *idem, From Paradise to the Promised Land*, p. 47 n. 7); Wenham, *Genesis 16–50*, pp. 99-103. Cf. M.A. O'Brien, 'The Story of Abraham and the Debate over Source Hypothesis', *AusBR* 38 (1990), pp. 3-6; Arnold, *Encountering the Book of Genesis*, p. 108.

2. Gen. 12.1-4a and Gen. 22.15-18 may be seen as an inclusio within an inclusio (see, for example, Mullen, *Ethnic Myths*, p. 143 n. 60). The precise function of the latter text in the Abraham narrative is discussed in detail below; cf. Section 4c.

3. Cf. Gen. 26.5.

4. Chew, '"Blessing for the Nations"', p. 104.

makes the assonances outlined above all the more striking. The second
is the apparent symmetrical arrangement of the Abraham cycle which
Wenham helpfully sets out as follows: [5]

A						Genealogy of Terah	11.26-32
	B					Call of Abram	12.1-9
		C				Sarah endangered	12.10-20
			D			Lot episodes 1	13.1–14.24
				E		Covenant with Abraham	15.1-21
					F	Birth of Ishmael	16.1-16
				E′		Covenant with Abraham	17.1-27
			D′			Lot episodes 2	18.1–19.38
		C′				Sarah endangered	20.1-18
	B′					Testing of Abraham	22.1-19
A′						Genealogy of Milcah	22.20-24

Thus as Wenham contends, 'this overall structure reinforces the sense
of parallel between Gen. 12.1-9, Abraham's call and 22.1-19, his testing. The first tells of Abraham's first encounter with God, the second of
his final encounter.'[6] On each occasion Abraham is given specific instructions to obey. In both passages a series of divine promises are consequent on Abraham's compliance.[7] Moreover, both chapters share several common motifs: the order to go to a place indicated by God; the
instruction to sever a family link; the promise of personal blessing,
nationhood and international blessing. Moster's conclusion is apt: 'these
[i.e. points of similarity between Gen. 12 and 22] are too numerous to
be attributed to coincidence. What we have here is a compositional

---

5.   Wenham, 'The Akedah: A Paradigm', p. 98. Cf. the palistrophes proposed
by Cassuto, *From Noah to Abraham*, pp. 294-96; Coats, *Genesis*, p. 28; Magonet,
'Abraham and God', p. 162; I.M. Kikiwada and A. Quinn, *Before Abraham Was:
The Unity of Genesis 1–11* (Nashville: Abingdon Press, 1985), p. 96; Rosenberg,
King and Kin, p. 84; Rendsburg, *The Redaction of Genesis*, pp. 28-29. Though their
palistrophes are marginally different, they all similarly pair Gen. 12.1-9 with 22.1-
19, suggesting that regardless of the presence or absence of a chiastic structure in
the narrative, it is clearly bracketed by this inclusio.

6.   Wenham, 'The Akedah: A Paradigm', p. 98. Admittedly, the inexplicable
omission in Wenham's chiastic structure of Gen. 21.1-34 undermines his structural
argument to some extent.

7.   In both Gen. 12.1-3 and Gen. 22.16-18 the promised blessing apparently
incorporates a personal, national and international dimension. The various elements
in both promissory passages are discussed below.

technique used to mark the beginning and end of a literary unit'.[8] Therefore a detailed analysis of each of these pericopes is essential for a
canonical reading of the main Abraham narrative, or as Moster has
aptly subtitled it, 'The Evolution of the Covenant Relationship between
God and Abraham'.[9]

3. A Detailed Analysis of Genesis 12.1-3

The pivotal importance of Gen. 12.1-3 in the present form of Genesis is
widely recognized.[10] Set against the dark backcloth of the primaeval
prologue (and in particular, the Babel incident), this text heralds a new
stage in God's dealings with humanity. It sets the agenda for the Abraham cycle and the patriarchal stories which follow in the book of
Genesis, and also introduces the key themes of the subsequent Pentateuchal narrative. As Wenham avers:

> by placing the promises to Abram right at the beginning of the patri-
> archal narratives the redactor is asserting their fundamental importance
> for the history of Israel and the world and indicating how the stories that
> follow ought to be understood.[11]

a. *The Translation of Genesis 12.1-3*
This speech pericope, bracketed by the narrator's comments (vv. 1, 4a),
contains a series of divine promises consequent on Abraham's compliance with Yahweh's instructions. Before a detailed analysis of the
contents of this pericope can be attempted, two important translation
problems must be addressed; viz. the force of the imperative form of

---

8. Moster, 'The Testing of Abraham', p. 239.
9. Moster, 'The Testing of Abraham', p. 239.
10. Cf. H.W. Wolff, 'The Kerygma of the Yahwist', *Int* 20 (1966), pp. 131-58
(145); Van Develder, 'Abrahamic Covenant Traditions', p. 51; von Rad, *Genesis*,
p. 154; A.K. Jenkins, 'A Great Name: Genesis 12.2 and the Editing of the Pentateuch', *JSOT* 10 (1978), pp. 41-57 (46, 53); C. Westermann, *The Promises to the
Fathers* (trans. D.E. Green; Philadelphia: Fortress Press, 1979), p. 156 (see also his
Genesis 12–36, p. 148); J.A. Emerton, 'The Origin of the Promises to the Patriarchs
in the Older Sources of the Book of Genesis', *VT* 32 (1982), pp. 14-32 (14); P.D.
Miller, 'Syntax and Theology in Genesis 12.3a', *VT* 34 (1984), pp. 472-76 (472);
Wenham, *Genesis 1–15*, pp. 268, 274-75; Turner, *Announcements of Plot*, p. 52;
McKeown, 'Unifying Themes', pp. 54-57.
11. Wenham, *Genesis 1–15*, p. 271.

היה at the end of v. 2, and the nuance of the niphal form of ברך at the
end of v. 3.

As P.D. Miller observes, 'The issues in understanding the syntax are
not merely superficial, for the meaning of the text is to a large degree
uncovered by a careful understanding of the relation of the clauses to
each other'.[12] Moreover, in that the translation of this programmatic
text may have important ramifications for the reading of the subsequent
Abraham narrative, it is important that these grammatical features of
the text are adequately examined. The Hebrew text of Genesis 12.1-4.a
is set out below:

ויאמר יהוה אל־אברם לך־לך מארצך וממולדתך ומבית אביך
אל־הארץ אשר אראך: ואעשך לגוי גדול ואברכך ואגדלה שמך
והיה ברכה: ואברכה מברכיך ומקללך אאר ונברכו בך כל
משפחת האדמה: וילך אברם כאשר דבר אליו יהוה

The first imperative and its initial corollaries are reasonably clear:
God gives Abraham the command to 'Go!' and promises nationhood ('a
great nation, blessing, and a great name').

The grammatical nuance of the second imperative in the Masoretic
Text (the verb היה in v. 2d) is more controversial. As it stands it may
be taken either as a second command in this divine speech (i.e. 'Be a
blessing!'),[13] or as an emphatic consequence clause (i.e. '…so that you
will effect blessing').[14]

12. Miller, 'Syntax and Theology', p. 472.

13. So many recent studies: see, for example, Mitchell, 'Abram's Understanding', p. 35; F.I. Andersen, *The Sentence in Biblical Hebrew* (Paris: Mouton,
1974), p. 108; R.W. Klein, 'The Yahwist Looks at Abraham', *CTM* 45 (1974), pp.
43-49 (44); Dequeker, 'Noah and Israel', p. 123; S. Terrien, *The Elusive Presence*
(San Francisco: Harper & Row, 1978), p. 73; P. Auffret, 'Essai sur la structure
littéraire de Gn 12.1-4aα', *BZ* 26 (1982), pp. 243-48 (247); W.J. Dumbrell, 'The
Covenant with Abraham', *RTR* 38 (1982), pp. 42-50 (42-43); Chew, ' "Blessing for
the Nations" ', p. 167; B. Och, 'Abraham and Moriah: A Journey to Fulfilment',
Judaism 38 (1989), pp. 293-309 (301); Clines, *What Does Eve Do To Help?*, p. 56;
Turner, *Announcements of Plot*, p. 55; G. Van Groningen, *Messianic Revelation in
the Old Testament* (Grand Rapids: Baker Book House, 1990), p. 134 n. 17; Janzen,
Genesis 12–50, p. 15; Alexander, 'Abraham Reassessed', p. 12. Though retaining
an imperative mood in his translation, Hamilton (*Genesis 1–17*) nevertheless interprets it as a consequence clause linked to the initial imperative in v. 1; cf. p. 369
n. 3 and p. 373 n. 12.

14. This interpretation has the support of some eminent Hebraists (for instance,
Driver, *Tenses in Hebrew*, p. 69; GKC, §110i; Joüon, §116h; Gibson, *Davidson's*

Alternatively, others have suggested emendations to the Masoretic Text. Following Rashi, some have re-pointed the consonantal text as וְהָיָה, giving the reading 'and it [i.e. 'your name', v. 2c] shall be a blessing'.[15] More radically, Coats has suggested inserting a yod after the conjunction to maintain the flow of imperfects with waw expressing consequence.[16]

However, Turner's observation is surely pertinent: 'If the passage wished to convey the impv. in this line (v. 2d)...it could not have done so any better than the present MT'.[17] This, and the fact that there does not seem to be any overwhelming argument for disallowing the usual imperative force here, justifies Terrien's conclusion that although the imperative phrase 'be a blessing' may be unusual, 'there is no valid reason to correct it (Gen 12.2c). This is the mission of Abraham and of Israel: "Be a blessing!"'[18]

Retaining an imperative reading of וְהָיָה is given further support by the fact that both imperatives in this pericope are directly followed by cohortatives. Normally such a construction expresses purpose or result.[19] It is therefore accurate to convey the Hebrew syntax of these conditional clauses by linking the promises to their related imperatives by 'so that'.[20] The fact that the first of these imperative-cohortative clauses in Gen. 12.2-3 expresses a conditional promise provides ample

Introductory Hebrew Grammar—Syntax, §86b, pp. 105-106), and is adopted by several commentators, see, for example, Wolff, 'Kerygma of the Yahwist', p. 137 n. 28; Van Develder, 'Abrahamic Covenant Traditions', p. 116; T. Vriezen, 'Bemerkungen zu Genesis 12.1-7', in M. Beek *et al.* (eds.), *Symbolae Biblicae et Mesopotamicae* (Festschrift F.M.T. de Liagre Böhl; Leiden: E.J. Brill, 1973)p. 387; E. Ruprecht, 'Vorgegebene Tradition und theologische Gestaltung in Genesis XII 1-3', *VT* 29 (1979), p. 180; Yarchin, 'Imperative and Promise', p. 171; Westermann, *Genesis 12–36*, p. 144; Wenham, *Genesis 1–15*, pp. 266, 276; Hamilton, *Genesis 1–17*, p. 373. This interpretation is also reflected in several English translations, e.g. RSV; NIV; NASB; NRSV.

15. So, for example, Gunkel, *Genesis*, p. 164; Skinner, *Genesis*, p. 244; Speiser, *Genesis*, pp. 85-86; NEB.

16. Coats, *Genesis*, p. 107.

17. Turner, *Announcements of Plot*, p. 53 n. 4.

18. Terrien, *Elusive Presence*, p. 74.

19. Cf. Chapter 3 Section 3b (n. 75) above.

20. Cf. Alexander, 'Genesis 22 and the Covenant', pp. 19-21 and 'Abraham Reassessed', p. 12; Turner, *Announcements of Plot*, p. 55; Janzen, *Genesis 12–50*, p. 15.

reason for taking an identical construction in the same pericope as a quite distinct conditional promise, and this is the premise of the translation given below.[21]

In relation to the second translation crux—the nuance of the niphal of ברך at the end of v. 3—there are again two main lines of interpretation: נברכו may be understood either in a passive sense (i.e. 'all the families of the earth shall *be blessed* through you'), or in a reflexive sense (i.e. 'by you all the families of the earth shall *bless themselves*').

It should also be noted that the precise nuance given to the debated niphal form here has a direct influence upon the translation of the following prepositional phrase בך. In agreement with a reflexive interpretation of נברכו it is possible to translate בך as 'by you'.[22] However, a local sense ('in you') or an instrumental sense ('through you') is equally possible, and as Dumbrell suggests, 'a somewhat parallel use of the phrase in Gen 21.12 ("for through Isaac shall your descendants be named" RSV) tips the scales in favour of an instrumental sense'.[23]

In support of the passive interpretation of Gen. 12.3 the following points may be noted:

1. Both the LXX (ἐνευλογηθήσονται ἐν σοὶ πᾶσαι αἱ φυλαὶ τῆς γῆς), followed by other ancient versions (e.g. Vulgate, Targums; cf. Sir. 44.21) and the New Testament (e.g. καὶ ἐν τῷ σπέρματί σου [ἐν]ευλογηθήσονται πᾶσαι αἱ πατριαὶ τῆς γῆς, Acts 3.25; 'ενευλογηθήσονται ἐν σοὶ πάντα τὰ ἔθνη, Gal. 3.8) indicate the antiquity of a passive interpretation.[24]

2. The niphal conjugation generally carries a passive voice, whereas a reflexive is normally indicated by means of the hithpael. If a reflexive voice were intended, this could have been communicated unambiguously through a consistent use of the hithpael.

3. A hithpael does not necessarily carry a reflexive force, but

21. See Section 3b.

22. So RSV; JB; NJPSV; NRSV (in footnote); NJB.

23. Dumbrell, 'The Covenant with Abraham', p. 49.

24. The decisive argument for R.L. Brawley ('For Blessing All Families of the Earth: Covenant Traditions in Luke–Acts', *CurTM* 22 [1995], pp. 18-26 [25]), for whom the LXX translation of Gen. 22.18 in the future passive 'obviates the ambiguity'.

may have a passive meaning in some contexts.[25] Therefore it is possible that the hithpael forms of בּרך should be read in the light of the niphals rather than vice versa. Not surprisingly, therefore, a passive interpretation has both past and present scholarly support.[26]

Those who advocate a reflexive translation,[27] however, make the following observations:

25. O.T. Allis ('The Blessing of Abraham', *Princeton Theological Review* 25 [1927], pp. 263-98 [281]) lists the following texts as examples: Gen. 37.35; Num. 31.23; Deut. 4.21; 23.9; 1 Sam. 3.14; 30.6; 1 Kgs 2.26; Job 15.28; 30.16, 17; Pss. 107.17, 27; 119.52; Isa. 30.29; Lam. 4.1; Ezek. 19.12; Dan. 12.10; Mic. 6.16. To these Hamilton (*Genesis 1–17*, p. 375) suggests the following additions: Prov. 31.30; Eccl. 8.10; Ps. 72.17.

26. See, for instance, KJV; E.W. Hengstenberg, 'The History of the Kingdom of God in the Old Testament', in *The Works of Hengstenberg* (4 vols.; repr., Cherry Hill: Mack, 1972 [1871]), pp. 125-27; J.C.L. von Hofmann, *Weissagung und Erfüllung im alten und neuen Testamente: Ein theologischer Versuch* (2 vols.; Nördlingen: C.H. Beck, 1841–44), I, pp. 96-98; König, *Die Genesis*, pp. 449-50; Allis, 'The Blessing of Abraham', pp. 263-98; Jacob, *Das Erst Buch der Tora*, pp. 338-39; R. Martin-Achard, *A Light to the Nations: A Study of the Old Testament Conception of Israel's Mission to the World* (trans. J.P. Smith; Edinburgh: Oliver and Boyd, 1962), pp. 32-37; Cassuto, *From Noah to Abraham*, p. 315; Kidner, *Genesis*, p. 114; Van Develder, 'Abrahamic Covenant Traditions', pp. 135, 145-48 (even though he translates it reflexively [p. 93]—he suggests that the passive/reflexive senses are not mutually exclusive, p. 128); C.L. Rogers, 'The Covenant with Abraham and its Historical Setting', *BSac* 127 (1970), pp. 241-56 (255); J.B. Payne, 'A Critical Note on Ecclesiasticus 44.21's Commentary on the Abrahamic covenant', *JETS* 15 (1972), pp. 186-87; von Rad, *Genesis*, pp. 160-61; J. Scharbert, 'בּרך brk', *TDOT*, II, p. 297 (also *idem*, *Genesis 12–50*, p. 128); Vriezen, 'Bemerkungen zu Genesis 12.1-7', pp. 388-89; W.C. Kaiser, Jr, *Toward an Old Testament Theology* (Grand Rapids: Zondervan, 1978), p. 13; Magonet, 'Abraham and God', p. 164; Dequeker, 'Noah and Israel', p. 123; Hamilton, *Genesis 1–17*, pp. 374-76; Mullen, *Ethnic Myths*, p. 129.

27. Such an interpretation has been predominant in scholarly exegesis since Rashi: RSV; JB; NEB; REB; NJB. Scholars adopting the reflexive interpretation include Delitzsch, *A New Commentary on Genesis*, I, pp. 378-80; Dillmann, *Genesis*, II, p. 12; Holzinger, *Genesis*, p. 137; Gunkel, *Genesis*, p. 165; J. Skinner, *Genesis*, p. 244; J. Muilenburg, 'Abraham and the Nations: Blessing and World History', *Int* 19 (1965), pp. 387-98 (391-93); B. Albrektson, *History and the Gods: An Essay on the Idea of Historical Events as Divine Manifestations in the Ancient Near East and in Israel* (ConBOT, 1; Lund: Gleerup, 1967), pp. 79-81; Vawter, *On Genesis*, p. 177; W.G. Plaut (ed.), *Genesis. The Torah: A Modern Commentary*

1. A passive connotation could have been unequivocally conveyed by means of the more frequent qal passive participle or
   the pual (a form of ברך admittedly not found in Genesis, but
   employed elsewhere in the Pentateuch; cf. Num. 22.6; Deut.
   33.13).
2. Elsewhere in Genesis the essential formula of 12.3 is cast in
   both the niphal (18.18; 28.14) and hithpael (22.18; 26.4)
   forms. The primarily reflexive hithpael form should be used to
   interpret the disputed niphal.
3. What is meant by the reflexive expression is to evoke blessing
   upon oneself using the name of Abraham, as is illustrated by
   several instances of this type of formula elsewhere (cf. Gen.
   48.20; Zech. 8.13; Ruth 4.11).

A major difficulty with the reflexive interpretation, however, is that
the promises are explicitly related to the person of Abraham rather than
to his name. Thus, he and not his name will be a source of blessing for
others. Indeed, as Vogels correctly observes:

> This corresponds much better with the whole context, in which the '*you*'
> is frequently used...'those who bless *you*' (v. 3), and not those who bless
> his name. In other words Abraham will be a cause of blessing for
> others.[28]

An additional difficulty for the reflexive interpretation is underlined
by Wehmeier, who insists that a reflexive interpretation of the verb is
not supported by the structure of the pericope:

> If in this context V. 3b would say that the nations *wished* to be blessed as
> Israel is, this would constitute a peculiar anticlimax. Rather we expect an
> indication that the nations *participate* in Israel's blessing. This is
> especially clear in the light of V. 3a... what is expected to be the normal

(New York: Union of American Hebrew Congregations, 1981), p. 116; M. Wein-
feld, 'The Old Testament—the Discipline and its Goals', in J.A. Emerton (ed.),
Congress Volume (VTSup, 32; Leiden: E.J. Brill, 1981), p. 426 n. 8; B. Dahlberg,
'The Unity of Genesis', in K.R.R. Gros Louis and J.S. Ackerman (eds.), *Literary
Interpretations of Biblical Narratives* (Nashville: Abingdon Press, 1982), II, p. 131;
Westermann, *Genesis 12–36*, pp. 151-52; Blum, *Vätergeschichte*, pp. 350-52;
O'Brien, 'Story of Abraham', p. 9; Janzen, *Genesis 12–50*, p. 15; S. Japhet, 'The
Trial of Abraham and the Test of Job: How Do They Differ?', *Henoch* 16 (1994),
pp. 153-72 (155).
    28. Vogels, *God's Universal Covenant*, p. 41.

action is expressed by the plural, that others bless Israel and consequently receive blessings themselves. In continuation of this statement
one should expect an indication that the nations participate in Israel's
blessing and not only that they wish to be blessed. Hence the context
does not favour the reflexive understanding of the Nif'al.[29]

Thus an exclusively reflexive interpretation of this text would appear
to be ruled out, a conclusion confirmed by the similar texts in which the
niphal is employed. The incongruity of a reflexive interpretation is most
transparent in Gen. 18.18, where a statement concerning a mere wish
expressed by other nations would hardly explain Abraham's significance. Rather, as Wehmeier observes, 'it is only because they *receive*
blessing through Abraham that the patriarch's role is so important'.[30]
The third text (Gen. 28.14) in which the niphal form occurs is evidently
citing the Gen. 12.3 clause verbatim, but adding 'and in your seed' from
22.18 and 26.4. If a reflexive interpretation cannot be sustained in Gen.
12.3, it is at least dubious that such a nuance was intended by the narrator citing this text in Gen. 28.14. Moreover, given that a text which
actually employs the hithpael is also alluded to, the use of the niphal (in
preference to the hithpael?) in Gen. 28.14 is perhaps significant. It
appears most improbable, therefore, that the compiler of Genesis intended his readers to interpret these occurrences of the niphal form
of ברך reflexively. Nevertheless, this leaves the use of the hithpael in
Gen. 22.18 and 26.4 unexplained. Wehmeier's explanation is less than
convincing. He maintains that both passages derive from the hand of a
relatively late redactor, the rogue hithpael verbs reflecting typical Deuteronomic antipathy towards non-Israelites. Unable to remove these
promises so deeply rooted in the patriarchal traditions, the Deuteronomic redactor deliberately attempted to weaken their force by rein-
terpreting this particular promise in a reflexive sense:

> While the Yahwist had emphasised that the nations participated in the
> blessing of Israel, and that this was the focal point of God's plans, the
> later redactor holds that the nations only *wished* to be blessed like Israel,
> but that they are not actually included in the intended scope of Yahweh's
> history with his people.[31]

---

29. G. Wehmeier, 'The Theme of "Blessing for the Nations" in the Promises to
the Patriarchs and in Prophetical Literature', *BangTF* 6 (1974), pp. 1-13 (5-6).
30. Wehmeier, 'The Theme of "Blessing for the Nations"', p. 6.
31. Wehmeier, 'The Theme of "Blessing for the Nations"', pp. 10-11.

Not only does this explanation depend on the rather dubious assertion that both these passages are later interpolations,[32] but it also raises an additional question: why could such a high-handed editor not simply have recast the niphal texts in hithpael form?

A more plausible solution to account for the enigmatic hithpael forms has been advocated by a number of scholars.[33] These scholars suggest giving the niphal a 'middle' sense (i.e. 'win/find blessing'), a translation which has the advantage of incorporating both a passive and reflexive meaning, thus explaining why the compiler of Genesis allowed both forms of the verb to stand unaltered in the final text. If a middle rather than a passive sense were intended, this would also explain why the more common qal passive participle or pual of ברך was not employed. Moreover, as Dumbrell correctly points out, 'Such a sense would also be more congruent with the general Old Testament position on mission, whereby the nations are consistently presented as seekers, as coming to a reconstituted Israel'.[34]

Such a medio-passive interpretation, however, while accommodating both the niphal and hithpael conjugations, still leaves unexplained the distribution of these two forms of ברך in the relevant texts (i.e. Gen. 12.3; 18.18; 22.18; 26.4; 28.14). Why is the niphal used in 12.3, 18.18 and 28.14, but the hithpael in 22.18 and 26.4? A close comparison of these texts discloses that where the niphal is deployed, a less direct situation is implied: the one through whom the nations will acquire blessing is Abraham (or, in the case of 28.14, Jacob).[35] In contrast, in

---

32. See Section 4b below.

33. See, for example, Procksch, *Die Genesis*, pp. 96-97; J. Schreiner, 'Segen für die Völker in der Verheissung an die Väter', *BZ* 6 (1962), pp. 1-31 (7); Wolff, 'Kerygma of the Yahwist', p. 137 n. 31; L. Schmidt, 'Israel ein Segen für die Völker? (Das Ziel des jahwistischen Werkes—eine Auseinandersetzung mit H.W. Wolff)', *TV* 12 (1975), pp. 135-51 (138-39) (cf. *idem*, 'Überlegungen zum Jahwisten', *EvT* 37 [1977], pp. 230-47 [239-40]); Vogels, *God's Universal Covenant*, p. 40 (also *idem*, *Abraham et sa Légende: Genèse 12,1–25,11* [Paris: Cerf, 1996], pp. 104, 110-11); Dumbrell, 'The Covenant with Abraham', p. 49; C.W. Mitchell, *The Meaning of BRK 'To Bless' in the Old Testament* (SBLDS, 95; Atlanta: Scholars Press, 1987), pp. 31-33; Wenham, *Genesis 1–15*, p. 266 n. 3f; McKeown, 'Unifying Themes', pp. 65-66; Scullion, *Genesis*, p. 110; C.A. Keller and G. Wehmeier, 'ברך *brk* pi. To bless', *TLOT*, I, p. 274.

34. Dumbrell, 'The Covenant with Abraham', p. 49.

35. Admittedly, 28.14 also includes mention of Jacob's 'seed'. Even so, the

contexts where the hithpael is found, the channel of blessing is the promised 'seed'—through whom the anticipated blessing will be directly communicated. Significantly, this more direct situation is implicit not only in both Genesis texts which use the hithpael ברך, but also in the two comparative occurrences in the Hebrew Bible (i.e. Ps. 72.17; Jer. 4.2).

It is perhaps preferable, therefore, to retain some distinction in connotation between the niphal and hithpael forms of ברך, rather than treating them as being entirely synonymous. For example, the hithpael form of the promise may be understood as what Waltke and O'Connor describe as a 'benefactive reflexive',[36] and translated as 'in your seed all the nations of the earth will acquire blessing for themselves'. The niphal may be understood as a middle and rendered 'through you all the families of the earth may/will experience blessing'.

b. *The Structure of Genesis 12.1-3*
Translating והיה (v. 2) in an imperative sense, there are clearly two main divisions in Gen. 12.1-3, each commencing with a divine command ('Go!' v. 1b; 'Be a blessing' v. 2d) with related promises ('national significance', v. 2abc; 'international significance', v. 3). The pericope is set out below with its command-promise, command-promise structure:

> Yahweh told Abram,
>> 'Leave your land, your clan and your father's house and go to the land that I will disclose to you,
>>> so that I may make you into a great nation, bless you and make you famous.
>> Be a blessing,
>>> so that I may bless those blessing you and curse whoever despises you and so that through you all the families of the ground may experience blessing.'
> Abram did as Yahweh said... (my translation).

Clearly the narrator's comments with regard to the introduction of Yahweh's speech and details of Abraham's response provide a

---

primary mediator of blessing referred to is Jacob, thus the niphal conjugation is used.

36. *IBHS*, §26.2e (p. 430). Such a reflexive 'refers to an action done on one's own behalf'.

structural framework for the pericope.[37] Between these comments there
are two sets of conditional promises related by the theme of blessing. In
the first segment (vv. 1-2c) Abraham is to be the recipient of blessing;
in the second segment (vv. 2d-3) Abraham is to be the mediator of
blessing.

This subtle distinction within this short pericope is further illustrated
by the fact that in the first part (vv. 1-2c) only two parties are explicitly
mentioned (i.e. Yahweh and Abraham), whereas third parties are specifically introduced in the second segment. The focus of the promises in
the two sections of this pericope (vv. 1-4a) is therefore not identical.
Thus a progression in vv. 1-3 can be discerned: the focus shifts from
primarily God and Abraham to others who are described in terms of
their relationship with Abraham. There is, nevertheless, a clear relation
between the two distinctive segments in these verses. The third parties
are recipients of God's blessing or curse, depending on their relationship with Abraham. As Janzen asserts, 'This widening movement suggests a deep relation between the call and destiny of Abram and his
descendants, and the call and destiny of all human communities'.[38]

Therefore the blessing promised in the second sub-section, while
remaining distinct, is in some way dependent upon the promise related
in the first; that is, Abraham's role as a mediator of blessing is contingent upon his being a recipient of blessing.

c. *The Meaning of Genesis 12.1-3*
There can be little doubt that the central theme of this pericope is that
of blessing. This is reflected, not only by the frequent occurrence of the
root ברך,[39] but also by its climactic position at the end of the speech.
Therefore, Alexander is surely correct in suggesting that

> the primary motive behind the call of Abraham is God's desire to bring
> blessing, rather than cursing, upon the families of the earth. The promise
> that Abraham will become a great nation...must be understood as being
> subservient to God's principal desire to bless all the families of the
> earth.[40]

37. Wenham's attempt (*Genesis 1–15*, p. 270) to detect a deliberate chiastic
pattern is not altogether convincing; in any case, the narrator's comments by themselves provide an adequate inclusio for this pericope regardless of any such additional literary device.
38. Janzen, *Genesis 12–50*, p. 17.
39. The root ברך is used five times in 12.2-3.
40. Alexander, 'Abraham Re-assessed', p. 13.

However, while there is general agreement that the central thrust of the pericope relates to blessing, retaining an imperative force for והיה in v. 2d does have important ramifications for precisely how the details are interpreted: it shifts attention to some extent to the conditions upon which the promises depend.[41] The second imperative indicates that there are two distinctive sets of promissory clauses, the realization of each being dependent on Abraham's compliance with the associated command. Thus Gen. 12.1-3 is not a purely gracious pronouncement;[42] rather, in order to achieve national prestige (v. 2a, b, c), Abraham must comply with the divine instruction to 'Go...!' (v. 1b). As Hamilton comments, 'the promise to give the land to Abram (v. 7) follows the promise to show the land to Abram (v. 1), and "show" becomes "give" only when Abram makes his move'.[43] Similarly, in order for others to 'find blessing' through him, Abraham must obey the divine injunction to 'Be a blessing!' (v. 2d).[44] It is important, therefore, that the promissory aspects in these verses are clearly defined and carefully distinguished. Even though there is a clear connection between the blessing promised to Abraham and the blessing promised through Abraham, a failure to demarcate these two prospects unfortunately obscures the meaning of this programmatic text in the Abraham narrative.

Related to the first imperative is the prospect of national status, conveyed in the threefold promise of 'a great nation, blessing, and a great name' (v. 2a, b, c). There is general agreement that each of these three promissory elements relates to the idea of national status, the 'great nation' and the 'great name' disclosing the precise nature of the anticipated 'blessing'.[45] Moreover, the use of the noun גוי in this context

---

41. Contrast Wenham's premise that 'the divine speech consists of a command ...followed by a series of promises (vv. 2-3) that heavily outweigh the command, showing where the chief interest of the passage lies' (*Genesis 1–15*, p. 274). In a similar vein Moberly (commenting on Gen. 22) suggests that 'one of the most notable features about the divine promises elsewhere in Genesis is that they always constitute a unilateral and unconditional offer on God's part' ('The Earliest Commentary on the Akedah', *VT* 38 [1988], pp. 302-23 [318]).

42. Contra Wenham and Moberly.

43. Hamilton, *Genesis 1–17*, p. 371.

44. How Abraham was to become a source of blessing is not spelt out explicitly, but when 12.2 is read in conjunction with 22.16-18, his personal faith and his future posterity appear to play a crucial role.

45. So Hamilton, *Genesis 1–17*, p. 372; Janzen, *Genesis 12–50*, p. 15; Carr, *Reading the Fractures*, p. 187. Cf. Dumbrell's observation ('The Covenant with

signifies that a geopolitical entity is being spoken of.[46] This is supported by the fact that

> their [i.e. Abraham's descendants] existence as a nation is closely tied to the promise of the possession of the land which is made to Abraham at the same time (12.7; cf. 17.8; 18.18). While the extended family of Abraham's descendants naturally constitutes an *'am*, it requires a territorial acquisition…before they can truly form a *goy* among the other *goyim* of the world.[47]

The 'great name' promised to Abraham again relates to the overarching promise of nationhood. This is indicated here not only by a deliberate contrast with the failed aspirations of the tower-builders of Babel (cf. Gen. 11.4) whose attempts at civil organization (nationhood) had been thwarted by divine judgment, but also by the fact that this same language is used in relation to David (2 Sam. 7.9) in the context of international prestige. As well as pointing to national prestige in the Hebrew Bible (cf. 2 Sam. 8.13; 1 Kgs 1.47), this phrase ('a great name') seems to perform a similar function in several royal inscriptions from early second-millennium Mesopotamia.[48]

On account of this association with David (cf. Ps. 72.17) and extra-biblical royal inscriptions, it might seem logical to see in this promise of 'a great name' an allusion to the Israelite monarchy, specifically, the Davidic-Solomonic era, an inference drawn by numerous scholars.[49]

Abraham', p. 47) that 'blessing in Gen. has the nationhood of the passage [12.1-3] primarily in view, i.e. it carries with it the notion of territory as well as descendants'. While H. Mowvley ('The Concept and Content of Blessing in the Old Testament', *BT* 16.2 [1965)], pp. 74-80) is certainly correct in identifying fertility as a key aspect of 'blessing', his thesis leans too heavily on questionable etymological connections between the root for 'bless' and the root for 'kneel'. Cf. Mitchell's critique (*The Meaning of BRK*, pp. 3-16) of Mowvley and others employing such methodology. Mitchell (pp. 29-36) has shown that the blessing promised in Gen. 12.2 is a much more multifaceted concept; for a similar conclusion, see also McKeown's detailed analysis, 'Unifying Themes', pp. 53-98.

46. The three major constitutional aspects of a גוי are identified by Clements as race, government and territory (*TDOT*, II, pp. 426-33); cf. Speiser, ' "People" and "Nation" ', pp. 157-63; Hulst, *TLOT*, II, pp. 896-919.

47. Clements, *TDOT*, II, p. 429.

48. E. Ruprecht, 'Der traditionsgeschichtliche Hintergrund der einzelnen Elemente von Gen XII 2-3', *VT* 29 (1979), pp. 444-64 (452).

49. See, for example, Wolff, 'Kerygma of the Yahwist', pp. 141-43; Clements, *Abraham and David*, pp. 57-58; Westermann, *Genesis 12–36*, p. 150; Jenkins, 'A

However, as Van Seters cautions,[50] this is not necessarily correct. Van
Seters maintains, rather, that

> what this statement has in mind is a purely ethnic form of identity with
> no necessity for a monarchy whatever. Abraham is not the beginning of a
> royal line but of all the families in Israel. Now in the Davidic-Solomonic
> period there does not seem to be any such sense of unity, even between
> Israel and Judah, let alone all the other disparate elements. The king was
> the fundamental and sole basis of unity, and there is not a hint anywhere
> of the monarchy being traced back to Abraham. So the significance of
> the statement must be otherwise.[51]

Although Van Seters rather overstates his case,[52] his fundamental observation that 'there is no reason to believe that the author had the Davidic
period specifically in mind' is reasonably secure.[53] What is not in question, however—even by Van Seters—is that 'the language used in this
promise [12.2-3] is drawn from royal ideology'.[54]

Thus the first part of this short pericope relates primarily to Abraham,
holding out to him the prospect of nationhood. As the rest of the
Pentateuch makes clear, the text has Israel in focus; Israel is the
geopolitical entity with which God promised to bless Abraham.

As observed above, however, there is a subtle shift in the focal point
of the second part of this divine speech. No longer is the emphasis on a
national entity that will stem from Abraham. Rather, the focus now is
on an international community. Indeed the fact that God no longer
speaks in terms of a גוי (or indeed גוים), but rather of כל משפחת
האדמה is perhaps significant. The expression is extremely rare, occurring in only two other places: Gen. 28.14 and Amos 3.2.[55] Though the

Great Name', p. 46; Ruprecht, 'Der traditionsgeschichtliche Hintergrund', pp. 460-
61; K. Berge, *Die Zeit des Jahwisten: Ein Beitrag zur Datierung jahwistischer
Vätertexte* (BZAW, 186; Berlin: W. de Gruyter, 1990), pp. 55, 72-73.

50. Van Seters, *Abraham*, pp. 271-72; *idem*, *Prologue to History*, pp. 253-56.
See also N.E. Wagner, 'Abraham and David?', in J.W. Wevers and D.B. Redford
(eds.), *Studies on the Ancient Palestinian World* (Festschift F.V. Winnett; Toronto:
University of Toronto Press, 1972), pp. 117-40.

51. Van Seters, *Abraham*, p. 271.

52. Cf. Gen. 17.6, 16; Gen. 35.11, texts which expressly link Abraham to the
future monarchy!

53. Van Seters, *Prologue to History*, p. 253.

54. Van Seters, *Prologue to History*, p. 253.

55. The Amos text employs the longer spelling of the construct noun (משפחות).
In Zech. 14.17 a synonymous phrase (replacing האדמה with הארץ) is employed.

term מִשְׁפָּחָה may be used with reference to a political entity,[56] the deliberate selection of this particular word in the present context may hint at the non-political nature of the blessing enshrined in this universal promise: Abraham will be a channel, not of ethnic or political blessing for the nations, but rather of spiritual blessing for humankind. The division of the earth's population into clans and nations recounted in Genesis 10 will be 'reversed' through the fulfilment of this aspect of the divine promise to Abraham.[57]

It is clear from 12.3a, however, that divine blessing will not come automatically to 'all the families of the ground'. Rather, such 'blessing' is contingent upon a specific response on their part. As Mitchell notes, 'The promise of blessing is conditional. Only those on good terms with Abraham will acquire blessing, while those hostile to him will be the object of God's devastating curse.'[58] In order to experience the divine 'blessing', potential recipients must 'bless' Abraham, which, like its antonym in Gen. 12.3 (i.e. 'disdain') denotes deeds rather than mere words.[59] How such 'blessing' or 'disdain' translates into action is not specified; only that one's relationship with Abraham is the determining factor in whether one obtains divine blessing or experiences divine curse.

Thus the two sections within this short pericope have in perspective two quite distinct prospects: the first section refers to Abraham in relation to the nation of Israel (i.e. the land to which he is being called and the nation of which he will be the progenitor); the second section refers to Abraham in relation to an international community (i.e. 'all the families of the earth', v. 3). The theme of 'blessing' in Gen. 12.1-3, therefore, is twofold: in the first section (vv. 1-2c) it concerns national

---

56. *Pace* Dumbrell, who narrowly defines the term as 'units with no real political structure and in which no system of final governmental headship operates' ('The Covenant with Abraham', p. 46). The term has a wider connotation than 'family' (for which בַּיִת is the closest Hebrew term); it was one of the units that made up a tribe (שֵׁבֶט). 'Clan' or 'extended family' captures the sense well. In Amos 3.2, where they are contrasted with Israel, 'nations' is at least implicit.

57. I concur with Van Develder ('Abrahamic Covenant Traditions', pp. 124-25) that this terminology is chosen because, like the concept of a 'name', it alludes to an important motif in the primaeval prologue.

58. Mitchell, *The Meaning of BRK*, p. 30.

59. For a defence of this interpretation, which certainly fits better with the concept of God blessing Abraham (v. 2) and blessing/cursing others (v. 3), see Mitchell, *The Meaning of BRK*, pp. 126-31.

blessing promised to Abraham; in the second section (vv. 2d-3) it relates to international blessing promised through Abraham. The two elements are nevertheless related; although Yahweh's purposes primarily concern Abraham and the nation which will derive from him, ultimately they have a much wider focus: 'all the families of the earth' who, through Abraham, will also experience blessing. As Hamilton concludes, 'Abram must be more than a recipient. He is both a receptacle for the divine blessing and a transmitter of that blessing.'[60]

In the light of this analysis, emphasis on both these distinctive roles in the ensuing narrative may be anticipated. Moreover, if these two distinct sets of conditional promises are to be ratified by covenant, it should not be surprising that more than one covenant is required. Therefore, careful study of this programmatic pericope in the Abraham narrative actually prepares the reader for the otherwise anomalous inclusion of two starkly different reports of covenants being made between God and Abraham.

4. *A Detailed Examination of Genesis 22.1-19*

a. *The Divine Test of Abraham in Genesis 22*
With the birth of the promised heir and his future inheritance secured (ch. 21), the reader might well have anticipated a shift away from Abraham and on to Isaac. However, Genesis 22 begins somewhat unexpectedly with the words:

ויהי אחר הדברים האלה והאלהים נסה את־אברהם

The drama that unfolds in the following verses underlines the sheer magnitude of this particular test in the Abraham story. Now, when Abraham may have expected no further complications in the fulfilment of the divine promises, he was to face the most acute embarrassment of all: a divine instruction to sacrifice the promised heir! As von Rad observes:

> One must be careful not to interpret the story in a general sense as a question about Abraham's willingness to obey and accordingly to direct all interest to Abraham's trial... Above all, one must consider Isaac, who is much more than simply a 'foil' for Abraham, i.e., a more or less accidental object on which his obedience is to be proved. Isaac is the child of promise. In him every saving thing that God has promised to do

60. Hamilton, *Genesis 1–17*, p. 373.

is invested and guaranteed. The point here is not a natural gift, not even the highest, but rather the disappearance from Abraham's life of the whole promise.[61]

The basic explanation of this otherwise bizarre episode in the Abraham narrative is contained in the opening clause: it was a *divine* test[62] (cf. the emphatic position and definite form of אלהים.[63]). Through skilful artistry the narrator then steadily builds up the tension to the critical point at which Isaac's life is spared: the divine instructions are graphically spelt out (vv. 1b-2); Abraham's compliance is recorded in rather laborious detail (vv. 3-10);[64] the divine intervention breaks into the story at the most intense moment of stress (vv. 11-12). The narrator could easily have concluded the episode with his comment on Abraham's subsequent itinerary (v. 19). Instead, however, the intervening verses record an aetiology and a reiteration of the divine promises of personal, national and international blessing (vv. 13-18). What was the compiler's rationale for the inclusion of this apparently superfluous material?

Though the divine speech in vv. 16-18 is commonly considered to be a secondary addition,[65] there are no such doubts in relation to the substitutionary sacrifice of the ram; this is generally accepted as an integral part of the original account. The problems inherent in an aetiological interpretation of this incident are discussed below.[66] In any case, such

---

61. Von Rad, *Genesis*, p. 244.

62. Despite the unconvincing attempt by H. Patcas ('Akedah, the Binding of Isaac', *Dor Le Dor* 14 [1985–86], pp. 112-14) to explain the verb etymologically in terms of 'God *uplifting* Abraham by the Akedah'. Rather than resulting from Abraham's misunderstanding of God's directive regarding Isaac (so Patcas, following Rashi), the Akedah was specifically designed as a divine test of Abraham's commitment to Yahweh. This the narrator makes clear from the outset.

63. As S.D. Walters ('Wood, Sand and Stars: Structure and Theology in Gn. 22.1-19', *TJT* 3 [1987], pp. 301-30 [304]) observes, 'The narrative heightens the story's tension slightly by saying that it is Abraham's own God who tests and who points out the place of sacrifice'. Cf. Joüon, §137*f*, I.2.

64. *Pace* D.M. Gunn and D.N. Fewell (*Narrative in the Hebrew Bible* [Oxford Bible Series; Oxford: Oxford University Press, 1993], pp. 90-100), whose scepticism with regard to Abraham's response involves as much reading into the passage as those commentators with whom they disagree, and necessitates a rather cynical (and unconvincing) interpretation of the divine response to Abraham's behaviour.

65. Cf. Section 4b below.

66. Cf. Section 4b below.

an interpretation fails to explain adequately the absolute necessity of an animal sacrifice on this occasion: would the direct intervention of Yahweh not have been sufficient in itself? The fact that a substitutionary sacrifice was still deemed necessary even after Isaac's life had been spared deserves some explanation. Westermann's assertion that 'the sacrificial action which had been commanded and begun must be brought to a conclusion; a sacrifice must be offered; only thus is the sacrifice of the child revoked and no longer required',[67] surely begs the question, 'Why?' The divine directive (v. 12) clearly prohibited the execution of the עלה as originally commanded. Moreover, in that Abraham had in principle carried out the divine command per se,[68] the subsequent offering of a ram seems initially puzzling and rather redundant. Nevertheless, Abraham's offering of the ram is explicitly said to have been substitutionary:

וילך אברהם ויקח את־האיל ויעלהו לעלה תחת בנו

This clearly indicates that an עלה on this occasion was still considered important. What was the *raison d'être* for what seemed an unnecessary offering in that the test had been passed? Why was a *sacrifice* necessary on this occasion? Did it have an integral connection with the nature and outcome of the divine test of Abraham?[69]

It is essential, therefore, that the following question be addressed: Why did God put Abraham through this particular test and what was achieved by it?[70]

---

67. Westermann, *Genesis 12–36*, p. 362.

68. Cf. Sir. 44.20; Wis. 10.5; *4 Macc.* 16.20; 18.11; Heb. 11.17.

69. A.M. Rodriguez (*Substitution in the Hebrew Cultus* [Berrien Springs: Andrews University Press, 1979]) puts these important questions to the text, but fails to answer them convincingly; cf. pp. 263-70.

70. J.I. Lawlor ('The Test of Abraham: Genesis 22.1-19', *GTJ* NS 1 [1980], pp. 19-35 [27]) recognizes the necessity of asking this question, but concludes (mistakenly, in my opinion) that 'there is no clear indication why He [Yahweh] deemed such a test necessary; only that he did'. Crenshaw's suggestion ('Journey into Oblivion', *Soundings* 58 [1975], p. 249) of misplaced loyalty on the part of Abraham is plausible, but there is little evidence of Abraham's alleged 'excessive love for the son of the promise coming dangerously close to idolatry' in the text. I concur with Moster's assertion ('The Testing of Abraham', pp. 239, 242) that 'to understand the *Akedah*, we must know the essence of Abraham's full covenant responsibilities… Only after the candidate passed the test did God's covenantal promise become binding'.

b. *The Function of the Divine Test in Genesis 22*
Given the literary structure of the Abraham narrative,[71] the divine test
of Abraham comes at a climactic point. As Wenham observes, 'The
account of the sacrifice of Isaac constitutes the aesthetic and theological
summit of the whole story of Abraham'.[72] This conventional appraisal
is further supported by the computer-assisted literary analysis conducted by R.D. Bergen.[73] The three primary observations underlined by
Bergen's study are as follows: the relative frequency of the key figure,
Abraham, as the subject of a narrative framework verb (30 times in 19
verses, 12 more than in any other section); the similar combined subject
frequency of Abraham or God in this pericope (almost twice as much as
the closest competitor, Gen. 18.16-33); the climactic location of this
pericope in its literary framework.[74] While any such computer-assisted
analysis is only as good as the methodology employed, Bergen's division of the Abraham cycle into 21 pericopes has much to commend it.
In any case, Bergen illustrates that more conventional literary analysis
supports the results of his computer-assisted analysis.[75]

However, while the importance of Gen. 22.1-19 in the Abraham
narrative is universally acknowledged and its literary value is certainly
appreciated, there is no consensus as to the function of this pericope
within its narrative framework. The theological purpose of Genesis 22
has been variously explained.[76] Davis broadly defines the main interpretations as follows.[77]

71. See Section 1 above.

72. Wenham, *Genesis 16–50*, p. 99.

73. Cf. R.D. Bergen, 'The Role of Genesis 22.1-19 in the Abraham Cycle: A
Computer-Assisted Textual Interpretation', *CTR* 4 (1990), pp. 313-26.

74. Bergen's computer-assisted analysis covered Gen. 11.27 to Gen. 25.11, the
contents of which he divided into 21 sub-sections delineated according to their
subject-matter or contents. For Bergen, two features strongly favour the identification of Gen. 22.1-19 as the narrator's intended centrepiece: its location within the
latter half of the overall text (i.e. within the section of the story where narrators in
all cultures have a tendency to place the most significant section); the degree of
repetition in Gen. 22.1-19 (verbs and subjects used elsewhere are found to a higher
degree in this episode than any other episode in the likely peak region) gives this
section the highest connectivity among the latter half of the Abraham cycle.

75. Bergen, 'The Role of Genesis 22.1-19', pp. 317-22.

76. An introduction to the history of interpretation is provided by D. Lerch,
Isaaks Opferung christlich gedeutet: eine auslegungsgeschichtliche Untersuchung
(BHT, 12; Tübingen: J.C.B. Mohr [Paul Siebeck], 1950); S. Spiegel, *The Last*

1. This story is about Israel's repudiation of the ritual practice of human sacrifice.
2. This story is about Abraham, the hero of existential faith.
3. This story is about Isaac, the victim who is faithful even to death.

The first of these approaches has been espoused by numerous traditio-historical critics,[78] and has in its favour not only comparative evidence (the marked difference between the official Israelite position on child sacrifice and that of Israel's ancient Near Eastern neighbours), but also its broad contextual plausibility (i.e. Israel's superior moral status, represented in the person of Abraham, demonstrates its suitability as a 'light to the nations'). However, this particular interpretation is funda-

---

Trial: The Akedah (trans. J. Goldin; repr., Woodstock: Jewish Lights Publishing, 1967); see also J.-L. Duhaime, 'Le sacrifice d'Isaac (Gn 22, 1-19): L'héritage de Gunkel', *ScEs* 33 (1981), pp. 139-56; J.D. Levenson, *The Death and Resurrection of the Beloved Son: The Transformation of Child Sacrifice in Judaism and Christianity* (New Haven: Yale University Press, 1993); F. Manns (ed.), *The Sacrifice of Isaac in the Three Monotheistic Religions: Proceedings of a Symposium on the Interpretation of the Scriptures Held in Jerusalem, March 16–17, 1995* (SBFA, 41; Jerusalem: Franciscan, 1995). A concise summary of the major interpretations is offered by E.F. Davis, 'Self-Consciousness and Conversation: Reading Genesis 22', *BBR* 1 (1991), pp. 27-40. For a more comprehensive survey of interpretation, see the recently published works by L. Kundert (*Die Opferung/Bindung Isaaks* [2 vols.; WMANT, 78 and 79; Neukirchen–Vluyn: Neukirchener Verlag, 1998]) and H.D. Neef (*Die Prüfung Abrahams: eine exegetisch-theologische Studie zu Gen 22,1-19* [Stuttgart: Calwer Verlag, 1998]).

77. Davis, 'Self-Consciousness and Conversation', p. 28.

78. See, for example, Gunkel, *Genesis übersetzt*, pp. 241-42; *idem, Genesis*, pp. 239-40); Driver, *The Book of Genesis*, p. 222 (though Driver also acknowledged that this passage also 'teaches the value set by God upon the surrender of self, and obedience'); Procksch, *Die Genesis*, p. 315; P. Volz and W. Rudolph, *Der Elohist als Erzähler. Ein Irrweg der Pentateuchkritik?* (BZAW, 63; Giessen: A. Töpelmann, 1933), pp. 40-44; Noth, *A History of Pentateuchal Traditions*, pp. 114-15. Although more recent commentators have generally soft-pedalled this approach (cf. von Rad, *Genesis*, p. 244; Davidson, *Genesis 12–50*, p. 93; Speiser, *Genesis*, p. 165; Westermann, *Genesis 12–36*, p. 358), aetiological interpretations have not been entirely abandoned; cf. Crenshaw, *A Whirlpool of Torment*, p. 26. For several traditio-historical critics the aetiology legitimizes a sacred place, rather than or as well as a sacred rite. S. Breibart ('The Akedah—a Test of God', *Dor Le Dor* 15 [1986], pp. 19-28) offers what is essentially a variation on the aetiological interpretation, taking the episode as one through which Abraham demonstrated the distinctiveness of his God vis-à-vis the deities of the surrounding peoples.

mentally flawed. The most incisive criticism is that such an apologetic interpretation is completely absent from the text: the passage nowhere suggests that the divine command to offer Isaac as an עלה accorded with established human custom, nor does it incorporate any general repudiation of child sacrifice. Rather, the narrative clearly depicts God as the initiator of these events and explicitly relates the assured blessing to Abraham's unquestioning compliance with the divine instructions. As Davis observes, 'In a narrative as carefully styled as this one, it is difficult to escape the impression that the author has deliberately directed our attention away from the historical and ethical issue as the context for interpretation'.[79]

The second approach to this episode in the Abraham cycle attempts to read the passage in its present literary setting.[80] The opening words of Gen. 22.2 point backwards to the fact that, after the expulsion of Hagar and Ishmael in ch. 21, there could be no uncertainty as to the significance of Isaac for the realization of the divine promises: it was on Isaac alone that Abraham's future hope rested. The divine instruction to slay Isaac was therefore a blatant contradiction as far as the promise of posterity was concerned. Thus the key issue in this passage is not ethical discernment but rather faith-generated obedience. 'Far from showing the awakening of new ethical insight, this story portrays in the starkest terms Abraham's blind unreasoning faith'.[81] As a comparison with other passages in which God (Elohim or Yahweh) is said to be the 'tester' demonstrates, 'the reason Yahweh deemed it necessary to test

79. Davis, 'Self-Consciousness and Conversation', p. 32; cf. Speiser's incisive comment (*Genesis*, p. 165) that 'the sacrifice is characterized at the outset as unreal, a gruesome mandate to be cancelled at the proper time. If the author had intended to expose a barbaric custom, he would surely have gone about it in a different way'.

80. Having the support of New Testament exegetes (cf. Heb. 11.17-19 and Jas 2.21-24), this was the view espoused by both Luther ('Lectures', ad loc. Gen. 22.3) and Calvin (*Genesis,* ad loc. Gen. 22.2, 4). In the mid-twentieth century perhaps its best known advocate was Søren Kierkegaard (*Fear and Trembling* [Garden City, NY: Doubleday, 1955]). It seems to be the current general consensus among both Christian and Jewish scholars. It is not, however, without some detractors; for instance, R. Gordis, 'Faith of Abraham: a Note on Kierkegaard's Teleological Suspension of the Ethical', *Judaism* 25 (1976), pp. 414-19 (esp. p. 414).

81. Davis, 'Self-Consciousness and Conversation', p. 34. A rather different reading is offered by L. Bodoff in his article, 'God Tests Abraham—Abraham Tests God', *BR* 9.5 (1993), pp. 52-56, 62; Bodoff interprets the narrated 'steps of Abraham's compliance' as evidence of subtle stalling on Abraham's part.

Abraham was to know what was in his heart, to test his obedience to and fear of Yahweh when his promised and beloved son was at stake'.[82]

In contrast with the previous two approaches, the third interpretation focuses on the role of Isaac rather than that of Abraham. A typological interpretation of Isaac's experience was in vogue among Christian interpreters from at least the second century CE, and there are possible allusions in the first century.[83] However, the early church did not have a monopoly on a typological interpretation of the Akedah, as the rabbinic midrash eloquently illustrates.[84] Isaac's voluntary suffering was interpreted as a model of submissiveness and faithfulness.

This third approach is seriously undermined by its inherent atomization of the text; Genesis 22 has been isolated entirely from its literary context and given an interpretation which is far removed from the biblical narrator's express intention (i.e. to narrate a test of *Abraham's* faith).

Although the second approach undoubtedly reflects the theological purpose of Genesis 22, the function of this significant chapter within its complete literary context has not been sufficiently explored. As Moster observes, 'Inadvertently, the *Akedah* story is usually isolated from the

82. So Lawlor, 'The Test of Abraham', p. 28. Other than Gen. 22, Lawlor identifies eight passages in which God is the subject of the verb נסה: Exod. 15.22-26; 16.4; 20.18-20; Deut. 8.2, 16; Judg. 2.21-22; 3.1-4; Ps. 26.2; 2 Chron. 32.31. In the first six of these passages Israel is the object of God's testing, and five of these six texts explicitly relate the motif of testing to God's concern over Israel's covenantal obedience. This connection between testing and obedience is at least implicit in Exod. 20.18-20, which shares with Gen. 22 the theme of the 'fear of God'. Moreover, in the two other passages (Ps. 26.2 and 2 Chron. 32.31) an emphasis on obedience is again implicit.

83. According to P.R. Davies ('The Sacrifice of Isaac and Passover', in E.A. Livingstone [ed.], *Studia Biblica: Papers on Old Testament and Related Themes* [JSOTSup, 11; Sheffield: JSOT Press, 1978], pp. 127-32) the earliest testimony to such typology is the Epistle of Barnabas and Melito of Sardis, with further testimony found in the writings of Clement of Alexandria, Irenaeus, Origen and Tertullian. R.M. Jensen ('The Binding or Sacrifice of Isaac: How Jews and Christians See Differently', *BR* 9.5 [1993], pp. 42-51) notes that 'this interpretative motif continued through the fourth and fifth centuries with Ambrose, John Chrysostom, Theodoret and Augustine' (p. 46), and she illustrates how it was popularized through church liturgy and artistic impressions (pp. 46-51). Suggested allusions in the New Testament include Rom. 8.32, Gal. 3.16 and possibly Jn 1.29 and 3.16.

84. *Gen. R.* 56.9; see also *Mek.* 7, 11. A concise discussion of the rabbinic interpretations of Gen. 22 is found in Kunin's article, 'The Death of Isaac', pp. 71-81.

rest of the Abraham episode and treated as an independent unit, whereas, properly to understand it, it should be considered as an integral part of an ongoing theme'.[85]

With the ascendancy of literary criticism in biblical studies, interest in the surgical removal of text from context has rapidly declined and scholars have focused less on the rather speculative question of a text's tradition history and more on how it functions in its received literary context. It is therefore appropriate to examine the role of Gen. 22.1-19, not simply within its immediate context (between chs. 21 and 22.20-21),[86] but within its total literary setting (the Abraham narrative in the book of Genesis).

As we have seen, it is Alexander's contention that Genesis 22 must be interpreted in the light of Genesis 17.[87] Together these chapters describe the establishment of a second covenant between God and Abraham (the first being recounted in Gen. 15), Genesis 17 announcing such a covenant and Genesis 22 describing its actual ratification. Alexander defends this reading by a careful comparison between these chapters and the establishment of the Noahic covenant described in Genesis 6–9, illustrated in Table 7.1, below.

Table 7.1. *Thematic Comparison of Genesis 6–9, 17 and 22.*

Theme	Genesis 6–9	Genesis 17, 22
The promise of a covenant	6.18	17.2, 7, 19
The obligations of the covenant	6.14-16, 19-21; 7.1-3	17.1, 9-14; 22.2
The fulfilment of the obligations	6.22; 7.5	17.23-27; 22.12
The offering of a sacrifice (עלה)	8.20	22.13
The establishment of the covenant	9.9-17	22.16-18

It cannot be denied that there are striking parallels between the two accounts, Abraham's actions mirroring those of Noah in several key

---

85. Moster, 'The Testing of Abraham', p. 237; cf. K.A. Deurloo, 'Because You have Hearkened to My Voice (Genesis 22)', in *Voices From Amsterdam*, p. 114.

86. As is profitably done, for example, by H.E. Schaalman in his exposition of 'The Binding of Isaac', in F.C. Holmgren and H.E. Schaalman (eds.), *Preaching Biblical Texts: Expositions by Jewish and Christian Scholars* (Grand Rapids: Eerdmans, 1995), pp. 36-45.

87. Alexander, 'Genesis 22 and the Covenant', pp. 17-22; cf. Turner, *Announcements of Plot*, p. 92, who is in 'broad agreement' with Alexander's thesis.

aspects. Though not all have found Alexander's analysis convincing,[88] it is at least plausible and certainly explains a number of the otherwise anomalous features of the Genesis 22 passage.

First, it provides a rationale for the test of Abraham, illustrating that Abraham has indeed met the conditions of the covenant announced in Genesis 17. No longer is Genesis 22 simply an aetiological story inserted into the Abraham narrative as a polemic against child sacrifice in Israel or as an explanation of a sacred place. Nor is the divine command so extraordinary or inexplicable. Abraham's 'blameless walk before God' had to be ascertained prior to the establishment of the eternal covenant.[89] This test revealed the full extent of Abraham's conformity to the divine will. As the text explicitly states, the purpose of the test was to ascertain whether or not Abraham 'feared God' (Gen. 22.12). If, as Wenham suggests,[90] Job 1.1 is analogous to this text in Genesis, then 'fearing God' is closely associated with being 'blameless and upright'. Thus the divine test functions in the Abraham narrative as a superb illustration of Abraham's blameless walk before God.

Secondly, it removes the enigma of the second divine speech (22.15-18) in that a sacrifice was necessary before God could solemnly confirm his earlier promises.

As Moberly observes, the oath pericope (22.15-18) has been generally neglected in the interpretation of the Akedah.[91] This is largely due, at least in modern critical study, to its dismissal as allegedly secondary material, although this does not account for its apparent neglect throughout the history of interpretation. However, the reasons for dismissing the pericope as a later editorial gloss are less than convincing. Moberly lists these as threefold: (1) the resolution of the test story by v. 14; (2) the stylistic difference between vv. 15-18 and vv. 1-14; (3) the

---

88. Cf. the favourable comments of A.G. Hunter ('Father Abraham: A Structural and Theological Study of the Yahwist's Presentation of the Abraham Material', *JSOT* 35 [1986], pp. 3-27 [23 n. 16]) and Garrett (*Rethinking Genesis*, p. 160 n. 1) with the rather more sceptical and/or dismissive responses of Moberly ('Akedah', p. 310), Hamilton (*Genesis 18–50*, p. 115 n. 68) and S. Prolow ('Isaac Unbound', *BZ* 40 [1996], pp. 84-91 [84 n. 6]).

89. Cf. Gen. 17.1, 'Walk before me and be blameless *so that* I may establish my covenant between me and you and increase you greatly' (Alexander's translation [emphasis mine] in 'Abraham Reassessed', p. 16).

90. Wenham, *Genesis 16–50*, p. 110.

91. Moberly, 'Akedah', pp. 302-303.

distinctive vocabulary in vv. 15-18.[92] As with source analysis generally, the latter point is undermined by the fact that vocabulary is largely determined by content. While it is true that the oath pericope 'contains two phrases which are otherwise unparalleled in Genesis but are common in prophetic literature',[93] the use of these phrases clearly serves to underline the significance of this occasion. To dismiss these verses as marginal to the story on account of the distinctive vocabulary is strangely to miss the narrator's point. For the redactor who gave the Abraham narrative its final form these verses are absolutely crucial for our understanding of the test pericope: it was Abraham's compliance with the divine command to sacrifice Isaac which secured the fulfilment of all the divine promises made to him.

Moberly's second point, that the narrative is terse while the promises are full, is at least partly a matter of genre. Significantly, both pericopes conform to the usual pattern of narrative and promise respectively: 'Throughout Genesis divine-promise speeches tend to employ synonyms, similes, and repetition, whereas narrative is terse and wastes few words recording events'.[94] Therefore the stylistic differences between the second divine speech and the rest of the chapter may be explained by the difference in literary genre, and thus do not necessarily betray a later redactor's hand.

Moberly's first point is more formidable, yet carries less force than might initially be assumed, as is illustrated by the incisive criticism that without these verses the test of Abraham is devoid of any clear purpose.[95] The latter is explicitly supplied in the second divine speech pericope. Thus it may be questioned whether or not the story of Abraham's test is in fact complete by v. 14. As Van Seters judiciously comments:

> it is the theme of 'testing' and of obedient response to that testing that is
> most basic to the whole story structure as we now have it. It seems easy
> enough to see the connection between the statement of the test in v. 1
> and the obedience that results in the rescue of the child in vv. 13-14. But
> if this were the end of the story, as so many propose, the whole purpose

---

92. Moberly, 'Akedah', pp. 304-308. Wenham ('The Akedah: A Paradigm', p. 96) counts six reasons offered by Moberly, but this larger figure has been reached through subdividing Moberly's arguments.

93. נשבעתי and נאם־יהוה (Moberly, 'Akedah', p. 308).

94. Wenham, 'The Akedah: A Paradigm', p. 97.

95. So Coats, 'Abraham's Sacrifice of Faith', p. 395; Van Seters, *Abraham*, p. 239; Alexander, 'Genesis 22 and the Covenant', pp. 17-22.

of testing would have no real consequence. Nothing would be changed. It is only with the inclusion, in the second speech, of the divine confirmation of the patriarchal promises, vv. 15-18, that the ultimate aim of the testing becomes clear. Because of Abraham's obedience his children will be blessed.[96]

Moreover, as Bergen observes, 'a literary and thematic analysis suggests that far from being an awkward appendage to the story, it [i.e. Gen. 22.15-18] is in fact the keystone'.[97] It is Bergen's contention that 'Gen 22.1-19 functions as the thematic crux of the Abraham story, bringing together in climactic fashion seven different pivotal motifs developed throughout the whole'.[98] These seven motifs are identified by Bergen as follows: Abraham Tested, Heir Denied, Altar-Building, Separation from Family, Faith, Blessing, and Possession of Land, the latter three being brought to a climax in Gen. 22.15-18. Without the second divine speech of Genesis 22, three themes of fundamental significance in the Abraham narrative would have been inexplicably omitted in the climactic part.

One further observation by Wenham is certainly pertinent. In the absence of the elucidating divine promise the 'resolution' of this traumatic test of Abraham's obedience would be rather anticlimactic.[99]

---

96. Van Seters, *Abraham*, p. 239; cf. *idem*, *Prologue to History*, pp. 261-64, in which he upholds the authenticity of the material in vv. 15-18, whose present position has been determined purely by literary considerations. A number of scholars have followed Coats and Van Seters in challenging the secondary nature of ch. 22.15-18; see, for example, Sternberg, *The Poetics of Biblical Narrative*, p. 55; Rendsburg, *The Redaction of Genesis*, pp. 33-34; P. Trible, 'Genesis 22: The Sacrifice of Sarah', in J.P. Rosenblatt and J.C. Sitterson (eds.), *'Not in Heaven': Coherence and Complexity in Biblical Narrative* (Bloomington: Indiana University Press, 1990), p. 251 n. 16; Bergen, 'The Role of Genesis 22.1-19', p. 324; Wenham, *Genesis 16–50*, pp. 101-103 and 'The Akedah: A Paradigm', pp. 95-96; Hamilton, *Genesis 18–50*, p. 115. Nevertheless, the secondary nature of these verses still has recent defenders; see, for example, Westermann, *Genesis 12–36*, pp. 354-56; Blum, *Vätergeschichte*, pp. 320-31; T. Veijola, 'Das Opfer des Abraham—Paradigma des Glaubens aus dem nachexilischen Zeitalter', *ZTK* 85 (1988), pp. 129-64 (159); Carr, *Reading the Fractures*, pp. 153-56; and most recently Kundert, *Die Opferung/Bindung Isaaks*, I, p. 31. Cf. McAfee ('The Patriarch's Longed-for Son', p. 246), who suggests that it is the first oracle (i.e. vv. 11-12) which is 'an insertion into an earlier form of the story'.

97. Bergen, 'The Role of Genesis 22.1-19', p. 324.

98. Bergen, 'The Role of Genesis 22.1-19', p. 322.

99. Wenham, *Genesis 16–50*, p. 102.

More problematic, however, is the fact that

> Both the Ishmael stories contain expansive promises of blessings on him
> and his descendants, that he would be a great nation too numerous to
> count (16.10; 21.18). Yet...deprived of 22.15-18, the Abraham cycle
> comes to an incongruous conclusion with the promises to Abraham
> apparently fulfilled through Ishmael. But included, 22.15-18 makes a
> fitting climax to the sequence of promises unfolded in the preceding
> chapters.[100]

Thus it is a great mistake to take the second angelic message of
Genesis 22 as anything other than an essential interpretative key to both
the verses immediately preceding and the entire Abraham cycle.[101] But
why is the speech inserted after, and not before, the sacrifice of the ram?
If, as Alexander suggests, a sacrifice was a necessary precursor to such
a covenantal oath, this speech simply could not have been incorporated
within the first angelic revelation. Therefore linking the sacrifice of v.
13 with ratification of the eternal covenant of Genesis 17 eliminates the
anomaly of a second divine speech. Moreover, identifying this sacrifice
as covenantal is not without justification. The fact that a 'ram' was
provided for this sacrifice may be significant in that the only earlier
point in Genesis which mentions a ram is Genesis 15, where a ram was
one of the divided animals of the covenant ratification rite.

Thirdly, if Genesis 17 and 22 belong together (as Alexander contends), this elucidates why Abraham's implicit obedience is presented
both here (ch. 22) and in Gen. 26.5 as the crucial factor which guaranteed the fulfilment of the divine promise. Such obedience was a prerequisite for the establishment of this particular covenant (Gen. 17.1-2).

The importance of Abraham's obedience is clearly seen in the fact
that the divine guarantee begins and concludes with explicit reference
to it (Gen. 22.16b, 18b). This emphasis, however, is not 'otherwise
unprecedented'.[102] On the contrary, from the very beginning God's

100. Wenham, 'The Akedah: A Paradigm', p. 100.
101. In any case, as Walters incisively comments ('Wood, Sand and Stars',
p. 326): 'the interpreter's primary responsibility is to the given text in its palpable
reality. The story, Gen. 22.1-19, exists in that form and only in that form... Why
should we expound the hypothetical rather than the real? No exposition of the story
which omits the promise can be considered true to the text.' Similarly Deurloo
('The Way of Abraham', p. 127) asserts that 'to omit 22.15-18 as a later addition is
to leave out essential information'.
102. *Pace* R.W.L. Moberly, 'Christ as the Key to Scripture: Genesis 22 Reconsidered', in Hess, Wenham and Satterthwaite (eds.), *He Swore an Oath*, p. 161.

promises to Abraham were conditional (cf. the imperatives in 12.1-3);
moreover, as suggested above, the covenant announced in Genesis 17
explicitly incorporated certain obligations on Abraham's part.[103] As
Alexander observes, 'From this it is evident that certain conditions are
placed upon Abraham which must be fulfilled before the covenant is
made'.[104] Therefore, rather than altering or transforming the terms of
the existing promise at this point, the divine guarantee is simply restat-
ing the conditional aspect of the divine promise. This promise can now
be ratified by divine oath in that the stated preconditions have been
fulfilled.

If Alexander's premise is correct (that ch. 22 recounts the establishment of the conditional covenant announced in ch. 17), then it is not
surprising that the divine guarantee (signifying the ratification of this
covenant) should be so intimately related to Abraham's obedience.
Such a divine assurance would have been impossible otherwise. As
reflected in Gen. 26.2-5, Abraham's obedience was a primary factor in
the establishment of the eternal covenant announced in Genesis 17.
Abraham's compliance with God's instructions demonstrated that he
had fulfilled the essential precondition of 'blamelessness'.[105]

c. *The Emphases of the Divine Guarantee in Genesis 22*
The significance of this particular divine promise in the Abraham
narrative is underlined by the unique way in which it is introduced.
Only here in Genesis is a divine oath introduced with Yahweh swearing
by himself (בי נשבעתי).[106] Furthermore, only here in Genesis is the
messenger formula, so common in the prophetic books of the Hebrew
Bible, used to reinforce the divine oath.[107] Together these two features
serve not only to emphasize the sincerity of the promise-maker, but also
the importance of the particular promises being made.

103. Cf. Chapter 5 Section 4 above.
104. Alexander, 'Genesis 22 and the Covenant', p. 19.
105. There is no suggestion here that the Genesis account portrays Abraham as
morally perfect; cf. his conduct in Gen. 12.10-20; 16; 20. Rather, the focus in Gen.
22.16, 18 and Gen. 26.5 is on the exemplary obedience which reflected his sincere
faith in the promises of God, on which their fulfilment was absolutely dependent.
106. H.C. White ('The Divine Oath in Genesis', *JBL* 92 [1973], pp. 165-79) has
provided a useful summary of the various formulae associated with divine oaths in
Genesis.
107. The only other place in which this messenger formula is employed in the
Pentateuch is Num. 14.28.

The opening and closing statements of this oracular blessing are significant, emphasizing the conditionality of the promises contained in this divine oath (cf. 'because you have done this', v. 16, and 'because you have obeyed my voice', v. 18). The sandwiching of the divine oath between these two causal clauses forges an undeniable link between Abraham's obedience and the realization of the promised blessing: it was Abraham's obedience which evoked this solemn guarantee in relation to the particular divine promises Yahweh made to him.[108] 'That the blessing pronounced in vv 17-18 is directly related to Abraham's willingness to offer Isaac is clearly established by the redundant expression of v. 16.'[109] The structure of the pericope therefore suggests that the fulfilment of the promises affirmed here and the binding of Isaac are intimately connected. Yahweh's solemn pledge issued directly from Abraham's act of submission. The Akedah was thus of key importance as far as the fulfilment of these particular promissory elements was concerned. As Turner perceives, 'Abraham's initiatives had previously placed the promise under threat; his unquestioning, passive obedience has now confirmed its permanence'.[110]

A close connection between the nature of Abraham's obedience and the reward for his exemplary behaviour is borne out also by a careful analysis of the promissory elements of the oath in Gen. 22.16-18, which may also provide additional links with the annunciation of the eternal covenant in Genesis 17.

The blessing guaranteed to Abraham is threefold: his seed 'will be numerous (v. 17a), victorious (v. 17b.), and influential (v. 18)'.[111] Although not particularly novel in content, in that they reflect ideas encapsulated within the earlier promissory speeches made by God to Abraham, there are dimensions of this promissory triad which are nevertheless noteworthy: namely, the subtle changes in precisely how these promissory elements are articulated here.

Perhaps the most striking difference between the blessing formula here and similar formulae previously used in the Abraham narrative is the emphatic way in which it is introduced: this is the only time in

---

108. This same emphasis on conditionality is repeated in Gen. 26.4-5, where essentially the same promises are transferred to Isaac on account of his father's obedience.

109. Lawlor, 'The Test of Abraham', p. 24.

110. Turner, *Announcements of Plot*, p. 178.

111. So Hamilton, *Genesis 18–50*, p. 115.

Genesis where the infinitive absolute is used to reinforce the verb ברך.
This clearly adds some significance to this particular promissory
speech, the last in a series made to Abraham personally.

In relation to the promise of numerous offspring the simile of the
stars in the sky has been employed before (cf. Gen. 15.5), but not that
of the 'sand on the seashore'.[112] Other than this there does not appear to
be any significant difference between this promise and its previous
expressions. What is significant, however, is that this is the only place
in Genesis where two similes are brought together in connection with
the promise of numerical increase. This has the effect of making this
element of the promise more emphatic on this occasion. It is perhaps
significant that the only other place where this dimension of the promise is stated emphatically is in Gen. 17.2: וארבה אותך במאד מאד ('I
will multiply you *very greatly*'). Therefore this feature common to both
passages supports the link between the two chapters observed above,
offering further reason for believing that the solemn oath of Gen. 22.16-
18 establishes the covenant promised in Gen. 17.2.

In contrast with the first promissory element in Gen. 22.17, the
second expression, 'possessing the gates of your enemies', is more of a
novelty. This clause has been taken by most commentators as a thinly
veiled allusion to the earlier promises regarding the possession of
territory (i.e. they connect this promise with the promises of territorial
inheritance, cf. Gen. 12.1, 7; 13.15-17; 15.7-8; 17.8, and understand the
clause in terms of military conquest).[113] While the interpretation of the
idiom as 'conquering one's enemies' is undisputed, the fact that this
expression ('possessing the gate of...') is so unusual invites careful
reflection. The only other occurrence is in Gen. 24.60. As Alexander
contends, the latter text should probably be understood in terms of the
divine oath (22.17-18), which presumably had been recounted by
Abraham's servant to Rebekah's family.[114] The use of the singular suffix ('his') on 'enemies' in both texts seems to confirm this, for, had the

112. It must be acknowledged, however, that Gen. 13.16 conveys a similar idea.
Even so, the exact simile found in Gen. 22 is new.

113. See, for example, Skinner, *Genesis*, p. 331; Speiser, *Genesis*, p. 164; Coats,
Genesis, p. 159; Youngblood, *The Book of Genesis*, p. 191; Wenham, *Genesis 16–
50*, p. 112. For von Rad (*Genesis*, p. 243) this feature betrays the secondary nature
of the second divine speech, since 'the promise that Abraham's seed "will possess
the gate of their enemies" is an idea still foreign to the basis of the promises'.

114. Alexander, 'Further Observations', pp. 366-67.

borrowing been in the opposite direction, one would surely have expected plural suffixes (especially if, as is generally understood, Rebekah's brothers were pronouncing this blessing on her posterity collec-
tively).[115] This raises an important issue which clearly has ramifications
for how this promised victory is to be interpreted; viz. the identity of
the 'seed' spoken of in Gen. 22.17b. If the 'seed' is a collective concept
here, then the territorial conquest by Isaac and Rebekah's physical
descendants (i.e. Israel's possession of Canaan) is undoubtedly intended. If, however, the 'seed' of this part of the oath is a singular descendant of Abraham, the interpretation of 'will possess the gate [sing.] of
his enemies' in terms of a series of military conquests needs to be re-
examined.

The identity of this 'seed' is not as straightforward as the collective interpretation reflected in contemporary English translations suggests.[116] Although the English reader might reasonably conclude that a
group of descendants is consistently in mind, the Hebrew text seems to
suggest otherwise. Admittedly the singular noun is not unusual per se
since the noun זֶרַע is often deployed with a collective meaning. This
collective sense is quite clear, for example, in Gen. 15.13-16, where the
common singular noun deployed in v. 13 is preceded by a singular
complement (גֵּר) but followed by a series of plural suffixes on related
prepositions and verbs. However, such a collective sense must not be
assumed uncritically elsewhere. As noted above, the syntax in both
Gen. 22.17b and 24.60 is rather unexpected. While there is nothing unusual about the noun (זֶרַע) being connected to a singular form of the verb
(יִרַשׁ), Alexander has recently suggested that the singular suffix attached
to the 'enemies' (שֹׂנְאָיו) of this 'seed' is very significant.[117] Alexander builds his case on the insights of Jack Collins, who maintains that
the precise meaning of זֶרַע in relation to 'offspring' is indicated in

115. Cf. J. Collins, 'A Syntactical Note [Genesis 3.15]: Is the Woman's Seed
Singular or Plural?', *TynBul* 48 (1997), pp. 139-48 (142-44), and the discussion
below.

116. Modern English versions render the phrase: 'your descendants/they will
possess the gate(s) of *their* enemies' (e.g. NASB; TEV; NIV; NKJV; NJPSV; NRSV;
NJB; NLT [emphasis mine])—reflecting a collective understanding of the term
'seed'. Wenham (*Genesis 16–50*, p. 98) inexplicably translates the phrase (in 22.17)
'so that *you* may possess the gate of *your* enemies' (emphasis mine), but clearly
understands this promise in terms of Abraham's descendants (cf. Wenham, *Genesis
16–50*, p. 116).

117. Alexander, 'Further Observations', pp. 363-67.

Hebrew syntax by the verb inflections and pronouns used in association with it.[118] Collins' argument relates primarily to Gen. 3.15, but his observations apply equally to Gen. 22.17b, as is cogently illustrated by Alexander. If Collins' thesis is correct, then the 'offspring' spoken of in Gen. 22.17b and 24.60 must of necessity be an individual descendant, rather than Abraham's 'offspring' in a collective sense. Collins himself appears to have overlooked the singular suffixes relevant to his discussion in 22.17 and 24.60, and his classifying of these texts as examples of זרע used in a collective sense is undoubtedly influenced by the fact that the preceding clauses refer to a plurality of 'offspring'. However, as Alexander has pointed out, the 'syntactical arrangement [the imperfect verb ירש is preceded by a non-converting ו] leaves open the possibility that the זֶרַע referred to in the final clause differs from that mentioned in the first part of the verse'.[119] It is possible, therefore, to maintain that the promise of Gen. 22.17b-18 relates not to a *group* of descendants, but rather to an *individual*.

Such an interpretation is further supported, as Alexander has highlighted,[120] by the only allusion to Gen. 22.17-18 outside the book of Genesis, viz. Ps. 72.17, where the inheritor of these patriarchal blessings is a royal individual. This, together with the fact that a synchronic reading of Genesis—indeed the whole of Genesis to Kings—suggests that an individual 'seed' is of special interest to the narrator,[121] places the burden of proof on those who wish to interpret 22.17b and 24.60 in a collective sense.

The third clause evidently reiterates the international dimension of Abraham's influence announced in Gen. 12.3 and repeated in Gen. 18.18, but there are two clear differences: (1) the hithpael of ברך

118. Collins, 'A Syntactical Note'. Unfortunately the LXX of Gen. 22.17 does not attach any pronoun to ὑπεναντίων, but the third person singular suffix in the MT is entirely consistent with the pattern where a single individual is in view.

119. Alexander, 'Further Observations', p. 365. Alexander's observation is made in relation to 22.17, but applies equally to 24.60.

120. Alexander, 'Further Observations', p. 365-66.

121. See T.D. Alexander, 'From Adam to Judah: the Significance of the Family Tree in Genesis', *EvQ* 61 (1989), pp. 5-19; *idem*, 'Genealogies, Seed and the Compositional Unity of Genesis', *TynBul* 44 (1993), pp. 255-70; *idem*, 'Messianic Ideology in the Book of Genesis', in P.E. Satterthwaite, R.S. Hess and G.J. Wenham (eds.), *The Lord's Anointed: Interpretation of Old Testament Messianic Texts* (Carlisle: Paternoster Press), pp. 19-39; *idem*, 'Royal Expectations in Genesis to Kings: Their Importance for Biblical Theology', *TynBul* 49 (1998), pp. 191-212.

replaces the niphal conjugation used in the previous texts; (2) Abraham's 'seed' has assumed the role which in each of the preceding texts had been delegated to Abraham; 'in your seed' (Gen. 22) has replaced 'through you' (Gen. 12 and 18). As observed above, each change is not only significant in itself, but is also related to the others.[122] However, even if no distinction in meaning is made between the niphal and hithpael verb forms, the substitution here of Abraham's 'seed' for Abraham himself must be of some consequence. This is especially so in that all three elements of the divine oath in Genesis 22 are intimately related by this particular focus on Abraham's 'seed'.

It is undeniable, therefore, that the promised blessing is inextricably bound up with the concept of 'seed'. This connection between the binding of Isaac, the promised heir of Abraham, and the blessing transferred to Abraham's promised 'seed' is of key importance. It was by obediently surrendering his promised heir that Abraham secured the blessing of his promised 'seed'. The blessing promised here will find fulfilment not in Abraham himself, but rather in his 'seed'.

If, as suggested above, Genesis 17 and 22 are related by the common theme of an eternal covenant between God and Abraham, one would expect this to be borne out by the promissory elements incorporated in the divine guarantee of Gen. 22.16-18, and Alexander maintains that this is indeed the case: 'The divine oath in 22.16-18 not only embraces the contents of the earlier promissory covenant regarding many descendants and land but also includes the additional aspect that all nations will be blessed through Abraham's "seed"'.[123]

While the latter is indeed expected if Alexander's premise is correct, the reference to the 'earlier promissory covenant' (Gen. 15) may be somewhat unexpected. Why should a divine oath ratifying the eternal conditional covenant anticipated in Genesis 17 mention this previous and distinct promissory covenant? Moreover, it is surely significant that in the reaffirmation to Isaac (cf. Gen. 26.2-5) both aspects of the divine promise (i.e. national and international blessing) are spoken of in terms of 'the oath that I swore to your father Abraham' (Gen. 26.3, NRSV). These two aspects of the divine promise are again closely related in the revelation to Jacob (cf. Gen. 28.13-15). Furthermore, in the only other

---

122. Cf. the discussion of the hithpael's significance in Section 3a above.

123. Alexander, 'Abraham Reassessed', p. 20. Covenant echoes in Gen. 22.15-18 are also picked up by Stek (' "Covenant" Overload', p. 31), although he does not draw such a close link with ch. 17.

place in Genesis where reference is made to God swearing an oath (i.e. Gen. 24.7), the focus is entirely on the promise of land.[124]

From this evidence it would appear that the nationhood element of God's original promise cannot be dismissed as an inconsequential aspect of the divine guarantee offered in Genesis 22. The promise of personal blessing (Gen. 12.2) is reiterated more categorically in Gen. 22.16; the promise of numerous progeny (Gen. 15.5; cf. 12.2) is reinforced with the additional simile of the sand on the seashore in Gen. 22.17; and the promise of territory (Gen. 12.1 [implicitly], 12.7 [explicitly]; 15.7-8) is given more concrete reiteration in the prospect of Abraham's descendant(s) possessing the gates of his (their) enemies (Gen. 22.17).[125] This is admittedly somewhat anomalous in a passage which allegedly records the establishment of a covenant focusing primarily on an altogether different element of the initial promissory pericope.

However, as noted in the previous chapter,[126] this apparent anomaly in Alexander's proposal is offset to some extent by the fact that the second promissory element in Gen. 12.1-3 is dependent upon the first: Abraham's role as a mediator of blessing is contingent upon his role as a recipient of blessing. In addition to this programmatic text, two other passages in the Abraham narrative seem to confirm this intimate connection between these two major aspects of the divine promise to Abraham: the allusion to the promise of nationhood in Gen. 17.8, and the uniting of both promissory elements in Gen. 18.18.

The reference in Gen. 22.17 to the nationhood aspect in the context of the international dimension of God's promise is therefore not quite so anomalous as it may at first appear. The former is a prerequisite for the latter, and since neither of these aspects of the divine promise is realized in the book of Genesis, it is important that divine reassurances incorporate both dimensions of the anticipated blessing.

Moreover, the literary function of Gen. 22.15-18 in the main part of the Abraham narrative must not be overlooked. As noted at the

124. Here the allusion seems to be to Gen. 15.18, therefore the 'oath' in this instance is probably not that of Gen. 22.16, but a similar divine affirmation offered at the time the initial covenant was ratified.

125. As noted above, however, this latter promise may need to be interpreted more broadly than simply in terms of Israel's territorial conquest of Canaan.

126. Cf. Chapter 6 Section 4 above.

beginning of this chapter, 22.16-18 forms an inclusio with 12.1-4a,[127] confirming the fulfilment of the promises given at the start. This being so, it is natural that in God's final speech to Abraham he should solemnly confirm both aspects of the initial divine promises, especially since neither aspect had yet materialized and the realization of the second (blessing for the nations) was entirely contingent upon the fulfilment of the first (nationhood). Although Gen. 24.1 indicates that Abraham had experienced the divine blessing promised in Gen. 12.2, it is nevertheless clear that this statement needs qualification: the fulfilment relates only to blessing on a personal level (i.e. as relating to posterity and prosperity). Obviously the fulfilment of the larger dimensions of the promise (i.e. national and international blessing) is not to be sought within the lifetime of Abraham (or even within the book of Genesis as a whole). Thus, given the future dimension of both major elements of the promise in the book of Genesis, and the fact that the realization of the second promissory element was dependent on the realization of the first, it is natural that the divine guarantee in Gen. 22.16-18 should encompass the promise of nationhood.

5. *Genesis 15 and 17 in the Context of Genesis 12.1–22.19*

As this chapter has shown, the covenantal promises and obligations relating to Abraham are bracketed by the inclusio of Gen. 12.1-3 and 22.15-18. The programmatic agenda is established in Gen. 12.1-3. Here two major promissory aspects are delineated, each of which is linked with a divine command. The first promissory aspect relates to Abraham becoming a 'great nation', and is contingent upon his obeying Yahweh's command to leave his country, clan and extended family and complete his journey to Canaan (12.1; cf. 11.31). For this promise of 'nationhood' to be realized, two things were vital: descendants and land that Abraham could call his own. The fact that Abraham was presently 'seedless' (11.30) and, if he obeyed the divine command, would be potentially 'landless', should not escape our attention. This promise of becoming a 'great nation' would have had a hollow ring to all but the ear of faith. It is not surprising, therefore, that immediately after Abraham has responded positively to the divine injunction and arrived in Canaan, Yahweh should reassure him with the words, 'I will give this *land* to your *seed*' (12.7).

127. Cf. Section 2 (n. 2) above.

In the stories that follow, these two prospects (i.e. land and descendants) are never far from view. The sojourn in Egypt (12.10-20) seems to place both prospects in jeopardy, although particularly the prospect of physical descendants through Sarah.[128] In the strife between the herdsmen of Abraham and Lot the promise of land is at stake, although if (at this stage) Abraham was entertaining any notion of Lot as a potential surrogate heir (cf. 15.2-3), this incident could have had ramifications for the entire promise of 'nationhood'. In any case, both aspects of the promise (i.e. 'land' and 'descendants') are reaffirmed as soon as Lot and Abraham have parted company (13.14-17). The next incident, Abraham's rescue of Lot and his encounter with Melchizedek, is significant in relation to the promise of nationhood for two reasons: not only does it present Abraham acting as a king himself, but it also introduces us to the priest-kings of Salem, with whom the royal line descended from Abraham was ultimately identified (cf. Ps. 110.4). Thus in Genesis 14 the prospect of Abraham becoming a 'great nation' and having a 'great name' is to some measure foreshadowed.[129] Yet it is only foreshadowed, for, as the following chapter makes clear, this promise of nationhood will not be fulfilled either in Abraham's lifetime (15.15) or in the immediate future (cf. 15.13, 16).

Significantly, the first place in the narrative where the patriarch expresses any doubts about the divine promises is in Genesis 15. Here Abraham expresses his reservations in connection with both aspects of the promise of nationhood (15.2, 8), and both aspects are guaranteed by divine oath in the 'covenant between the pieces' (15.18). Significantly, after Genesis 15 no further questions are asked by Abraham in relation to the promise of 'land'. Indeed, this dimension of the promise clearly recedes into the background.[130] Thus by the end of Genesis 15, the land aspect of the promise of nationhood has been firmly resolved in Abraham's mind. While Abraham may have been initially sure that the other dimension of the divine oath would also materialize (cf. 15.6),

128. Despite the discouraging comment in 11.30, it appears that Abraham and Sarah did not give up hope of having a child together until some ten years after the episode in Egypt (cf. Abraham's age in 12.4 and 16.16).

129. See J.G. McConville, 'Abraham and Melchizedek: Horizons in Genesis 14', in Hess, Wenham and Satterthwaite (eds.), *He Swore an Oath*, pp. 93-118.

130. In fact, the territorial aspect of the promise is only mentioned twice in the ensuing chapters of the Abraham narrative (17.8; 24.7). On both occasions the context is the establishment of a specific line of Abrahamic descent.

this aspect had not been so clearly delineated. Although Yahweh had guaranteed that Abraham would have biological descendants, apparently he had not expressly said whether or not such descendants would come through Sarah. Thus beginning with Genesis 16, there is a shift in emphasis in the Abraham narrative. No longer is the promissory focus on the nationhood aspect per se, but rather on the question of the legitimate line of Abrahamic descent, a matter complicated by the birth of a son to Abraham by Sarah's Egyptian maidservant (16.1-16).

It is this potential for confusion which necessitated the announcement in Genesis 17 that God would establish (i.e. perpetuate) a covenant, not with Ishmael, but with Isaac, the son who was yet to be born to Sarah (17.19-21). Unlike the earlier 'covenant between the pieces', however, this 'eternal covenant' involves mutual obligations, and encompasses more than the promise of nationhood. This covenant concerns primarily the other main aspect of the divine promissory agenda set out in Gen. 12.1-3; viz. the promise that 'through Abraham all the familes of the ground would obtain blessing'. Little, if any, attention has been paid to this international aspect of the divine programme involving Abraham in the intervening narrative.[131] The nations come into sharp focus, however, in Genesis 17. Indeed, the thrust of the divine covenant announced in this chapter is that Abraham will be 'father [in the metaphorical sense of benefactor] of a multitude of nations' (vv. 4-6; cf. v. 16). How this will materialize is elucidated in 17.6b-8. This covenant will be established (i.e. perpetuated) through a particular line of Abraham's descendants, who alone will inherit the blessings promised to Abraham (the promise of becoming 'a great nation' through which blessing will be mediated to the nations). This special line of Abrahamic descent will begin with Isaac, and from it will come a royal line of 'seed' (the 'kings' of 17.6, 16; cf. 35.11). It is this feature which unites these two different aspects of the divine promise, for these 'kings' will reign in the 'great nation' promised to Abraham, and through this royal 'seed' Abraham will become the 'father [the spiritual benefactor] of many nations'. Thus, while Genesis 17 encompasses both the national and international aspects of Gen. 12.1-3,

131. A number of commentators (e.g. Coats, *Genesis*, p. 120; Wenham, *Genesis 1–15*, pp. 321-22; Ross, *Creation and Blessing*, pp. 293-94) suggest allusions to it in Gen. 14. Given the royal associations found in that chapter, such allusions are perhaps unsurprising.

the focus is primarily on the 'seed' through whom *both* aspects of the programmatic agenda will be fulfilled.

This focus on the special line of 'seed' through whom these promises will be fulfilled is maintained in the subsequent chapters of the Abrahamic narrative. The miracle needed to establish this special line of 'seed' is underlined in 18.1-15. The incidents that follow, involving Abraham's intercession for Sodom (18.16-33) and Lot's survival despite its destruction (19.1-29), seem to highlight not only Abraham's potential to mediate blessing to other nations, but also that these other nations will share in the divine blessing of Abraham only if they emulate his righteous behaviour (18.17-19). The latter text is significant because, as well as bringing together both aspects of the promissory agenda (i.e. nationhood and international blessing), it underlines that the ethical obligation demanded of Abraham (17.1) was expected of all those who wished to share in the blessings encompassed by this covenant (18.19).[132] This may also be implicit in the final episode involving Lot (19.30-38). Lot's daughters, through their incestuous relationship with their father, each established a line of 'seed' which differed markedly from the 'seed' of Abraham.

In the final chapters of the Abraham narrative the focus on the special line of Abrahamic descent is sharpened even more.[133] Once again Abraham places in jeopardy all the promises, but primarily that relating to the promised 'seed', by the deceitful ploy of passing his wife off as his sister (20.1-18). Yet again God intervenes (cf. 20.18; 21.1), and the son promised to Abraham and Sarah is born at last (21.1-7). The special line of Abrahamic 'seed', anticipated in ch. 17, is finally established. With this, however, the issue of Abraham's promised 'seed' and legitimate heir becomes of tantamount importance. Therefore it is not surprising that this is the next matter to be resolved in the narrative (21.8-21). Ishmael, because he is a genuine 'seed' of Abraham, will enjoy some of the blessings guaranteed to Abraham (21.13; cf. 17.20). Isaac, however, is Abraham's unique 'seed' and covenant heir (21.12;

---

132. As suggested above, such an ethical requirement was probably implicit in the 'covenant sign' of circumcision. As well as focusing attention on the special line of 'seed' through whom all nations would be blessed, this rite was a perpetual reminder of the submissive walk that was an integral part of this 'eternal covenant'.

133. For a fuller discussion of the role of Gen. 20–22 within the Abraham narrative, see Alexander, *Abraham in the Negev*, ch. 7.

cf. 17.19, 21). Thus Isaac is accurately introduced in the Akedah account as Abraham's 'only son' (22.2).

The narrative significance of Abraham's tryst with the Philistines (21.22-34) is, admittedly, initially more obscure,[134] although it is clearly an integral part of its present setting (i.e. chs. 20–22).[135] Abimelech's concern, not only for himself, but for his 'seed', probably indicates that Abraham shared such concerns; therefore the narrator has not shifted too far from his primary focus on Abraham's 'seed'. The emphasis on Abimelech's benevolent attitude toward Abraham, his recognition of the special relationship between Abraham and God (21.22), and the fact that a covenant relationship was formally established between Abimelech and Abraham (21.31; cf. v. 23) is also consequential. There are clear allusions here to the promises of 12.3, which again suggests that the narrator is primarily concerned with the fulfilment of the second aspect of the promissory agenda (i.e. the mediation of blessing to the nations).

However, this episode may be significant for another reason: it relates the making of a covenant between people involving mutual obligations. Not only is this the first such covenant actually established in Genesis, but also this covenant is established by the 'swearing of an oath' (21.31). This pericope may well serve, therefore, among other things, to alert the astute reader to the covenantal significance of the following chapter, the first place in the Hebrew Bible where we read of God himself 'swearing' an oath. The covenant of ch. 21 may thus provide the hermeneutical cue for understanding the swearing of an oath in 22.16-18 as synonymous with the making of a covenant (cf. 21.27-31).

Before such a covenant is established, however, Abraham's submission to God must first be demonstrated, as is anticipated in the earlier divine injunctions ('Behave in an exemplary fashion so that I may establish my covenant with both you and your descendants, and greatly

---

134. Wenham's assessment (*Genesis 16–50*, p. 90) is a little too negative; cf. Alexander, *Abraham in the Negev*, pp. 108-09.

135. For instance, this episode clearly assumes the reader's knowledge of the earlier incident involving Abimelech (cf. 21.22 with 20.1). In addition, 20.1 and 21.34 seem to encompass all the intervening material. Moreover, without this episode, 22.19 would be most obscure. Before 21.31, Beersheba is mentioned only in connection with Hagar and Ishmael in 21.14. Abraham's treaty with Abimelech explains (a) where Beersheba is, and (b) why Abraham and his servants should have returned there.

increase your numbers', 17.1-2; and 'Be a blessing!' which prefaces the promise of mediating blessing to others in 12.3). By means of the Akedah incident, Abraham is subjected to the ultimate test of his loyalty and faith: is he prepared to obey God despite the promises, or does his commitment to God depend on the promises? Abraham's willingness to comply with this most demanding divine request not only proved the genuine quality of his relationship with God, but also vindicated God's choice of him as the one through whom 'all the familes of the ground will experience blessing'. And so the eternal covenant, announced in ch. 17, is at last established (22.16-18). Here, both promissory aspects of the programmatic agenda (12.1-3) are encompassed in the divine oath: Abraham's 'seed' will become very numerous (22.17a; cf. 13.16; 15.5). The 'great nation' of 12.2 will be established. However, this numerical proliferation of Abraham's 'seed' is in no way restricted to Abraham's genealogical descendants. Rather, as anticipated in 17.1-6, there will also be such numerical proliferation on an international scale. As well as being the physical progenitor of a 'great nation', Abraham will be the spiritual benefactor of a 'multitude of nations'. And it is to this latter dimension of the promissory agenda that 22.17b-18 relates. Abraham will become the father of an international community by mediating blessing to them through an individual royal descendant.[136]

6. Conclusion

This synchronic reading of the main section of the Abraham narrative illustrates that Gen. 12.1–22.19 is bound together by two major promissory themes:[137] Abraham as the physical progenitor of a 'great nation', and Abraham as the spiritual benefactor of 'all the nations of the earth'. The establishment of the 'great nation' is the primary focus up to and

---

136. While Gen. 22.17b-18 does not explicitly state that this individual 'seed' of Abraham will be of royal status, this is a logical deduction to make from (a) the otherwise obscure mention of 'kings' in connection with Abraham's promised 'seed' in 17.6, 16; (b) the fact that Ps. 72 (the only clear allusion to this divine oath outside the book of Genesis) clearly associates its fulfilment with an ideal royal figure.

137. For a concise explanation of why Gen. 22.20–25.11 should be treated as an appendix to the main section of the Abraham narrative, see Alexander, 'Royal Expectations', p. 202 n. 26.

including the covenant established in Genesis 15. From this point on, however, attention is chiefly paid to the 'seed' through whom Abraham will mediate blessing to 'many nations'. This emphasis culminates in the establishment of an eternal covenant (in Gen. 22) that will be perpetuated exclusively through the special 'seed' who will descend from Abraham through Isaac.

In the final composition of the book of Genesis, therefore, chs. 15 and 17 serve to introduce two separate yet related covenants. Together, these covenants solemnly guarantee that the divine promises made to the patriarch at the beginning of the Abraham narrative (12.1-3) will be fulfilled. The first covenant, ratified by the smoking fire-pot and blazing torch passing between the divided animals, confirmed God's promise to make Abraham the father (i.e. the physical progenitor) of a nation. The second covenant, concluded by the sacrifice of the ram and subsequent divine oath in ch. 22, confirmed God's promise to make Abraham the 'father' (i.e. the spiritual benefactor) of an international community. While these covenants have their own distinctive emphases they are not unrelated. Rather, they are connected: a royal descendant will come from the nation, and through this individual 'seed' of Abraham 'all the nations of the earth will experience/acquire for themselves blessing'.

Chapter 8

SUMMARY AND CONCLUSION

The inclusion within the Abraham cycle of two episodes dealing with the establishment of a covenant between God and Abraham raises important questions both for a literary analysis and for a theological appreciation of the Abraham narrative as we now have it: Why did the redactor(s) include two accounts of a divine-human covenant? What function in the overall narrative does each pericope serve? How significant is this for the interpretation of the theological theme(s) of this section of Genesis and the book as a whole?

As Chapter 2 has illustrated, several explanations of this enigma have been put forward by previous writers. Most scholars embracing a diachronic approach have seen the 'solution' in postulating two different underlying sources or traditions of the same covenant, both of which have been preserved by the final redactor of the material. From a synchronic perspective, opinion has been more divided. Some have suggested that Genesis 15 and 17 are to be viewed as two stages in the making of a single divine–human covenant. Others have maintained, rather, that Genesis 17 constitutes a renewal or reaffirmation of the covenant that was established in Genesis 15. Still others have argued that the two chapters introduce two very different covenants (in terms of their focus and/or function).

This synchronic investigation into the relationship between the divine–human covenants in the Abraham narrative has not only exposed the inherent weaknesses in the first three explanations of the relationship between Genesis 15 and 17. It has also shown that it is reasonable to conclude—from the elements of continuity and discontinuity—that these chapters focus on two distinct, yet related, covenants established between God and Abraham. This deduction, arrived at through a detailed final-form analysis of the biblical text, has been supported by the following observations.

First, Genesis 15 and 17 cannot be read as two accounts of the same event in the life of Abraham; a close reading reveals that the chapters differ in both major and minor details. Whereas the promissory emphasis in Genesis 15 is clearly on nationhood (i.e. the promises of 'seed' and 'land'), in Genesis 17 the focus is on Abraham as the 'father [i.e. spiritual benefactor] of a multitude of nations'. The covenant depicted in Genesis 15 is unconditional, yet the covenant announced in Genesis 17 involves mutual obligations. There is no analogous feature in Genesis 15 to the covenant 'sign' of circumcision, a feature that receives considerable attention in Genesis 17. In Genesis 15 Abraham is childless, whereas in Genesis 17 Abraham is already the father of a son. A covenant ritual is enacted and a covenant is made in Genesis 15. In Genesis 17, however, there is no such ritual enactment, and the establishment of the covenant is consistently referred to in the future tense. In the light of these and other irreconcilable features, it is difficult to see in what sense these pericopes can be labelled 'parallel accounts'. To interpret Genesis 15 and 17 as 'doublets' is clearly a gross oversimplification.

Secondly, although there is too much discontinuity between the two covenant pericopes to merit reading them as 'parallel accounts' or even as two 'stages' of a single covenant, there is enough continuity between them to warrant seeing them as in some sense connected. While the promissory emphasis of each chapter is indisputably distinct, it is nevertheless clear that there are important points of thematic contact between them. Genesis 17 clearly encompasses both elements of the 'covenant between the pieces' (i.e. 'innumerable descendants' and 'territorial inheritance'). Significantly, however, there is no anticipation in Genesis 15 of the 'international' dimension that is emphasized so strongly in Genesis 17 (i.e. Abraham becoming 'father of a multitude of nations'). This suggests that whereas the promise of Abraham becoming 'father of many nations' is dependent in some way on the promise of 'nationhood', the latter is not dependent on the former. Abraham could become a 'great nation' without necessarily becoming 'father of a multitude of nations'. He could not, however, become 'father of a multitude of nations' unless he first became the father of a 'great nation'. The promise of nationhood, therefore, has chronological priority over the promise relating to the nations. The latter is dependent on the former. So while it is wrong to conclude that Genesis 15 and 17 represent 'parallel accounts' or two 'stages' of a single divine–human covenant, it is equally mistaken to treat them as two unrelated episodes.

Thirdly, the different emphases in Genesis 15 and 17 mirror the two separate strands set out in the promissory agenda of Gen. 12.1-3. Each covenant picks up different aspects from the divine programme of anticipated blessing. Genesis 15 concentrates on the divine promise to make Abraham a 'great nation', whereas Genesis 17 focuses more on the divine promise that through Abraham 'all the families of the ground will experience blessing'. Although these promissory aspects are to some degree related, each covenant pericope serves a different function within its present literary context. Genesis 15 guarantees the fulfilment of the first promissory aspect outlined in Gen. 12.1-3 (i.e. nationhood). Genesis 17, while encompassing this promissory aspect, anticipates a similar divine guarantee in relation to the second promise in the programmatic agenda (i.e. the blessing of the nations). Such anticipation was necessitated by the need for clarification in relation to the identity of Abraham's 'seed' and 'covenant heir'.

Fourthly, the overarching theme in Genesis 15 and 17 relates to this question of Abraham's 'seed' and 'heir'. While the covenant depicted in Genesis 15 has firmly guaranteed that Abraham would have an heir, the events narrated in the following chapter underline that Sarah's role in the establishment of such a 'seed' had not been made clear. With the birth of Ishmael, and the imminent arrival of Isaac, clarification was needed over the status of each of these two boys in relation to the 'seed' through whom God's promises to Abraham will be fulfilled. Therefore the main point in Genesis 17 is that, although those related to Abraham may share in the promised blessings, God will perpetuate his 'eternal covenant' exclusively through a particular line of 'seed'. This line will commence with Isaac, and will evolve into a royal line (the enigmatic 'kings' of Gen. 17.6, 16; cf. 35.11), through whom Abraham will become 'father [i.e. spiritual benefactor] of a multitude of nations'.

Fifthly, Genesis 17 should not be read in isolation, but in conjunction with the Akedah episode of Genesis 22; this helps to explain the most enigmatic aspects of both these pericopes, viz. the anticipation of a covenant in Genesis 17, and the necessity of a test and sacrifice in Genesis 22. The 'eternal covenant' anticipated in Genesis 17 is not actually ratified in that chapter. Such ratification can only take place after Abraham has demonstrated the prerequisite highlighted in Gen. 17.1 (i.e. submissive loyalty to God). This he illustrates admirably through the Akedah incident. Thus, in response to Abraham's obedience (cf. 22.16,

18; 26.5), God establishes the 'eternal covenant' anticipated in ch. 17, solemnly guaranteeing the fulfilment of both aspects of his original promissory agenda. Abraham's 'seed' (pl.) *will* become extremely numerous (the 'great nation' of 12.2). In addition, Abraham's 'seed' (sing.) *will* conquer his enemies and so, through this particular 'seed' of Abraham, 'all the nations of the earth *will* acquire blessing for themselves'. The sacrificing of the ram and God's swearing of an oath demonstrate the fact that this is indeed a covenant-making occasion.

Together these points offer convincing reasons for understanding the 'covenant between the pieces' and the 'covenant of circumcision' as two distinct, yet related, divine–human covenants. This hypothesis best explains the inclusion of Genesis 15 and 17 by the final redactor of the Abraham narrative. Moreover, it offers the most adequate answers to the important exegetical questions set out at the beginning of this book.[1] It accounts for the presence of two quite different pericopes pertaining to the establishment of covenants between God and Abraham. It provides a cogent explanation for how the two covenants are related thematically. And, most importantly, it explains the distinctive emphasis of each pericope within the context of a synchronic reading of the Abraham narrative.

Such a reading of Genesis 15 and 17 has important ramifications for the interpretation, not only of the book of Genesis, but of all of Genesis–Kings.[2] In relation to the former it highlights the significance of 'seed' as a central theme in the book as a whole. Through a number of recent articles,[3] Alexander has made an impressive case for understanding 'seed' as a *Leitwort* in the book of Genesis. If my understanding of Genesis 15 and 17 is correct, then this *Leitwort* (or rather, *Leitmotif*) is the central thread—the thematic lynchpin—that connects the distinctive promissory emphasis of each covenant pericope. This is something which, notwithstanding his considerable insights into the material, Alexander has perhaps not articulated as clearly as possible.[4]

---

1.   See Chapter 1.
2.   Whatever their diachronic history, the final redaction of Genesis–Kings suggests that these books were framed to form a unified narrative. Cf. Alexander, 'Royal Expectations', pp. 193-96.
3.   Cf. Chapter 7 (n. 120) above.
4.   This is due, in some measure, to his over-emphasis on the 'international' dimension of the promises reflected in Gen. 17. By failing to pay close enough attention to the national dimensions encompassed within this chapter, Alexander

This emphasis on Abraham's 'seed' illustrates that both Genesis 15 and 17, despite their distinctive emphases, are *primarily* interested in the 'seed' whose lineage is traced throughout the book of Genesis.[5] This 'seed' motif would also account for the inclusion of the Lot episodes in the Abraham narrative (esp. 19.30-38). As in the primaeval narrative and the post-Abrahamic patriarchal material,[6] alternative lines of 'seed' are contrasted with the special line of 'seed' through which the catastrophe of Genesis 3 will be reversed and God's creative purposes for all humankind realized.

However, as Genesis is not a literary island, this synchronic analysis of the relationship between Genesis 15 and 17 impinges also on the interpretation of Genesis–Kings as a whole. This twin-covenant thesis has important ramifications for how the rest of the material that unfolds in this body of literature relates to each covenant. For example, how do subsequent divine–human covenants function in relation to the promissory emphasis of each of these pericopes in the Abraham narrative? This question is of particular significance for the interpretation of the Davidic covenant,[7] given the clear allusions in 2 Samuel 7 and related texts to blessings and obligations associated with Abraham.[8] Certainly my understanding of the 'eternal covenant' of Genesis 17 throws considerable light on why God should establish such a covenant with David in relation to 'his seed after him' (cf. 2 Sam. 7.11-16; Ps. 89.4, 29, 36). A strong case could be made for interpreting the Davidic covenant as a divine guarantee that the promise of 'international blessing' which God made to Abraham will ultimately be fulfilled through a

---

has not spelt out clearly (at least in his discussion of ch. 17) the crucial significance of 'nationhood' for the fulfilment of the 'international promise'.

5.   The importance of this theme in Genesis is reflected, not only by the *tôlᵉdôt* formulae with which the book is framed (cf. 2.4; 5.1; 6.9; 10.1; 11.10, 27; 25.12, 19; 36.1, 9; 37.2), but by the disproportionate occurrences of the term זרע in Genesis vis-à-vis the rest of the Hebrew Bible (a ratio of 1:3 according to Alexander, 'Royal Expectations', p. 203).

6.   Cf. 3.15; 4.17-24; 10.1-20; 19.30-38; 25.12-18; 36.1-43.

7.   While the term 'covenant' is not used explicitly in 2 Sam. 7, it is clear from elsewhere that this chapter depicts the making of such (cf. 2 Sam. 23.5; Pss. 89.3, 28, 34; 132.11-12).

8.   For instance, the promise of 'a great name' (2 Sam. 7.9); the assurance of victory over enemies (2 Sam. 7.11; Ps. 89.23); the obligation of keeping God's laws (2 Sam. 7.14; Pss. 89.30-32; 132.12); a divine–human relationship (2 Sam. 7.24; Ps. 89.26); the prospect of fulfilment in a single royal descendant (2 Sam. 7.12-13).

royal descendant of David. This, in turn, would explain the transference of the Abrahamic promises to a future Davidic king in Psalm 72. In other words, the Davidic covenant serves to identify at a later stage in Genesis–Kings the promised line of 'seed' which will mediate blessing to all the nations of the earth. While a more detailed examination of the connection between the Abrahamic and Davidic covenants (as well as the other covenants in Genesis–Kings) lies outside the scope of the current investigation, clearly further research is required in the light of my analysis of the Abraham narrative.

While there can be no doubt that Genesis–Kings traces the fulfilment of the programmatic promises that God made to Abraham, the extent of fulfilment must be reassessed in the light of the twin-covenant interpretation of the Abrahamic material advocated in this study. Clearly the promises of 'land' and 'seed' are portrayed as fulfilled (at least provisionally) in the period covered by Genesis–Kings.[9] The book of Exodus begins by emphasizing the numerical proliferation of Abraham's descendants in Egypt (1.6-10). This phenomenal increase is further underlined by the notoriously large numbers given for the Exodus generation in 12.37, and the comparable totals of the subsequent census figures in the book of Numbers (chs. 1 and 26). The later population 'figures' of the Davidic-Solomonic Empire reinforce the same point (cf. 2 Sam. 17.11; 24.9; 1 Kgs 3.9; 4.20).

A similar pattern can be discerned with respect to the territorial promise. The promise of land was in some measure fulfilled by the series of military campaigns conducted under Joshua's leadership (Josh. 21.43-45; 23.14).[10] Without question, the fulfilment of the territorial promise was more comprehensive in the time of the Davidic-Solomonic Empire (cf. 2 Sam. 22.1; 1 Kgs 4.21, 24). So the promise of nationhood

---

9.   While the promises of 'innumerable descendants' and 'possession of land' have been realized (at least in a primary sense) by the end of the Former Prophets, it is clear from the Latter Prophets that the ultimate realization of these promises was still in the future (for the promise of 'innumerable seed', cf. Hos. 1.10-11; [Isa. 48.19]; Jer. 23.3; Ezek. 36.10-11, 37-38; 37.26; for the promise of 'land', cf. Isa. 14.1; 57.13; 60.21; Jer. 3.16-17; 12.15; Ezek. 11.15-17; 36.6-12; Zech. 2.11-12; 14.9-11). For a fuller discussion of the provisional nature of the fulfilment of the Abrahamic promises in the Hebrew Bible, see Williamson, 'Abraham, Israel and the Church'.

10.   These rather idealistic statements, however, are tempered by the more realistic picture presented elsewhere (cf. Josh. 13–19; Judg. 1–2).

is depicted as fulfilled in the Former Prophets.[11] Given that this promise
had been guaranteed unconditionally by the 'covenant between the
pieces', its primary fulfilment in Genesis–Kings is hardly surprising.

But what about the international dimension of the programmatic
agenda? The establishment in the nation descended from Abraham
through Isaac and Jacob of a dynastic monarchy immediately recalls the
promise of 'kings' in Genesis (17.6, 16; 35.11). Moreover, the fact that
these kings are descended from Judah provides another link with the
way that Abraham's special line of 'seed' is traced in the patriarchal
narratives. Not only is particular attention drawn in Genesis 38 to Perez
(Judah's 'seed'),[12] but also Judah is the only one of the twelve tribes
with which regal imagery is expressly associated (49.8-12). Nevertheless, even though Abraham has become a 'great nation'—a nation ruled
over by 'kings' descended from Isaac, Jacob, Judah and Perez (i.e.
Abraham's 'seed' and covenant heirs)—there is little indication that
this has culminated in blessing being mediated to 'all the nations of the
earth'. While, admittedly, there are foreshadowings of the latter in the
persons of Joseph (cf. Gen. 41.57) and Solomon (cf. 1 Kgs 4.34;
9.26-10.25), readers are left with the distinct impression that this promissory aspect of the programmatic agenda has somehow failed to materialize.

The distinction which has been drawn in this study between the two
divine–human covenants in the Abraham narrative may shed considerable light on the reason why this is so. If the fulfilment of the divine
promise of international blessing was dependent on the moral blamelessness, not only of Abraham (cf. 17.1; 22.16, 18; 26.5), but also of his
'royal seed' (as encapsulated in the rite of circumcision and further
alluded to in the lifestyle demanded of the nation generally in the
Mosaic covenant; cf. Deut. 18.14-20), then no such royal 'seed' had yet
emerged. Not only does this explain the projection of the Abrahamic
promise onto the ideal (and morally blameless) king of Psalm 72, but it
also explains the New Testament's emphasis on the fact that Jesus

11. For a concise discussion of the fulfilment of the nationhood promise in
Genesis–Kings, see Alexander, 'Royal Expectations', pp. 196-98.

12. The significance of Perez is indicated by at least three features: (1) this
sordid episode involving Judah and Tamar interrupts the story of Joseph, the
obvious candidate for covenant heir; (2) the motif of 'seed' is emphasized in 38.8-9;
(3) there are striking similarities between the births of Perez and Jacob (cf. 25.24-
26; 38.27-30).

Christ was a morally blameless descendant of both Abraham and David (i.e. he was the royal 'seed' of Abraham in whom all nations would be blessed).

Therefore this synchronic analysis of the relationship between Genesis 15 and 17 raises important questions which require further research: How do subsequent divine–human covenants in Genesis–Kings relate to the covenants established between God and Abraham? To what extent are the distinctive promissory emphases of each covenant pericope (Gen. 15 and 17) fulfilled in Genesis–Kings? Is the 'covenant between the pieces' superseded in Genesis–Kings by the 'covenant of circumcision'? While these issues lie outside the parameters of the present study, the fact that the relationship between Genesis 15 and 17 does have such widespread ramifications underlines how important this investigation is. As well as impinging on a theological appreciation of the Hebrew Bible, it has a significant bearing on the relationship between the two Testaments of the Christian Bible.

For too long the theological relationship between Genesis 15 and 17 has remained unexplored; inadequate solutions have been proposed but not rigorously critiqued. When examined within the context of the narrative as a whole, the divine–human covenants in the Abraham cycle are best understood as relating to different promissory aspects which are held together by a common thread: God's plan to mediate blessing to all the nations of the earth through Abraham and his 'seed'.

BIBLIOGRAPHY

Aalders, G.C., *Genesis* (trans. W. Heynen; Bible Student's Commentary; 2 vols.; repr., Grand Rapids: Zondervan, 1981 [1949]).

Abela, A., 'Genesis 15: A Non-Genetic Approach', *MelT* 37.2 (1986), pp. 9-40.

—*The Themes of the Abraham Narrative* (Zabbar, Malta: Veritas, 1989).

Aberbach, M., and B. Grossfeld, *Targum Onkelos to Genesis: A Critical Analysis Together with an English Translation* (Denver: Ktav Publishing House, 1982).

Adar, Z., *The Book of Genesis: An Introduction to the Biblical World* (Jerusalem: Magnes Press, 1990).

Albrektson, B., *History and the Gods: An Essay on the Idea of Historical Events as Divine Manifestations in the Ancient Near East and in Israel* (ConBOT, 1; Lund: Gleerup, 1967).

Albright, W.F., 'Abram the Hebrew: A New Archaeological Interpretation', *BASOR* 163 (1961), pp. 36-54.

—'The Hebrew Expression for "Making a Covenant" in Pre-Israelite Documents', *BASOR* 121 (1951), pp. 21-22.

Alexander, T.D., *Abraham in the Negev: A Source-Critical Investigation of Genesis 20.1– 22.19* (Carlisle: Paternoster Press, 1997).

—'Abraham Re-assessed Theologically: The Abraham Narrative and the New Testament Understanding of Justification by Faith', in Hess, Wenham and Satterthwaite (eds.), *He Swore an Oath*, pp. 7-28.

—'From Adam to Judah: The Significance of the Family Tree in Genesis', *EvQ* 61 (1989), pp. 5-19.

—*From Paradise to the Promised Land: An Introduction to the Main Themes of the Pentateuch* (Carlisle: Paternoster Press, 1995).

—'Further Observations on the Term "Seed" in Genesis', *TynBul* 48 (1997), pp. 363-67.

—'Genealogies, Seed and the Compositional Unity of Genesis', *TynBul* 44 (1993), pp. 255-70.

—'Genesis 22 and the Covenant of Circumcision', *JSOT* 25 (1983), pp. 17-22.

—'A Literary Analysis of the Abraham Narrative in Genesis' (PhD thesis; The Queen's University of Belfast, 1982).

—'Messianic Ideology in the Book of Genesis', in P.E. Satterthwaite, R.S. Hess and G.J. Wenham (eds.), *The Lord's Anointed: Interpretation of Old Testament Messianic Texts* (Carlisle: Paternoster Press, 1995), pp. 19-39.

—'Royal Expectations in Genesis to Kings: Their Importance for Biblical Theology', *TynBul* 49 (1998), pp. 191-212.

—*The Servant King: The Bible's Portrait of the Messiah* (Leicester: InterVarsity Press, 1998).

Allen, L., 'Circumcision', *NIDOTE*, IV, pp. 474-76.

Allis, O.T., 'The Blessing of Abraham', *Princeton Theological Review* 25 (1927), pp. 263-98.

—*God Spake By Moses: An Exposition of the Pentateuch* (Philadelphia: Presbyterian and Reformed, 1951).

Alter, R., *The Art of Biblical Narrative* (New York: Basic Books, 1981).

—*Genesis: Translation and Commentary* (New York: W.W. Norton, 1996).

—*The World of Biblical Literature* (New York: Basic Books, 1992).

Anbar, M., 'Abrahamic Covenant: Gen. 15' (Hebrew), *Schnaton* 3 (1978–79), pp. 34-52.

—'Additional Notes to *Schnaton* 3' (Hebrew), *Schnaton* 4 (1980), pp. 275-79.

—'Genesis 15: A Conflation of Two Deuteronomic Narratives', *JBL* 101 (1982), pp. 39-55.

Andersen, F.I., 'The Scope of the Abrahamic Covenant', *The Churchman* 74 (1960), pp. 239-44.

—*The Sentence in Biblical Hebrew* (The Hague: Mouton, 1974).

Andersen, F.I., and N. Freedman, *Hosea* (AB; New York: Doubleday, 1980).

Anderson, A.A., *Psalms 1–72* (NCBC; London: Marshall, Morgan & Scott, 1972).

Anderson, B.W., 'Abraham, the Friend of God', *Int* 42 (1988), pp. 353-66.

—*Contours of Old Testament Theology* (Minneapolis: Fortress Press, 1999).

Arnold, B.T., *Encountering the Book of Genesis* (Encountering Biblical Studies; Grand Rapids: Baker Book House, 1998).

Astruc, J., *Conjectures sur les mémoires originaux dont il paraît que Moyse s'est servi pour composer le livre de la Genèse* (Brussels: Chez Fricx, 1753).

Atkinson, B.F.C., *The Book of Genesis* (The Pocket Commentary of the Bible; Chicago: Moody Press, 1957).

Auffret, P., 'Essai sur la structure littéraire de Gn 12.1-4 aα', *BZ* 26 (1982), pp. 243-48.

Baker, D.L., 'Typology and the Christian Use of the Old Testament', *SJT* 29 (1976), pp. 137-57.

Baldwin, J., *The Message of Genesis 12–50* (Bible Speaks Today; Leicester: InterVarsity Press, 1986).

Baltzer, K., *The Covenant Formulary in Old Testament, Jewish and Christian Writings* (Oxford: Basil Blackwell, 1971).

Barr, J., 'Some Semantic Notes on the Covenant', in H. Donner, R. Hanhart and R. Smend (eds.), *Beiträge zur alttestamentlichen Theologie* (Festschrift W. Zimmerli; Göttingen: Vandenhoeck & Ruprecht, 1977), pp. 23-38.

—'The Synchronic, the Diachronic and the Historical: A Triangular Relationship?', in J.C. De Moor (ed.), *Synchronic or Dychronic? A Debate on Method in Old Testament Exegesis* (OTS, 34; Leiden: E.J. Brill, 1995), pp. 1-14.

Barth, L.M., 'Genesis 15 and the Problems of Abraham's Seventh Trial', *Maarav* 8 (1992), pp. 245-63.

Baumann, A., 'המה *hāmāh*', *TDOT*, III, pp. 414-18.

Beckwith, R.T., 'The Unity and Diversity of God's Covenants', *TynBul* 38 (1987), pp. 92-118.

Beecher, W.J., *The Prophets and the Promise* (repr., Grand Rapids: Baker Book House, 1963 [1905]).

Begg, C.T., 'The Birds in Genesis 15.9-10', *BN* 36 (1987), pp. 7-11.

—'Doves and Treaty-Making: Another Possible Reference', *BN* 48 (1989), pp. 8-11.

—'Rereading the "Animal Rite" of Genesis 15 in Early Jewish Narratives', *CBQ* 50 (1988), pp. 36-46.

Ben Zvi, E., 'The Dialogue between Abraham and YHWH in Gen. 18.23-32: A Historical-Critical Analysis', *JSOT* 53 (1992), pp. 27-46.

Berge, K., *Die Zeit des Jahwisten. Ein Beitrag zur Datierung jahwistischer Vätertexte* (BZAW, 186; Berlin: W. de Gruyter, 1990).

Bergen, R.D., 'The Role of Genesis 22.1-19 in the Abraham Cycle: A Computer-Assisted Textual Interpretation', *CTR* 4 (1990), pp. 313-26.

Berkhof, L., *Systematic Theology* (Grand Rapids: Eerdmans, 1941).

Biddle, M.E., 'The "Endangered Ancestress" and Blessing for the Nations', *JBL* 109 (1990), pp. 599-611.

Blaising, C.A., and D.L. Bock, *Progressive Dispensationalism* (Wheaton: Victor, 1993).

Blenkinsopp, J., *The Pentateuch: An Introduction to the First Five Books of the Bible* (London: SCM Press, 1992).

Blum, E., *Die Komposition der Vätergeschichte* (WMANT, 57; Neukirchen–Vluyn: Neukirchener Verlag, 1984).

—*Studien zur Komposition des Pentateuch* (BZAW, 189; Berlin: W. de Gruyter, 1990).

Blythin, I., 'The Patriarchs and the Promise', *SJT* 21 (1968), pp. 56-73.

Bodoff, L., 'God Tests Abraham—Abraham Tests God', *BR* 9.5 (1993), pp. 52-56, 62.

Boer, P.A.H. de, 'Quelques remarques sur l'Arc dans la Nuée', in C. Brekelmans (ed.), *Questions disputées d'Ancien Testament: Méthode et théologie* (Leuven: Leuven University Press, 2nd edn, 1989), pp. 105-14.

Boorer, S., 'The Importance of a Diachronic Approach: The Case of Genesis–Kings', *CBQ* 51 (1989), pp. 195-208.

—*The Promise of the Land as Oath: A Key to the Formation of the Pentateuch* (BZAW, 205; Berlin: W. de Gruyter, 1992).

Bovon, F., and G. Rouiller (eds.), *Exegesis: Problems of Method and Exercises in Reading (Genesis 22 and Luke 15)* (trans. D.G. Millar; Pittsburgh: Pickwick Press, 1978).

Braswell, J.P., ' "The Blessing of Abraham" versus "the Curse of the Law" ', *WTJ* 53 (1991), pp. 73-91.

Brawley, R.L., 'For Blessing All Families of the Earth: Covenant Traditions in Luke–Acts', *CurTM* 22 (1995), pp. 18-26.

Bray, G., 'The Promises Made to Abraham and the Destiny of Israel', *SBET* 7 (1989), pp. 69-87.

Breibart, S., 'The Akedah—a Test of God', *Dor Le Dor* 15 (1986), pp. 19-28.

Brett, M., *Biblical Criticism in Crisis? The Impact of the Canonical Approach on Old Testament Studies* (Cambridge: Cambridge University Press, 1991).

Bright, J., *Covenant and Promise: The Future in the Preaching of the Pre-Exilic Prophets* (London: SCM Press, 1977).

Brock, S., 'Where was Sarah?', *ExpTim* 96 (1984), pp. 14-17.

Brueggemann, W., *Genesis: A Bible Commentary for Teaching and Preaching* (Interpretation; Atlanta: John Knox Press, 1982).

—'Genesis 17.1-22', *Int* 45 (1991), pp. 55-59.

—*The Land: Place as Gift, Promise, and Challenge in Biblical Faith* (OBT; Philadelphia: Fortress Press, 1977).

Buchanan, G.W., *The Consequences of the Covenant* (Leiden: E.J. Brill, 1970).

Buttrick, D.G., 'Genesis 15.1-18', *Int* 42 (1988), pp. 393-97.

Calvin, J., *Commentaries on the Minor Prophets* (Edinburgh: Calvin Translation Society, 1846).

—*A Commentary on Genesis* (Geneva Commentaries; repr., London: Banner of Truth Trust, 1965).

Campbell, A.F., and M.A. O'Brien, *Sources of the Pentateuch: Texts, Introductions, Annotations* (Minneapolis: Fortress Press, 1993).

Caquot, A., 'L'alliance avec Abram (Genèse 15)', *Sem* 12 (1962), pp. 51-66.

Carpenter, E., 'מול', *NIDOTE*, II, pp. 869-70.

Carr, D.M., 'Βίβλος γενέσεως Revisited: A Synchronic Analysis of Patterns in Genesis as Part of the Torah', Parts 1 and 2, *ZAW* 110 (1998), pp. 159-72, 327-47.

—'Controversy and Convergence in Recent Studies of the Formation of the Pentateuch', *RelSRev* 23 (1997), pp. 22-31.

—review of *Genesis 15. Eine Erzählung von der Anfängen Israels* (Würzburg: Echter Verlag, 1988) by H. Mölle, in *JBL* 110 (1991), pp. 505-507.

—*Reading the Fractures of Genesis: Historical and Literary Approaches* (Louisville, KY: Westminster / John Knox Press, 1996).

Carroll, R.P., *Jeremiah* (OTL; London: SCM Press, 1986).

Cassuto, U., *A Commentary on the Book of Genesis. II. From Noah to Abraham* (trans. I. Abrahams; Jerusalem: Magnes Press, 1964).

—*The Documentary Hypothesis* (trans. I. Abrahams; Jerusalem: Magnes Press, 1961).

Cazelles, H., 'Connexions et structure de Gen. XV', *RB* 69 (1962), pp. 321-49.

Charlesworth, J.H. (ed.), *The Old Testament Pseudepigrapha* (2 vols.; London: Darton, Longman & Todd, 1983–85).

Charny, I.W., 'And Abraham Went to Slay Isaac: A Parable of Killer, Victim, and Bystander in the Family of Man', *JES* 10 (1973), pp. 304-18.

Chew, H.C., 'The Theme of "Blessing for the Nations" in the Patriarchal Narratives of Genesis' (PhD thesis; University of Sheffield, 1982).

Childs, B.S., *Biblical Theology of the Old and New Testaments* (London: SCM Press, 1992).

Christensen, D.L., 'The Akedah in Genesis 22.1-19: An Invitation to Jewish–Christian Dialogue', *ABQ* 4 (1985), pp. 340-46.

Clements, R.E., *Abraham and David: Genesis 15 and its Meaning for Israelite Tradition* (SBT, 2.5; London: SCM Press, 1967).

—'גוי *gôy*', *TDOT*, II, pp. 426-33.

Clines, D.J.A., *The Theme of the Pentateuch* (JSOTSup, 10; Sheffield: Sheffield Academic Press, 2nd edn, 1997).

—*What Does Eve Do to Help? And Other Readerly Questions to the Old Testament* (JSOTSup, 94; Sheffield: JSOT Press, 1990).

Coats, G.W., 'Abraham's Sacrifice of Faith: A Form-Critical Study of Genesis 22', *Int* 27 (1973), pp. 389-400.

—'The Curse in God's Blessing: Gen 12, 1-4a in the Structure and Theology of the Yahwist', in J. Jeremias and L. Perlitt (eds.), *Die Botschaft und die Boten* (Festschrift H.W. Wolff; Neukirchen–Vluyn: Neukirchener Verlag, 1981), pp. 31-41.

—*Genesis, with an Introduction to Narrative Literature* (FOTL; Grand Rapids: Eerdmans, 1983).

Coffin, E.A., 'The Binding of Isaac in Modern Israeli Literature', in M.P. O'Connor and D.N. Freedman (eds.), *Backgrounds to the Bible* (Winona Lake, IN: Eisenbrauns, 1987), pp. 293-308.

Cohn, R.L., 'Narrative Structure and Canonical Perspective in Genesis', *JSOT* 25 (1983), pp. 3-16.

Collins, J., 'A Syntactical Note [Genesis 3.15]: Is the Woman's Seed Singular or Plural?', *TynBul* 48 (1997), pp. 139-48.

Crenshaw, J.L., 'Journey into Oblivion: A Structural Analysis of Gen 22.1-19', *Soundings* 58 (1975), pp. 243-56.

—*A Whirlpool of Torment* (OBT; Philadelphia: Fortress Press, 1984).

Crüsemann, F., 'Die Eigenständigkeit der Urgeschichte. Ein Beitrag zur Diskussion um den "Jahwisten"', in J. Jeremias and L. Perlitt (eds.), *Die Botschaft und die Boten* (Festschrift H.W. Wolff; Neukirchen–Vluyn: Neukirchener Verlag, 1981), pp. 11-29.

—'Le Pentateuque, une Tora: Prolégomènes à l'interprétation de sa forme finale', in A. de Pury (ed.), *Le Pentateuque en question: Les origines et la composition des cinq premiers livres de la Bible à la lumière des recherches récentes* (Geneva: Labor & Fides, 1989), pp. 339-60.

Dahl, N.A., *The Crucified Messiah and Other Essays* (Minneapolis: Augsburg, 1974).

Dahlberg, B., 'The Unity of Genesis', in K.R.R. Gros Louis and J.S. Ackerman (eds.), *Literary Interpretations of Biblical Narratives* (Nashville: Abingdon Press, 1982), II, pp. 126-33.

Dahood, M., 'Ugaritic Lexicography', in *Mélanges Eugène Tisserant* (Studi e Testi, 231; Rome: Pontifical Biblical Institute, 1964), pp. 81-104.

—'Zecharia 9,1 'ên 'Ādām', *CBQ* 25 (1963), pp. 123-24.

Daly, R.J., *The Origins of the Christian Doctrine of Sacrifice* (London: Darton, Longman & Todd, 1978).

—'The Soteriological Significance of the Sacrifice of Isaac', *CBQ* 39 (1977), pp. 45-75.

Davidson, R., 'Covenant Ideology in Ancient Israel', in R.E. Clements (ed.), *The World of Ancient Israel: Sociological, Anthropological and Political Perspectives* (Cambridge: Cambridge University Press, 1989), pp. 323-47.

—*Genesis 12–50* (CBC; Cambridge: Cambridge University Press, 1979).

Davies, P.R., 'Abraham and Yahweh: A Case of Male Bonding', *BR* 11.4 (1995), pp. 24-33, 44-45.

—'The Sacrifice of Isaac and Passover', in E.A. Livingstone (ed.), *Studia Biblica: Papers on Old Testament and Related Themes* (JSOTSup, 11; Sheffield: JSOT Press, 1978), pp. 127-32.

Davies, P.R., and B. Chilton, 'The Aqedah: A Revised Tradition History', *CBQ* 40 (1978), pp. 514-46.

Davies, W.D., *The Gospel and the Land: Early Christianity and Jewish Territorial Doctrine* (repr.; The Biblical Seminar, 25; Sheffield: JSOT Press, 1974).

Davis, E.F., 'Self-Consciousness and Conversation: Reading Genesis 22', *BBR* 1 (1991), pp. 27-40.

Davis, J.J., *Paradise to Prison: Studies in Genesis* (Grand Rapids: Baker Book House, 1975).

Day, J., 'Pre-Deuteronomic Allusions to the Covenant in Hosea and Psalm LXXVIII', *VT* 36 (1986), pp. 1-12.

Decker, R.J., 'The Church's Relationship to the New Covenant', *BSac* 152 (1995), pp. 291-305.

Delitzsch, F., *A New Commentary on Genesis* (trans. S. Taylor; 2 vols.; Edinburgh: T. & T. Clark, 1888).

De Moor, J.C. (ed.), *Synchronic or Diachronic? A Debate on Method in Old Testament Exegesis* (OTS, 34; Leiden: E.J. Brill, 1995).

Dequeker, L., 'Noah and Israel: The Everlasting Divine Covenant with Mankind', in C. Brekelmans (ed.), *Questions disputées d'Ancien Testament: Méthode et théologie* (Leuven: Leuven University Press, 2nd edn, 1989), pp. 115-29.

Deurloo, K.A., 'Because You have Hearkened to My Voice (Genesis 22)', in M. Kessler (ed. and trans.), *Voices from Amsterdam* (Atlanta: Scholars Press, 1994), pp. 113-30.

—'Narrative Geography in the Abraham Cycle', in A.S. Van der Woude (ed.), *In Quest of the Past: Studies on Israelite Religion, Literature and Prophetism* (OTS, 26; Leiden: E.J. Brill, 1990), pp. 48-62.

—'The Way of Abraham', in M. Kessler (ed. and trans.), *Voices from Amsterdam* (Atlanta: Scholars Press, 1994), pp. 95-112.

DeWitt, D.S., 'The Generations of Genesis', *EvQ* 48 (1976), pp. 196-211.

Dillmann, A., *Genesis Critically and Exegetically Expounded* (trans. W.B. Stevenson; 2 vols.; Edinburgh: T. & T. Clark, 1897).

Dion, H.M., 'The Patriarchal Traditions and the Literary Form of the "Oracle of Salvation"', *CBQ* 29 (1967), pp. 198-206.

Dods, M., *The Book of Genesis* (The Expositor's Bible; London: Hodder & Stoughton, 11th edn, 1888).

Domeris, W.R., 'המה', *NIDOTE*, I, pp. 1041-43.

Doukhan, J.B., 'The *Aqedah* at the "Crossroad": Its Significance in the Jewish–Christian–Muslim Dialogue', *AUSS* 32.1-2 (1994), pp. 29-40.

—'The Centre of the Aqedah: A Study of the Literary Structure of Genesis 22.1-19', *AUSS* 31.1 (1993), pp. 17-28.

Driver, S.R., *The Book of Genesis* (Westminster Commentaries; London: Methuen, 11th edn, 1920).

—*A Treatise on the Use of the Tenses in Hebrew and other Syntactical Questions* (Oxford: Clarendon Press, 3rd edn, 1892).

Duhaime, J.-L., 'Le sacrifice d'Isaac (Gn 22, 1-19): L'héritage de Gunkel', *ScEs* 33 (1981), pp. 139-56.

Dumbrell, W.J., *Covenant and Creation: A Theology of the Old Testament Covenants* (Exeter: Paternoster Press, 1984).

—'The Covenant with Abraham', *RTR* 38 (1982), pp. 42-50.

—'Creation, Covenant and Work', *EvRT* 13 (1989), pp. 137-56.

—'The Prospect of Unconditionality in the Sinaitic Covenant', in A. Gileadi (ed.), *Israel's Apostasy and Restoration* (Festschrift R.K. Harrison; Grand Rapids: Baker Book House, 1988), pp. 141-55.

Dun, J., 'Der Jacobbund Gen 15.8ff', *ZAW* 80 (1968), pp. 35-38.

Eichrodt, W., 'Covenant and Law: Thoughts on Recent Discussion', *Int* 20 (1966), pp. 302-21.

Eilberg-Schwartz, H., *The Savage in Judaism: An Anthropology of Israelite Religion and Ancient Judaism* (Bloomington: Indiana University Press, 1990).

Ellington, J., 'Translating God's Promises to Abraham', *BT* 45 (1994), pp. 201-207.

Ellis, E.E., *Paul's Use of the Old Testament* (Grand Rapids: Eerdmans, 1957).

Emerton, J.A., 'An Examination of Some Recent Attempts to Defend the Unity of the Flood Narrative in Genesis: Part I', *VT* 37 (1987), pp. 401-20.

—'An Examination of Some Recent Attempts to Defend the Unity of the Flood Narrative in Genesis: Part II', *VT* 38 (1988), pp. 1-21.

—'The Origin of the Promises to the Patriarchs in the Older Sources of the Book of Genesis', *VT* 32 (1982), pp. 14-32.

—review of *The Making of the Pentateuch: A Methodological Study* (Sheffield: JSOT Press, 1987), by R.N. Whybray, in *VT* 39 (1989), pp. 110-16.

Eslinger, L.M., 'Knowing Yahweh: Exod 6.3 in the Context of Genesis 1–Exodus 15', in L.J. de Regt, J. de Waard and J.P. Fokkelmann (eds.), *Literary Structure and Rhetorical Strategies in the Hebrew Bible* (Assen: Van Gorcum, 1996), pp. 188-98.

Ewald, H., *Die Komposition der Genesis kritisch untersucht* (Braunschweig: L. Lucius, 1923).

Feinberg, C.L., 'Jeremiah', in F.E. Gaebelein (ed.), *The Expositors Bible Commentary* (12 vols.; Grand Rapids: Zondervan, 1986), VI, pp. 355-691.

Fensham, F.C., 'The Covenant as Giving Expression to the Relationship between OT and NT', *TynBul* 22 (1971), pp. 82-94.

Firestone, R., 'Abraham's Son as the Intended Sacrifice (*Al-Dbabīḥ, Qur'ān* 37.99-113): Issues in *Qur'ānic* Exegesis', *JSS* 34 (1989), pp. 95-131.

Fishbane, M., *Biblical Interpretation in Ancient Israel* (Oxford: Clarendon Press, 1985).

Fisher, M.C., 'נָתַן (*nātan*) give', *TWOT*, II, pp. 608-609.

Flavel, J., *The Works of John Flavel* (6 vols.; repr., London: Banner of Truth Trust, 1968).

Flesseman-van Leer, E., 'Abraham, the Father of Believers', in H.-G. Link (ed.), *The Roots of Our Common Faith* (Faith and Order Paper, 119; Geneva: World Council of Churches Publications, 1984), pp. 35-39.

Fohrer, G., *Introduction to the Old Testament* (trans. D.E. Green; Nashville: Abingdon Press, 1968).

Fokkelmann, J.P., *Narrative Art in Genesis: Specimens of Stylistic and Structural Analysis* (Assen: van Gorcum, 1975).

—'On the Mount of the Lord there is Vision: A Response to Francis Landy Concerning the Akedah', in J.C. Exum (ed.), *Signs and Wonders: Biblical Texts in Literary Focus* (SBLSS; Atlanta: Scholars Press, 1989), pp. 41-57.

—'Time and the Structure of the Abraham Cycle', in A.S. Van der Woude (ed.), *New Avenues in the Study of the Old Testament* (VTSup, 32; Leiden: E.J. Brill, 1989), pp. 96-109.

Fox, E., 'Can Genesis Be Read as a Book?', *Semeia* 46 (1989), pp. 31-40.

—*In the Beginning: A New English Rendition of the Book of Genesis* (New York: Schocken Books, 1983).

Fox, M.V., 'The Sign of the Covenant: Circumcision in the Light of the Priestly *'ôt* Etiologies', *RB* 81 (1974), pp. 557-96.

France, R.T., *Jesus and the Old Testament* (Leicester: InterVarsity Press, 1971).

Franxman, T.W., *Genesis and the Jewish Antiquities of Flavius Josephus* (Rome: Biblical Institute Press, 1979).

Freedman, D.N., 'Divine Commitment and Human Obligation—The Covenant Theme', *Int* 18 (1964), pp. 419-31.

Fretheim, T., 'The Book of Genesis', in J.A. Keller *et al.* (eds.), *The New Interpreter's Bible* (12 vols.; Nashville: Abingdon Press, 1994), I, pp. 321-674.

—*The Pentateuch* (Nashville: Abingdon Press, 1996).

Friedman, R.E., 'Some Recent Non-Arguments Concerning the Documentary Hypothesis', in M.V. Fox, V.A. Hurowitz, M.L. Klein, B.J. Schwartz and N. Shupak (eds.), *Texts, Temples and Traditions* (Festschrift M. Haran; Winona Lake, IN: Eisenbrauns, 1996), pp. 87-101.

—'The Recession of Biblical Source Criticism', in R.E. Friedman and H.G.M. Williamson (eds.), *The Future of Biblical Studies: The Hebrew Scriptures* (Atlanta: Scholars Press, 1987), pp. 81-101.

—'Torah (Pentateuch)', *ABD*, IV, pp. 605-22.

Fritz, V. , 'Jahwe und El in den vorpriesterschriftlichen Geschichtswerden', in *Studien zur Literatur und Geschichte des alten Israel* (SBA, 22; Stuttgart: Katholische Bibelwerk, 1997), pp. 51-66.

Fuller, D.P., *Gospel and Law: Contrast or Continuum?* (Grand Rapids: Eerdmans, 1980).

Galy, A., 'Une lecture de Genèse 22', in A. Vanel (ed.), *L'ancien Testament approches et lectures: des procédures de travail à la théologie* (Le Point Théologique, 24; Paris: Editions Beauchesne, 1977), pp. 157-77.

Garrett, D., *Rethinking Genesis: The Sources and Authorship of the First Book of the Pentateuch* (Grand Rapids: Baker Book House, 1991).

Genest, O., 'Analyse sémiotique de Gn 22, 1-19', *ScEs* 33 (1981), pp. 157-77.

Gerstenberger, E., 'Covenant and Commandment', *JBL* 84 (1965), pp. 38-51.

Gibson, J.C.L., *Davidson's Introductory Hebrew Grammar—Syntax* (Edinburgh: T. & T. Clark, 4th edn, 1994).

—*Genesis* (DSB; 2 vols.; Edinburgh: Saint Andrew Press, 1982).

Ginsberg, H.L., 'Abram's "Damascene" Steward', *BASOR* 200 (1970), pp. 31-32.

Goldingay, J., 'Diversity and Unity in Old Testament Theology', *VT* 34 (1984), pp. 153-68.

—'The Patriarchs in Scripture and History', in A.R. Millard and D.J. Wiseman (eds.), *Essays on the Patriarchal Narratives* (Leicester: InterVarsity Press, 1980), pp. 11-42.

—'The Place of Ishmael', in P.R. Davies and D.J.A. Clines (eds.), *The World of Genesis: Persons, Places, Perspectives* (JSOTSup, 257; Sheffield: Sheffield Academic Press, 1998), pp. 146-49.

Golka, F.W., 'The Aetiologies in the Old Testament', *VT* 26 (1976), pp. 410-28.

—'Die theologischen Erzählungen im Abrahamkreis', *ZAW* 90 (1978), pp. 186-95

Gordis, R., 'Faith of Abraham: A Note on Kierkegaard's Teleological Suspension of the Ethical', *Judaism* 25 (1976), pp. 414-19.

Gordon, R.P., 'Preaching from the Patriarchs: Background to the Exposition of Genesis 15', *Them* 1 (1975), pp. 19-23.

Gosse, B., 'Genèse 13,15 et le don de la terre à Abraham', *RHPR* 74 (1994), pp. 395-97, 475.

Green, R.M., 'Abraham, Isaac, and the Jewish Tradition: An Ethical Reappraisal', *JRE* 10 (1982), pp. 1-21.

Greenberg, M., *Introduction to Hebrew* (Englewood Cliffs, NJ: Prentice Hall, 1965).

Grisanti, M.A., 'נתן', *NIDOTE*, III, pp. 205-11.

Gros Louis, K.R.R., 'Abraham' (I and II), in K.R.R. Gros Louis and J.S. Ackerman (eds.), *Literary Interpretations of Biblical Narratives* (Nashville: Abingdon Press, 1982), II, pp. 53-84.

Gross, H., 'Glaube und Bund. Theologische Bemerkungen zu Genesis 15', in G. Braulik (ed.), *Studien zum Pentateuch* (Festschrift W. Kornfeld; Vienna: Herder, 1977), pp. 25-37.

—'Zur theologischen Bedeutung von *halak* (gehen) in Abraham-Geschichten (Gen 12– 25)', in M. Görg (ed.), *Die Väter Israels: Beiträge zur Theologie der Patriarchen-*

überlieferungen im Alten Testament (Festschrift J. Scharbert; Stuttgart: Katholisches Bibelwerk, 1989), pp. 73-82.

Grudem, W., *Systematic Theology: An Introduction to Biblical Doctrine* (Leicester: InterVarsity Press, 1994).

Gunkel, H., *Genesis* (trans. M. Biddle; Macon: Mercer University Press, 1997).

—*Genesis übersetzt und erklärt* (Gottingen: Vandenhoeck & Ruprecht, 3rd edn, 1910).

Gunn, D.M., and D.N. Fewell, *Narrative in the Hebrew Bible* (Oxford Bible Series; Oxford: Oxford University Press, 1993).

Ha, J., *Genesis 15: A Theological Compendium of Pentateuchal History* (BZAW, 181; Berlin: W. de Gruyter, 1989).

Haag, E., 'Die Abrahamtradition in Gen 15', in M. Görg (ed.), *Die Väter Israels: Beiträge zur Theologie der Patriarchenüberlieferungen im Alten Testament* (Festschrift J. Scharbert; Stuttgart: Katholisches Bibelwerk, 1989), pp. 83-106.

Habel, N.C., 'The Gospel Promise to Abraham', *CTM* 40 (1969), pp. 346-55.

—*The Land is Mine: Six Biblical Land Ideologies* (OBT; Minneapolis: Fortress Press, 1995).

Hagelia, H., *Numbering the Stars: A Phraseological Analysis of Genesis 15* (ConBOT, 39; Stockholm: Almquist & Wiksell, 1994).

Halpern-Amaru, B., *Rewriting the Bible: Land and Covenant in Postbiblical Jewish Literature* (Valley Forge, PA: Trinity Press International, 1994).

Halprin, B., 'Be a Blessing and All the Families of the Earth Shall be Blessed by You (Gen. 12. 1-3)' (Hebrew), *Beth Mikra* 35 (1989–90), pp. 325-33.

Hamilton, V.P., *The Book of Genesis, Chapters 1–17* (NICOT; Grand Rapids: Eerdmans, 1990).

—*The Book of Genesis, Chapters 18–50* (NICOT; Grand Rapids: Eerdmans, 1995).

—*Handbook on the Pentateuch* (Grand Rapids: Baker Book House, 1982).

Harper, W.R., *Amos and Hosea* (ICC; Edinburgh: T. & T. Clark, 1905).

Harrison, R.K., 'Genesis', *ISBE*, II, pp. 436-37.

—*Introduction to the Old Testament* (Grand Rapids: Eerdmans, 1969).

Hartley, J.E., 'שמר (shāmar)', *TWOT*, II, pp. 939-41.

Hasel, G.F., 'The Meaning of the Animal Rite in Genesis 15', *JSOT* 19 (1981), pp. 61-78.

Hays, J.D., 'An Exegetical and Theological Study of the Abrahamic Covenant in a Canonical Context' (PhD thesis; Southwestern Baptist Theological Seminary, Fort Worth, Texas, 1992).

Hayward, C.T.R., *Saint Jerome's 'Hebrew Questions on Genesis'* (Oxford: Clarendon Press, 1995).

Heinisch, P., *Das Buch Genesis übersetzt und erklärt* (HSAT; Bonn: Peter Hanstein, 1930).

Held, M., 'Philological Notes on the Mari Covenant Rituals', *BASOR* 200 (1970), pp. 32-40.

Helfmeyer, F.J., 'אות 'ôth', *TDOT*, I, pp. 167-88.

—'הלך hālakh', *TDOT*, III, pp. 388-403.

Helyer, L.R., 'The Separation of Abram and Lot: Its Significance in the Patriarchal Narratives', *JSOT* 26 (1983), pp. 77-88.

Hengstenberg, E.W., *Christology of the Old Testament* (2 vols.; Mac Dill, FL: MacDonald, n.d.).

—'The History of the Kingdom of God in the Old Testament', in *The Works of Hengstenberg* (4 vols.; repr., Cherry Hill: Mack, 1972 [1871]).

Henninger, J., 'Was bedeutet die rituelle Teilung eines Tieres in zwei Hälften? Zur Deutung von Gen. 15,9ff', *Bib* 34 (1953), pp. 344-53.

Henry, M., 'Genesis to Deuteronomy', in *Matthew Henry's Commentary on the Whole Bible* (6 vols.; McLean, VA: MacDonald, n.d.).

Herbert, A.S., *Genesis 12–50: Abraham and his Heirs* (Torch Biblical Commentaries; London: SCM Press, 1962).

Herczeg, Y.I.Z., Y. Petroff and Y. Kamenetsky, *The Torah: With Rashi's Commentary Translated, Annotated, and Elucidated* (New York: Mesorah Publications, 1995).

Hess, R.S., 'The Slaughter of the Animals in Genesis 15: Genesis 15.8-21 and its Ancient Near East Context', in Hess, Wenham and Satterthwaite (eds.), *He Swore an Oath*, pp. 55-65.

Hess, R.S., G.J. Wenham and P.E. Satterthwaite (eds.), *He Swore an Oath: Biblical Themes from Genesis 12–50* (Carlisle: Paternoster Press, 2nd edn, 1994).

Hillers, D.R., *Covenant: The History of a Biblical Idea* (Baltimore: The Johns Hopkins University Press, 1969).

—'Delocutive Verbs in Biblical Hebrew', *JBL* 86 (1967), pp. 320-24.

—'A Note on Some Treaty Terminology in the Old Testament', *BASOR* 176 (1964), pp. 46-47.

Hirsch, S.R., *The Pentateuch Translated and Explained by Samuel Raphael Hirsch*. I. *Genesis* (trans. I. Levy; New York: Judaica Press, 2nd edn, 1971).

Hoeksema, H., *Reformed Dogmatics* (Grand Rapids: Reformed Free Publishing Association, 1966).

Hoenig, S.B., 'Circumcision: The Covenant of Abraham', *JQR* 53 (1962–63), pp. 322-34.

Hofmann, J.C.L. von, *Weissagung und Erfüllung im alten und neuen Testamente: Ein theologischer Versuch* (2 vols.; Nördlingen: C.H. Beck, 1841–44).

Hoftijzer, J., *Die Verheissung an die drei Erväter* (Leiden: E.J. Brill, 1956).

Holmgren, F.C., 'Abraham and Isaac on Mount Moriah: Genesis 22.1-19' (Part 1), *CovQ* 39.3 (1981), pp. 3-40.

—'Abraham and Isaac on Mount Moriah: Genesis 22.1-19' (Part 2), *CovQ* 40.1 (1982), pp. 75-85.

—'Faithful Abraham and the *'ᵃmānâ* Covenant: Nehemiah 9,6–10,1', *ZAW* 104 (1992), pp. 249-54.

Hölscher, G., *Geschichtsschreibung in Israel: Untersuchungen zum Jahvisten und Elohisten* (Lund: C.W.K. Gleerup, 1952).

Holzinger, H., *Genesis* (KHAT; Tübingen: J.C.B. Mohr [Paul Siebeck], 1898).

Hoppe, L.J., 'Israel and the Nations', *TBT* 25 (1987), pp. 289-90.

Horst, F., 'Der Eid im Alten Testament', *EvT* 17 (1957), pp. 366-84.

Houk, C.B., 'A Syllable-Word Structure Analysis of Genesis 12–23', in C.L. Meyers and M. O'Connor (eds.), *The Word of the Lord Shall Go Forth* (Festschrift D.N. Freedman; Winona Lake, IN: Eisenbrauns, 1983), pp. 191-201.

Howard, G.E., 'Christ is the End of the Law: The Meaning of Romans 10.4ff.', *JBL* 88 (1969), pp. 331-37.

Hubbard, D.A., *Hosea* (TOTC; Leicester: InterVarsity Press, 1989).

Huffmon, H.B., 'The Covenant Lawsuit in the Prophets', *JBL* 78 (1959), pp. 1-26.

Hulst, A.R., נוי/עם *'am / gôy* people', *TLOT*, II, pp. 896-919.

Hunter, A.G., 'Father Abraham: A Structural and Theological Study of the Yahwist's Presentation of the Abraham Material', *JSOT* 35 (1986), pp. 3-27.

Hupfield, H., *Die Quellen der Genesis und die Art ihrer Zusammensetzung von neuem untersucht* (Berlin: Wieganat und Grieben, 1853).

Hyatt, J.P., 'Circumcision', *IDB*, I, pp. 629-31.

Isaac, E., 'Circumcision as a Covenant Rite', *Anthropos* 59 (1964), pp. 444-56.

Ishida, T., 'The Structure and Historical Implications of the Lists of Pre-Israelite Nations', *Bib* 60 (1979), pp. 461-90.

Jacob, B., *Das erste Buch der Tora: Genesis übersetzt und erklärt* (Berlin: Schocken Books, 1934).

—*The First Book of the Bible: Genesis* (abridged trans. E.I. Jacob and W. Jacob; New York: Ktav Publishing House, 1974).

Janzen, J.G., *Genesis 12–50: Abraham and All the Families of the Earth* (ITC; Grand Rapids: Eerdmans, 1993).

Japhet, S., 'The Trial of Abraham and the Test of Job: How Do They Differ?', *Henoch* 16 (1994), pp. 153-72.

Jenkins, A.K., 'A Great Name: Genesis 12.2 and the Editing of the Pentateuch', *JSOT* 10 (1978), pp. 41-57.

Jenks, A.W., 'Elohist', *ABD*, II, pp. 478-82.

—*The Elohist and North Israelite Traditions* (SBLMS, 22; Missoula, MT: Scholars Press, 1977).

Jensen, R.M., 'The Binding or Sacrifice of Isaac: How Jews and Christians See Differently', *BR* 9.5 (1993), pp. 42-51.

Jones, D.R., *Jeremiah* (NCBC; Grand Rapids: Eerdmans, 1992).

Jones, G.H., 'Abraham and Cyrus: Type and Antitype?', *VT* 22 (1972), pp. 304-19.

Kaiser, O., 'Traditionsgeschichtliche Untersuchung von Genesis 15', *ZAW* 70 (1958), pp. 107-26.

Kaiser, W.C., Jr, 'The Davidic Promise and the Inclusion of the Gentiles (Amos 9.9-15 and Acts 15.13-18): A Test Passage for Theological Systems', *JETS* 20 (1977), pp. 97-111.

—*The Messiah in the Old Testament* (Carlisle: Paternoster Press, 1995).

—'The Promised Land: A Biblical-Historical View', *BSac* 138 (1981), pp. 302-11.

—'Salvation in the Old Testament: With Special Emphasis on the Object and Content of Personal Belief', *Jian Dao* 2 (1994), pp. 1-18.

—*Toward an Old Testament Theology* (Grand Rapids: Zondervan, 1978).

Karlberg, M.W., 'Covenant and Common Grace', *WTJ* 50 (1988), pp. 323-37.

—'Reformed Interpretation of the Mosaic Covenant', *WTJ* 43 (1980), pp. 1-57.

Keil, C.F., 'The Minor Prophets', in C.F. Keil and F. Delitzsch, *Biblical Commentary on the Old Testament* (10 vols.; repr., Grand Rapids: Eerdmans, 1976–77), X.

—'The Pentateuch', in C.F. Keil and F. Delitzsch, *Biblical Commentary on the Old Testament* (10 vols.; repr., Grand Rapids: Eerdmans, 1976–77), I.

Keller, C.A., and G. Wehmeier, 'ברך *brk* pi. To bless', *TLOT*, I, pp. 266-82.

Keown, G.L., P. Scalise and T.G. Smothers, *Jeremiah 26–52* (WBC, 27; Dallas: Word Books, 1995).

Kessler, M., 'The Shield of Abraham?', *VT* 14 (1964), pp. 494-97.

Kidner, D., *Genesis* (TOTC; Downers Grove: InterVarsity Press, 1967).

Kierkegaard, S., *Fear and Trembling* (Garden City, NY: Doubleday, 1955).

Kikiwada, I.M., 'Unity in Genesis 12.1-9', in A. Shinan (ed.), *Proceedings of the Sixth World Congress of Jewish Studies*, I (Jerusalem: Jerusalem Academic Press, 1977), pp. 229-35.

Kikiwada, I.M., and A. Quinn, *Before Abraham Was: The Unity of Genesis 1–11* (Nashville: Abingdon Press, 1985).

Kilian, R., *Isaaks Opferung. Zur Überlieferungsgeschichte von Genesis 22* (SBS, 44; Stuttgart: Katholisches Bibelwerk, 1970).

—*Die vorpriesterlichen Abrahamsüberlieferungen, literarkritisch und traditions-geschichtlich untersucht* (BBB, 24; Bonn: Peter Hanstein, 1966).

Klein, R.W., 'Call, Covenant, and Community: The Story of Abraham and Sarah', *CurTM* 15 (1988), pp. 120-27.

—'The Message of P', in J. Jeremias and L. Perlitt (eds.), *Die Botschaft und die Boten* (Festschrift H.W. Wolff; Neukirchen–Vluyn: Neukirchener Verlag, 1981), pp. 57-66.

—'The Yahwist Looks at Abraham', *CTM* 45 (1974), pp. 43-49.

Kline, M.G., 'Abram's Amen', *WTJ* 31 (1968), pp. 1-11.

—*By Oath Consigned: A Reinterpretation of the Covenant Signs of Circumcision and Baptism* (Grand Rapids: Eerdmans, 1969).

—'Canon and Covenant', *WTJ* 32 (1969–70), pp. 49-67, 179-200.

—'Canon and Covenant', *WTJ* 33 (1970), pp. 45-72.

—'Law Covenant', *WTJ* 27 (1964), pp. 1-21.

—'The Old Testament Origins of the Gospel Genre', *WTJ* 38 (1975), pp. 1-27.

Knierim, R., 'Criticism of Literary Features, Form, Tradition, and Redaction', in D.A. Knight and G.M. Tucker (eds.), *The Hebrew Bible and its Modern Interpreters* (Minneapolis: Fortress Press, 1985), pp. 123-65.

Köckert, M., review of *Genesis 15: Eine Erzählung von den Anfängen Israels* (Würzburg: Echter Verlag, 1988), by H. Mölle, in *Bib* 73 (1992), pp. 568-75.

—*Vätergott und Väterverheißungen. Eine Auseinandersetzung mit Albrecht Alt und seinen Erben* (FRLANT, 142; Göttingen: Vandenhoeck & Ruprecht, 1988).

König, E., *Die Genesis eingeleitet, übersetzt und erklärt* (Gütersloh: C. Bertelsmann, 3rd edn, 1925).

Kreuzer, S., 'Das Opfer des Vaters—die Gefährdung des Sohnes—Genesis 22', *Amt und Gemeinde* 37 (1986), pp. 62-70.

Kruger, P.A., 'אוֹת', *NIDOTE*, I, pp. 331-33.

Kruse, H., 'David's Covenant', *VT* 35 (1985), pp. 139-64.

Kselman, J.S., 'The Book of Genesis: A Decade of Scholarly Research', *Int* 45 (1991), pp. 380-92.

Külling, S.R., 'The Dating of the So-Called "P-Sections" in Genesis', *JETS* 15 (1972), pp. 67-76.

—*Zur Datierung der 'Genesis-P-Stücke': Namentlich des Kapitels Genesis 17* (Kampen: Kok, 1964).

Kundert, L., *Die Opferung/Bindung Isaaks: Gen 22, 1-19 im Alten Testament, im Frühjudentum und im Neuen Testament* (WMANT, 78; Neukirchen–Vluyn: Neukirchener Verlag, 1998).

—*Die Opferung/Bindung Isaaks: Gen 22, 1-19 in frühen rabbinischen Texten* (WMANT, 79; Neukirchen–Vluyn: Neukirchener Verlag, 1998).

Kunin, B.D., 'The Death of Isaac: Structuralist Analysis of Genesis 22', *JSOT* 64 (1994), pp. 57-81.

Kutsch, E., 'Gesetz und Gnade. Probleme des alttestamentlichen Bundesbegriffs', *ZAW* 79 (1967), pp. 18-35.

—'Gottes Zuspruch und Anspruch. *bᵉrît* in der alttestamentlichen Theologie', in C. Brekelmans (ed.), *Questions disputées d'Ancien Testament: Méthode et théologie* (Leuven: Leuven University Press, 2nd edn, 1989), pp. 71-90.

—'*kārat bᵉrît*, eine Verpflichtung festsetzen', in H. Gese and H.P. Rüger (eds.), *Wort und Geschichte* (Festschrift K. Elliger; Neukirchen–Vluyn: Neukirchener Verlag, 1973), pp. 121-27.

—*Verheißung und Gesetz: Untersuchungen zum sogennanten 'Bund' im Alten Testament* (Berlin: W. de Gruyter, 1973).

Labuschagne, C.J., 'נתן *ntn* to give', *TLOT*, II, pp. 774-91.

Lack, R., 'Le sacrifice d'Isaac—Analyse structurale de la couche élohiste dans Gen 22', *Bib* 56 (1975), pp. 1-12.

Lambdin, T.O., *Introduction to Biblical Hebrew* (London: Darton, Longman & Todd, 1973).

Landy, F., 'Narrative Techniques and Symbolic Transactions in the Akedah', in J.C. Exum (ed.), *Signs and Wonders: Biblical Texts in Literary Focus* (SBLSS; Atlanta: Scholars Press, 1989), pp. 1-40.

Lawlor, J.I., 'The Test of Abraham: Genesis 22.1-19', *GTJ* NS 1 (1980), pp. 19-35.

Lemaire, A., 'Cycle primitif d'Abraham et contexte géographico-historique', in A. Lemaire and B. Otzen (eds.), *History and Traditions of Early Israel* (Festschrift E. Nielsen; OTS, 50; Leiden: E.J. Brill, 1993), pp. 62-75.

Lerch, D., *Isaaks Opferung christlich gedeutet: eine auslegungsgeschichtliche Untersuchung* (BHT, 12; Tübingen: J.C.B. Mohr [Paul Siebeck], 1950).

Leupold, H.C., *Exposition of Genesis* (Columbus: The Wartburg Press, 1942).

Levenson, J., 'The Davidic Covenant and its Modern Interpreters', *CBQ* 41 (1979), pp. 205-19.

—*The Death and Resurrection of the Beloved Son: The Transformation of Child Sacrifice in Judaism and Christianity* (New Haven: Yale University Press, 1993).

Levine, B., *In the Presence of the Lord: A Study of Cult and Some Cultic Terms in Ancient Israel* (SJLA, 5; Leiden: E.J. Brill, 1974).

Lewis, T., and C.E. Armerding, 'Circumcision', *ISBE*, I, pp. 700-702.

Libolt, C.G., 'Canaan', *ISBE*, I, pp. 585-91.

Loewenstamm, S.E., 'The Divine Grants of Land to the Patriarchs', *JAOS* 91 (1974), pp. 509-10.

—'גוי', *Encyclopaedia Biblica* (8 vols.; Jerusalem: Bialik Institute, 1965–82), II, col. 457.

—'Zur Traditionsgeschichte des Bundes zwischen den Stücken', *VT* 18 (1968), pp. 500-506.

Lohfink, N., *Die Landverheissung als Eid: Eine Studie zu Gn 15* (SBS, 28; Stuttgart: Katholisches Bibelwerk, 1967).

Long, B.O., *The Problem of Etiological Narrative in the Old Testament* (BZAW, 108; Berlin: Alfred Töpelmann, 1968).

Longenecker, R.N., *Biblical Exegesis in the Apostolic Period* (Grand Rapids: Eerdmans, 1975).

—'The "Faith of Abraham" Theme in Paul, James and Hebrews: A Study in the Circumstantial Nature of New Testament Teaching', *JETS* 20 (1977), pp. 203-12.

Loretz, O., 'Mgn—"Geschenk" in Gen 15.1', *UF* 6 (1974), p. 492.

Lowe, J.H., *'Rashi' on the Pentateuchal Genesis* (London: Hebrew Compendium Publishing, 1928).

Lundblom, J.R., 'Abraham and David in the Theology of the Yahwist', in C.L. Meyers and M. O'Connor (eds.), *The Word of the Lord Shall Go Forth* (Festschrift D.N. Freedman; Winona Lake, IN: Eisenbrauns, 1983), pp. 203-209.

Luther, M., 'Lectures on Genesis 15–20', in J. Pelikan and H.T. Lehmann (eds.), *Luther's Works* (56 vols.; Saint Louis: Concordia Publishing House; Philadelphia: Fortress Press, 1955–72), III, pp. 1-394.

Lyke, L.L., 'Where does "the Boy" Belong? Compositional Strategy in Genesis', *CBQ* 56 (1994), pp. 637-48.

MacRae, A.A., 'Abraham and the Stars', *JETS* 8 (1965), pp. 97-100.

—עלם ('*lm*)', *TWOT*, II, pp. 672-73.

Magonet, J., 'Abraham and God', *Judaism* 33 (1984), pp. 160-70.

—*Bible Lives* (London: SCM Press, 1992).

Maher, M., *Genesis* (OTM, 2; Wilmington: Michael Glazier, 1982).

—*Targum Pseudo-Jonathan: Genesis* (The Aramaic Bible, Ib; Edinburgh: T. & T. Clark, 1992).

Mann, T.W., '"All the Families of the Earth": The Theological Unity of Genesis', *Int* 45 (1991), pp. 341-53.

—*The Book of the Torah: The Narrative Integrity of the Pentateuch* (Atlanta: John Knox Press, 1988).

Manns, F. (ed.), *The Sacrifice of Isaac in the Three Monotheistic Religions: Proceedings of a Symposium on the Interpretation of the Scriptures Held in Jerusalem, March 16–17, 1995* (SBFA, 41; Jerusalem: Franciscan, 1995).

Martens, E.A., *God's Design: A Focus on Old Testament Theology* (Leicester: InterVarsity Press, 2nd edn, 1994).

Martin-Achard, R., *Actualité d'Abraham* (Neuchâtel: Delachaux & Niestlé, 1969).

—*A Light to the Nations: A Study of the Old Testament Conception of Israel's Mission to the World* (trans. J.P. Smith; Edinburgh: Oliver & Boyd, 1962).

Martinez, E.R., *Hebrew-Ugaritic Index to the Writings of Mitchell J. Dahood: A Bibliography with Indices of Scriptural Passages, Hebrew and Ugaritic Words and Grammatical Observations* (Scripta Pontificii Instituti Biblica, 116; Rome: Pontifical Biblical Institute, 1967).

Martyn, J.L., 'A Law-Observant Mission to Gentiles: The Background of Galatians', in M.P. O'Connor and D.N. Freedman (eds.), *Backgrounds to the Bible* (Winona Lake, IN: Eisenbrauns, 1987), pp. 199-214.

Mayer, G., 'מוּל *mûl*', *TDOT*, VIII, pp. 158-62.

Mays, J.L., 'God Has Spoken: A Meditation on Genesis 12: 1-4', *Int* 14 (1960), pp. 413-20.

—*Hosea* (OTL; London: SCM Press, 1969).

Mazor, Y., 'Genesis 22: The Ideological Rhetoric and the Psychological Composition', *Bib* 67 (1986), pp. 81-88.

McAfee, E.C., 'The Patriarch's Longed-for Son: Biological and Social Reproduction in Ugaritic and Hebrew Epic' (PhD thesis; Harvard University, 1996).

McBride, S.D., 'Transcendent Authority: The Role of Moses in Old Testament Traditions', *Int* 44 (1990), pp. 229-39.

McCarthy, D.J., 'Berit and Covenant in the Deuteronomistic History', in P.A.H. de Boer (ed.), *Studies in the Religion of Ancient Israel* (VTSup, 23; Leiden: E.J. Brill, 1972), pp. 65-85.

—'*bᵉrît* in Old Testament History and Theology', *Bib* 53 (1972), pp. 110-21.

—'Covenant in the Old Testament: The Present State of Inquiry', *CBQ* 27 (1965), pp. 217-40.

—'Covenant-Relationships', in C. Brekelmans (ed.), *Questions disputées d'Ancien Testament: Méthode et théologie* (BETL, 33; Leuven: Leuven University Press, 1989), pp. 91-103.

—*Der Gottesbund im Alten Testament* (Stuttgart: Katholisches Bibelwerk, 1967).

—*Institution and Narrative: Collected Essays* (Rome: Biblical Institute Press, 1985).

—*Old Testament Covenant: A Survey of Current Opinions* (Oxford: Basil Blackwell, 1973).

—'The Symbolism of Blood Sacrifice', *JBL* 88 (1969), pp. 166-76.

—'The Symbolism of Blood Sacrifice', *JBL* 92 (1973), pp. 205-10.

—'Three Covenants in Genesis', *CBQ* 26 (1964), pp. 179-89.

—*Treaty and Covenant: A Study in the Form in the Ancient Oriental Documents and in the Old Testament* (AnBib, 21a; Rome: Biblical Institute Press, 1978).

McComiskey, T.E., *The Covenants of Promise: A Theology of the Old Testament Covenants* (Leicester: InterVarsity Press, 1985).

McConville, J.G., 'בְּרִית', *NIDOTE*, I, pp. 747-55.

—'Abraham and Melchizedek: Horizons in Genesis 14', in Hess, Wenham and Satterthwaite (eds.), *He Swore an Oath*, pp. 93-118.

McCullough, W.S., 'Sign in the OT', *IDB*, IV, pp. 345-46.

McEvenue, S., *The Narrative Style of the Priestly Writer* (AnBib, 50; Rome: Biblical Institute Press, 1971).

McKane, W., *Studies in the Patriarchal Narratives* (Edinburgh: Handsel Press, 1979).

McKeown, J., 'A Study of the Main Unifying Themes in the Hebrew Text of the Book of Genesis' (PhD thesis; The Queen's University of Belfast, 1991).

McNamara, M., *Targum Neofiti: Genesis* (The Aramaic Bible, Ia; Edinburgh: T. & T. Clark, 1992).

Meissner, S., 'Paulinische Soteriologie und die "Aqedat Jitzchaq"', *Judaica* 51 (1995), pp. 33-49.

Mendenhall, G.E., 'The Nature and Purpose of the Abraham Narratives', in P.D. Miller, P. Hanson and S. McBride (eds.), *Ancient Israelite Religion* (Festschrift F.M. Cross; Philadelphia: Fortress Press, 1987), pp. 337-57.

—'Puppy and Lettuce in Northwest Semitic Covenant Making', *BASOR* 133 (1954), pp. 26-30.

Mendenhall, G.E., and G.A. Herion, 'Covenant', *ABD*, I, pp. 1179-1202.

Milgrom, J., *The Binding of Isaac: The Akedah, a Primary Symbol of Jewish Thought and Art* (Berkeley: Bibal, 1988).

—'Priestly (Source)', *ABD*, V, pp. 454-61.

Miller, P.D., 'Syntax and Theology in Genesis 12.3a', *VT* 34 (1984), pp. 472-76.

Mitchell, C.W., *The Meaning of BRK 'To Bless' in the Old Testament* (SBLDS, 95; Atlanta: Scholars Press, 1987).

Mitchell, J.J., 'Abram's Understanding of the Lord's Covenant', *WTJ* 32 (1969), pp. 24-48.

Mitchell, S., *Genesis: A New Translation of the Classic Biblical Stories* (New York: HarperCollins, 1996).

Moberly, R.W.L., *At the Mountain of God: Story and Theology in Exodus 32–34* (JSOTSup, 22; Sheffield: JSOT Press, 1983).

—'Christ as the Key to Scripture: Genesis 22 Reconsidered', in Hess, Wenham and Satter-thwaite (eds.), *He Swore an Oath*, pp. 143-73.

—'The Earliest Commentary on the Akedah', *VT* 38 (1988), 302-23.

—*Genesis 12–50* (OTG; Sheffield: JSOT Press, 1992).

—*The Old Testament of the Old Testament: Patriarchal Narratives and Mosaic Yahwism* (OBT; Minneapolis: Fortress Press, 1992).

Mölle, H., *Genesis 15: Eine Erzählung von den Anfängen Israels* (FzB, 62; Würzburg: Echter Verlag, 1988).

Morrice, W.G., 'New Wine in Old Wine-Skins, XI Covenant', *ExpTim* 86 (1975), pp. 132-36.

Moster, J.B., 'The Testing of Abraham', *Dor Le Dor* 17 (1988–89), pp. 237-42.

Motyer, J.A., 'Covenant and Promise', *Evangel* 1.1 (1983), pp. 2-4.

—'Covenant, Law and Sacrifice', *Evangel* 1.3 (1983), pp. 3-5.

—'The Normative Covenant', *Evangel* 1.2 (1983), pp. 3-5.

—'The Perfection of the Covenant', *Evangel* 1.4 (1983), pp. 3-5.

—*The Prophecy of Isaiah* (Downers Grove: InterVarsity Press, 1993).

Mowvley, H., 'The Concept and Content of Blessing in the Old Testament', *BT* 16.2 (1965), pp. 74-80.

Muilenburg, J., 'Abraham and the Nations: Blessing and World History', *Int* 19 (1965), pp. 387-98.

—'The Form and Structure of the Covenantal Formulations', *VT* 9 (1959), pp. 347-69.

Mullen, E.T., Jr, *Ethnic Myths and Pentateuchal Foundations: A New Approach to the Formation of the Pentateuch* (SBLSS; Atlanta: Scholars Press, 1997).

Müller, H.-P., 'Segen im Alten Testament. Theologische Implikationen eines halb verges-senen Themas', *ZTK* 87 (1990), pp. 1-32.

Murtonen, A., 'The Use and Meaning of the Words *lᵉbārek* and *bᵉrākāh* in the Old Testa-ment', *VT* 9 (1959), pp. 158-77.

Naor, M., 'And They Shall Come Back Here in the Fourth Generation (Gen 15.16)', (Hebrew) *Beth Mikra* 27 (1981–82), pp. 40-45.

Neef, H.D., *Die Prüfung Abrahams: eine exegetisch-theologische Studie zu Gen 22,1-9* (Stuttgart: Calwer Verlag, 1998).

Nelson, R.N., 'Was Not Abraham Justified by Works?', *Dialog* 22 (1983), pp. 258-63.

Neusner, J., *Genesis Rabbah: The Judaic Commentary to the Book of Genesis: A New American Translation* (3 vols.; Atlanta: Scholars Press, 1985).

Nicholson, E.W., 'The Covenant Ritual in Exodus xxiv 3-8', *VT* 32 (1982), pp. 74-86.

—*God and his People: Covenant and Theology in the Old Testament* (Oxford: Clarendon Press, 1986).

—'P as an Originally Independent Source in the Pentateuch', *IBS* 10 (1988), pp. 192-206.

—'The Pentateuch in Recent Research: A Time for Caution', in J.A. Emerton (ed.), *Congress Volume: Leuven 1989* (VTSup, 43; Leiden: E.J. Brill, 1991), pp. 10-21.

—*The Pentateuch in the Twentieth Century: The Legacy of Julius Wellhausen* (Oxford: Clarendon Press, 1998).

Niehaus, J.J., *God at Sinai: Covenant and Theophany in the Bible and Ancient Near East* (SOTBT; Carlisle: Paternoster Press, 1995).

Noble, P., 'Synchronic and Diachronic Approaches to Biblical Interpretation', *JLT* 7.2 (1993), pp. 130-48.

Noegel, S.B., 'A Crux and a Taunt: Night-Time Then Sunset in Genesis 15', in P.R. Davies and D.J.A. Clines (eds.), *The World of Genesis: Persons, Places, Perspectives* (JSOTSup, 257; Sheffield: Sheffield Academic Press, 1998), pp. 128-35.

Noort, E., '"Land" in the Deuteronomistic Tradition. Genesis 15: The Historical and Theological Necessity of a Diachronic Approach', in J.C. De Moor (ed.), *Synchronic or Diachronic? A Debate on Method in Old Testament Exegesis* (OTS, 34; Leiden: E.J. Brill, 1995), pp. 129-44.

Noth, M., *Exodus* (trans. J.S. Bowden; OTL; London: SCM Press, 1962).

—*A History of Pentateuchal Traditions* (trans. B.W. Anderson; Englewood Cliffs, NJ: Prentice-Hall, 1972).

—*The Laws in the Pentateuch and Other Essays* (trans. D.R. Ap-Thomas; London: Oliver & Boyd, 1966).

O'Brien, M.A., 'The Story of Abraham and the Debate over Source Hypothesis', *AusBR* 38 (1990), pp. 1-17.

Och, B., 'Abraham and Moriah: A Journey to Fulfilment', *Judaism* 38 (1989), pp. 293-309.

Oeming, M., 'Ist Genesis 15 ein Beleg für die Anrechnung des Glaubens zur Gerechtigkeit?', *ZAW* 95 (1982), pp. 182-97.

Owen, J., *The Works of John Owen* (16 vols.; repr., London: Banner of Truth Trust, 1965–68).

Pagolu, A., *The Religion of the Patriarchs* (JSOTSup, 277; Sheffield: Sheffield Academic Press, 1998).

Pailin, D.A., 'Abraham and Isaac: A Hermeneutical Problem before Kierkegaard', in R.L. Perkins (ed.), *Kierkegaard's Fear and Trembling: Critical Appraisals* (Alabama: University of Alabama Press, 1981), pp. 10-42.

Patcas, H., 'Akedah, the Binding of Isaac', *Dor Le Dor* 14 (1985–86), pp. 112-14.

Payne, J.B., 'A Critical Note on Ecclesiasticus 44.21's Commentary on the Abrahamic Covenant', *JETS* 15 (1972), pp. 186-87.

Peck, W.J., 'Murder, Timing and the Ram in the Sacrifice of Isaac', *ATR* 58 (1976), pp. 23-43.

Peckham, B., *The Composition of the Deuteronomistic History* (HSM, 35; Atlanta: Scholars Press, 1985).

Pedersen, J., *Israel* (2 vols.; London: Oxford University Press, 1926).

Pelcovitz, R.R., *Sforno Commentary on the Torah: Translation and Explanatory Notes* (New York: Mesorah Publications, 1987).

Perlitt, L., *Bundestheologie im Alten Testament* (Neukirchen–Vluyn: Neukirchener Verlag, 1969).

Petersen, D.L., 'Covenant Ritual. A Traditio-Historical Perspective', *BR* 22 (1977), pp. 7-18.

Pierce, R.W., 'Covenant Conditionality and a Future for Israel', *JETS* 37 (1994), pp. 28-39.

Pieters, A., *The Seed of Abraham: A Biblical Study of Israel, the Church, and the Jew* (Grand Rapids: Eerdmans, 1950).

Plaut, W.G. (ed.), *Genesis. The Torah: A Modern Commentary* (New York: Union of American Hebrew Congregations, 1981).

Poole, M., *A Commentary on the Holy Bible* (3 vols.; repr., London: Banner of Truth Trust, 1962).

Porter, J.R., *The Extended Family in the Old Testament* (Occasional Papers in Social and Economic Administration, 6; London: Edutext Publications, 1967).

Portnoy, S.L., and D.L. Petersen, 'Genesis, Wellhausen and the Computer: A Response', *ZAW* 96 (1984), pp. 421-25.

Preuss, H.D., ' "Ich will mit dir sein" ', *ZAW* 80 (1968), pp. 139-73.

Prewitt, T.J., *The Elusive Covenant: A Structural-Semiotic Reading of Genesis* (Bloomington: Indiana University Press, 1990).

Procksch, O., *Die Genesis, übersetzt und erklärt* (KAT; Leipzig: A. Deichertsche Verlagsbuchhandlung, 2nd edn, 1924).

Prolow, S., 'Isaac Unbound', *BZ* 40 (1996), pp. 84-91.

Propp, W.H., 'That Bloody Bridegroom', *VT* 43 (1993), pp. 495-518.

Pury, A. de, 'La tradition patriarcale en Genèse 12–35', in A. de Pury (ed.), *Le Pentateuque en question: Les origines et la composition des cinq premiers livres de la Bible à la lumière des recherches récentes* (Geneva: Labor & Fides, 1989), pp. 259-70.

—'Yahwist ("J") Source', *ABD*, VI, pp. 1012-19.

Pury, A. de, and T. Römer, 'Le Pentateuque en question: Position du problème et brève histoire de la recherche', in A. de Pury (ed.), *Le Pentateuque en question: Les origines et la composition des cinq premiers livres de la Bible à la lumière des recherches récentes* (Geneva: Labor & Fides, 1989), pp. 9-80.

Pyne, R.A., 'The "Seed", the Spirit, and the Blessing of Abraham', *BSac* 152 (1995), pp. 211-22.

Rad, G. von, *Genesis: A Commentary* (trans. J.H. Marks; OTL; London: SCM Press, rev. edn, 1972).

—*Das Opfer des Abraham* (Munich: Chr. Kaiser Verlag, 1976).

—*The Problem of the Hexateuch and Other Essays* (trans. E.T. Dicken; Edinburgh: Oliver & Boyd, 1966).

Radday, Y.T., and H. Shore, *Genesis: An Authorship Study in Computer-Assisted Statistical Linguistics* (AnBib, 103; Rome: Biblical Institute Press, 1985).

Radday, Y.T., H. Shore, M.A. Pollatschek and D. Wickmann, 'Genesis, Wellhausen and the Computer', *ZAW* 94 (1982), pp. 467-81.

Ramban, *Commentary on the Torah: Genesis* (New York: Shilo Publishing House, 1971).

Rashkow, I.N., 'Intertextuality, Transference, and the Reader in/of Genesis 12 and 20', in D. Fewell (ed.), *Reading between Texts: Intertextuality and the Hebrew Bible* (Louisville, KY: Westminster/John Knox Press, 1992), pp. 57-73.

Redford, D.B., *A Study of the Biblical Story of Joseph (Genesis 37–50)* (VTSup, 20; Leiden: E.J. Brill, 1970).

Rendsburg, G.A., 'David and his Circle in Gen xxxviii', *VT* 36 (1986), pp. 438-46.

—'Notes on Genesis XV', *VT* 42 (1992), pp. 266-72.

—*The Redaction of Genesis* (Winona Lake, IN: Eisenbrauns, 1986).

Rendtorff, R., *Die 'Bundesformel': Eine exegetisch-theologische Untersuchung* (Stuttgart: Katholisches Bibelwerk, 1995).

—' "Covenant" as a Structuring Concept in Genesis and Exodus', *JBL* 108 (1989), pp. 385-93.

—'Directions in Pentateuchal Studies', *CRBS* 3 (1997), pp. 43-65.

—'Genesis 15 im Rahmen der theologischen Bearbeitung der Vätergeschichten', in R. Albertz, H.P. Müller, H.W. Wolff and W. Zimmerli (eds.), *Werden und Wirken des Alten Testaments* (Festschrift C. Westermann; Göttingen: Vandenhoeck & Ruprecht, 1980), pp. 74-81.

—*The Problem of the Process of Transmission in the Pentateuch* (trans. J.J. Scullion; JSOTSup, 89; Sheffield: JSOT Press, 1990).

—'The Yahwist as Theologian? The Dilemma of Pentateuchal Criticism', *JSOT* 3 (1977), pp. 2-10.

Reventlow, H., *Opfere deinen Sohn. Ein Auslegung von Genesis 22* (Biblische Studien, 53; Neukirchen–Vluyn: Neukirchener Verlag, 1968).

Rickards, R.R., 'Genesis 15: An Exercise in Translation Principles', *BT* 28 (1977), pp. 213-20.

Robertson, O.P., *The Christ of the Covenants* (Grand Rapids: Presbyterian and Reformed, 1980).

—'Current Reformed Thinking on the Nature of the Divine Covenants', *WTJ* 40 (1978), pp. 63-76.

—'Genesis 15.6: A New Covenant Exposition of an Old Testament Text', *WTJ* 42 (1980), pp. 259-89.

Rodriguez, A.M., *Substitution in the Hebrew Cultus* (Berrien Springs: Andrews University Press, 1979).

Rogers, C.L., 'The Covenant with Abraham and its Historical Setting', *BSac* 127 (1970), pp. 241-56.

Römer, T.C., 'La formation du Pentateuque selon l'exégèse historico-critique', in C.-B. Amphoux and B. Outtier (eds.), *Les premières traditions de la Bible* (Lausanne: Zèbre, 1996), pp. 17-55.

—'Genesis 15 und Genesis 17: Beobachtungen und Amfragen zu einem Dogma der "neueren" und "neuesten" Pentateuchkritik', *DBAT* 26 (1989–90), pp. 32-47.

—*Israels Väter: Untersuchungen zur Vaterthematik im Deuteronomium und in der deuteronomistischen Tradition* (OBO, 99; Göttingen: Vandenhoeck & Ruprecht, 1990).

Römer, T.C. (ed.), *Abraham: Nouvelle jeunesse d'un ancêtre* (Essais Bibliques, 28; Geneva: Labor & Fides, 1997).

Rosenbaum, M., and A.M. Silbermann, *Pentateuch with Targum Onkelos, Haphtaroth and Rashi's Commentary: Genesis* (New York: Hebrew Publishing Company, n.d.).

Rosenberg, J., *King and Kin: Political Allegory in the Hebrew Bible* (Bloomington: Indiana University Press, 1986).

Ross, A.P., *Creation and Blessing: A Guide to the Study and Exposition of Genesis* (Grand Rapids: Baker Book House, 1988).

Rost, L., (ed.), *Das kleine Credo und andere Studien zum Alten Testament* (Heidelberg: Quelle & Meyer, 1965).

Ruppert, L., *Das Buch Genesis. I. Kap.1–25, 18* (Düsseldorf: Patmos, 1975).

Ruprecht, E., 'Der traditionsgeschichtliche Hintergrund der einzelnen Elemente von Gen XII 2-3', *VT* 29 (1979), pp. 444-64.

—'Vorgegebene Tradition und theologische Gestaltung in Genesis XII 1-3', *VT* 29 (1979), pp. 171-88.

Ryle, H.E., *The Book of Genesis in the Revised Version with Introduction and Notes* (Cambridge Bible for Schools and Colleges; Cambridge: Cambridge University Press, 1914).

Sailhamer, J.H., 'Genesis', in F.E. Gaebelein (ed.), *The Expositor's Bible Commentary* (12 vols.; Grand Rapids: Zondervan, 1990), II, pp. 1-284.

—'The Mosaic Law and the Theology of the Pentateuch', *WTJ* 53 (1991), pp. 241-61.

—*The Pentateuch as Narrative: A Biblical-Theological Commentary* (Library of Biblical Interpretation; Grand Rapids: Zondervan, 1992).

Saldarini, A.C., 'Interpretation of the *Akedah* in Rabbinic Literature', in R. Polzin and E. Rothman (eds.), *The Biblical Mosaic: Changing Perspectives* (SBLSS; Chico, CA: Scholars Press, 1982), pp. 149-65.

Sarna, N.M., 'Abraham', *EncJud*, II, cols. 111-15.

—*Genesis* (JPS Torah Commentary; Philadelphia: Jewish Publication Society, 1989).

—*Understanding Genesis: The Heritage of Biblical Israel* (New York: Schocken Books, 1970).

Schaalman, H.E., 'The Binding of Isaac', in F.C. Holmgren and H.E. Schaalman (eds.), *Preaching Biblical Texts: Expositions by Jewish and Christian Scholars* (Grand Rapids: Eerdmans, 1995), pp. 36-45.

Scharbert, J., '"Bᵉrit" im Pentateuch', in M. Carrez, J. Doré and P. Grelot (eds.), *De la Tôrah au Messie. Etudes d'exégèse et d'herméneutique bibliques* (Festschrift H. Cazelles; Paris: Desclée, 1981), pp. 163-70.

—'ברך *brk*', *TDOT*, II, pp. 279-308.

—' "Fluchen" und "segnen" im Alten Testament', *Bib* 39 (1958), pp. 8-14.

—*Genesis 12–50* (Die Neue Echter Bibel, 5; Würzburg: Echter Verlag, 1986).

—'Die Geschichte der *Bārûk*-Formel', *BZ* 17 (1973), pp. 1-28.

—'Die Landverheißung als "Urgestein" der Patriarchen-Tradition', in A. Caquot, S. Légasse and M. Tardieu (eds.), *Mélanges bibliques et orientaux* (Festschrift M.M. Delcor; AOAT, 215; Neukirchen–Vluyn: Neukirchener Verlag, 1985), pp. 359-68.

Schedl, C., 'Berufung Abrahams, des Vaters der Glaubigen: Logotechnische Analyse von Gen. 12.1-9', *BZ* 28 (1984), pp. 255-59.

Schmid, H.H., 'Gerechtigkeit und Glaube: Genesis 15.1-6 und sein biblisch-theologischer Kontext', *EvT* 40 (1980), pp. 396-420.

—*Der sogennante Jahwist: Beobachtungen und Fragen zur Pentateuchforschung* (Zürich: Theologischer Verlag, 1976).

Schmid, R., *Das Bundesopfer in Israel: Wesen, Ursprung und Bedeutung der alttestamentlichen Schelamim* (Munich: Kösel-Verlag, 1964).

Schmidt, L., 'Israel ein Segen für die Völker? (Das Ziel des jahwistischen Werkes—eine Auseinandersetzung mit H.W. Wolff)', *TV* 12 (1975), pp. 135-51.

—'Überlegungen zum Jahwisten', *EvT* 37 (1977), pp. 230-47.

—'Vaterverheißungen und Pentateuchfrage', *ZAW* 104 (1992), pp. 1-27.

Schmitt, H.C., 'Redaktion des Pentateuch im Geiste der Prophetie', *VT* 32 (1982), pp. 170-89.

Schreiner, J., 'Segen für die Völker in der Verheissung an die Väter', *BZ* 6 (1962), pp. 1-31.

Schulz, A., '*Eliʿezer*?', *ZAW* 75 (1963), pp. 317-19.

Schwantes, M., ' "Lege deine Hand nicht an das Kind". Überlegungen zu Genesis 21 und 22', in F. Crüsemann, C. Hardmeier and R. Kessler (eds.), *Was ist der Mensch...? Beiträge zur Anthropologie des Alten Testaments* (Festschrift H.W. Wolff; Munich: Chr. Kaiser Verlag, 1992), pp. 164-78.

Scullion, J.J., *Genesis: A Commentary for Students, Teachers and Preachers* (Collegeville, MN: Liturgical Press, 1992).

Sebass, H., 'Gen 15.2b', *ZAW* 75 (1963), pp. 317-19.

—'Landverheissung an die Väter', *EvT* 37 (1977), pp. 210-29.

Segal, M.H., *The Pentateuch: Its Composition and its Authorship and Other Biblical Studies* (Jerusalem: Magnes Press, 1967).

Sheriffs, D., *The Friendship of the Lord: An Old Testament Spirituality* (Carlisle: Paternoster Press, 1996).

Siebesma, P.A., *The Function of the Niph'al in Biblical Hebrew* (Studia Semitica Nierlandica; Assen: Van Gorcum, 1991).

Siker, J.S., *Disinheriting the Jews: Abraham in Early Christian Controversy* (Louisville, KY: Westminster/John Knox Press, 1991).

Ska, J.L., *'Our Fathers Have Told Us': Introduction to the Analysis of Hebrew Narratives* (Rome: Pontifical Biblical Institute, 1990).

—'Quelques remarques sur Pg et la dernière rédaction du Pentateuque', in A. de Pury (ed.), *Le Pentateuque en question: Les origines et la composition des cinq premiers livres de la Bible à la lumière des recherches récentes* (Geneva: Labor & Fides, 1989), pp. 95-125.

Skinner, J., *A Critical and Exegetical Commentary on Genesis* (ICC; Edinburgh: T. & T. Clark, 2nd edn, 1930).

Slager, D.J., 'The Use of Divine Names in Genesis', *BT* 43 (1992), pp. 423-29.

Smick, E.B., 'מול (mûl)', *TWOT*, I, pp. 494-95.

Smith, W.R., *The Old Testament in the Jewish Church* (Edinburgh: A. & C. Black, 1881).

Snijders, L.A., 'Genesis XV: The Covenant with Abram', in P.A.H. De Boer (ed.), *Studies on the Book of Genesis* (OTS, 12; Leiden: E.J. Brill, 1958), pp. 261-79.

Speiser, E.A., *Genesis* (AB; New York: Doubleday, 1964).

—'"People" and "Nation" of Israel', *JBL* 79 (1960), pp. 157-63.

Spiegel, S., *The Last Trial: The Akedah* (trans. J. Goldin; repr., Woodstock: Jewish Lights Publishing, 1967).

Steck, O.H., 'Genesis 12.1-3 und die Urgeschichte des Jahwisten', in H.W. Wolff (ed.), *Probleme Biblischer Theologie* (Festschrift G. von Rad; Munich: Chr. Kaiser Verlag, 1971), pp. 525-54.

Steinberg, N., 'The Genealogical Framework of the Family Stories in Genesis', *Semeia* 46 (1989), pp. 41-50.

—*Kinship and Marriage in Genesis: A Household Economics Perspective* (Minneapolis: Fortress Press, 1993).

Stek, J.H., '"Covenant" Overload in Reformed Theology', *CTJ* 29 (1994), pp. 12-41.

Sternberg, M., *The Poetics of Biblical Narrative: Ideological Literature and the Drama of Reading* (Bloomington: Indiana University Press, 1985).

Stolz, F., 'אות 'ôt sign', *TLOT*, I, pp. 67-70.

Strickman, H.N., and A.M. Silver, *Ibn Ezra's Commentary on the Pentateuch: Genesis (Bereshit)* (New York: Menorah, 1988).

Stuart, D., *Hosea–Jonah* (WBC, 31; Waco, TX: Word Books, 1987).

Sutherland, D., 'The Organization of the Abraham Promise Narratives', *ZAW* 95 (1983), pp. 337-43.

Syrén, R., *The Forsaken Firstborn: A Study of a Recurrent Motif in the Patriarchal Promise* (JSOTSup, 133; Sheffield: JSOT Press, 1993).

Terrien, S., *The Elusive Presence* (San Francisco: Harper & Row, 1978).

Thompson, J.A., *The Book of Jeremiah* (NICOT; Grand Rapids: Eerdmans, 1980).

Thompson, T.L., *The Historicity of the Patriarchal Narratives* (BZAW, 133; Berlin: W. de Gruyter, 1974).

—*The Origin Tradition in Ancient Israel*. I. *The Literary Formation of Genesis and Exodus 1–23* (JSOTSup, 55; Sheffield: JSOT Press, 1987).

Tigay, J.H., 'Conflation as a Redactional Technique', in *idem* (ed.), *Empirical Models for Biblical Criticism* (Philadelphia: University of Philadelphia Press, 1985), pp. 53-95.

—'The Evolution of the Pentateuchal Narratives in the Light of the Evolution of the *Gilgamesh Epic*', in *idem* (ed.), *Empirical Models for Biblical Criticism*, pp. 21-52.

—'The Stylistic Criterion of Source Criticism', in *idem* (ed.), *Empirical Models for Biblical Criticism*, pp. 149-73.

Townsend, J.L., 'Fulfillment of the Land Promise in the Old Testament', *BSac* 142 (1985), pp. 320-37.

Trible, P., 'Genesis 22: The Sacrifice of Sarah', in J.P. Rosenblatt and J.C. Sitterson, Jr (eds.), *'Not in Heaven': Coherence and Complexity in Biblical Narrative* (Bloomington: Indiana University Press, 1990), pp. 170-91.

Turner, L.A., *Announcements of Plot in Genesis* (JSOTSup, 96; Sheffield: JSOT Press, 1990).

Unger, M.F., 'Some Comments on the Text of Gen 15.2-3', *JBL* 72 (1953), pp. 49-50.

Van Develder, F.R., 'The Form and History of the Abrahamic Covenant Traditions' (PhD thesis; Drew University, Madison, NJ, 1967).

Van Gelder, C., 'The Covenant's Missiological Character', *CTJ* 29 (1994), pp. 190-97.

Van Groningen, G., *Messianic Revelation in the Old Testament* (Grand Rapids: Baker Book House, 1990).

Van Seters, J., *Abraham in History and Tradition* (New Haven: Yale University Press, 1975).

—*Prologue to History: The Yahwist as Historian in Genesis* (Louisville, KY: Westminster/John Knox Press, 1992).

—*The Life of Moses: The Yahwist as Historian in Exodus–Numbers* (Kampen: Kok, 1994).

Van Wieringen, A.L.H.M., 'The Reader in Genesis 22.1-19: Textsyntax—Textsemantics —Textpragmatics', *EstBíb* 53 (1995), pp. 289-304.

Vawter, B., *On Genesis: A New Reading* (Garden City, NY: Doubleday, 1977).

Veijola, T., 'Das Opfer des Abraham—Paradigma des Glaubens aus dem nachexilischen Zeitalter', *ZTK* 85 (1988), pp. 129-64.

Vermes, G., 'New Light on the Sacrifice of Isaac from 4Q225', *JJS* 47 (1996), pp. 140-46.

Vetter, D., *Seherspruch und Segensschilderung* (Theologische Monographien; Stuttgart: Calwer Verlag, 1974).

Victor, P., *The Theme of Promise in the Patriarchal Narratives* (unpublished PhD thesis; University of St Andrews, 1972).

Vogels, W., 'Abraham et l'offrande de la terre (Gn 13)', *SR* 4 (1974), pp. 51-57.

—*Abraham et sa légende: Genèse 12,1–25,11* (Paris: Cerf, 1996).

—*God's Universal Covenant: A Biblical Study* (Ottawa: University of Ottawa Press, 1979).

Volz, P., and W. Rudolph, *Der Elohist als Erzähler. Ein Irrweg der Pentateuchkritik?* (BZAW, 63; Giessen: A. Töpelmann, 1933).

Vos, G., *Biblical Theology* (repr., Edinburgh: Banner of Truth Trust, 1948).

Vriezen, T., 'Bemerkungen zu Genesis 12.1-7', in M. Beek *et al.* (eds.), *Symbolae Biblicae et Mesopotamicae* (Festschrift F.M.T. de Liagre Böhl; Leiden: E.J. Brill, 1973), pp. 380-92.

Wagner, N.E., 'Abraham and David?', in J.W. Wevers and D.B. Redford (eds.), *Studies on the Ancient Palestinian World* (Festschrift F.V. Winnett; Toronto: University of Toronto Press, 1972), pp. 117-40.

—'A Literary Analysis of Genesis 12–36' (PhD thesis; University of Toronto, 1965).

Waldow, H.E. von, 'Israel and her Land: Some Theological Considerations', in H. Bream, R.D. Heim, and C.A. Moore (eds.), *A Light Unto My Path* (Festschrift J.M. Myers; Philadelphia: Temple University Press, 1974), pp. 493-508.

Walker, N., 'A New Interpretation of the Divine Name "Shadd(a)i"', *ZAW* 72 (1960), pp. 64-66.

Wallace, R.S., *Abraham: Genesis 12–23* (London: SPCK, 1981).

Walters, S.D., 'Wood, Sand and Stars: Structure and Theology in Gn. 22.1-19', *TJT* 3 (1987), pp. 301-30.

Waltke, B.K., 'The Phenomenon of Conditionality within Unconditional Covenants', in A. Gileadi (ed.), *Israel's Apostasy and Restoration* (Festschrift R.K. Harrison; Grand Rapids: Baker Book House, 1988), pp. 123-39.

Walton, J.H., *Chronological and Background Charts of the Old Testament* (Grand Rapids: Zondervan, 1994).

—*Covenant: God's Purpose, God's Plan* (Grand Rapids: Zondervan, 1994).

Wcela, E.A., 'The Abraham Stories, History and Faith', *BTB* 10 (1980), pp. 176-81.

Wehmeier, G., *Der Segen im Alten Testament: Eine semasiologische Untersuchung der Wurzel brk* (Theological Dissertations, 6; Basel: Friedrich Reinhardt, 1970).

—'The Theme of "Blessing for the Nations" in the Promises to the Patriarchs and in Prophetical Literature', *BangTF* 6 (1974), pp. 1-13.

Weimar, P., 'Genesis 15. Ein redaktionskritischer Versuch', in M. Görg (ed.), *Die Väter Israels: Beiträge zur Theologie der Patriarchenüberlieferungen im Alten Testament* (Festschrift J. Scharbert; Stuttgart: Katholisches Bibelwerk, 1989), pp. 361-411.

—'Gen 17 und die priesterschriftliche Abrahamsgeschichte', *ZAW* 100 (1988), pp. 22-60.

—*Untersuchungen zur Redaktionsgeschichte des Pentateuch* (BZAW, 146; Berlin: W. de Gruyter, 1977).

Weinfeld, M., 'ברית *berîth*', *TDOT*, II, pp. 253-79.

—'*Berît*. Covenant vs. Obligation', *Bib* 56 (1975), pp. 120-28.

—'The Covenant of Grant in the Old Testament and in the Ancient Near East', *JAOS* 90 (1970), pp. 184-203.

—'The Loyalty Oath in the Ancient Near East', *UF* 8 (1976), pp. 379-414.

—'The Old Testament—the Discipline and its Goals', in J.A. Emerton (ed.), *Congress Volume* (VTSup, 32; Leiden: E.J. Brill, 1981), pp. 423-34.

—'The Period of the Conquest and of the Judges as Seen by the Earlier and Later Sources', *VT* 17 (1967), pp. 93-113.

—*The Promise of the Land: The Inheritance of the Land of Canaan by the Israelites* (Berkeley: University of California Press, 1993).

Weisman, Z., 'National Consciousness in the Patriarchal Narratives', *JSOT* 31 (1985), pp. 55-73.

Wellhausen, J., *Die Composition des Hexateuchs und der historischen Bücher des Alten Testaments* (Berlin: W. de Gruyter, 4th edn, 1963).

—*Geschichte Israels: Erster Band—Prolegomena zur Geschichte Israels* (Berlin: G. Reimer, 1883) (ET *Prolegomena to the History of Israel* [Edinburgh: A. & C. Black, 1885]).

Wells, P., 'Covenant, Humanity, and Scripture: Some Theological Reflections', *WTJ* 48 (1986), pp. 17-45.

Wenham, G.J., 'The Akedah: A Paradigm of Sacrifice', in D.P. Wright, D.N. Freedman and A. Hurvitz (eds.), *Pomegranates and Golden Bells: Studies in Biblical, Jewish, and Near Eastern Ritual, Law, and Literature* (Festschrift J. Milgrom; Winona Lake, IN: Eisenbrauns, 1995), pp. 93-102.

—'The Coherence of the Flood Narrative', *VT* 28 (1978), pp. 336-48.

—'Genesis: An Authorship Study and Current Pentateuchal Criticism', *JSOT* 42 (1988), pp. 3-18.

—*Genesis 1–15* (WBC, 1; Waco, TX: Word Books, 1987).

—*Genesis 16–50* (WBC, 2; Dallas: Word Books, 1994).

—'Method in Pentateuchal Source Criticism', *VT* 41 (1991), pp. 84-109.

—'Pentateuchal Studies Today', *Them* 22.1 (1996), pp. 3-13.

—'The Religion of the Patriarchs', in A.R. Millard and D.J. Wiseman (eds.), *Essays on the Patriarchal Narratives* (Leicester: InterVarsity Press, 1980), pp. 157-88.

—'The Symbolism of the Animal Rite in Genesis 15: A Response to G.F. Hasel, *JSOT* 19 (1981)', *JSOT* 22 (1982), pp. 134-37.

Westermann, C., *Blessing in the Bible and the Life of the Church* (trans. K. Crimm; OBT; Philadelphia: Fortress Press, 1978).

—'Genesis 17 und die Bedeutung von Berit', *TLZ* 101 (1976), cols. 161-70

—*Genesis 1–11* (trans. J.J. Scullion; London: SPCK, 1984).

—*Genesis 12–36* (trans. J.J. Scullion; London: SPCK, 1986).

—*The Promises to the Fathers* (trans. D.E. Green; Philadelphia: Fortress Press, 1979).

Wette, W.M.L. de, *Beiträge zur Einleitung in das Alte Testament* (2 vols.; Halle: Schwimmelpfennig, 1806–1807) (trans. T. Parker; *A Critical Introduction to the Canonical Scriptures of the Old Testament* [2 vols.; Boston: Little, Brown, 1843]).

Whiston, W., *The Works of Flavius Josephus Complete and Unabridged* (Peabody, MA: Hendrikson Publishers, 1987).

White, H.C., 'The Divine Oath in Genesis', *JBL* 92 (1973), pp. 165-79.

—*Narration and Discourse in the Book of Genesis* (Cambridge: Cambridge University Press, 1991).

—'Word Reception as the Matrix of the Structure of the Genesis Narrative', in R. Polzin and E. Rothman (eds.), *The Biblical Mosaic: Changing Perspectives* (SBLSS; Chico, CA: Scholars Press, 1982), pp. 61-83.

Whybray, R.N., *An Introduction to the Pentateuch* (Grand Rapids: Eerdmans, 1995).

—*The Making of the Pentateuch: A Methodological Study* (JSOTSup, 53; Sheffield: JSOT Press, 1987).

Williamson, P.R., 'Abraham, Israel and the Church', *EvQ* 72 (2000), pp. 99-118.

Willis, J.T., *Genesis* (Austin: Sweet, 1979).

Winnett, F.V., *The Mosaic Tradition* (Toronto: Toronto University Press, 1949).

Wiseman, D.J., 'Abraham in History and Tradition. Part I: Abraham the Hebrew', *BSac* 134 (1977), pp. 123-30.

—'Abraham in History and Tradition. Part II: Abraham the Prince', *BSac* 134 (1977), pp. 228-37.

—'Abraham Reassessed', in A.R. Millard and D.J. Wiseman (eds.), *Essays on the Patriarchal Narratives* (Leicester: InterVarsity Press, 1980), pp. 139-56.

Wiseman, P., *New Discoveries in Babylonia about Genesis* (London: Marshall, 1936) (reissued as *Ancient Records and the Structure of Genesis* [Nashville: Nelson, 1985]).

Witsius, H., *The Economy of the Covenants between God and Man: Comprehending a Complete Body of Divinity* (trans. and rev. W. Crookshank; 2 vols.; repr., Escondido, CA: The den Dulk Christian Foundation, 1990 [1822]).

Wolff, H.W., *Hosea* (Hermeneia; Philadelphia: Fortress Press, 1974).

—'The Kerygma of the Yahwist', *Int* 20 (1966), pp. 131-58.

Wood, J.E., 'Isaac Typology in the New Testament', *NTS* 14 (1968), pp. 583-89.

Wright, C.J.H., 'אָב', *NIDOTE*, I, pp. 219-23.

Wright, N.T., *The Climax of the Covenant: Christ and the Law in Pauline Theology* (Edinburgh: T. & T. Clark, 1991).

Wynn-Williams, D.J., *The State of the Pentateuch: A Comparison of the Approaches of M. Noth and E. Blum* (BZAW, 249; Berlin: W. de Gruyter, 1997).

Yarchin, W., 'Imperative and Promise in Genesis 12.1-3', *StudBT* 10 (1980), pp. 164-78.

Yonge, C.D. (ed.), *The Works of Philo: Complete and Unabridged* (Peabody: Hendrikson, 1993).

Youngblood, R.F., 'The Abrahamic Covenant: Conditional or Unconditional?', in M. Inch and R.F. Youngblood (eds.), *The Living and Active Word of God* (Festschrift S.J. Schultz; Winona Lake, IN: Eisenbrauns, 1983), pp. 31-46.

—*The Book of Genesis: An Introductory Commentary* (Grand Rapids: Baker Book House, 2nd edn, 1991).

Zakovitch, Y., 'Juxtaposition in the Abraham Cycle', in D.P. Wright, D.N. Freedman and A. Hurvitz (eds.), *Pomegranates and Golden Bells: Studies in Biblical, Jewish, and Near Eastern Ritual, Law, and Literature* (Festschrift J. Milgrom; Winona Lake, IN: Eisenbrauns, 1995), pp. 509-24.

Zenger, E. (ed.), *Der neue Bund im Alten: Studien zur Bundestheologie der beiden Testamente* (Quaestiones disputatae, 146; Freiburg: Herder, 1993).

Zimmerli, W., *1. Mose 12–25: Abraham* (ZBK; Zürich: Theologischer Verlag, 1976).

—'Promise and Fulfilment', in C. Westermann (ed.), *Essays on Old Testament Interpretation* (trans. J.L. Mays; London: SCM Press, 1963), pp. 89-122.

—'Sinaibund und Abrahambund: Ein Beitrag zum Verständnis der Priesterschrift', *TZ* 16 (1960), pp. 268-80 (reprinted in W. Zimmerli, *Gottes Offenbarung: Gesammelte Aufsätze zum Alten Testament* [Munich: Chr. Kaiser Verlag, 1963], pp. 205-16).

Zlotowitz, M., and N. Scherman, *Bereishis: Genesis: A New Translation with a Commentary Anthologized from Talmudic, Midrashic and Rabbinic Sources* (2 vols.; New York: Mesorah Publications, 1986).

Zuidema, W. (ed.), *Isaak wird wieder gepfert. Die 'Bindung Isaaks' als Symbol des Leidens Israels* (Neukirchen–Vluyn: Neukirchener Verlag, 1987).

Zwickel, W., 'Der Altarbau Abrahams zwischen Bethel und Ai (Gen 12f.)', *BZ* 36 (1992), pp. 207-19.

INDEXES

INDEX OF REFERENCES

OLD TESTAMENT

JOURNAL FOR THE STUDY OF THE OLD TESTAMENT
SUPPLEMENT SERIES